Where the Domino Fell

America and Vietnam, 1945 to 1995

Second Edition

Where the Domino Fell

America and Vietnam, 1945 to 1995

Second Edition

James S. Olson
Randy Roberts

New York   St. Martin's Press

Sponsoring Editor: Katherine E. Kurzman
Managing editor: Patricia Mansfield Phelan
Associate project editor: Jennifer Valentine
Production associate: Melissa Kaprelian
Art director: Lucy Krikorian
Photo research: Barbara Salz
Cover design: John Harmon
Cover photo: © Charles Bonnay/Black Star

Library of Congress Catalog Card Number: 94-80114

Copyright © 1996 by St. Martin's Press, Inc.

Manufactured in the United States of America.

0 9 8 7 6
f e d c b a

For information, write:
St. Martin's Press, Inc.
175 Fifth Avenue
New York, NY 10010

ISBN: 0-312-08431-5

Contents

Preface

A 1990 issue of *Time,* devoted to "Vietnam: 15 Years Later," said it all. The cover photograph showed a Vietnamese peasant walking through a rice field. "In America, the pain endures," the cover read. "In Cambodia, the killing continues." The lead story claimed that "guilt and recrimination still shroud America's perceptions of the only war it ever lost."

Vietnam remains with us. In fact, it has become part of the popular culture as well as the political culture of the United States. Middle-aged Americans are still trying to sort out their feelings about the war, and a new generation of young adults has grown up wondering what all the fuss is about. Both groups are now ready for answers. The years since 1975, when the last helicopter lifted off the roof of the United States embassy in Saigon (Ho Chi Minh City), may be too brief a time for definitive judgments, but it is enough time to have gained perspective about the war, to have learned whatever lessons there are to learn.

Unfortunately, however, there still isn't much perspective about the war, at least not in the public mind. The idea for this book was born in a classroom at Sam Houston State University in Huntsville, Texas, several years ago when a student vociferously argued that the United States lost the war by not really trying, by holding back on its might and power. When we asked him to elaborate on his argument, he cited the movie *Rambo II.* We wondered how an intelligent American college student could have had his ideas about the war shaped by such a film, and we decided there was a need for a book about Vietnam that focused on the people involved and how the war developed out of their convictions, hopes, and fears. We wanted to show how and why the United States lost the war.

Our point of view, which will of course soon become obvious to the reader, is that for the United States the Vietnam War was the wrong war in the wrong place at the wrong time. War is, above all else, a political event. Wars are won only when political goals are achieved. Military firepower and troops are—like diplomacy and money—essentially tools to achieve political objectives. The United States went into Indochina after World War II with imprecise, muddled political objectives. It departed in 1975 after a thirty-year effort with a political focus just as blurred as it was in the beginning. The war was unwinnable because the United States never decided what it was trying to achieve politically.

We are grateful to the reference librarians at Sam Houston State University and Purdue University for their assistance. We appreciate the help of Louise Waller and Lynnette Blevins. We would also like to thank the following reviewers who offered useful comments: Truman R. Clark, Tomball College; Anthony O. Edmonds, Ball State University; Ben F. Fordney, James Madison University; Katherine K. Reist, University of Pittsburgh at Johnstown; and Clifford H. Scott, Indiana University–Purdue University at Fort Wayne. Finally, we would like to thank the hundreds of students in our Vietnam War classes who have helped us shape our own ideas about the war.

James S. Olson
Randy Roberts

Where the Domino Fell

America and Vietnam, 1945 to 1995

Second Edition

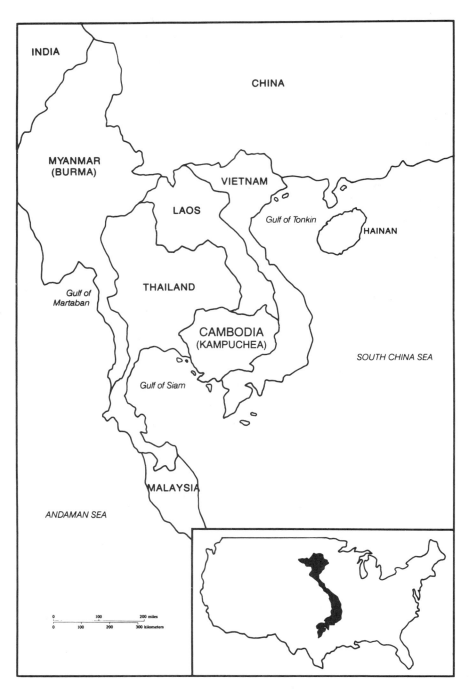

Indochina, 1995. *Inset:* A comparison in size between Vietnam and the United States.

Prologue: The Future as History

In 1975, when the helicopters took off from the United States embassy in Saigon, bringing an end to the Vietnam War, most Americans, for a complex variety of reasons, were disgusted with the conflict and the politicians who had brought it about. The United States had lost its first war. Because of its peculiar nature—so bloody yet undeclared, so efficient yet so unpopular—the Vietnam War has exerted an extraordinary impact on American culture and foreign policy, shaping the way Americans view themselves, their history, and their view of the world. Few experiences in American history have been more painful or confusing. W.D. Earhart, in his novel *Vietnam-Perkasie* (1983), captures that pain in describing the battle for the city of Hue in 1968:

> I fought back passionately, in blind rage and pain, without remorse, conscience or deliberation. I fought back . . . at the Pentagon Generals and the Congress of the United States, and the *New York Times*; at the draft-card burners, and the Daughters of the American Revolution . . . at the teachers who taught me that America always had god on our side and always wore white hats and always won; at the Memorial Day parades and the daily Pledge of Allegiance . . . at the movies of John Wayne and Audie Murphy, and the solemn statements of Dean Rusk and Robert McNamara (p. 214).

Americans spent the next fifteen years trying to come to terms with Vietnam, trying to figure out how the war got so out of control, why so many millions of people, on both sides, had been wounded and killed, how so much moral capital had been so foolishly dissipated.

George Santayana, the Spanish-American poet and philosopher, once warned that "those who forget the past are destined to relive it." The crusade against Saddam Hussein and Iraq in 1990–1991 tested Santayana's prophecy. The Gulf War ended in the spring of 1991, and the GIs gradually began returning home from Saudi Arabia and Iraq. The demobilization was a slow, steady process. The troops were treated as conquering heroes; no ancient Roman Legion marching down the Appian Way from adventures abroad ever received a more enthusiastic welcome. Small towns and large cities across the country rolled out the red carpet and staged military parades complete with tanks, armor, high school marching bands, overhead jet fighters flying in formation, artillery pieces, Boy Scout and Girl Scout troops, and soldiers, lots of soldiers. The demand for soldiers to march in parades was so high that large military bases in the United States actually had some of their day-to-day operations disrupted by the need to supply units for the weekly parades.

The most striking image in those parades was not the military hardware or spit-polished young men and women marching in unison. The victory celebrations also attracted tens of thousands of middle-aged warriors—balding, overweight men, many of them amputees, wearing flak jackets and faded military green, walking down the streets of America, or rolling down them in wheelchairs, with smiles on their faces. They had pinned their old medals on again. The Vietnam vets were finally getting their due, their parades, delayed by fifteen or twenty or twenty-five years of guilt, *angst*, and anger over what had taken place in Indochina and in the United States. For millions of Americans, the Gulf War provided the opportunity for an act of mass, collective repentance. After a decade of films and books like *Coming Home, Platoon, Born on the Fourth of July*, and *Full Metal Jacket*, the whole country wanted to atone for the wretched way they had treated those same Vietnam veterans a generation ago.

But more than expiation was involved in the relationship between Vietnam and Desert Storm. As President George Bush said when Iraq finally capitulated in 1992, "We finally have the Vietnam monkey off our backs." Politicians wanted to make sure that this war was handled better, that firepower was used more effectively and efficiently, and that the political objectives of the war were clearly communicated to the American people. Military leaders desperately wanted to rewrite their image, to erase the memories of depressed GIs smoking marijuana and fragging their officers, and to appear competent and professional once again. And the public wanted a victory, a memory more akin to the mass celebrations in Times Square in 1945 than to the television pictures of helicopters rescuing the last Americans from the roof of the United States embassy in Saigon in 1975. And everybody got what they wanted.

There was something unnerving, however, about the easy analogies between Desert Storm and Vietnam, proof of how vulnerable we are to political rhetoric and our own short memories. When the desert dust finally settled in Saudi Arabia and Iraq, large numbers of Americans were convinced that the Gulf War and the war in Vietnam were similar conflicts that should have had similar outcomes, that the reasons for our defeat in Vietnam were exactly the same as the explanations for our victory in Desert Storm. Victory in the Persian Gulf came because we did not "fight with one hand tied behind our back." Who can forget the exhilaration, the technological orgasm, so many Americans felt when General H. Norman Schwarzkopf showed the films of "smart bombs" sneaking their way down the air shafts of Baghdad buildings? The obvious implication, of course, is that Vietnam, too, could have been a glorious American victory if only we had fought "the right way"—to win.

If only life, and history, were that simple. They are not. Vietnam and the Persian Gulf were separated by more than a continent and a generation. They took place in completely different worlds, even different realities. In the Gulf War of 1991–1992, Saddam Hussein, a third-rate dictator, invaded tiny Kuwait to secure control of rich oil fields there and to elevate his political stature in the region. Kuwait appealed to the United States and the United Nations to force an Iraqi withdrawal. President George Bush enjoyed the massive support of the American people, who understood the oil-related national security interests at stake, and marshaled a broad coalition of European powers and Arab nations. The United Nations endorsed the effort. The strategic military objective was clear-cut—drive Saddam Hussein and the Iraqi army out of Kuwait—and its achievement, along with a sense of military victory, was easily measurable. The Gulf War was tactically conventional, fought in open, desert spaces where Allied armor and air power were most effective. The Iraqis did not stand a chance. The war was over in weeks.

Policymakers who try to compare apples and oranges engage in a treacherous business. The Gulf War was not Vietnam, and Somalia was not the Gulf War. Convinced that the "Vietnam monkey was off our backs," flush with the success of the Gulf War, President George Bush decided to send American soldiers into Somalia late in 1992. The world media broadcast daily images of starving Somali children unable to find food because of the civil war raging throughout the country. Desperately poor and plagued for centuries with interclan rivalry and violence, Somalia was a political quagmire. In the beginning, the military objective appeared simple enough: disarm the roving bands of bloodthirsty "technicals" and feed starving children. Hungry Somalis at first greeted the GIs with open arms, welcoming them to the Horn of Africa. But within a matter of months, Somalia deteriorated into a bloody quagmire. American troops took sides in the civil war and soon found themselves the objects of ambushes and guerrilla attacks. Six months into the Clinton administration in 1993, GIs started dying there. One especially troubling image made its way into the prime-time news. Technicals from one of the marauding clans took the body of a dead American marine, stripped him naked, and paraded him through the streets of Mogadishu. Somali crowds lined the streets, laughing, shouting, and celebrating. If the dead Marine got close enough, they kicked and spit at him. The American public was up in arms. In a man-on-the-street interview, a reporter asked a retired St. Louis construction worker what he thought about Somalia. "Somalia is a toilet," the worker replied. "It's always been a toilet; it will always be a toilet. Let's get out. I don't want my boy dying in that shithole." Bill Clinton withdrew the troops a few months later. The Vietnam monkey was back.

Eternal War:
The Vietnamese Heritage

Vietnam is nobody's dog.

—Nguyen Co Thach, 1978

He was just a wisp of a man, thin and gaunt, frail and seemingly vulnerable, his stringy goatee elongating an already long face. After seventy-six years of world wandering, hiding, and escaping, he was finally declining, wrinkled brown skin now only translucently covering his bones. Over the years his rivals had easily, and quite casually, misjudged him, confusing frailty and shyness with weakness, never realizing, until it was too late, the fire that possessed him. Ho Chi Minh was ill in 1966, and he calmly waited for old age to do what imperial police and foreign soldiers had never been able to do—silence him. He had a weakness for American cigarettes and Maurice Chevalier records, but he had little use for anything else the United States and France had produced, particularly the havoc they had wreaked upon his homeland.

Late in 1966, with the war in Vietnam reaching its peak, Ho Chi Minh remarked to Jean Sainteny, an old French diplomat and friend: "The Americans . . . can wipe out all the principal towns of Tonkin [northern Vietnam]. . . . We expect it, and, besides, we are prepared for it. But that does not weaken our determination to fight to the very end. You know, we've already had the experience, and you have seen how that conflict ended." It was only a matter of time before the Americans went the same way as the Chinese, Japanese, and French. Vietnam was for the Vietnamese, not for anyone else, and that passion had driven Ho Chi Minh throughout his life.

That key to Ho Chi Minh's passion was the fundamental theme of Vietnamese history. Long ago a Chinese historian remarked, "The people of Vietnam do not like the past." No wonder. Vietnam developed in the shadow of Chinese imperialism. In 208 B.C. the Han dynasty expanded into southern China and Vietnam, declaring the region a new Chinese province—Giao Chi. Their informal name for the region was Nam Viet, which meant "land of the southern Viets." Over the centuries the Chinese brought their "mandarin" administrative system, technology, language, writing, and Confucian social philosophy to Vietnam. But control did not translate into assimilation. Intensely ethnocentric, the Vietnamese, while welcoming many Chinese institutions, refused to accept a Chinese identity. The historian Frances FitzGerald describes that dilemma in Vietnamese history: "The Vietnamese leaders assumed Chinese political culture while rejecting . . . Chinese political domination."

Periodically, the Vietnamese violently resisted, giving Vietnam such national heroes as the Trung sisters, who led an anti-Chinese insurrection in A.D. 40; Trieu Au, the Vietnamese Joan of Arc who led a rebellion in A.D. 248; and Ngo Quyen, the military leader of Vietnam's successful revolution in 938. An old Vietnamese proverb captures the region's history: "Vietnam is too close to China, too far from heaven." Even after they had achieved independence in 938, the Vietnamese had to deal periodically with Chinese or Mongol expansionism. Vietnam fought major wars against invaders from the north in 1257, the 1280s, 1406–1428, and 1788. Tran Hung Dao, the great thirteenth-century Vietnamese general, defeated the enemy after having all his soldiers tattoo the inscription "Kill the Mongols" on their right arms. He wrote: "We have seen the enemy's ambassadors stroll about in our streets with conceit. . . . They have demanded precious stones and embroidered silks to satisfy their boundless appetite. . . . They have extracted silver and gold from our limited treasures. It is really not different from bringing meat to feed hungry tigers."

In the centuries-long struggle against China, Vietnam developed a hero cult that elevated martial qualities as primary virtues. Vietnamese art glorified the sword-wielding, armor-bearing soldiers riding horses or elephants into battle. War, not peace, was woven into the cloth of Vietnamese history. The historian William Turley writes that out "of this experience the Vietnamese fashioned a myth of national indomitability. . . . The Vietnamese forged a strong collective identity . . . long before the Europeans appeared off their shores." Vietnam's enemies learned that lesson the hard way.

But there was also a patience to Vietnamese militarism, an unwillingness to be intimidated, a conviction that a small country could prevail against an empire if it bided its time and waited for its moment. Between 1406 and 1428, led by the great Le Loi, the Vietnamese attacked the Chinese through hit-and-run guerrilla warfare, letting rugged mountains and thick rain forests do much of their work for them, wearing down the enemy, sapping its spirit, confusing its objectives, finally delivering a death blow, a strategic offensive to drive the Chinese back across the border. That story became legendary in Vietnamese military history.

Anti-Chinese resistance became the cutting edge of Vietnamese identity. A prominent eighteenth-century Chinese emperor lamented the stubbornness of the Vietnamese. They are not, he said, "a reliable people. An occupation does not last very long before they raise their arms against us and expel us from their country." Suspicion of the Chinese permeated Vietnamese history. In 1945, for example, with the French ready to return to Vietnam and Chinese troops occupying much of northern Vietnam, Ho Chi Minh agreed to cooperate temporarily with France. When some of his colleagues protested, Ho remarked that it "is better to sniff French shit for a while than to eat Chinese shit all our lives."

For Ho Chi Minh, the "French shit" was still bad enough. France came to Vietnam in two stages, first in the seventeenth century and again in the nineteenth century. Father Alexandre de Rhodes, a French Jesuit, came to Hanoi in 1627, converted thousands of Vietnamese to Roman Catholicism, and created a Latin alphabet for the Vietnamese language. Although suspicious Vietnamese leaders expelled de Rhodes in 1630 and again in 1645, he planted the seeds of the French empire.

The French returned in force to Vietnam in 1847 when a naval expedition arrived at Tourane (later called Danang) and, within a few weeks, fought a pitched battle with local Vietnamese. Two more French warships fought another battle at Tourane in 1856. A French fleet captured Tourane in 1858 and conquered Saigon in 1859. Vietnamese resistance drove the French out, but in 1861 they returned to Saigon to stay. After signing a treaty with Siam in 1863, France established a protectorate over Cambodia. France extended its control over southern Vietnam, or Cochin China, during the rest of the decade. France then turned north, and in 1883 a naval expedition reached the mouth of the Perfume River, just outside Hue. After the French fleet shelled the city, a Vietnamese leader gave France a protectorate over Annam (central Vietnam) and Tonkin (northern Vietnam), although it took France years to assert its control in those regions. To provide uniform government over the colonies, France established the French Union in 1887. After securing a protectorate over Laos by signing another treaty with Siam (now Thailand) in 1893, France had five regions in the Union: Cochin China, Annam, Tonkin, Cambodia, and Laos.

The Vietnamese were no more satisfied with French domination than with Chinese. The most resentful Vietnamese lived in Nghe An Province, located in Annam in central Vietnam, a low coastal plain bordered by the Annamese mountains. Nghe An and the surrounding provinces were the most densely populated areas of Vietnam, and by far the poorest. The soil was leached and dry, the weather alternating between torrential monsoon rains and hot summer winds.

The French called the Nghe Annese the "Buffaloes of Nghe An" because of their reputation for stubbornness. The Vietnamese referred to them as the "People of the Wooden Fish." The Vietnamese love a special sauce known as *nuoc mam*. They alternate layers of fish and layers of salt in a barrel and let the brew ferment in the heat several weeks. The fish decompose into a mush and the fluid into a salty brine. *Nuoc mam* is to Vietnamese fish what catsup is to American french fries. The Nghe Annese were too poor to afford fish, the proverb says, so they carried a wooden fish in their pockets to dip into *nuoc mam* at restaurants. Nghe Annese, the jesters claimed, licked the wooden fish

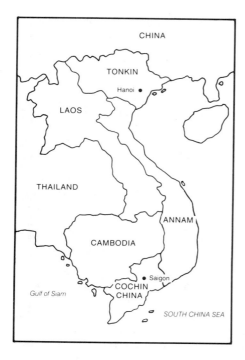

Vietnam under French control in the late nineteenth century.

until they were kicked out, only to repeat the culinary charade somewhere else.

But Nghe An, with its neighboring Ha Tinh Province, was not known only for its poverty. Year after year the prizewinning poets, musicians, and scholars at the imperial court at Hue came from Nghe An and Ha Tinh. They were thinkers and tinkerers, creative people who looked at life from unique perspectives, refused to believe what they were told, and insisted on having things proven to them. Their skepticism bred unhappiness. By the 1800s the best schools at Hue no longer accepted applicants from Nghe An and Ha Tinh, no matter how high their scores. Central Vietnamese, "the people of the wooden fish," were troublemakers, dreaming of a better world.

Born in 1890 as Nguyen Sinh Cung, Ho Chi Minh grew up in Nghe An. Near his birthplace was the *den*, a monument to Le Loi. The Vietnamese believe that the spirit of an honored individual lives on in a *den*. Ho Chi Minh visited the *den* as a child and listened to tales of how Le Loi expelled the hated Chinese. His father, Nguyen Sinh Sac, was the son of peasants who became a scholar and a ferocious anti-French nationalist. His sister was a renowned balladeer, and her folk songs railed at China and France. Sac passed the mandarin examinations and found a job at the imperial palace at Hue, but the imperial court was full of pro-French

Vietnamese sycophants or tradition-bound mandarins. "The French," said Phan Boi Chau, an early twentieth-century nationalist, "used honeyed words and great rewards to entice the Vietnamese. They offered high government positions and benefits of all sorts to make some of us into their hunting dogs."

For a while in the late 1890s and early 1900s Nguyen Sinh Sac was a minor government official in Hue. Ho Chi Minh's mother died in 1900, and Sac, along with his two sons and a daughter, lived in a tiny, dingy one-room apartment facing the opulent splendor of the Palais de la Censure where the Vietnamese emperor and the mandarin court ruled Vietnam. Ho Chi Minh bore the brunt of ridicule from the children of the court mandarins, and he developed an instinctive dislike for intellectual snobbery. Throughout his life, he frequently quoted the poet Tuy Vien: "Nothing is more contemptible than to seek honors through literature."

Although the Vietnamese had thrown off the Chinese yoke in 938, over the centuries they gradually adopted the Chinese mandarin system to govern the nation. Eventually, mandarin teachers and bureaucrats became a self-conscious elite. To pass the civil service examinations and secure the best jobs, Vietnamese scholars immersed themselves in the Chinese language and Confucian values, which gradually distanced them from Vietnamese peasants. The mandarins also adopted many Chinese institutions—a centralized tax system, a judicial hierarchy, and the royal palace architecture complete with gates, moats, bridges, and pools. For all their resentment of Chinese expansionism, the Vietnamese accepted Chinese culture. Confucianism promoted rule by a paternalistic elite committed to morality and fairness, and it demanded unswerving obedience from the governed. The essence of personal behavior is obedience, submissiveness, and peaceful acquiescence in the social hierarchy.

The mandarin system was also conservative to a fault. Mandarins were suspicious of all change. They opposed science, technology, industrialization, and democracy, any one of which might dislodge them from their positions of privilege. A popular late nineteenth-century Vietnamese poem reflected the growing resentment of the mandarin class:

> Becoming a mandarin you treat your servants as dirt,
> And steal every bit of money the people have.
> Although you scoop in who knows how much money,
> Do the people get any help from you?

On top of the mandarin elite, the French imposed the colonial bureaucracy. They ruled Vietnam through local clients—French-speaking Roman Catholic Vietnamese, who soon became a new elite, competing with the mandarins for influence. Eventually, the French abolished the mandarin examinations, prohibited the teaching of Chinese, and displaced the mandarins as power brokers. Except for the French bureaucrats themselves, the Francophile Vietnamese enjoyed the finest homes, the best jobs, the fanciest clothes—the good life.

Nguyen Sinh Sac's job at the imperial court gave him a living but no dignity. Indeed, he came to view the post as a dishonor. "Being a mandarin," he said many times, "is the ultimate form of slavery." Sac refused to let Ho Chi Minh even study for the examinations. He refused to speak French, arguing that doing so "would corrupt my Vietnamese," and openly advocated the abolition of the mandarin class and the disintegration of the French empire. Nguyen Sinh Sac was one of Nghe An's most troublesome children. The French fired him.

The father passed on those passions to his children. His daughter Nguyen Thanh worked in Vinh supervising a French military mess hall and smuggled rifles and ammunition to the De Tham guerrillas, a group already fighting against the French. When French police arrested and convicted her of treason, the mandarin judge gave her a life sentence and an epitaph: "Other women bring forth children, you bring forth rifles." Her brother Nguyen Khiem was just as militant. He repeatedly wrote eloquent letters to French officials protesting Vietnamese poverty and calling for freedom.

But it was the other son—Nguyen Sinh Cung, later known as Ho Chi Minh—who realized Sac's dream. At five years old, Ho was running messages back and forth to members of the anti-French underground. The house was a beehive of political talk, always around the theme of Vietnamese independence. A frequent visitor, and occasional fugitive, was Phan Boi Chau, the most prominent of Vietnam's early nationalists. Other Nghe An acquaintances of Nguyen Sinh Sac included Phan Chu Trinh, the constitutionalist who wanted to overthrow the mandarin bureaucracy.

The Nguyen Sinh Sac family was also a "brown canvas" household. The traditional dress of the Vietnamese was the *ao dai*, the *non*, and the *quoc*. For women, the *ao dai* was a long dress worn over black or white trousers that fit loosely around the legs. A rectangular piece of material formed a panel reaching down from the waist in the front and the back. For men the dress was only knee length. The embroidery on the cloth indicated the station in life of the wearer. Gold brocade was reserved for the imperial family. High-ranking mandarins used purple embroidery, and low-ranking mandarins used blue. Peasants could have only the plainest cloth. The *non* was the ubiquitous conical hat made of latania leaves, and the *quoc* were the wooden shoes. Radicals adopted brown canvas clothes as a symbolic protest of mandarin authority and a gesture to blur class lines. By the late 1880s large numbers of men in Nghe An wore brown canvas, in spite of mandarin edicts to the contrary. For much of his life Ho Chi Minh wore brown canvas clothes except at the most formal occasions.

Nguyen Sinh Sac listened carefully to all the Vietnamese nationalists, but the philosophical debate really revolved around the conflicting
ideas of Phan Boi Chau and Phan Chu Trinh. Phan Boi Chau had been
born in Nghe An in 1867. His father had passed the mandarin examinations but refused to work for the government, becoming a teacher in a
small village. Phan Boi Chau joined the Scholars' Revolt in 1885, a
resistance movement of Vietnam's emperor Ham Nghi and a number of
mandarin officials against French rule. In 1893 he participated in Phan
Dinh Phung's unsuccessful Nghe Tinh uprising against the French.

By the early 1900s Phan Boi Chau was convinced that Vietnam could
enter the modern world only if the French were expelled from Indochina.
For a teenaged Ho Chi Minh, Phan Boi Chau must have been an imposing figure. Phan Boi Chau's round face and wire-rimmed spectacles gave
him a scholarly, almost mandarin look, as did the full goatee. But he was
no simple scholar. He was a man of intense passion and commitment.
"The French," he said, "treat our people like garbage. . . . The meek are
made into slaves, the strong-minded are thrown into jail. The physically
powerful are forced into the army, while the old and weak are left to
die. . . . The land is splashed with blood." There was also an ascetic look
to Phan Boi Chau, as if he had transcended mundane pursuits for a
grander cause. If Vietnam was to flower, France must fall.

In 1907, a few years after visiting with the family of Nguyen Sinh
Sac, Phan Boi Chau led the abortive Poison Plot, in which low-ranking
Vietnamese soldiers tried to poison French officers in Hanoi. The conspiracy was uncovered before it took too large a toll, but Phan Boi Chau
earned a reputation as the first violent revolutionary in modern Vietnam. He spent years moving about in Japan, China, and Siam, with
French police always on his trail. The Chinese arrested him in Shanghai
in 1913. He was released from prison in 1917 and spent the rest of his
life in China. He died there in 1940.

Phan Boi Chau was rivaled only by Phan Chu Trinh, another Nghe
Annese. Born to a well-to-do family in 1872, Phan Chu Trinh passed the
mandarin examinations. A 1903 meeting with Phan Boi Chau changed
his life. Phan Chu Trinh resigned his government post two years later,
convinced that the Vietnamese emperor and his mandarin "lackeys"
would doom Vietnam to oblivion. But he parted company with Phan Boi
Chau on two accounts; Phan Chu Trinh did not believe in radical violence, and he was convinced that the imperial court and mandarin bureaucracy, not the French empire, should be destroyed first. He wanted
to work with the French in replacing the mandarins with a modern,
democratic political and educational system.

Although neither Phan Boi Chau nor Phan Chu Trinh was able to
implement his ideas in the early 1900s, they left a rich legacy. From
Phan Boi Chau came the conviction that only revolutionary violence
would dislodge the French, and from Phan Chu Trinh came the cer-

tainty that the mandarin system was rotten, corrupted by its elitism, agrarianism, and conservatism. Ho Chi Minh would eventually have to decide which to destroy first—the French empire or the mandarin court—but by the time he was a young man he already knew his destiny. Nghe An had produced yet another radical.

Ho Chi Minh left Nghe An Province at the end of 1910. He spent nearly a year in Phan Thiet teaching at a school financed by a *nuoc mam* factory. Late in 1911 he headed south to Saigon, where he enrolled in a vocational school, but he was unhappy learning a trade that the French would only use to exploit him. He left school early in 1912, signed up as a mess boy on a French ocean liner, and left Saigon for the other side of the world. Traveling under the alias of "Van Ba," Ho Chi Minh got a glimpse of much of the world in the next several years. In North Africa he saw what France was doing to the Algerians; in South Africa he noted what the English and the Boers were doing to the blacks; and in other ports of call he observed the imperial rule of the English, French, Dutch, and Portuguese. He worked in New York City, whetting his curiosity about American democracy, and on the eve of World War I, Ho Chi Minh was in London working as a cook at the Carlton Hotel.

During Ho Chi Minh's thirty-year absence from home, Vietnam became an even more oppressive place for native Vietnamese. The French viewed the Vietnamese as children at best and savages at worst. They refused to learn the Vietnamese language, and in 1878 they declared French and *quoc ngu*, the Latin alphabet Father Alexandre de Rhodes had developed, the official languages of the colony. They replaced the local legal code with their own version of Roman law. Convinced that the word "Vietnam" was symbolic of protest, the French outlawed it, insisting that "French Indochina" was the proper term. Centuries-old Buddhist pagodas were often bulldozed when prime land was needed to construct Roman Catholic churches.

The imposition of the French language and French law accelerated the alienation of peasant land. There were widespread poverty and millions of landless peasants in Vietnam before the French, but most peasants owned at least a small plot, and historically the emperor had discouraged the development of large estates. But between 1880 and 1930 the French changed landholding patterns. Many peasants lost their property because they could not pay high French taxes, could not contest claims against the land in French courts, or fell into debt to French or Vietnamese creditors who foreclosed on their property. The number of landless peasants, tenant farmers, and debt peons rose. In Tonkin 9 percent of the population came to own 52 percent of cultivated land, and 250 people owned 20 percent. They included French settlers and wealthy Vietnamese. It was the same in Cochin China. Tenant farmers paid up to 70 percent of their harvest to the landlord, and farmers borrowing money to finance production on their own land paid interest rates of 100 percent.

French companies had monopolies on the production of alcohol, opium, and salt, robbing peasant farmers of another source of income.

With imported rubber trees, the French created a new industry. By 1940 there were more than six hundred rubber plantations in Vietnam, but a handful of French companies controlled them. Poverty forced thousands of Vietnamese peasants to leave home for years to work the French plantations. Finally, the French bureaucracy was top-heavy, and the taxes the French imposed on Vietnamese peasants were too high. In a 1920 speech, Ho Chi Minh said: "French imperialism . . . conquered our country with bayonets. Since then we have not only been oppressed and exploited shamelessly, but also tortured and poisoned pitilessly. . . . Prisons outnumber schools and are always overcrowded. . . . Thousands of Vietnamese have been led to a slow death or massacred." Though not so eloquent, millions of Vietnamese felt the same way. To them France was a nation of police, soldiers, pimps, tax collectors, and labor recruiters.

Almost as bad was the Vietnamese elite who did the French bidding. For any Vietnamese to succeed in the French colony, he or she had to be a French-speaking Roman Catholic who carried out the edicts of the empire. If these Vietnamese were not mandarins in their educational background, they were just as elitist, just as hierarchical, and just as conservative. They got the best government posts, the finest homes, and the largest estates. Ho Chi Minh referred to them as *colonis indigèniae* (indigenous colonists): "If you take the largest and strongest member of the herd and fasten a bright substance to its neck, a gold coin or a cross, it becomes completely docile. . . . This weird . . . animal goes by the name of *colonis indigèniae*, but depending on its habitat it is referred to as Annamese, Madagascan, Algerian, Indian."

Ho Chi Minh moved to Paris in 1918 and quickly immersed himself in anticolonial politics. There were 100,000 Vietnamese in Paris, and Ho found good restaurants in which to eat his favorite dishes. He met the exiled Phan Chu Trinh and listened to him preach against the evils of the Vietnamese imperial court at Hue and the virtues of democracy and industrialization. Ho Chi Minh met frequently with French socialists, pressing them on the question of empire, trying to discern if they really wanted to change the world. He supported himself by touching up photographs and writing newspaper articles, adopting the name "Nguyen Ai Quoc" (Nguyen the Patriot) or "Nguyen O Phap" (Nguyen Who Hates the French). In the Vietnamese community, Ho Chi Minh became a leading nationalist, and the French secret police kept track of him.

But then overnight, Ho Chi Minh became *the* leading nationalist, a genuine hero. At the Paris Peace Conference negotiating the end of World War I, Ho Chi Minh electrified Vietnamese nationalists when he submitted an eight-point set of demands that included Vietnamese representation in the French parliament; freedom of speech, press, and association; release of all political prisoners; and full equality under the law for the Vietnamese in Indochina. If France would not meet those demands, the empire was morally bankrupt and would surely be destroyed. Looking back on that moment in 1919, the Vietnamese student Bui Lam remembered: "It was like a flash of lightning. . . . Here was a Vietnamese insisting that his people be accorded their rights. . . . No two Vietnamese residing in France could meet, after this, without mentioning the name of Nguyen Ai Quoc."

Ho Chi Minh was soon the soul of the expatriate Vietnamese community. The Vietnamese sought him out, no longer looking to Phan Chu Trinh as their leader. Ho Chi Minh was a charismatic leader. Perhaps it was the combination of a revolutionary soul and a Confucian personality. His hatred of the French empire knew no bounds, nor did his love for his country. But at the same time Ho Chi Minh was a man of the *luc duc*, the six virtues Confucianism demanded of all leaders: *Tri* (wisdom), *Nhan* (benevolence), *Tin* (sincerity), *Nghia* (righteousness), *Trung* (moderation), and *Hoa* (harmony). He seemed unassuming, a "brown canvas" man from Nghe An.

Paris solidified Ho Chi Minh's political philosophy. For several years he had been a member of the French Socialist party, but he grew weary of its unwillingness to do anything more than sympathize on the "colonial question." Ho Chi Minh decided the socialists were "capitalist souls in syndicalist bodies," too given to parliamentary debate, political compromise, and intellectual moderation to help the Vietnamese. His decision in 1920 to part company with the socialists left him with the problem of finding the real key to Vietnamese liberation. Along with a large faction of French socialists, he decided in 1920 to convert the organization into a French Communist party. His conversion came when a French communist gave him a copy of Vladimir Lenin's "Thesis on the National and Colonial Questions." Lenin argued that imperialism was the natural consequence of capitalism. Industrial monopolies, to secure new sources of raw materials and new markets, expand into the underdeveloped world and exploit colonial peoples. The imperial powers enrich themselves by pushing the colonies into poverty. But Lenin also argued that there were two enemies to be confronted: Western imperialists and Asian feudalists. A tiny minority of Asian natives, protected by European technology, controlled enormous economic assets, intensifying the suffering of peasants and workers. Revolution was the answer. Throw off the imperial yoke and redistribute property to the peasant masses.

Ho Chi Minh later recalled his introduction to Lenin. "What emotion, enthusiasm, clear-sightedness and confidence it instilled in me! I was overjoyed. Though sitting alone in my room I shouted aloud as if addressing large crowds: 'Dear martyrs, compatriots! This is what we need, this is our path to liberation.' " Here was the solution to the long debate between Phan Boi Chau and Phan Chu Trinh. In the name of Phan Boi

Chau, the people of Vietnam must destroy the French colonial apparatus, and in the name of Phan Chu Trinh they must promote revolution in Vietnam, wiping out the last vestiges of mandarin elitism and stripping wealthy, Francophile Vietnamese of their huge estates.

After years of searching, Ho Chi Minh had an ideology to match his passion. In later years, people would debate which was his true love, nationalism or communism? In the United States, anticommunists would see only his communism, arguing that nationalism was just a subterfuge. Antiwar critics, on the other hand, claimed that deep down Ho Chi Minh was a nationalist, that communism was simply the most effective tool for bringing about independence. But both points of view were naive. Ho hated the French empire for what it had done to his country, but he also hated the French-speaking Vietnamese Catholics who enriched themselves at the expense of poor peasants. Ho Chi Minh was a devout communist because in communism he saw the resolution of both evils. Communism fit the hand of Nghe Annese radicalism like a glove.

Ho Chi Minh's conversion to communism transformed his life. He was a founding member of the French Communist party, and in 1921 he established the Intercolonial Union, a communist-front group to work against imperialism. He spent 1923 and 1924 in Moscow. Late in 1924 the Soviets asked him to go to Canton as an adviser to the Soviet envoy. There Ho discovered a large Vietnamese expatriate community coalescing around Phan Boi Chau, the old family friend. But the joy of the reunion was short-lived. Ho Chi Minh talked at length with him about revolution, but Phan Boi Chau's commitment stopped at talk. Perhaps he was just too old—the fire had dimmed. Ho Chi Minh also found him conservative, willing to get rid of the French but not the Vietnamese elite in a genuine revolution.

Young Vietnamese nationalists in Canton gravitated to Ho Chi Minh's leadership. One of them was Pham Van Dong. Born in Quang Nam Province of central Vietnam in 1906 to a mandarin family, Dong studied at the French lycée in Hue. His father was exiled to the French colony of Reunion in 1915 for fomenting rebellion among the Vietnamese troops recruited to fight in World War I. As a student, Pham Van Dong became intensely anti-French, and he moved to Canton to escape the secret police. He was captivated by Ho Chi Minh's "shining simplicity." Nguyen Luong Bang, another young nationalist born in Hai Hung Province in 1904, met Ho Chi Minh in Canton and saw him "healthy-looking, extremely bright-eyed . . . with an engagingly gentle way of speaking." With Pham Van Dong, Nguyen Luong Bang, and several other young Vietnamese, Ho Chi Minh founded the Revolutionary Youth League of Vietnam in 1925. It was the first purely Marxist organization in Indochina.

French secret agents and Chinese police went after the rebels, and Ho

Chi Minh urged his associates to return to Vietnam and organize anti-French communist cells. He went to Moscow in 1927, attended conferences in Europe later in the year, and in 1928 lived in Bangkok as a Buddhist monk organizing the Vietnamese emigrant community. Ho traveled to Hong Kong in 1929 and met Le Duc Tho, another Vietnamese nationalist. Tho, born in Nam Ha Province in 1910 to a mandarin family, became an anti-French nationalist while attending school. With Le Duc Tho, Pham Van Dong, Nguyen Luong Bang, and several other Vietnamese in Hong Kong, Ho Chi Minh established the Indochinese Communist party in June 1929. Its leaders wanted to "overthrow French imperialism, feudalism and the reactionary Vietnamese capitalist class." Another young Vietnamese nationalist soon joined them. Vo Nguyen Giap, born in Quang Binh Province in 1912, came from a well-to-do family. He earned a law degree at Hanoi University. By the time he was a teenager, Giap hated the French. Although he had never met Ho Chi Minh, Giap was familiar with his revolutionary nationalism and joined the Indochinese Communist party.

The Vietnamese first emerged as a self-conscious people several thousand years ago in Tonkin. Central Vietnam was dominated by Champa, a kingdom established by the Cham people, who had originally been seafaring merchants from India. The Mekong River Delta in southern Vietnam was the land of the Khmer—ethnic Cambodians. In the eleventh century ethnic Vietnamese expanded into Annam, eventually defeating Champa. But early in the sixteenth century a dynastic struggle erupted in Tonkin, with two families—the Nguyen and the Trinh—vying for control of the Vietnamese imperial court. The Nguyen lost and escaped south into Annam and Cochin China, where they built their own power base. On and off for nearly two hundred years the Trinh tried unsuccessfully to conquer the Nguyen. At one point in the early 1600s the Nguyen constructed two 20-foot-high walls stretching eleven miles to block the Trinh advance. The families finally achieved a truce in 1673. The Nguyen consolidated their power by crushing Cham and Khmer power.

The two regions of Vietnam evolved very differently. Northerners looked down on southerners as a lazy, backward people with little sense of community. Southerners viewed northerners as pushy and aggressive. Life in southern Vietnam was easy, at least compared to Tonkin. The Mekong River flowed gently, slowly, and predictably, its annual flooding at the end of July and again in September providing rich new alluvial soils for the rice crop, which farmers planted between July and September. They harvested the crop from December through February, with as much as 1,500 pounds of rice coming from each acre. North of Saigon, in the central lowlands of southern Vietnam, yields were less, but farmers were capable of producing two rice crops a year. Southern Vietnam was the breadbasket of Indochina. Land had been readily available in southern Vietnam after the defeat of the Khmer, and a frontier spirit had developed, with farmers acquiring relatively large landholdings and developing self-serving lifestyles. Population density in southern Vietnam was less than in the north. A more rural culture developed.

In Tonkin, the Red River Delta was rich but unpredictable. The river flowed swiftly out of the Laotian mountains, and it flooded unpredictably. Crop yields were low when compared to those of southern Vietnam, and rice had to be imported, even in good years. Over the centuries, the north Vietnamese had to work together to build and supervise thousands of miles of dikes. Population density was heavier there and demanded more political and economic organization. Peasant landholdings were much smaller, but the sense of community much stronger. Northerners were more urbane than southerners and considered themselves superior, but they needed southerners if Vietnam ever hoped to achieve economic self-sufficiency.

Religion contributed to the differences. Buddhism came to Vietnam from two different sources. The Chinese brought Mahayana Buddhism to Vietnam, but the Indians brought Theravada Buddhism to Champa and the Khmer. Theravada Buddhism was conservative. It viewed salvation as a future state distinct from the present; individuals find nirvana by transcending the present and detaching themselves from worldly cares. In Tonkin, however, there was only Mahayana Buddhism. It was progressive and rested on the belief that anybody could become Buddha and enjoy salvation. Mahayana Buddhism identified morally redeemed people as those committed to acts of love and charity, who focused on the present and postponed their own salvation until they helped others achieve theirs. Mahayana Buddhism bequeathed a communal spirit to northerners that was not as well developed in the south. When the time came to resist the French and the Japanese, the communal nature of northern culture provided an ideal atmosphere for political organization. In the south, where more individualist concerns prevailed, unified political action developed more slowly. It was in northern Vietnam, not the south, that the revolution began.

It started in Nghe An. The Great Depression depressed rice prices, eroding peasant income and creating an epidemic of economic misery and political discontent. Widespread tax revolts erupted spontaneously throughout central Vietnam, and more sporadic eruptions took place in the Mekong Delta. But in Nghe An, radicals organized peasants into Red Soviets—local councils demanding the end of rents, massive tax cuts, and land redistribution.

On September 12, 1930, more than 6,000 Nghe An peasants marched on Vinh, the provincial capital. Although the march began as a peaceful demonstration, the French called in an air strike, killing more than 174 people. Later in the day, when relatives drifted in to claim the bodies, aircraft killed another fifteen people. A French journalist called the second attack "an awkward error which had a bad effect." Bad effect, indeed! The repression of the Nghe An Revolt was a seminal event, proof that France would stop at nothing to keep the empire. For the French, the revolt was sobering testimony to the power of Vietnamese peasants if anyone organized them. For the mandarins, the revolt was the future if communists ever took over. The "Vietnamese reactionary class," as Ho Chi Minh described them, would lose everything.

But the collapse of the Nghe An Revolt taught Ho Chi Minh and his followers another lesson. Nobody would overthrow the French empire without first creating a broad-based political organization reaching all the way down to the peasant masses. As far back as 1924, Ho Chi Minh said that in "all the French colonies . . . conditions have combined to further an uprising of the peasants. Here and there they have rebelled, but their rebellions have been drowned in blood. If the peasants remain pacific today it is because they lack organization and a leader." Revolution depended on the support of millions of peasants. Success in Vietnam would be more a political question than a military one.

After the suppression of the Nghe An Revolt, the French went after all revolutionary nationalists. Pham Van Dong was arrested in 1930 and sent to the dreaded "tiger cages" at Con Son Island, where he spent the next eight years. Nguyen Luong Bang held out for a year, but he was put in a French prison in 1931. Tho spent years in hiding and in French jails during the 1930s. Vo Nguyen Giap went into exile in 1939, but the French arrested his wife and baby. Both died in prison in 1941, giving Vo Nguyen Giap a vendetta to accompany his nationalism. The French tried Ho Chi Minh in absentia, convicted him of treason, and sentenced him to death. Under pressure from the French, British authorities imprisoned him in Hong Kong. Rumors quickly spread that he died there, a story both the French and Soviets believed.

But late in 1932 some British contacts smuggled Ho Chi Minh out of Hong Kong and drove him to Shanghai, where he met with Soviet officials who helped him get to Moscow in 1933. Five years later, Ho Chi Minh returned to China, and the next year he met Vo Nguyen Giap for the first time. Pham Van Dong made it out of the French prison in 1939 and headed for China as well. There the three of them planned their next move, hoping that the turmoil in the world would provide them with an opportunity. It came in June 1940 when Germany conquered France. Nazi successes fit in well with Japan's designs for Asia. Indochina seemed like a ripe plum, and Japan picked it. In September 1940 Japanese troops moved south out of China into Tonkin. They occupied the rest of Annam and Cochin China by July 1941. Ho Chi Minh now faced another foreign power. Japan became the new enemy. Ho Chi Minh quietly left China and returned to Vietnam. His thirty-year odyssey was over.

In 1945, Vo Nguyen Giap (left) and Ho Chi Minh (right) were worried about Chinese designs on Vietnam as well as about the French commitment to maintaining its empire there.
AP/WIDE WORLD PHOTOS

Ho Chi Minh and his followers took up refuge in a limestone cave near Pac Bo in the mountains of Cao Bang Province. Ho knew only too well that he was not the first Vietnamese to plan the destruction of the French empire. Dozens of anti-French crusades had been launched over the years, but all failed. The Can Vuong movement of the late 1800s demanded restoration of Vietnamese royalty, but in doing so it did not address the resentments of the peasant masses for the mandarin elite. Phan Boi Chau and Phan Chu Trinh had tried but failed; their isolated, poorly planned uprisings were easy prey for the efficient French colonial administrators. Phan Boi Chau's close associate Hoang Hoa Tham organized the De Tham war against the French, but the effort was poorly structured and ended with Hoang Hoa Tham's assassination in 1913. Nguyen Thai Hoc established the Viet Nam Quoc Dan Dang, or Vietnam Nationalist party, in 1929 and launched an abortive uprising against the

French at Yen Bay, but the movement, composed exclusively of middle- and upper-class Vietnamese, disintegrated. Nguyen Thai Hoc died at the guillotine in 1930.

After 1910, urban nationalists appeared in the cities. Such groups as Bui Quang Chieu's Constitutional party and Nguyen An Ninh's Hopes of Youth were influenced by Western values. They wanted reform, not revolution, and definitely not any sort of violence. They failed to capture the mantle of Vietnamese nationalism because they were isolated from peasants, not just in their use of the French language but in their abandonment of Confucian symbols. The leaders were primarily intellectuals, given to endless ideological squabbles. It was also easy for French authorities to keep track of urban nationalists.

A different approach had to be taken, one that would absorb Vietnamese from all classes. Ho Chi Minh remembered Lenin's advice that Asian communists should form alliances with each nationalist organization while keeping their independence from all of them. Ho downplayed communism, not wanting to give his French critics anything to use against him. The organization to liberate Vietnam had to be based on nationalism, not revolution, at least in the beginning. Only then was there any hope of bringing together large numbers of Vietnamese in a resistance movement. In May 1941, outside the cave in Cao Bang Province, Ho Chi Minh established the political organization for implementing his dream: the Viet Nam Doc Lap Dong Minh, or Vietminh—the League for Vietnamese Independence. Ho Chi Minh declared: "Our people suffer under a double yoke: they serve not only as buffaloes and horses to the French invaders but also as slaves to the Japanese plunderers. . . . Rich people, soldiers, workers, peasants, intellectuals, employees, traders, youth, and women who warmly love your country. . . . Let us unite together!"

The Vietminh were about to inherit the mantle of Vietnamese nationalism. They built a coalition of urban intellectuals and peasants. French-educated Vietnamese intellectuals found in Marxism a scientific, anti-imperialist ideology that explained history and provided, in its moralistic fervor, a neo-religion to replace the void they felt in rejecting Confucian traditionalism. Peasants saw in the Vietminh a passionate movement dedicated to getting rid of the French and providing them with economic relief. Above all else, the Vietminh enjoyed the charisma of Ho Chi Minh.

Shortly after the formation of the Vietminh, Ho Chi Minh went back to China to seek assistance from Jiang Jieshi in fighting the Japanese. Just before leaving, Ho Chi Minh announced to his closest associates that he was changing his name from Nguyen Ai Quoc, by which he had been known among Vietnamese nationalists for more than thirty years, to "Ho Chi Minh" (He Who Enlightens). In China, Jiang Jieshi had Ho Chi Minh arrested, and he spent more than a year in prison, almost dying from the conditions. He was released late in 1943 when some Chinese leaders decided he might be useful after all in fighting Japan. Ho Chi Minh returned to Cao Bang Province.

By that time Ho Chi Minh was ready to look toward a new source for assistance. Ever since his visit to New York City in 1913, he had a bemused curiosity about the United States. Although American capitalism created classes and exploited the poor, there was nevertheless a powerful sense of opportunity there. The Americans had, after all, been the first colony to revolt successfully against a European imperial power, and their Declaration of Independence was eloquent in its proclamation of human equality. American imperialism was even more intriguing. The United States acquired the Philippines in 1898 and then fought a bloody war against Filipino insurrectionists who had no interest in replacing their Spanish yoke with an American one. U.S. troops crushed the rebellion, but not before a guerrilla war took thousands of lives. But the Americans had made good on their promise. The Tydings-McDuffie Act of 1934 launched the Philippines on the road to independence, with a twelve-year timetable before the American withdrawal. Maybe the Americans were as good as their Declaration of Independence proclaimed?

Ho Chi Minh had no illusions about why the Americans might be willing to help him. They opposed Japan's expansion into Indochina in 1940 and 1941 not because of any sympathy with the national aspirations of the Vietnamese. Instead, the United States had been worried about its own access to the French rubber plantations, about British and Dutch oil reserves in Malaya and the East Indies, about the future of the Philippine Islands, and about the fate of the Open Door policy in China. But Ho thought that perhaps the Americans might be willing, if not to liberate Vietnam from the French, at least to help expel the Japanese invaders. Japan was simply the latest foreign power trying its imperial wings in Vietnam. True, the Japanese had defeated, or at least displaced, the French, but Ho Chi Minh took little comfort in that. Using Japanese soldiers to battle French bureaucrats was fraught with danger, like hunting "the tiger," he said, "only to be eaten by the wolves."

So Ho Chi Minh sought American assistance. The Office of Strategic Services (OSS), forerunner of the Central Intelligence Agency (CIA), wanted to develop good intelligence sources in Southeast Asia. Ho made himself available, promising to return downed American fliers and escaped prisoners of war as well as provide information on Japanese troop movements. OSS leaders knew he was a communist, but they also knew he had no use for Japan. Ho courted American support. He wanted arms shipments, first to fight the Japanese and then the French. After securing a promise that the weapons would be used against the Japanese and not the French, the OSS airlifted 5,000 guns to the Vietminh. The OSS agent who brought the guns remembered Ho Chi Minh as "an awfully sweet old guy. If I had to pick out one quality about that little old man sitting on his hill in the jungle, it was his sweetness."

Steely resolve undergirded the sweetness, and Ho Chi Minh's associates shared it. Vo Nguyen Giap, the lawyer and history teacher turned revolutionary, emerged as a brilliant military tactician, and from that mountain cave he expanded Vietminh power into the other northern provinces. By 1945 the Vietminh exercised widespread authority in Cao Bang, Phong Tho, Ha Giang, Yen Bay, Tuyen Quang, and Bac Kan provinces. Ho Chi Minh, not France or Japan, ran those provinces. Pham Van Dong led the effort to recruit more peasant soldiers into the Vietminh, and on several occasions whole garrisons deserted the French and came over.

By the spring of 1945, Giap was itching for a large-scale military effort. Ho Chi Minh, gifted with an uncanny sense of timing, was more cautious, not wanting to see a repeat of the Nghe An slaughter of 1930. The Vietminh should stay with their guerrilla tactics, attacking French and Japanese forces only when victory was certain, not taking unnecessary risks. The Vietminh should be, he said, "like the elephant and the tiger. When the elephant is strong and rested . . . we will retreat. And if the tiger ever pauses, the elephant will impale him on his mighty tusks. But the tiger will not pause and the elephant will die of exhaustion and loss of blood."

Ho Chi Minh convinced Giap to continue to fight like a tiger, not like an elephant. A large-scale military confrontation was probably unnecessary anyway. By 1945 the Americans were pounding the last nails into the Nazi coffin in Europe, and they were preparing an invasion of Japan. With the Japanese empire collapsing and the French empire still in limbo, Ho Chi Minh believed strongly that "we will not even need to seize power since there will be no power to seize." Why waste men and resources in a military escalation when victory was at hand?

Suddenly, in August 1945, after the Americans dropped nuclear weapons on Hiroshima and Nagasaki, the war was over. Bao Dai, the last Vietnamese emperor whom Japan recognized as a puppet head of state, tried to assert himself as the leader of the new nation. But on August 17, 1945, when Bao Dai supporters held a rally in Hanoi, 150,000 people showed up, many of them waving Vietminh flags. Soon the Vietminh leaders had the crowd marching through the streets of Hanoi, leaving the court mandarins sitting alone on an empty dais. In Vinh, Hue, Saigon, Haiphong, Danang, and Nha Trang, the Vietminh staged similar people's rallies.

Two days later, a few thousand Vietminh soldiers took control of Hanoi. Emperor Bao Dai, ensconced in the imperial palace at Hue, sent a message to the French warning them that their return to Vietnam would be problematic at best because of "the desire for independence that has been smoldering in the bottom of all hearts." If the French colonial apparatus is reconstructed, he said, "it will no longer be obeyed; each village would be a nest of resistance, every enemy a former friend." When Bao Dai proposed a coalition government with the Vietminh, he was roundly rejected. On August 25, 1945, Bao Dai abdicated the Vietnamese throne. Ho Chi Minh entered Hanoi the same day, wearing a brown canvas shirt, short pants, and a brown pith helmet. A week later, on September 2, he announced the creation of the Democratic Republic of Vietnam with a simple message:

> We hold these truths that all men are created equal, that they are endowed by their Creator with certain unalienable Rights, among these are Life, Liberty and the pursuit of Happiness. . . .
>
> The French have fled, the Japanese have capitulated, Emperor Bao Dai has abdicated; our people have broken down the fetters which for over a century have tied us down; our people have at the same time overthrown the monarchic constitution that reigned supreme for so many centuries and instead have established the present Republican government.

At independence celebrations later that day, United States military officials were invited guests. A Vietminh band played "The Star-Spangled Banner." America was a friend. Vietnam was free. Or so Ho Chi Minh thought.

2

The First Indochina War, 1945–1954

In war, a great disaster always indicates a great culprit.
—Napoleon, 1813

With artillery shells bursting continuously on the base at Dienbienphu, Colonel Charles Piroth, the French artillery commander, went into a deep depression. He had lost his left arm to German shrapnel during World War II, but his commitment to soldiering was so intense that his superiors had not forced his retirement. For months Piroth bragged that the end was near for the Vietminh, that they would not be able to go toe-to-toe with his "big guns." But on March 15, 1954, Piroth realized the truth. He apologized to his comrades, claiming that "it is all my fault," lay down on the cot, held a grenade with his hand, and pulled the pin with his teeth.

Ten years earlier, President Franklin D. Roosevelt could have almost predicted Piroth's death. He believed World War II would destroy European colonialism. In March 1943 Roosevelt suggested to the British foreign secretary, Anthony Eden, that when the war was over Indochina should be placed under international trusteeship. In a private conversation with Secretary of State Cordell Hull in 1944, the president remarked, "France has had the country—thirty million inhabitants—for nearly one hundred years, and the people are worse off than they were at the beginning. . . . The people of Indochina are entitled to something better than that." Eventually, Roosevelt backed down, primarily because of intense British and French opposition.

Roosevelt died on April 12, 1945, and the new president did not share his concern. Southeast Asia was another world to Harry Truman. Born and reared in Missouri, Truman had the traditional strengths—and a few of the weaknesses—of the Midwest. Decent, honest, hard working, he took a man at his word and the world as he found it. Harry's father, who had a speculator's optimism, was prone to economic failures, and by the time Truman graduated from high school there was no money for college. He worked in a bank for a while, then he farmed a full section of land. When President Woodrow Wilson asked for a declaration of war against Germany in 1917, Truman left the plow and picked up a rifle.

The war took him to France, where as a captain he successfully commanded troops in battle.

Peace returned Truman to his childhood love, and the newlyweds moved to Kansas City, where he opened a haberdashery. The store went bankrupt in 1922, and for the next twenty years—almost to the time he became president—Truman was strapped for money. And so he turned to politics. There he discovered his métier. Equipped with valuable political assets—honesty, dedication, and a likeable personality—Truman rose through the Kansas City political machine. In 1934 he won a seat in the United States Senate, where he was a loyal if undistinguished party man. In 1944 the Democratic party turned to the well-liked but obscure Truman for the vice-presidential nomination; he seemed the candidate least likely to hurt FDR in the election. The American electorate responded with an amazed "Who's Truman?" Even John Bricker, the Republican vice-presidential candidate, remarked in a press conference, "Truman—that's his name, isn't it? I never can remember that name." On April 12, 1945, people remembered the name.

Grave matters greeted the new president. Germany was in flames but not yet defeated. Japan was losing the war but refused to entertain the fact. There were troubles in Palestine, a meeting was scheduled with Joseph Stalin, and, of course, there was the entire question of the bomb. In short, Truman faced difficult and momentous decisions. Indochina was not one of them. At the Potsdam Conference in July 1945, the Allied governments quickly worked out a plan for the Japanese surrender in Indochina. The Chinese would accept the surrender of Japanese forces north of the sixteenth parallel, and the British troops would land in Saigon and deal with the Japanese south of the line.

Whatever hopes Ho Chi Minh had for securing American assistance died in anticommunist paranoia. With Germany and Japan defeated, President Truman and American policymakers saw the Soviet Union as a new threat to world peace. They wanted to rebuild Western Europe—create an economic and military barrier to Soviet expansion. In 1947 George Kennan, the future ambassador to the Soviet Union, proposed his "containment policy"—the United States should confine the Soviet Union to its existing sphere of influence. The fulcrum of a stable Western Europe was France. But the French were still irritated over Roosevelt's position on Indochina. The State Department urged Truman to repair the rift by assuring France that the United States would not prevent a French return to Indochina. Not wanting to raise French ire over Indochina, Truman acquiesced in the revival of the empire. In the summer of 1945 he told Charles de Gaulle that the United States would not undermine the French there.

Although the State Department still felt that an independent anticommunist Vietnam was the best political arrangement, policymakers had to soft-pedal the idea in 1946 and 1947. The French economy was in bad shape, and the French Communist party was on the rise. Moderate French politicians warned that even the most benign discussions of colonial independence played into the hands of French communists. Truman did not want to contribute to that, so he adopted a position of pro-French neutrality on the colonial question and provided the Marshall Plan to rebuild the French economy. The Vietminh would get nothing from the United States.

Ho Chi Minh was prepared to go it alone if necessary. World War II created an unprecedented opportunity for him. When the Vietnamese saw Japanese troops defeating French soldiers, the myth of French superiority vanished. When World War II ended, a seething hatred for the Japanese as well as the French existed throughout the Vietnamese peasantry. In 1943 Japan had ordered French soldiers to seize the Vietnamese rice harvest for export to Japan or for fuel in Vietnamese factories. Small farmers went bankrupt the first year and starved to death in 1944. Somewhere between 500,000 and 2 million Vietnamese men, women, and children died in the famine.

Ho Chi Minh used the famine to build his movement. Using "Destroy the paddy granaries and solve the famine" as a call to arms, Ho's guerrillas attacked granaries and distributed rice to peasants. They assassinated local landlords or Vietnamese officials working for the French and the Japanese. They recruited new followers. Vietminh political organizers spread out into central and south Vietnam preaching antiforeign messages. When World War II ended, more than 500,000 people in Vietnam considered themselves loyal to Ho Chi Minh. The Vietminh ruled whole sections of the country as a quasi-government. By August 1945, when Ho Chi Minh entered Hanoi, the Vietminh had armed 5,000 people. By the end of the year, that number had increased to 70,000.

On September 13, 1945, the British under General Douglas D. Gracey entered Saigon with 2,000 Indian troops, most of them famed Gurkha soldiers. Another 18,000 were scheduled to arrive soon. General Lu Han left southern China with 200,000 soldiers and entered Tonkin on September 20. Most of the Chinese troops were barefooted and starving. When they reached the shops in Tonkin, they ate everything in sight, including bars of soap and wrapped packages, which they had never seen before and mistook for food. Sporadic fighting broke out between the ancient enemies. A month before, Ho Chi Minh marched triumphantly into Hanoi, convinced that independence was imminent. Now he faced 20,000 British troops, 200,000 Chinese troops, and, though still unarmed, several thousand French troops.

Ho Chi Minh's dream of independence was quickly fading. General Gracey had no sympathy for the Vietminh. Two weeks before arriving in Saigon, he announced that "civil and military control by the French is only a question of weeks." Gracey rearmed French troops so they could protect French citizens from the Vietminh. On September 22, the

French rioted in Saigon, attacking police stations, stores, and private homes, and mugging or shooting Vietnamese civilians on the streets. On September 24, the Vietminh declared a general strike. Water and electricity went off in Saigon, trams stalled in their tracks, rickshaws disappeared, and Vietminh roadblocks paralyzed commercial traffic. Vietminh agents went into a French suburb and murdered 150 people. Gracey rearmed Japanese soldiers, and the combined force of Japanese, Gurkha, and French troops went after the Vietminh.

There was a small American contingent in Saigon. Prime among them was A. Peter Dewey who parachuted into Tonkin in 1945 to harass the Japanese. He soon developed a close relationship with Ho Chi Minh, and in August 1945 he headed up the OSS team in Saigon. An outspoken opponent of French imperialism, Dewey clashed repeatedly with Gracey. Their personal battle came to a head late in September when Gracey would not let Dewey fly the American flag on the fender of his OSS jeep. On the way to Tan Son Nhut airport in Saigon on September 26, 1945, Vietminh soldiers fired on the flagless jeep, killing Dewey instantly. Just before leaving for the airport, Dewey had written, "Cochin China is burning, the French and British are finished here, and we ought to clear out of Southeast Asia." When he learned of Dewey's death, Ho Chi Minh formally apologized. Gracey, on the other hand, remarked that Dewey "got what he deserved." A. Peter Dewey was the first United States soldier to die in Vietnam.

The Vietminh were also on the run in Tonkin, where Chinese troops removed the Vietminh from power and replaced them with a pro–Jiang Jieshi group that wanted independence without communism. By the end of September, while British, French, and Japanese troops hounded the Vietminh in southern Vietnam, the Chinese reduced Vietminh-controlled territory in Tonkin. In just a month, Ho Chi Minh found himself dealing with all of Vietnam's enemies—the Chinese, French, and Japanese—as well as the British.

Although Great Britain was officially neutral about the French return to Indochina, most British officials were worried about their own empire. Insurgent nationalists were active in Malaya and Burma, and Mohandas Gandhi was steadily gaining power in India. When their responsibility for disarming Japanese troops ended in December 1945, the British withdrew from southern Vietnam. Each departing group of British-Indian troops was replaced by French soldiers wearing American fatigues, helmets, boots, and ammunition belts, carrying M-1 carbines, and driving Jeeps and Ford trucks. In Tonkin, the Chinese and French reached a formal agreement in February 1946: China would withdraw from Tonkin, and France would surrender the commercial concessions a Franco-Chinese treaty had granted in the 1890s. The last Chinese troops were out of Vietnam in October.

The French were back, and Ho Chi Minh's political instincts dictated compromise, even though most of his colleagues opposed rapprochement. General Jacques Philippe Leclerc, temporary head of French military forces in Vietnam, also favored compromise. Even though he had 35,000 soldiers at his disposal, Leclerc lost his enthusiasm for fighting an open-ended war against the Vietminh. Late in January, he toured the Mekong Delta and the Iron Triangle, a Vietminh stronghold twenty miles northwest of Saigon. "Fighting the Viet Minh," Leclerc decided, "will be like ridding a dog of its fleas. We can pick them, drown them, and poison them, but they will be back in a few days." On February 5, 1946, Leclerc remarked, "France is no longer in a position to control by arms an entity of 24 million people."

In that atmosphere the French and Vietminh negotiated the Franco-Vietminh Accords on March 6, 1946. France extended diplomatic recognition to Ho Chi Minh's regime—calling it a "free state . . . within the French Union"—and promised to hold free elections in the "near future" to determine if Cochin China would come under Ho Chi Minh's control. Ho agreed to have 25,000 French troops replace Chinese soldiers north of the sixteenth parallel and stay until 1951. Both sides consented to have a Vietminh delegation travel to Paris later in the year to work out details of the agreement.

But when Ho Chi Minh went to Paris in the summer of 1946, he was in for a big surprise. Georges Thierry d'Argenlieu was the culprit. A graduate of the French Naval Academy, he took vows in the Carmelite Order in 1920 but then returned to active naval duty in 1940. In 1943 he became commander in chief of the Free French Naval Forces. D'Argenlieu was a devout Roman Catholic, a man who lived permanently in the past—"the most brilliant mind of the twelfth century," according to his closest adviser. D'Argenlieu believed that Adolf Hitler's victory over France was a fluke, a brief pause in France's reign as the premier nation on earth. Buoyed by the Allied victory in 1945, d'Argenlieu expected France to return to its former splendor. With that vision, he became high commissioner for Indochina in August 1945.

On June 1, 1946, the day after Ho Chi Minh sailed for Paris, d'Argenlieu created the Republic of Cochin China, a new, separate colony in the French Union. Ho Chi Minh felt "raped." Unification was as important to him as independence. In fact, the two were synonymous, not just because of a nationalist dream but because of pure economics. Northern Vietnam was overpopulated and poor, unable to feed itself, while the nutrient-rich Mekong Delta produced rice surpluses. In Paris, to keep Ho Chi Minh away from the Vietnamese émigré community, French officials moved him out to Biarritz in southwest France. The conference was held out of the press limelight at the isolated Fontainebleau Palace. For eight weeks Ho Chi Minh tried to get France to recognize Vietnamese independence, but the French preferred total control over French colonies. Desperate for assistance, Ho Chi Minh contacted the American embassy, promising to open up Vietnam to United States investment and lease a naval base at Cam Ranh Bay in return for help in keeping the French out. Rebuffed, he remarked to an American reporter, "We . . . stand quite alone; we shall have to depend on ourselves." Before returning to Hanoi in mid-September, Ho Chi Minh signed a document in which France agreed to a unification referendum in Cochin China in 1947, but he had few illusions about France's real intentions. During his last meeting with Georges Bidault, the French prime minister, on September 14, 1946, Ho Chi Minh warned: "If we must fight, we will fight. You will kill ten of our men, and we will kill one of yours. Yet, in the end, it is you who will tire."

Ho Chi Minh was back in Tonkin in October 1946. The battle for Vietnam began a month later over the collection of customs duties in Haiphong. The French insisted it was their right; the Vietminh insisted it was not. When gunfire erupted between Vietminh and French soldiers, d'Argenlieu decided to "teach the Viets a lesson." On November 23, after giving the Vietminh two hours to evacuate Haiphong, the French attacked guerrilla hideouts in the city. French infantry and armored units swept through Haiphong; French aircraft provided tactical air support; and the French cruiser *Suffren* unloaded a sustained artillery bombardment. When the day was over, much of Haiphong was rubble. Six thousand people, including a few Vietminh, were dead.

Four weeks later, on December 19, 1946, the Vietminh retaliated in Hanoi, destroying the city's electrical power plant and assassinating several French officials. Ho Chi Minh fled the city and established new Vietminh headquarters in the jungle sixty miles from Hanoi, where he controlled several provinces with 40,000 Vietminh troops. General Etienne Valluy, who replaced Leclerc, announced that if "those gooks want a fight, they'll get it." General Vo Nguyen Giap told the Vietminh, "I order all soldiers and militia in the center, south, and north to stand together, go into battle, destroy the invaders, and save the nation." The war was on.

Firmly in control of Tonkin's major cities, the French high command knew it would have to conquer the Red and Mekong River Deltas to deprive the guerrillas of their rice supplies and the mountains near the Laotian and Chinese borders to strip them of their sanctuaries. General d'Argenlieu's strategic approach seemed logical: build isolated military outposts (hedgehogs), man them with crack troops, and roam into the countryside seeking out and destroying the Vietminh. Eventually, d'Argenlieu assumed, the Vietminh would run out of hiding places and be forced into a conventional set-piece battle, where superior French firepower would annihilate them.

The French hoped to conclude a quick victory; otherwise, the war would be expensive, both politically and financially. Among the greatest challenges facing French soldiers, and later their American counterparts, was the climate, especially in southern Vietnam. Beginning in September, monsoon winds hit central Vietnam from the northeast, blowing across the South China Sea, picking up enormous amounts of water, and dropping them on the countryside until early February. Rainfall averages 100 to 200 inches a year there. Meteorologists classify it as "tropical monsoon," but French troops dubbed it "wet hell." Farther south, in the region of Saigon and the Mekong Delta, a "tropical savanna" climate prevails. Summers receive large amounts of rainfall, with temperatures and humidity hovering in the nineties. French soldiers on summer patrols, especially if they were working their way through swamps and wetlands, often joked that they could not tell where the waterline stopped and the air began. Jean Dubé, a French soldier stationed in Cochin China in the late 1940s, recalled in the mid-1960s, "I know what those GIs are going through. It really didn't matter if we were wading through swamps or grasslands. We sweat so much we got just as wet in either place." But the Vietnamese were not going to give them a quick victory.

Ho Chi Minh and Vo Nguyen Giap prepared for guerrilla war. They assumed that France would not have the resources to stay for the long haul. French politics was already a quagmire, with socialists and communists calling for an end to the war. A bloody guerrilla war of ambushes, booby traps, and assassinations, with high casualties but no set-piece battles—at least not yet—was Giap's strategy. While the French saw the war in military terms—defeating the Vietminh on the battlefield—Ho Chi Minh saw it in political terms—destroying the French will to continue.

Throughout 1948 and 1949 the French established their hedgehogs—on Route 3 from Bac Ninh to Cao Bang, Route 18 from Bac Ninh to Haiphong, Route 5 from Hanoi to Haiphong, Route 1 from Hanoi to Lang Son, and Route 4 from Cao Bang to Lang Son. In the Mekong Delta, they sought out the guerrillas in search-and-destroy missions. On the political front, the French had Bao Dai, whom they restored to the throne in 1946, sign the Elysée Agreement on March 8, 1949, which created the State of Vietnam as an independent nation but with France in control of defense, finance, and diplomacy. France promised elections to incorporate Cochin China into a unified Vietnam and held them one month later. Convinced the elections were a sham, the Vietminh boycotted them. Only 1,700 people showed up at the polls, and they voted overwhelmingly to join the State of Vietnam. D'Argenlieu proclaimed that democracy had prevailed.

But in 1949 the war became part of a much larger global struggle between the United States and the Soviet Union. From 1945 to 1948, anticommunist rhetoric had grown shrill in Washington. President Truman announced the Truman Doctrine in 1947 to provide $400 million in military and economic assistance to Greece and Turkey in the fight against leftist-backed guerrillas. The fall of Greece and Turkey, Truman

Like their French predecessors, American GIs learned that the weather and terrain in Vietnam could make life, to say nothing of military operations, a daunting task.

UPI/THE BETTMANN ARCHIVE

argued, would threaten all the eastern Mediterranean and the Mideast. To save Western Europe, Truman announced the Marshall Plan in 1948—a $12.6 billion program of American economic assistance.

Three events in 1949, however, elevated anticommunism in the United States from fear to paranoia. In 1948, hoping to starve West Berlin into surrender, the Soviets blocked the highway from West Germany to West Berlin. Truman responded with the Berlin Airlift, an unprecedented daily resupply of a city of 2 million people. Tension escalated well into 1949 until the Soviets backed down. When the Soviet Union detonated an atomic bomb in 1949, a wave of fear swept throughout the United States. Finally, at the end of 1949, Mao Zedong and the Chinese communists drove Jiang Jieshi and the Chinese nationalists off the mainland out to the island of Taiwan.

Americans accepted at face value the idea of monolithic communism. Many Americans were convinced that an international communist conspiracy was set to take over the world from Moscow. Whenever communists caused any trouble anywhere, the Truman administration blamed Moscow. Late in 1948 Republican Congressman Richard M. Nixon of

California accused Alger Hiss, a Democrat and former State Department official, of being a communist. The trial, which resulted in Hiss's conviction for perjury, generated headlines throughout much of 1949. Early in 1950 Senator Joseph McCarthy, a Republican from Wisconsin, charged that 205 communists were working in the State Department. Congress passed the Internal Security Act in September 1950 requiring registration of communist and communist-front organizations. Communist subversives seemed to be everywhere.

American policymakers began seeing the war in Indochina from another perspective. Ever since President Franklin D. Roosevelt's pronouncements on the inherent problems of French imperialism, prominent Americans had at least been able to recognize the existence of Vietnamese nationalism. But as the fear of communism increased, most prominent Americans lost sight of Vietnamese nationalism. All they could see through their new ideological glasses was Ho Chi Minh's communism, which they believed tied him inextricably to the Soviet conspiracy. They had no idea of the extent of Ho Chi Minh's political independence.

A few people expressed a different point of view. In Paris, General Leclerc repeated his conviction that "anti-communism will be a useless tool unless the problem of nationalism is resolved." Raymond Fosdick, a State Department expert on Asia, claimed that whether "the French like it or not, independence is coming to Indochina. Why, therefore, do we tie ourselves to the tail of their battered kite?" But Leclerc and Fosdick were lonely voices. Far more typical was Dean Acheson, Truman's secretary of state. In 1949 Acheson remarked that whether "Ho Chi Minh is as much nationalist as Commie is irrelevant. . . . All Stalinists in colonial areas are nationalists."

Out of that fear of Indochinese communism emerged the "domino theory." As Soviet-American relations deteriorated in the late 1940s and early 1950s, the domino theory became a mainstay of United States foreign policy. For a time in the 1950s and early 1960s, it was central to the way Americans interpreted the world. It appeared as if the whole free world depended on the survival of French Indochina. If Ho Chi Minh succeeded in conquering Tonkin, Annam, and Cochin China, it would only be a matter of time before Laos and Cambodia fell. With Indochina in communist hands, dominoes would fall in two directions: Thailand and Burma would go under, then Pakistan and India. Afghanistan, Iran, and the rest of the Middle East would follow. Then communism would infect North Africa and the entire Mediterranean.

As recent historians like Andrew Rotter and Gabriel Kolko have pointed out, there was more to the domino theory than anti-Soviet rhetoric and anticommunist paranoia. Communist expansion was no idle threat in the region. The Philippines was already dealing with communist guerrillas, and in Malaya and Burma the British government faced similar threats. Radical insurgents in Indonesia were undermining the

Dutch colonial regime. Political leaders in Australia and New Zealand were genuinely concerned about the prospects of a communist victory in Vietnam. The fall of Vietnam might topple Malaya, the Philippines, and Indonesia, and once Indonesia fell, so would Australia and New Zealand.

In strategic and economic terms, Southeast Asia was also critical to American interests. The fall of Southeast Asia would threaten the island chain stretching from Japan to the Philippines, cutting off American air routes to India and South Asia and eliminating the first line of defense in the Pacific. Australia and New Zealand would be isolated. The region was loaded with important natural and strategic resources, including tin, rubber, rice, copra, iron ore, copper, tungsten, and oil. Not only would the United States be cut off from those resources, but huge potential markets for American products would be threatened. Communist victories in Indochina, Malaya, and Indonesia would also place a geopolitical noose around the Philippines. How long could the Philippines stay free of communism if its neighbors fell?

The United States was also particularly concerned about the relationship between Southeast Asia and Japan. The Japanese economy was notoriously resource poor, and with China now in communist hands, one reliable source of raw materials for the Japanese economy was gone. If the Japanese economy stagnated, the possibility of Japanese communists gaining power was very real. One way to preserve the economic integrity of Japan was to effect an economic integration of Japan and Southeast Asia. But if Southeast Asia fell to communism, such an integration would be impossible. A 1952 National Security Council (NSC) memo specifically stated that concern: "In the long run the loss of Southeast Asia, especially Malaya and Indonesia, could result in such economic and political pressures in Japan as to make it extremely difficult to prevent Japan's eventual accommodation to the Soviet Bloc."

There also seemed to be a connection between Southeast Asia and the survival of Western Europe. In 1949 Great Britain was still in the economic doldrums and dangerously low in dollar reserves. Recovery required huge capital investments, and the entire British empire needed to increase its exports to the United States. Southeast Asia was critical to that process. Before World War II a vigorous triangular trade existed between Great Britain, the United States, and British Malaya, which had valuable rubber and tin assets. That trade needed to be revived. Nor could the French economy be restored to health as long as the war in Indochina was such a financial drain. American policymakers looked carefully at all these issues. The United States abandoned nationalism in Southeast Asia because the survival of Great Britain, France, and Japan as noncommunist allies seemed more important.

The domino theory became the foreign-policy expression of these political, economic, and ideological needs, and as McCarthyism fanned the flames of anticommunism, the image of falling dominoes captured the public imagination. On September 20, 1951, during a visit to Washington, General Jean de Lattre de Tassigny, the commander in chief of French Indochina, described a chain of dominoes reaching from Tonkin to Europe: "Once Tonkging [*sic*] is lost, there is really no barrier before Suez. . . . The loss of Asia would mean the end of Islam, which has two-thirds of its faithful in Asia. The fall of Islam would mean upheavals in North Africa jeopardizing strategic defense bases situated there."

American leaders preferred to describe a row of dominoes in the other direction. Secretary of State John Foster Dulles said in 1953 that if "Indo-China should be lost, there would be a chain reaction throughout the Far East and South Asia," posing a "grave threat to Malaya, Thailand, Indonesia, the Philippines, Australia and New Zealand." Thomas Dewey, the Republican governor of New York, went even further, claiming that the "French are holding Indo-China, without which we would lose Japan and the Pacific." In 1965 Senator Thomas J. Dodd of Connecticut carried the domino theory to its extreme: "If we fail to draw the line in Vietnam we may find ourselves compelled to draw a defense line as far back as Seattle and Alaska, with Hawaii as a solitary outpost."

Throughout 1950 political events in Asia seemed to confirm American fears. Early in 1950, the Soviet Union and China extended diplomatic recognition to Hanoi, which for Dean Acheson revealed "Ho in his true colors as the mortal enemy of native independence in Indochina." The United States responded quickly, confirming the Elysée Agreement by recognizing Bao Dai's State of Vietnam as an "independent part of the French Union." In February the National Security Council recognized "that the threat of Communist aggression against Indochina is only one phase of anticipated Communist plans to seize all of Southeast Asia." On May 15, 1950, President Harry Truman announced his decision to supply $15 million in military assistance to France to fight the Vietminh.

A few weeks later the strategic atmosphere in Asia changed dramatically. When North Korea invaded South Korea in June, the Truman administration became convinced that the Soviet Union wanted all of Asia. Truman increased the American commitment to France, sending more than $133 million in Indochina aid at the end of the year. Truman committed another $50 million for economic and technical assistance. A contingent of DC-3 Dakota aircraft landed in Saigon in June. Waiting on the runway with paintbrushes, the French enraged American pilots when they replaced the aircrafts' white star markings with the French tricolor insignia. Late in November, Chinese troops joined the Korean War, killing thousands of United States soldiers. To most Americans, the international communist conspiracy was well under way.

In Hanoi, Vo Nguyen Giap was not thinking about any international communist conspiracy. From Mao Zedong's writings on revolutionary warfare, Vo Nguyen Giap developed a three-stage formula for defeating the French. During the first stage, the Vietminh would just survive, avoiding confrontations until they built up their reserves. If they could achieve surprise and complete superiority, they would strike, but otherwise the Vietminh bided their time. Vo Nguyen Giap's fear of premature battle was not sentimental. He possessed a unique philosophy about death. "Every minute," he remarked to a French reporter, "hundreds of thousands of people die on this earth. The life or death of a hundred, a thousand, tens of thousands of human beings, even our compatriots, means little." What he did not want was an engagement that destroyed his fledgling army. Stage one characterized Vietminh operations in 1946 and 1947.

The second stage employed guerrilla tactics—ambushes, road destruction, hit-and-run attacks, and assassinations. At night the Vietminh placed booby traps along French patrol routes. Their favorite ones were sharpened bamboo "punji stakes" dipped in human feces or poison and driven into holes, rice paddies, or attached to bent saplings; hollowed-out coconuts filled with gunpowder and triggered by a trip wire; walk bridges with ropes almost cut away so they would collapse when someone tried to cross; a buried bamboo stub with a bullet on its tip, activated when someone stepped on it; the "Malay whip log," attached to two trees by a rope and triggered by a trip wire; and boards studded with iron barbs and buried in stream beds and rice paddies. Vo Nguyen Giap's attacks on the French in 1948 and 1949 represented the second stage.

By 1949 Vo Nguyen Giap thought he was almost ready for the third stage. He wanted a real fight with the French Expeditionary Corps. Between 1945 and 1947, he built the People's Army from a ragtag group of 5,000 to more than 100,000, most of them irregular troops but also including thousands of highly disciplined, well-trained Vietminh soldiers. Events in 1949 made the general offensive even more inviting. Mao Zedong's victory gave Vo Nguyen Giap a sanctuary at his rear. Vietnamese peasants constructed four roads from the Chinese border to army-staging areas, and Chinese and Soviet supplies began to arrive. By 1950 he had five fully equipped infantry divisions, along with an artillery and engineering division. It was time for the third stage—the "general counteroffensive."

Vo Nguyen Giap set his sights on the French outpost at Dong Khe. The hedgehog sat astride Route 4, a road the French considered the Vietminh "jugular vein" in northern Tonkin. They reasoned that control of Route 4 would cut Vietminh supply lines from China and stall their troop movements. French truck convoys supplied Dong Khe on a daily basis, but in early 1950 Vo Nguyen Giap blocked all shipments to the garrison. On May 26, 1950, with monsoon rains drenching the land and Vietminh infantry surrounding the outpost, he began the artillery bombardment. Two days later, thousands of Vietminh soldiers stormed the garrison. It fell on May 28. Although French paratroopers retook Dong Khe a few days later, the Vietminh successfully attacked again on

September 18. Early in October, they took Cao Bang, the northernmost city on Route 4, and over the next several months the French abandoned Lang Son, their southern outpost on Route 4, and Thai Nguyen, the city on Route 3 between Hanoi and Cao Bang. Vo Nguyen Giap killed or captured 6,000 French troops and eliminated the French presence all along the Chinese border.

Heads rolled in Hanoi and Saigon. France fired most senior officials and conferred joint military and political command on General Jean de Lattre de Tassigny, who became high commissioner and commander in chief of Indochina in December 1950. A hero of both world wars, de Lattre had an ability matched by his ego. Handsome, confident, and obsessed with victory, he rebuilt French outposts in the Red River Valley, betting that Vo Nguyen Giap, flushed with success, would push too far.

De Lattre was right. Vo Nguyen Giap wanted to drive the French back into Hanoi, so he decided to attack Vinh Yen, a reinforced garrison thirty miles northwest of the capital. De Lattre was ready. The Vietminh attacked but failed to overrun the base. Giap tried an attack up the Day River southeast of Hanoi but was repulsed again. He threw the Vietminh against Nam Dinh, a French garrison twenty miles south of Haiphong. Bernard de Lattre, the general's son, had orders to hold Nam Dinh at all costs. He died obeying his father. By the end of May 1951, the Vietminh had 6,000 dead and Vo Nguyen Giap retreated from Vinh Yen. The general returned to stage two.

De Lattre was barely able to savor the victories. He was terminally ill with stomach cancer and died seven months later in Paris. General Raoul Salan replaced him, but he was little more than a caretaker. De Lattre had created the Vietnamese National Army, on paper a 115,000-man force, to at least make it appear that Bao Dai's government was really fighting the communists. In the meantime, Giap replenished his divisions. At the end of May 1953 Salan was relieved of his command. By that time the war was a bottomless pit. Since 1945 the war had cost France 3 dead generals, 8 colonels, 18 lieutenant colonels, 69 majors, 341 captains, 1,140 lieutenants, 9,691 enlisted men, and 12,109 French Legionnaires, along with 20,000 missing in action and 100,000 wounded. Saint-Cyr, the French military academy, was not graduating officers fast enough to replace the dead in Indochina.

The military situation was even worse. From the Chinese border in northern Vietnam to the Ca Mau Peninsula on the South China Sea, the Vietminh controlled two-thirds of the country. Their army, including regular and irregular troops, numbered in the hundreds of thousands, and in the words of journalist Theodore White, "has become a modern army, increasingly skillful, armed with artillery, organized into divisions." French control had been reduced to enclaves around Hanoi, Haiphong, and Saigon, as well as a strip of land along the Cambodian border.

It was time for a change. Salan's replacement was Henri Navarre, a veteran of both world wars who believed French forces could bring the Vietminh to their knees within a year. Navarre joined the French infantry in 1916 after graduating from Saint-Cyr as a cavalry officer. Except for duty in North Africa during World War II, his career was in army intelligence. Supremely self-confident, dictatorial, and righteously committed, Navarre was an instant celebrity in the French social circuits of Hanoi and Saigon. In both cities he outfitted himself with air-conditioned command posts complete with the best in French wine and cuisine. When he arrived in Saigon to assume his command, Navarre predicted an early end to the war: "Now we can see it clearly—like light at the end of a tunnel."

Navarre decided that French strategy needed an overhaul. After eight years of fighting, the French were no closer to winning than they had been back in 1946. The Vietminh were steadily growing, and Vo Nguyen Giap was preparing to widen the war into Laos. For Navarre, France was wasting men and resources fighting scattered guerrillas in a conflict that had no end. The key to victory was conventional war. He would seduce the Vietminh into a major engagement where French firepower would annihilate them.

What became known as the Navarre Plan was actually an elaborate military scheme devised in Washington and Paris. Because American troops were tied down in Western Europe and Korea, the United States insisted that France, with massive financial and matériel assistance, take care of Indochina itself. The plan called for a large increase in the size of the Vietnamese National Army and nine new French battalions. Navarre proposed removing his troops from isolated outposts, combining them with the new French troops, and taking the offensive in the Red River Valley. He hoped to be able to use the Vietnamese National Army elsewhere in Vietnam.

But in the fall of 1953, Vo Nguyen Giap countered with increased guerrilla attacks throughout the Red River Delta as well as an invasion of central and southern Laos. He also readied three Vietminh divisions for an invasion of northern Laos. Already at the limits of their economic and military commitment, the French became obsessed with keeping the Vietminh out of Laos, where the Pathet Lao, a communist-backed guerrilla force, was already causing enough trouble. Navarre began considering a new option—going after the Vietminh in western Tonkin along the Laotian border, even though it meant rescattering his forces to isolated areas.

Navarre scoured the map looking for the perfect place and found it near Laos at the village of Dienbienphu. There Navarre would establish a "mooring point," a center of operations from which French patrols could go out into the hills in search of the Vietminh. A large French garrison at Dienbienphu, Navarre surmised, would make it more difficult for Vo Nguyen Giap to ship supplies through Laos to southern Vietnam or invade Laos. Finally, Dienbienphu was the center of Vietminh opium production; revenues from the drug traffic financed weapons purchases. By suppressing opium production, Navarre hoped to cut Vietminh revenues.

Navarre was convinced that Ho Chi Minh would not be able to abide the French presence at Dienbienphu. In order to push ahead with his plans for domination of Indochina, Ho Chi Minh would have to destroy the French garrison. Anticipating massive, human-wave assaults like the Chinese had launched in Korea and the Vietminh at Dong Khe and Vinh Yen, Navarre planted the base in the center of the valley, with vast stretches of flat territory separating it from the neighboring mountains, where dozens of howitzers were aimed. Colonel Charles Piroth, the one-armed commander of French artillery, predicted that "no Vietminh cannon will be able to fire three rounds before being destroyed by my artillery." If the Vietminh attacked, they had to cross thousands of yards of open fields where French tanks, machine guns, and tactical aircraft would cut them to pieces. With complete air superiority, the French built an airstrip and thought they could hold out indefinitely, resupplying themselves by air from Hanoi.

Navarre wanted to double the size of the Vietnamese National Army to relieve the French Expeditionary Corps of its obligations to fight a nonstop war against Vietminh guerrillas and assume the offensive. French advisers would remain in the countryside to work with the Vietnamese National Army in suppressing the guerrillas. At the same time, Navarre assembled a new, powerful army corps to occupy Dienbienphu and engage the Vietminh in battle.

But where would Navarre find the men and the money? In France the Indochina War was increasingly unpopular, a bottomless pit swallowing men and matériel with no victory in sight. Conscription was out of the question; there was no way the government could get the necessary legislation through the French National Assembly. Public debate was already at a fever pitch. Instead, Navarre turned to the other colonies, putting together a polyglot army of French Legionnaires and volunteers from France, Lebanon, Syria, Chad, Guadeloupe, and Madagascar. For money Navarre looked to the United States. Ever since 1950, when Congress appropriated the first $15 million, American assistance steadily increased. Navarre wanted even more, and the administration of Dwight Eisenhower, worried about the domino theory, was quick to agree. By the end of 1953 the United States was supplying Navarre with 10,000 tons of equipment a month, at an annual cost of $500 million. That amount increased to $1.1 billion in 1954, nearly 78 percent of France's war expenses. Navarre had money and men.

Navarre placed Colonel Christian de Castries in command of Dienbienphu. An aristocrat, horseman, and athlete, Castries had won the world high jump championship in 1933 and the long jump championship in 1935, and during World War II he made the transition from cavalry to armor and was wounded several times. The Germans captured him in 1941, but he escaped in 1944 and rejoined French fighting forces. Known to show off at parties by chewing glass, Castries said life was sweet if a man "had a horse to ride, an enemy to kill, and a woman in his bed."

Beginning in November 1953, Castries supervised the construction of the base at Dienbienphu. He was immediately identifiable by his red cap, flaming red scarf, and riding crop in his hand. He put the main base at the center of the valley and then put up three major artillery bases: one three miles to the south, which he designated Isabelle; another about a mile to the northeast, which was Béatrice; and a third nearly two miles to the north, which he called Gabrielle. A notorious womanizer, Castries was supporting three mistresses by these names, and he wanted to immortalize them. Castries named other firebases and French posts after earlier conquests: Anne Marie, Françoise, Dominique, Eliane, Claudine, and Huguette. Castries manned the base with 13,200 paratroopers. In a radio broadcast on January 1, 1954, General Navarre announced that he expected "total victory after six more months of hard fighting."

Navarre's commander of the Tonkin theater was not as sanguine. René Cogny came from humble stock, but with scholarships he graduated from Saint-Cyr in artillery and then earned degrees in political science and law. The Germans captured him in 1940, but he escaped in 1941, only to be captured again in 1943. He spent the rest of the war at the Buchenwald concentration camp, where torture left him with a permanent limp. In the eight years after his release, Cogny enjoyed a spectacular rise through the ranks of the officer corps, from captain to major general. He feared the Navarre Plan. He wanted to avoid battles in the highlands, except for minor skirmishes; maintain a permanent offensive against the Vietminh in the Red River Delta; and frequently raid enemy supply lines and infiltration routes. When he first heard about the plan from Navarre, Cogny remarked to his chief of staff: "Dienbienphu will become, whether we like it or not, a drain on manpower . . . as soon as it is pinned down by a single regiment. . . . The consequences of such a decision may be very serious."

From his post in the mountains above Dienbienphu, Vo Nguyen Giap was dumbfounded. The locations of the artillery bases were ludicrous. Because Navarre had decided that Vo Nguyen Giap would attack the main base in an all-out human-wave attack, Navarre wanted his artillery prepared to blast the open fields outside the perimeter from several directions. But all Vo Nguyen Giap had to do was attack the artillery bases one by one, and then go after the main base. He knew that the Navarre Plan represented a significant shift in French strategy, and he was in a quandary at first about how to deal with the change. His

Major General René Cogny (left) supervised French military operations in
northern Vietnam in 1954. General Henri Navarre (right) was commander in
chief of French forces in Indochina. Together, they planned the military
strategy that led to the disaster at Dienbienphu.
HOWARD SOCHUREK/*LIFE* MAGAZINE

philosophy about such confrontations with the French had always been
consistent: "Strike to win, strike only when success is certain. If it is not,
then do not strike." Vo Nguyen Giap's biggest mistake, trying to overrun
the French base at Vinh Yen in 1951, had made him more prudent and
deliberate, more willing to wait until victory was certain.

Vo Nguyen Giap could not understand why the French picked Dienbienphu. The roads were narrow and exposed; the Vietminh would never
let supply trucks reach the valley; and Vietminh artillery would prevent
supply aircraft from landing at the hastily constructed airfield. The
valley was a wet bottomland of the Nam Yum River. After heavy rains
the valley turned into mud and drained very slowly. Torrential rains
during the monsoon season turned the valley into a quagmire. French
tanks would be immobilized. Any competent engineer or hydrologist
could have taken a look at Dienbienphu and concluded that tank warfare would be problematic at best. Even in dry weather the ground was
covered with heavy, vined brush that would clog tank tracks. The
French had also assumed that the Vietminh did not have any decent
artillery pieces and that even if they did they would not be able to place

them in the mountains above Dienbienphu. There were no roads up there for trucks to make deliveries.

When Vo Nguyen Giap calculated the deficiencies of the French position, he concluded that Vietminh victory was certain. The terrain would destroy armor mobility; tanks would become stationary artillery pieces. By assaulting Gabrielle, Isabelle, and Béatrice in sequence, Giap could eliminate French artillery. He was also counting on his own artillery. The Chinese had captured hundreds of American-built 105-mm howitzers and 120-mm potbellied mortars in Korea, and they were on their way. Vo Nguyen Giap intended to destroy the airfield and put Dienbienphu under siege. Nor was he worried about the vast open spaces between the mountain slopes and the French perimeter. He would dig hundreds of miles of tunnels and trenches from the mountain slopes toward the base, eliminating the French tactical advantage.

For years the French had waited for the set-piece battle in which their firepower would prevail, assuming, of course, that they would win such a contest. Jean de Lattre de Tassigny, Raoul Salan, and Henri Navarre all prayed for the confrontation. Castries put it best in January 1954: "If he [the Vietminh] comes down, we've got him. It may be a tough fight, but we shall halt him. And we shall at last have what we have always lacked: a concentrated target that we can smash." The French were convinced that if Vo Nguyen Giap attacked Dienbienphu, the Vietminh would suffer a decisive defeat.

Slowly and steadily Vo Nguyen Giap did the impossible—he put four Vietminh divisions into the mountains surrounding Dienbienphu. Navarre completely underestimated Giap's ability to move the Vietminh. Even though most of them had only cut-up rubber tires for shoes, Giap got twenty to fifty miles a day out of them, each carrying a rifle, a large bag of rice, clothing, a shovel, and a water bottle. When French aircraft bombed the small roads heading for Dienbienphu, Giap repaired them. Along Routes 13B and 41, he had 10,000 workers who repaired roads within an hour of the attack.

By early March 1954 Vo Nguyen Giap had 50,000 combat-hardened Vietminh troops and another 50,000 support troops in place, along with 100,000 Vietnamese porters carrying supplies on their backs. On March 12, 1954, the Vietminh taught the French a lesson in the art of war. General Navarre was confident that Giap would not be able to bring heavy artillery into battle, that French artillery and tactical air support would put Giap at a tremendous firepower disadvantage. Suddenly 105-mm shells began to rain on the airstrip at Dienbienphu, pockmarking it with craters and rendering it unsafe for supply landings. The French had expected Giap to move the artillery into place the way they did—on large trucks over visible roads. But Giap disassembled each artillery piece, organized thousands of porters to carry the elements to Dienbienphu, and then reassembled the artillery there.

The shelling on March 12 was just a preview. The main feature started at 5:00 P.M. the next day when Vietminh artillery exploded all over the French artillery bases. By midnight Vietminh troops seized outpost Béatrice. The bombardment of Gabrielle began at dusk the next day. Nine hours later Gabrielle fell. The Vietminh sustained thousands of casualties, but in less than fifteen hours Castries had lost most of his artillery. Isabelle was so far south of the main base that in order to protect it Castries had to move a large troop contingent there. Instead of attacking, Vo Nguyen Giap left Isabelle alone, rendering the French troops there useless. The next day the Vietminh bombardment became so heavy that aircraft could no longer land. French soldiers could only be supplied by air, and on March 17, 1954, American and French pilots began flying C-119s and C-47s over Dienbienphu, dropping food, weapons, and ammunition to the besieged soldiers. That same day armed Montagnard tribesmen, allied with the French, realized their plight and fled Dienbienphu. France needed help.

On March 20, General Paul Ely, chief of staff of the French armed forces, flew to Washington for a meeting with President Dwight Eisenhower, Secretary of State John Foster Dulles, and Admiral Arthur Radford, chairman of the Joint Chiefs of Staff. A member of the West Point class of 1915—called the "Class on Which the Stars Fell" because 59 of its 164 graduates rose to the rank of brigadier general or higher—Ike was perhaps the best of the group. General George C. Marshall passed over 350 senior officers to promote Eisenhower to major general. In 1942 Ike was made the commander of the European theater of operations and put in charge of the invasion of North Africa. In 1943 he commanded the invasions of Italy and Sicily. And in 1944 he led the invasion of Europe. Ike had a reputation for decisiveness, energy, intelligence, and skill in handling temperamental and egotistical individuals. Said FDR's press secretary of Ike: "To acquire these characteristics he worked constantly, sleeping only five hours a day . . . and laboring seven days a week and holidays. Chain smoking cigarettes, he had an inexhaustible supply of nervous energy."

Once in the White House, Eisenhower seemed more subdued. White House reporters recall not his energy and precise thinking but rather his mangled syntax and his fondness for golfing and bridge. But behind the mild facade Ike was still in charge. In foreign affairs, he made all the key decisions. Intellectuals and English teachers could fault his syntax, but as Fred I. Greenstein notes, Eisenhower "had geometric precision in stating the basic conditions shaping a problem, deducing their implications, and weighing the costs and benefits of alternative possible responses." As Ely talked, the geometry of Ike's mind was calculating.

The French general wanted to make sure that American assistance would continue under Eisenhower. Ely readily admitted that Dienbienphu was doomed, although he did not know how the communists could "continue to suffer the losses they have been taking . . . I don't know how they can stay in the battle." He made no specific request for anything more than continued American financial support. When the meeting concluded, Eisenhower asked Radford to see if the United States could offer some more assistance to the French. Without the knowledge of Eisenhower, Dulles, or even other joint chiefs, Radford had, with the assistance of American and French officers in Saigon, hatched a rescue plan. A graduate of the U.S. Naval Academy in Annapolis, Radford commanded aircraft carriers in the Pacific during World War II. In May 1953, when President Eisenhower toured the Pacific and East Asia to assess the Korean situation, Radford was commander of naval forces in the Pacific. He spent some time with Eisenhower during the tour and impressed the president with his grasp of Asian affairs. Eisenhower named Radford chief of naval operations in 1953 and chairman of the Joint Chiefs of Staff.

By that time Radford was a saber-rattling darling of the Republican right. A zealous convert to complicated weapons technology and air power, Radford endeared himself to a number of conservative politicians during World War II when he said the only approach to the Japanese was "to kill the bastards scientifically." Infantry combat "was messy and wasted personnel." Strategic and tactical bombing, on the other hand, was "precise and clean." Radford was convinced that Asia, not Europe, would be central to American foreign policy for the rest of the twentieth century. Late in 1953, when the president expressed concern about the defense budget, Radford became the author of the "New Look," a "more-bang-for-the buck" approach to military spending. Radford urged, and Eisenhower and Dulles accepted, the notion that instead of planning for a variety of military contingencies—strategic nuclear war, conventional war, limited nuclear war, and guerrilla war—the United States should plan for a war in which nuclear weapons would be used whenever they were strategically advantageous. Such an approach would be less expensive than a more comprehensive response system. Secretary of State John Foster Dulles used Radford's logic in his famous "massive retaliation" speech of January 12, 1954, when he threatened to use strategic nuclear weapons whenever and wherever the Soviet Union fomented rebellion.

When Radford learned of the desperate situation at Dienbienphu, he was anxious to use air power. It was the perfect place, he thought, to try out the New Look defense policy. He proposed Operation Vulture—the use of Philippine-based B-29s, accompanied by aircraft from the carriers USS *Essex* and USS *Boxer,* to knock out Vietminh artillery. Without artillery the Vietminh could not destroy the outpost. The airstrip could be repaired, and a full-scale resupply resumed. In case the air strike did not lift the siege, Radford was prepared to use atomic weapons. In his memoirs, Radford recalled: "We could have helped the French with air strikes. Whether these alone would have been successful in breaking the siege of Dien Bien Phu is debatable. If we had used atomic weapons, we probably would have been successful." Arthur Radford was playing for keeps.

The proposal triggered an intense debate. The other chiefs of staff, especially General Matthew Ridgway of the army, were opposed. Fresh from his command of United Nations forces in Korea, Ridgway felt sure the bombing would fail to lift the siege and that only ground troops—seven to ten full divisions—could rescue Dienbienphu. The Korean War had already proven how difficult Asian land wars could be, and the terrain of Indochina was far worse, the stuff of which bloody, endless guerrilla wars are made. Eisenhower listened carefully to Ridgway; the two infantry commanders understood one another.

Vice President Richard Nixon supported Operation Vulture. On March 13, the day the Vietminh overran Gabrielle, Nixon announced, "We have adopted a new principle. Rather than let the communists nibble us to death all over the world in little wars, we will rely in the future on massive, mobile retaliatory forces." In a press conference Nixon claimed that there "is no reason why the French forces should not remain in Indo-China and win. They have greater manpower, and a tremendous advantage over their adversaries, particularly air power." Like Radford, Nixon was prepared to use atomic bombs to lift the siege.

Eisenhower listened to Radford. He listened to Ridgway and Nixon. Never threatened by conflicting viewpoints, Ike believed in the value of good advice and well-reasoned arguments. Walter Bedell Smith, Eisenhower's World War II chief of staff and close friend, recalled that during the war Ike constantly sought advice: "One of his most successful methods in dealing with individuals is to assume that he himself is lacking in detailed knowledge and liable to make an error. . . . This was by no means a pose, because he . . . values the recommendations . . . he receives, although his own better . . . judgment might cause them to be disregarded." And so Eisenhower listened to opinions bold and cautious—and then he made his decision. He knew from experience that wars are seldom as neat as they seem in strategic papers, and that the "fog of battle" confounds the best laid plans. He was intrigued with Radford's plan. He would not, however, go forward without the support of Congress and the British.

On March 31, President Eisenhower publicly stated that he "could conceive of no greater tragedy than for the United States to become involved in an all-out war in Indochina," but privately he wanted to help the French. Ever since 1949 the Republican right wing had made enormous political capital on how the "Democrats had lost China," and he was not anxious to be blamed for losing Indochina. But at the same time, he perceived public skepticism about American involvement in Vietnam. The Korean armistice was just a few months old. Most Americans did not want another war in Asia. With congressional elections at the end of the year, Eisenhower did not want to "go it alone," so on April 3 he had Dulles and Radford try to sell the idea to a congressional delegation that included Senators William Knowland and Lyndon Johnson and Congressmen Joseph Martin and John McCormack.

Eisenhower was not asking for an immediate air strike. He was more cautious than that. What he wanted to know was whether they would give him the discretionary authority to use American forces if a Vietminh victory at Dienbienphu would lead to the fall of Indochina. The legislators were skeptical. They worried about what would happen if the bombing failed. Would ground troops be committed? They also were concerned about the United States' taking unilateral action. Why not coordinate a United Nations or an international effort to save Dienbienphu? They did have one unequivocal answer for Ike: no more Koreas, where the United States supplied 90 percent of the combat troops.

Because of the debate within the administration and congressional reservations, Eisenhower decided that American intervention would have to be contingent on securing cooperation from other North Atlantic Treaty Organization (NATO) powers, and getting France to make plans for granting independence for its Indochinese colonies. That was going to take some time, time Dienbienphu did not have. Convinced that Operation Vulture was the only way of saving Dienbienphu, the French asked Eisenhower for an immediate air strike, leaving the question of joint allied military operations for later discussions. He summarily rejected the request, chastising Radford for misleading the French but agreeing to explore the possibility of subsequent American intervention if European allies would cooperate. Eisenhower asked Dulles to go to Europe and secure NATO support. Dulles set out to achieve what he call "United Action."

Travel was as much a part of John Foster Dulles's life as diplomacy and breathing. He used airplanes like other men used cabs. No trip was too long to take for diplomacy. Dulles and Eisenhower made an odd couple. Compared to the warm, friendly president, the secretary of state seemed cold and distant. In fact, compared to almost anyone Dulles *was* cold and distant. The nation called Eisenhower "Ike," but no one called Dulles "Jack." Historian Townsend Hoopes describes Dulles as a "solid tree trunk of a man gnarled and durable . . . a rectangular brow and aquiline nose, a thin and drooping mouth, a strong jaw, the whole creating an effect of ultimate seriousness and at the same time of ultimate plainness." Proud of the history of foreign service in his family—his grandfather had been secretary of state for Benjamin Harrison and his uncle had held the same position for Woodrow Wilson—Dulles had been part of the Versailles peace mission in 1919, a Wall Street lawyer with clients across the globe, a delegate to the United Nations, and a lifelong student of foreign relations. As Eisenhower told reporters, there is "only one man I know who has seen *more* of the world and talked with more people and *knows* more than Dulles does—and that's me."

Dulles began a dizzying round of shuttle diplomacy, traveling back and forth between Europe and the United States trying to line up allies. Back home the president tried to drum up public support for intervention, using the domino theory in an April 7 press conference: "You have a row of dominoes set up and you knock over the first one, and what will happen to the last one is the certainty that it will go over very quickly. . . . The loss of Indochina will cause the fall of Southeast Asia like a set of dominoes." But while Eisenhower and Dulles were trying to line up the allies, General Ridgway torpedoed the idea. He was furious with Radford. Ridgway was convinced that Ike would not use atomic weapons; in 1945 he had advised Truman against employing them on the Japanese. Ridgway was right. At a meeting of the National Security Council in late April, when the issue came up again, the president finally interrupted a discussion with a frustrated outburst: "You boys must be crazy. We can't use those awful things against Asians for the second time in less than ten years. My God!" Ridgway also felt that conventional air strikes would not lift the siege. Intervention with ground troops would be inevitable. In a memo to President Eisenhower, Ridgway shared his misgivings: "How deep was the water over the bar at Saigon? What are the harbor and dock facilities? Where could we store the . . . supplies we would need? How good was the road network— how could supplies be transported as the fighting forces moved inland, and in what tonnages? What of the climate? The rainfall? What tropical diseases would attack the combat soldier?" Eisenhower understood. The next day Dulles informed Henri Bonnet, the French ambassador to the United States, that American intervention might not be forthcoming.

Operation Vulture and the larger proposal for United Action was compromised by French intransigence. During the discussions with the French, Eisenhower became more and more frustrated. He complained that the French "want us to come in as junior partners and provide materials, etc., while they themselves retain authority in that region." In the previous months they had balked at the notion of United Action themselves, fearing that French power would be subordinated in a multinational force. Nor were the French willing even to talk of independence for Vietnam. That, too, bothered Eisenhower, who wrote to a friend that France had employed "weasel words in promising independence . . . and through this reason . . . have suffered reverses that have been inexcusable." The French would not even cooperate with the Military Assistance and Advisory Group (MAAG), an American mission sent to Vietnam in 1950 to coordinate United States economic and military aid. France wanted American money, not American advice.

Skepticism among the NATO allies also doomed United Action. Dulles shuttled back and forth between London and Paris, pushing collective action, sometimes browbeating the British and French, but they would not budge. The French did not like the idea because they had no intention of freeing their colonies; they intended to remain indefinitely. The British thought Ho Chi Minh was a highly independent communist who would not let the Chinese, any more than the French, take over his country. When Dulles predicted the apocalypse if Dienbienphu fell, the British calmly replied that the United States was viewing the situation through ideological blinders. Foreign Minister Anthony Eden predicted that India, Burma, Pakistan, Thailand, Malaya, Indonesia, the Philippines, and Japan would survive even if Ho Chi Minh took over Vietnam. Dulles left London empty-handed on April 14. Prime Minister Winston Churchill was relieved to see Dulles go. Years later he summarized his feelings: "Dulles is the only case of a bull I know who carries his china closet around with him."

Everything also went wrong at Dienbienphu. Navarre's plans to increase the size of the Vietnamese National Army failed miserably. The government of Bao Dai sent 94,000 draft orders late in 1953, but only 5,400 new soldiers reported for duty. The Vietnamese National Army never exceeded the 115,000 level, and by early 1954 the desertion rate reached nearly 4,000 men a month. In a country where nationalism, communist and noncommunist, ran very deep, the French plan to develop a highly effective army of colonial troops was incredibly naive. The idea of turning the war over to the Vietnamese was no closer to reality in 1954 than it had been in 1951 when General de Lattre first created the Vietnamese National Army.

In Dienbienphu, French problems mounted. Monsoon rains immobilized French tanks in the heavy mud and prevented resupply from Hanoi. French troops rationed food and water. Ho Chi Minh, aware that the Geneva Conference was about to convene, was intent on destroying the French fortress. The shovels Vietminh soldiers carried into Dienbienphu were as useful as their rifles. They dug trenches and tunnels. Twenty-four hours a day, day after day, antlike, tens of thousands of Vietminh extended the trenches, inching their way toward the French outpost, steadily reducing the French perimeter, eliminating the stretches of open space the French had relied on. By the end of April, the Vietminh outnumbered the French ten to one, and the French perimeter, which once had a circumference of fifteen miles, was reduced to a thousand-yard square.

With Vo Nguyen Giap closing the circle on Dienbienphu, the Geneva Conference convened in Switzerland. The negotiators were aware that Dienbienphu was in trouble. Pham Van Dong, representing the Vietminh, had his own agenda. He snubbed Bao Dai's ministers. John Foster Dulles did not want to be there at all and was committed to making sure that the Geneva Accords resulting from the conference did "not give one inch of territory to the Communists." Described as a "card carrying Christian," Dulles equated communism with all the sins of atheism.

Once on hearing Jiang Jieshi and Syngman Rhee spoken of in unflattering terms, Dulles became excited and said, "No matter what you say about them, those two gentlemen are modern-day equivalents of the founders of the church. They are Christian gentlemen who have suffered for their faith." Dulles found it impossible to compromise with the Vietminh, and he behaved badly at Geneva, "like a puritan in a house of ill repute," according to his biographer. The representatives of Laos and Cambodia refused to deal with Pham Van Dong because they felt sure the Vietminh were bent on conquering all of Indochina. Only the British foreign minister, Anthony Eden, was prepared to deal with every constituency at Geneva.

The complexities of the personalities at Geneva paled next to the interests they represented. Pham Van Dong wanted a complete political settlement leading to the withdrawal of French forces and establishment of a new, independent government under Ho Chi Minh. France only wanted a military ceasefire. Georges Bidault headed the French delegation. The fall of Dienbienphu, Bidault realized, would doom the French in the north, but he hoped to regroup in Cochin China and maintain the empire. Laos and Cambodia sided with Bidault. They were already dealing with internal communist rebellions and assumed that French withdrawal, combined with a Vietminh triumph, would destroy the French Union and condemn Indochina to communism. Zhou Enlai and the Chinese wanted to partition Vietnam. They did not want a united Vietnam—French or Vietnamese—to the south. The Soviets were also conciliatory. Joseph Stalin's death in 1953 removed the most militant voice in Moscow, and they did not want a confrontation with the United States, not over a faraway place like Indochina. Only the Soviets and the British came to Geneva without a firm political agenda. They emerged as the leaders of the conference.

The various delegations spent their first two weeks at Geneva on other questions before turning their attention to Indochina. On May 6, just when the talks began, Vo Nguyen Giap attacked the French fortress, hitting it with new Soviet Katyusha field rockets, which the French dubbed "Stalin's organs" because of their roar, and sending thousands of Vietminh out of the trenches, through the exploding shells, and into the base. On the afternoon of May 7, after bitter, hand-to-hand combat, Vietminh entered the French headquarters and struck the flag. In a final radio message, Castries cried: "Our resistance is going to be overwhelmed. The Viets are within a few meters of the radio transmitter where I am speaking. I have given orders to carry out maximum destruction. We will not surrender. We will fight to the end. . . . Long live France!" The Vietminh seized him moments later, along with more than 10,000 of his comrades. The French prisoners spent the next ten weeks in horrible prison camps before their repatriation began on July 20.

Vo Nguyen Giap's troops had sustained 22,900 casualties (7,900 killed and 15,000 wounded), while the French buried 2,080 dead and treated 5,613 wounded. But Giap was still the victor. He regrouped his four divisions at Dienbienphu and marched them east toward the Red River Delta and Hanoi. Certain that a general French defeat was near, General Navarre rearranged his troops in the Red River Delta and placed them around Hanoi and along Highways 5 and 18 between Hanoi and Haiphong, the last escape route out of Tonkin.

Soon after news of Dienbienphu reached Geneva, the conference stalled as the various delegations doggedly pursued their own narrow objectives. The defeat toppled the French government. Prime Minister Joseph Laniel resigned on June 12 and Pierre Mendes-France, a radical socialist, became prime minister. He stunned the French Chamber of Deputies by announcing, "I promise to resign if, one month from now, on July 20, I have failed to obtain a cease-fire in Indochina." Mendes-France was committed to ending the war that had brought only humiliation to his country.

The Eisenhower administration realized that a settlement in Geneva was inevitable and that the communists would gain part of Indochina. On June 24 Dulles told congressional leaders the United States would have to look beyond Geneva and try to salvage something in Southeast Asia. In particular, he talked of assuming the responsibility for making sure that not another domino fell in Indochina. In order to "keep freedom alive," Dulles wanted a NATO-like regional alliance system in Southeast Asia. Nobody realized it at the time, but the United States had just assumed a responsibility that would lead a decade later to the Vietnam War.

Mendes-France's promise and the change in the American position breathed new life into the Geneva talks. Anthony Eden began playing a central role in the conference, as did Vyacheslav Molotov, the Soviet representative. Along with Zhou Enlai, they convinced Pham Van Dong and the Vietminh to accept a temporary partitioning of Vietnam to be followed by reunification elections. The French and the Vietminh hotly debated the question of where to divide Vietnam and when to hold the elections. Bidault wanted the dividing line as far north and the elections as far into the future as possible. Pham Van Dong wanted the dividing line as far south and the elections as soon as possible. Unlike Dienbienphu, the French won this battle. The Geneva Accords divided Vietnam at the seventeenth parallel into North Vietnam and South Vietnam. With that division in place, the accords imposed a ceasefire and provided for the withdrawal of French forces from North Vietnam and Vietminh forces from South Vietnam within the next three hundred days. Both the French and the Vietminh were to withdraw their troops from Laos and Cambodia. Finally, the accords provided for free elections in 1956, with the goal of reunifying the two Vietnams. An International Control

Commission composed of representatives from India, Canada, and Poland was established to monitor compliance with the accords.

Signed on July 21, 1954, the Geneva Accords received a wholesale endorsement only from France, Great Britain, China, and the Soviet Union. Pham Van Dong signed the agreement for the Democratic Republic of Vietnam, but Vietminh leaders were privately bitter about the partitioning. The Geneva Accords accomplished little. Pham Van Dong left the conference expecting free elections in 1956 to bring about the long-awaited unification of Vietnam. But Georges Bidault and the French left hoping to maintain French authority in Saigon and the Mekong Delta. They dreamed of bringing Tonkin back into the French Union. Ngo Dinh Diem, the anticommunist Vietnamese nationalist who became prime minister of the State of Vietnam on July 7, refused to sign the accords. Secretary of State John Foster Dulles told the American delegation to leave the accords unsigned. The first Indochina War was over, and the second was beginning.

Ho Chi Minh's 1946 prediction that France would kill ten Vietnamese for every dead French soldier proved prophetic. When the mud dried around Dienbienphu, the eight years of war had resulted in the deaths of nearly 300,000 Vietminh and up to a million Vietnamese civilians. France counted 95,000 dead. But the war was not a body count, a simple military equation in which the victor piled up more kills. As Ho Chi Minh believed all along, the first Indochina War had been a political conflict in which the Vietminh outlasted the French. It was a lesson the United States would have to learn the hard way.

3

The Making of a Quagmire, 1954–1960

There are profound differences between the Vietnamese and American people, in customs, outlook, political training, and philosophy. I hope we can find a bridge between Eastern and Western cultures.

—Ngo Dinh Diem, 1961

Although the Geneva Accords divided Indochina at the seventeenth parallel, promised free elections in 1956, and brought peace after so much war, Vietnam faced enormous challenges. Intoxicated with his victory, convinced that he would win the elections in 1956 and take over South Vietnam, and anxious to prove his communist credentials, Ho Chi Minh set out on a misguided crusade in 1954. With the French gone, he was determined to right the other great wrong in Vietnam—upper-class Vietnamese landlords who exploited peasants. Actually, few North Vietnamese peasants owned more than three or four acres, but Ho Chi Minh created Agricultural Reform Tribunals in every village to identify landlords. Accusations, lies, informants, and a neighbor-against-neighbor atmosphere prevailed. The tribunals had quotas of landlords to identify and kill, and their justice, if it could be called that, was as swift as it was capricious.

Within a year, thousands of alleged landlords were dead and tens of thousands more were in labor camps for "reeducation." The whole process was a political disaster. By the summer of 1956, Ho Chi Minh decided the whole campaign had gone too far. On August 17, he wrote a public letter apologizing that "all this has caused us to commit errors and meet with shortcomings carrying out land reform." Of the people who had been executed, Ho Chi Minh simply said, "One cannot wake the dead." In Nghe An Province, however, his apology did not completely satisfy his constituency. Early in November, farmers in Quynh Luu district, angry about the land reform program as well as the government's official anti-Catholicism, openly rioted, requiring government troops to restore order. Vo Nguyen Giap later described the campaign as "an extraordinary error. . . . We did not emphasize the necessity for caution and for avoiding unjust punishment of honest people . . . [and] resorted to terror on a wide scale." With the end of the Agricultural Reform Tribunals, political life in North Vietnam settled down.

South Vietnam was not so lucky. In the Mekong Delta, formerly Cochin China, debt burdens and farm tenancy rates had risen in the last years of the war. The country depended on rice and rubber exports, as well as French money, to keep the economy going, and that source of funds was about to dry up. There was a wealth of peasant resentment of the French and the pro-French Vietnamese. Rural South Vietnam was ripe for rebellion. The region was also a bewildering caldron of competing ethnic, religious, economic, and political groups. Most of them were at least reasonably happy that the French were gone, but there was nothing approaching a consensus about who would fill the vacuum and rule the country. In Hanoi, there was only one power center in 1954. In South Vietnam there were many.

The least of the South Vietnamese power centers was the remains of the three-hundred-year-old Nguyen dynasty. Emperor Bao Dai had abdicated the throne at Ho Chi Minh's insistence in 1945, but when the French resumed power in 1946, he became a figurehead emperor. Born as Prince Nguyen Vinh Thuy in 1913, Bao Dai was tutored by French nannies and teachers from birth. In 1921 he left Vietnam for Paris. When his father, Emperor Khai Dinh, died in 1925, Bao Dai returned to Vietnam for the funeral, but the French whisked him back to Paris. He did not return to Vietnam until 1932; by that time his French was better than his Vietnamese.

In Paris, Bao Dai learned more than French literature and history. He spent his spare time in high-class Paris brothels and cabarets, becoming more infatuated with sexual acrobatics and mirrored ceilings than he had ever been with Rousseau or Voltaire. Bao Dai was round faced with a high brow, husky and full but not fat, a face reflecting the cherubic complacency of a man who had never missed a meal. S. J. Perelman met Bao Dai in Hanoi in 1946 and unflatteringly described him: "Bao Dai was seated in a snug alcove surrounded by several hostesses. . . . The royal exile, a short, slippery-looking customer rather on the pudgy side and freshly dipped in Crisco, wore a fixed, oily grin that was vaguely reptilian." Bao Dai was intelligent, but he suffered from a fatal political weakness. He was a "man who resisted nobody." When Ho Chi Minh called for his abdication in 1945, Bao Dai was quick to agree, not wanting, in his own words, "to make the same mistake Louis XVI made."

Bao Dai was careful in public to wear the regal, gold-brocaded *ao dai*, speak Vietnamese, and conduct himself with regal reserve. In private, he preferred to wear double-breasted suits, speak French, and hunt, dance, eat, and enjoy women. When the Japanese occupied Indochina during World War II, Bao Dai compromised himself even more, serving as the head of state for the Japanese occupation. Bao Dai was still on hand in 1954, but most Vietnamese held him in contempt.

France designated Bao Dai as the future emperor of Vietnam and sent him to Paris to be educated and trained. There, he became more French than Vietnamese.

THE BETTMANN ARCHIVE

Another major source of political power in South Vietnam was the Hoa Hao movement. Born in the Mekong Delta village of Hoa Hao in 1919, Huynh Phu So had a sickly childhood, but he also had a mystical sense about him. In 1939 he entered a Buddhist monastery where, in his own words, he underwent a "vision and miraculous cure." An extraordinary speaker and gifted practitioner of herbal medicine and acupuncture, Huynh Phu So returned to the Mekong Delta and began preaching a curious mixture of Buddhism and nationalism. He believed people should pray four times a day to Buddha as well as such ancient Vietnamese heroes as the Trung sisters, Ly Bon, Tran Hung Dao, and Le Loi. Bitterly anti-French, he began attracting attention, converting thousands of southern Vietnamese and raising the ire of French police, who called him the "Mad Monk." The French arrested Huynh Phu So in 1940 and placed him in a mental hospital, where he converted his psychiatrist and most of the staff.

Hoa Hao conversions skyrocketed during World War II. Enjoying the protection of the Japanese, Huynh Phu So raised a personal army of 15,000 troops in the Mekong Delta. In 1946 he established the Dan Xa, or Social Democratic party, to oppose the French, but in 1947 Ho Chi Minh, concerned about Huynh Phu So's growing power, ordered his death. Vietminh assassins killed him that year. One of the new Hoa Hao leaders was a man named Ba Cut. A committed nationalist, Ba Cut sliced off the tip of his forefinger in 1947 to remind himself how much he hated the French. By the early 1950s the Hoa Hao had more than 1.5 million followers in South Vietnam. Most of them were anticommunists.

Another powerful Buddhist sect in South Vietnam was the Cao Dai. Born in Cholon in 1878, Ngo Van Chieu was deeply involved with spiritualism and séances. Claiming to have received a visit from the supreme power—the Cao Dai—Ngo Van Chieu established the Cao Dai religion. He became infatuated with movies, which he watched in the theaters of Saigon. Buddhism, Christianity, and the movies fused in Cao Dai theology. Cao Daists prayed to Buddha, Confucius, Jesus Christ, Joan of Arc, Victor Hugo, Charlie Chaplin, Laurel and Hardy, and a host of other religious, historical, and pop culture figures. Their pagodas were plastered with posters of the Cao Dai symbol—the huge, all-seeing eye. The Cao Dai faith spread rapidly in the Mekong Delta and frightened the French, who harassed its leaders. Centered around Tay Ninh, about sixty miles northwest of Saigon, the Cao Dai evolved into a semiautonomous state, eventually maintaining their own army. Ngo Van Chieu died in 1932. By the early 1950s, under their new leader Pham Cong Tac, the Cao Dai claimed 2 million adherents and an army of 25,000 troops.

Regular Buddhist monks were another political force. Buddhist monks lived in nearly every village, maintaining pagodas, working in the fields, living side-by-side with peasants. Normally well educated, they knew a great deal about philosophy, medicine, and astrology. Buddhist political life functioned on a local level, trying to maintain balance and peace in the villages. The monks did not look to Hanoi or Saigon for their crusades, unless politics in Hanoi or Saigon disrupted village life. They turned against the French for just that reason. In promoting Roman Catholicism and harassing Buddhist priests, the French committed the unforgivable sin—they brought dissonance to the villages. With the French gone, the monks returned to local concerns, but they were still capable of causing trouble.

No less important were the Binh Xuyen. Led by a ruthless cutthroat, Bay Vien, the Binh Xuyen were the Vietnamese Mafia. They were centered in Cholon, the Chinese suburb of Saigon. By the early 1950s they were a powerful political faction, complete with an army of 25,000 soldiers. Bay Vien's complex in Saigon was legendary. The Grande Monde was a huge gambling complex capable of taking two piasters from a Vietnamese drunk or a million francs from a wealthy French businessman. Down the block was the world's largest brothel, the infamous Hall of Mirrors, where a thousand tricks could be performed at once. Further down the block, an opium factory refined a high-grade product for distribution throughout Indochina. Bay Vien's opulent home was separated from his complex by a moat occupied by dozens of alligators. Outside his bedroom, on a very long chain, was a full-grown leopard. Pythons slithered up the two posts on the front porch. A huge Siberian tiger lived in a cage; its door could be tripped open from inside the house. It was not uncommon to find bits of cloth and human bones inside the cage. Bao Dai accepted payoffs from the Binh Xuyen, and in return, with French consent, he made Bay Vien a general in the South Vietnamese army and head of the national police, with authority over casinos, prostitution, opium traffic, gold smuggling, and currency manipulation. Bay Vien had little use for the communists.

The most troublesome political group were the Vietminh. At the time of the French surrender at Dienbienphu, there were more than 100,000 Vietminh soldiers in South Vietnam, most of them native southerners. They controlled one-third of the country and were especially powerful in the Ca Mau Peninsula and along the Cambodian border. When the Geneva Accords were signed, Ho Chi Minh ordered most Vietminh to move to North Vietnam until after the 1956 elections. About 10,000 stayed behind with orders to return to their villages, work in the fields, and organize the peasants for the 1956 elections. The Vietminh had no doubt they would win a free election. But if the elections were postponed or canceled, the Vietminh were to become the heart of a new guerrilla movement. They were revolutionary nationalists. They hated the French and the Chinese, as well as the Vietnamese emperor and his upper-class mandarins. Although Ho had pulled most of the Vietminh out of the South, they were potentially the most powerful political force in the country.

In addition to the political and religious sects, South Vietnam had a number of ethnic minorities. In 1954 there were almost 1 million Chinese in South Vietnam, most of them in the Saigon suburb of Cholon. The Vietnamese nurtured an intense dislike for the Chinese, not just because of China's periodic invasions of Indochina but because of their control of business and commerce. For their part, the Chinese were hardly bent on gaining political power. On the contrary, they were economic opportunists ready to work with whatever regime came to power, as long as goods moved and profits flowed. What the Chinese did have was an intense anticommunism. The French, the mandarins, the Nguyen emperors, even the Japanese—anybody, as far as the Chinese were concerned—would be better for business than the communists.

The second-largest ethnic minority were the Khmer. Totaling more than 600,000 people, the Khmer, or ethnic Cambodians, were concentrated northwest of Saigon around Tay Ninh, southwest of Saigon near Phu Vinh, and throughout An Xuyen Province in the Mekong Delta. They hated the French for conquering Cambodia, but they also despised the Vietnamese. Hundreds of years ago, the Khmer controlled the Mekong Delta, but beginning in the eleventh century the Vietnamese expanded slowly out of Tonkin, down the spine of Annam, and into the Mekong Delta, crushing the Khmer and pushing them up the Mekong

River into present-day Cambodia. The Vietnamese looked down upon the Khmer as backward, ignorant people, and the Khmer resented that. After World War II, Khmer guerrillas, known as the Khmer Kampuchea Krom, began fighting the French, hoping to bring the Mekong Delta back under Cambodian sovereignty. Periodically, the Krom also fought the Vietminh and the Vietnamese National Army. When the French surrendered at Dienbienphu, the Krom launched a small-scale guerrilla war against the Vietnamese. Although the Khmer did not exercise great power, they were an important South Vietnamese constituency.

The last of the ethnic minorities were the Montagnard, or "Mountain People"—more than forty tribes of hunters and foragers in the Central Highlands. They hated the Vietnamese because of the annual tribute payment the emperors collected, and they had little use for the French, who also taxed them heavily. During the first Indochina War, the French and the Vietminh recruited the Montagnard. General Vo Nguyen Giap in 1946 claimed that "to seize and control the highlands is to solve the whole problem of South Vietnam." The rugged mountains of the Central Highlands were perfect hiding places for guerrillas, and the Montagnard were perfect guides. The French tried to buy Montagnard support and occasionally succeeded. One French sergeant remarked that he had "the Sedangs as allies. They are great big good-looking fellows with nothing on except paint and tattooing and magic charms." More often than not, the Montagnard sided with the Vietminh. In the late 1940s, Ho Chi Minh brought thousands of Montagnard to Vietminh schools in Tonkin for training as teachers, nurses, and political agents. He promised them that once the French were gone and the imperial court at Hue was destroyed, there would be no more tribute payments.

Roman Catholics were another formidable political minority. Converted by French missionaries in the eighteenth and nineteenth centuries, South Vietnamese Catholics numbered 600,000 people in 1954. They were a privileged minority who had worked for the French and received the benefits of land, education, and place. Graduates of the French lycées in Hue and Saigon, they often received postgraduate training at military schools and universities in France. In South Vietnam they dominated the professions, colleges, civil service, and military. Among most Vietnamese Buddhists, the Roman Catholics were despised, suspect people tied to foreigners. Ho Chi Minh had targeted them long ago. Once the French were gone, the South Vietnamese elite had to go as well.

But in the 1950s and 1960s, South Vietnam was not destined to be ruled by the Hoa Hao, Cao Dai, Binh Xuyen, Buddhists, Vietminh, Chinese, Khmer, or Montagnard. Power went to Roman Catholics, and at the center of that elite was the Ngo family. The Ngo had formed a short-lived political dynasty in the tenth century and then served in the mandarinate at the imperial court for centuries. Early in the 1700s they converted to Catholicism. They were deeply religious. In the 1880s Buddhist monks led anti-Catholic riots that nearly destroyed the Ngo family. A Buddhist mob attacked the parish church at Dai Phong during mass. More than one hundred of the Ngo family were burned at the stake later that day.

One family member was not there. Ngo Dinh Kha was in Malaya studying for the priesthood. When he received news that his parents, grandparents, brothers, sisters, aunts, uncles, and cousins were dead, Ngo Dinh Kha returned to Hue and tried to rebuild. He passed the mandarin examinations and, fluent in French, moved quickly up the civil service ladder. Ngo's first wife died soon after their marriage, but his second wife had nine children. The third of them was Jean Baptiste Ngo Dinh Diem, born on January 3, 1901.

Ngo Dinh Diem remembered growing up Confucian and Catholic. Every morning at 6:00, seven days a week, the family put on their best robes and attended mass, and nearly every day their father spoke to them about duty, fidelity, and loyalty. Diem attended the French lycée in Hue and became thoroughly engrossed in French history, language, and literature.

Of all the Ngo children, Diem was the most religious. He did not play with other children, and as soon as he could read he spent hours each day by himself studying catechisms and religious histories. At the age of fifteen he entered a Catholic seminary in Hue to begin studying for the priesthood. His older brother, Ngo Dinh Thuc, was doing the same thing. But it soon became apparent that Diem was not meant to be a priest. Thuc urged him to leave the seminary, arguing that he "was too unworldly for the church." Another friend put it more clearly: "A priest at least learns of the world through the confessional. Diem is a monk living behind stone walls. He knows nothing." Diem left the seminary but took with him his vow of celibacy, which he kept throughout his life. He attended the French College for Administration in Hanoi and graduated at the top of his class in 1921. Back in Hue, Diem rose through the civil service ranks, becoming a district chief and then a provincial administrator, coming to the attention of the French in 1929 when he uncovered plans for a communist-inspired uprising. There were no distractions in Diem's life, no women or movies or gambling, only work and prayer. In 1933 Bao Dai appointed him minister of the interior. At the age of thirty-two, Ngo Dinh Diem seemed destined to become prime minister.

Like so many other Vietnamese, Diem longed for the day when France would leave Vietnam. But in Bao Dai's cabinet, Diem realized that the French, while talking about reform, restricted the imperial court, transforming the emperor and his civil servants into mere puppets. Ngo Dinh Diem resigned from the cabinet in protest late in 1933.

Diem retired to the family home in Hue, where he spent his days reading, praying, horseback riding, hunting, working in a rose garden, attending mass, and talking with his mother. During the 1930s and early 1940s, except for an abortive attempt to become prime minister in the Japanese puppet regime, Diem was out of sight and out of mind. The family believed he was destined for greatness, and they supported him financially until an opportunity came. In letters to members of the family, Diem often wrote, "We must continue the search for the Kingdom of God and Justice. All else will come of itself."

Although a nationalist, Diem kept faith in the Confucian virtues—loyalty, acquiescence, and social place. He wanted the French out, but he did not want the social structure turned upside down. Diem's opposition to communism was intensely personal after 1945. His older brother Ngo Dinh Khoi, a former governor of Quang Ngai Province, was anti-French and anticommunist, but he spoke out too strongly against the Vietminh. Vietminh arrested Khoi and his young son, convicted them in a kangaroo court, and executed them by burying Khoi and the boy alive. Ngo Dinh Diem never forgave the Vietminh. The Vietminh caught up with Diem in Tuy Hoa. They moved him to the highlands of North Vietnam, where he remained in custody for several months, and sent him to Hanoi in January 1946. Interested in gaining the support of Vietnam's leading Catholic layman, Ho Chi Minh offered Diem a cabinet position. Diem refused, calling Ho an "accomplice and a criminal" in Khoi's death. Diem was released in March 1946 as part of the Franco-Vietminh Accords.

During the next nine years Diem traveled around the world, staying away from home to avoid the Vietminh. He spent more than three years in the United States, living at the Maryknoll Seminary in Lakewood, New Jersey. At the time the United States was assisting France against the Vietminh but also hoping to find an anticommunist Vietnamese leader around whom a stable government could be built. Diem appeared to be that leader. Wesley Fishel, professor of political science at Michigan State University, met Diem in Japan and spoke at length with him about Indochina. Diem seemed perfect. He was a well-educated Roman Catholic who wanted an anticommunist, independent Vietnam. That Diem was not a believer in democracy mattered little to Fishel. "The people of Southeast Asia are not," Fishel said, "sufficiently sophisticated to understand . . . democracy."

Fishel saw to it that Diem met a number of prominent Americans, including Richard Cardinal Spellman, the Roman Catholic archbishop of New York; Senators John F. Kennedy of Massachusetts, Mike Mansfield of Montana, and Lyndon B. Johnson of Texas; and Supreme Court Justice William O. Douglas. In 1953 Douglas called Diem "a hero . . . revered by the Vietnamese because he is honest and independent and stood firm against the French influence." These men became the core of what was called the Vietnam Lobby, or the American Friends of Vietnam, who continually promoted Ngo Dinh Diem in 1953 and 1954. When the Geneva Accords divided Vietnam in 1954, Diem had strong supporters in the United States. On June 18, 1954, destiny called. Bao Dai invited Diem to serve as prime minister in a new government.

Although Ngo Dinh Diem seemed to be a candidate to build an anti-communist South Vietnam, official Washington debated the issue in 1954 and 1955. The French were dead set against Diem. They hoped to stay in South Vietnam and keep their empire. What the French really knew was that Diem was too much of a nationalist to allow France to remain in South Vietnam. They could manipulate Bao Dai, but not Diem. The French reservations concerned President Eisenhower. It was nothing profound, just an uneasiness about Diem's penchant for a solitary life and his extraordinary commitment to his family. Eisenhower also worried whether Diem could really rule a large Buddhist majority when he was such a devout Roman Catholic. But the real debate in American policy-making circles raged around the strongly negative and strongly positive views of Diem expressed by two Americans living in South Vietnam in 1954 and 1955: J. Lawton Collins and Edward G. Lansdale.

Nicknamed "Lightning Joe" by his army troops, Collins commanded the Twenty-fifth Infantry Division at Guadalcanal and then the VII Corps at the D-Day invasion of Europe during World War II. After the war Collins served as army chief of staff before President Dwight Eisenhower sent him to Saigon in 1954 as a special envoy to train the South Vietnamese. Collins despised Diem—his political base was too narrow and his sense of destiny too broad. "Lightning Joe" was convinced that Diem would self-destruct and create a political vacuum, which Ho Chi Minh would fill. Collins strongly advised Washington to shift support away from Diem. For his part, Diem hated Collins, whom he viewed as a self-righteous American given to pompous advice. Diem wanted American money, not American advice. Collins represented both. In private Diem could be quite animated and often put on a mime act for family members in which he pretended to be Collins, waving his finger in people's faces and talking loudly about what to do and how to do it. Much more to Ngo Dinh Diem's liking was Edward G. Lansdale.

An air force officer and former intelligence agent, Lansdale came to Saigon in 1954 as CIA station chief. He had already helped the Philippines crush the communist-backed Huk Rebellion. Assigned to conduct CIA paramilitary operations against North Vietnam, Lansdale spread rumors and leaflets about Ho Chi Minh, littered North Vietnam with counterfeit currency, warned northern Catholics that communists would persecute them, and destroyed weapons supplies north of the seventeenth parallel. He arranged for several hundred South Vietnamese soldiers to dress up as civilians, infiltrate North Vietnam, and spread rumors that the Vietminh wanted Chinese soldiers to come and rape Vietnamese women. This one backfired. The troops went into North Vietnam but did not return, at least not until a few years later, when they came back as guerrillas loyal to Ho Chi Minh.

Lansdale became a close friend of Diem, one of the few confidants

Diem had outside his family. To Lansdale, Diem was "a man with a terrible burden to carry and in need of friends, and I tried to be an honest friend." Lansdale thought Diem was a dedicated nationalist who loved Vietnam, hated communism, and wanted the best for his people. There was no other individual capable of governing South Vietnam. Ngo Dinh Diem was the only game in town. John Foster Dulles agreed. Dulles's brother Allen, head of the CIA, told the secretary of state that Lansdale was an astute judge of character and that Diem could be trusted. John Foster Dulles passed that on to Eisenhower, who remained skeptical about Diem's ability.

Dulles was also desperate for a South Vietnamese leader with enough mettle to pull the country together. In July 1954, the National Security Council committed the United States to "maintain a friendly non-communist South Vietnam and to prevent a Communist victory through all-Vietnam elections." In September 1954 Dulles established the Southeast Asia Treaty Organization (SEATO), a regional security alliance signed by the United States, Great Britain, France, Australia, New Zealand, Thailand, the Philippines, and Pakistan. South Vietnam, Laos, and Cambodia were forbidden by the Geneva Accords from joining, but a subsequent protocol to the treaty stated that if any one of them fell to communism, it would pose a threat to the alliance and justify a military response.

A few people were skeptical. Secretary of Defense Charles E. Wilson urged Eisenhower to get out as "completely and as soon as possible." The most eloquent dissent was Graham Greene's novel *The Quiet American* (1955). Gloria Emerson, who read the novel in 1956, later recalled, "It was a first warning to me, but I dismissed the book as brilliant but cynical, until it came back to haunt me." It is a novel of good intentions, idealism, lack of insight, and dangerous innocence. The quiet American is Alden Pyle, a character based on Edward Lansdale. Pyle believes in a coldly passionate way in abstractions—democracy, freedom, monolithic communism, falling dominoes, and the love of God. The novel is written from the viewpoint of Thomas Fowler, a British journalist who is as committed to reality as Pyle is to abstraction. Trying to convince Pyle of the error of his theories, Fowler observes:

> I know the record. Siam goes. Malaya goes. Indonesia goes. What does "go" mean? If I believed in your God and another life, I'd bet my future harp against your golden crown that in five hundred years there may be no New York or London, but they'll be growing paddy in these fields. . . . Thought's a luxury. Do you think the peasant sits and thinks of God and Democracy when he gets inside his mud hut at night? . . . Isms and ocracies. Give me facts.

Of course Pyle is impervious to Fowler's logic. He continues with the best intentions to ruin lives and kill innocent people. When one of his plans goes awry and several innocent Vietnamese are killed, Pyle observes: "They were only war casualties. . . . It was a pity, but you can't always hit your target. Anyway they died in the right cause. . . . In a way you could say they died for democracy."

Greene intended his novel to expose the absence of a moral vision in American policy in Vietnam. Stationed in Saigon as a war correspondent in the early 1950s, Greene witnessed the transference of power from France to the United States. He watched the arrival of fresh Pyles—men with crew cuts and "wide campus gazes" who seemed "incapable of harm" and who were determined to do good "not to any individual person but to a country, a continent, a world." But, of course, harm was implicit in a mission that framed good and evil in universal abstract terms. This central truth Greene recognized and addressed. In 1955, however, Americans were not prepared to listen. Only after the war was over would Michael Herr observe in his brilliant book *Dispatches* (1977), "Maybe it was already over for us in Indochina when Alden Pyle's body washed up under the bridge at Dakao, his lungs full of mud."

Robert Gorham Davis, reviewing *The Quiet American* for the *New York Times Book Review*, suggested that Greene's work was anti-American: "Pyle . . . does not remind Fowler of the thousands of individuals who make desperate escapes from Communist countries every week in order to live as humans." For Americans in the mid-1950s this was the crux of the matter—Vietnam was fighting communism and communism was a threat to humanity. That confidence kept the United States in Vietnam and wedded to Ngo Dinh Diem. In October 1954 the Eisenhower administration decided to channel economic and military assistance directly to Diem rather than through the French mission in Saigon. Late in 1954 the CIA foiled several coup attempts against Diem. On the shoulders of Ngo Dinh Diem rested American hopes to save Southeast Asia, strengthen the Japanese economy, rebuild Europe, and preserve the United States defensive picket line in the western Pacific.

Because of the complexity of South Vietnamese politics, it would have taken a political genius to control the centrifugal interests of Catholics and Buddhists, Hoa Hao and Cao Dai, Montagnard and Khmer, Chinese and Binh Xuyen. Ngo Dinh Diem was not a politician; he was a Confucian mandarin who expected to rule with "the mandate of heaven," to preside over a people who looked to him as their father and behaved obediently. The word "compromise" was not in Diem's vocabulary. Nor was "democracy." Diem clearly stated his political philosophy: "Our political system has been based not on the concept of management of the public affairs by the people or their representatives, but rather by an enlightened sovereign." His sister-in-law, Madame Ngo Dinh Nhu, stated it more symbolically: "If we open the window not only sunlight but many bad things will fly in also." The historian William Turley writes that Diem was "heir to a dying tradition, member of an elite that had been superbly prepared by birth, training, and experience to lead a Vietnam which no longer existed."

Instead of opening the window, Diem tried to eliminate every ray of sunlight. He brooked no opposition and expected total obedience, nothing more, nothing less. In April 1955 Diem asked Bay Vien and the Binh Xuyen to lay down their arms and close the opium dens and brothels. Bay Vien refused and dared Diem to come into Cholon. Diem called his bluff and invaded Cholon with tanks. As the Binh Xuyen retreated, they set fire to hundreds of homes and buildings. French authorities in Saigon, hoping Diem would meet his Waterloo, assisted the Binh Xuyen. It was civil war in Cholon. Bay Vien escaped to the jungles northwest of Saigon and from there to Paris. By that time thousands of people were dead, most of them Chinese civilians. Diem crushed the Binh Xuyen but in the process earned the enmity of the Chinese. Thousands of Binh Xuyen soldiers fled into the Mekong Delta and Central Highlands, where they vowed to continue the fight against Diem.

The crushing of the Binh Xuyen resolved the dispute between Edward Lansdale and J. Lawton Collins. Diem exercised brutal power, but he had done it successfully. American praise was quick in coming. John Foster Dulles was explicit in a cable he sent to the French: "Diem is the only means U.S. sees to save South Vietnam and counteract the revolutionary movement. . . . U.S. sees no one else who can. Whatever U.S. view has been in the past, today U.S. must support Diem wholeheartedly."

Flush with victories in Saigon and Washington, Diem set out to consolidate his power. He turned first on Bao Dai. Diem considered Bao Dai a morally bankrupt whoremonger whose ties to the Binh Xuyen were unforgivable: Imagine—the Nguyen emperor, the symbol of a dynasty that had ruled Vietnam for centuries, taking kickbacks from pimps and drug dealers! In 1955 Diem called for the abdication of Bao Dai. He set up a national referendum to decide the question. In an election that saw 605,000 of Saigon's 405,000 registered voters cast ballots, Diem received 98.2 percent. On October 23, 1955, he proclaimed the Republic of Vietnam, with himself as president.

Diem then attacked the Hoa Hao. Late in 1955 Diem sent troops into the Mekong Delta to destroy the Hoa Hao army. The Hoa Hao fought a bloody guerrilla war against the Army of the Republic of Vietnam (ARVN), but in April 1956 Ba Cut was arrested. He had a curious look about him. The short finger still reminded him of the French, but when he heard news of the partitioning of Vietnam in 1954, he had vowed not to cut his hair until the country was reunited. Uncombed and unwashed, the hair tangled down his shoulders. To the sharkskin-suited Diem, Ba Cut was disgusting and dangerous. In July 1956 Diem sent him to the guillotine. Surviving Hoa Hao soldiers scattered throughout the rural countryside.

Diem also worked on the Cao Dai. He bought off some Cao Dai leaders. It took $1 million to get Cao Dai general Trinh Minh The to change sides. ARVN troops invaded Tay Ninh Province late in 1955 to disarm the Cao Dai army. The Cao Dai fought for a time, but they knew of Diem's ruthlessness and did not want to go the way of the Binh Xuyen and Hoa Hao. In February 1956 Pham Cong Tac, the Cao Dai leader, escaped into Cambodia. Most Cao Dai soldiers surrendered their arms, but others escaped into the Mekong Delta.

With Bao Dai in France, the Binh Xuyen crushed, and the sects in disarray, Diem fulfilled his dream. In a speech on January 19, 1956, he announced, "The presence of foreign troops, no matter how friendly . . . [is] incompatible with Vietnam's concept of full independence." He told the French to leave. The French empire in Vietnam finally died on April 10, 1956, when the last of 10,000 French troops left Saigon.

Nor did Diem have any use for the Khmer Kampuchea Krom. Krom troops were powerful in An Xuyen Province, and early in 1956 ARVN troops moved against them. Dressed in the distinctive button-down jacket and skirts with the lower end brought between the legs and tucked in at the waist, Krom soldiers were indistinguishable from Khmer peasants working the rice paddies. ARVN troops, indiscriminate at best, killed thousands of Khmer civilians in their operations against the Krom. In return the Krom launched their own guerrilla war against Diem.

Ngo Dinh Diem soon had the Khmer even angrier at him, along with the Buddhists and the Montagnard. As soon as the Geneva Accords divided the country, Diem, Lansdale, and CIA operatives encouraged northern Catholics to move south, arguing that the communists would persecute them if they stayed where they were. They sent messages that the Virgin Mary was living in Saigon. More than 600,000 Catholics moved to South Vietnam. Another 300,000 North Vietnamese—former soldiers in the Vietnamese National Army, colonial administrators, and businessmen afraid of what the communists would do to them—also left. They emigrated in complete village units, led by the parish priest, with nothing but what they could carry.

Once in South Vietnam these people increased the Roman Catholic population to 1.5 million people. A northern Catholic himself, Diem was sympathetic to their plight. Those with good educations moved into the South Vietnamese civil service. For others the government established 319 villages, giving the immigrants land and financial support until they could establish an economic foothold. The controversy came over the land they received. More than 400,000 settled in the Mekong Delta, most of them on land that had traditionally been worked by the Khmer. The Khmer sense of alienation only strengthened.

Diem placed nearly 100,000 immigrant Catholics in the Central Highlands, giving them Montagnard land. Diem believed the Montagnard should learn to speak Vietnamese, leave the mountains, study a useful trade, and adopt Vietnamese values. He approached the Montagnard much as Americans treated the Indians in the nineteenth century. The South Vietnamese developed programs to relocate the Montagnard and provided them with schools, all the while giving their land to other Vietnamese. In the meantime the Vietminh promised the Montagnard that once the Diem government had been eliminated their land would be returned.

Northern Catholics were intensely anti-Buddhist. Led by Father Hoang Quynh, they joined the Luc Luong Dai Doan Ket, or Greater Unity Force, which demanded the conversion of all of South Vietnam. Quynh asked Diem to promote Catholics over Buddhists and destroy infidelity. Diem's personal inclinations were less militant, but he had a political problem. Northern Catholics were his strongest supporters, and Buddhist monks knew it. They were uneasy with Catholic political strength and suspicious of Diem. Large numbers of Buddhists, Montagnard, and Khmer saw their land go to Catholic refugees. Diem's refusal to promote land reform was hardly surprising. Taking land from well-to-do South Vietnamese would rob him of a loyal constituency. By 1960, in the Mekong Delta, nearly 50 percent of cultivated land was owned by 2 percent of the people.

Finally, to consolidate his power in the countryside, Diem abolished local elections and appointed his supporters to official village posts. It was a colossal mistake. For centuries, even under the Nguyen imperial court and the French, local politics had been governed by the ancient slogan, "The empire stops at the village gates." Peasants elected their own officials to govern local affairs, and neither the emperor nor the French had interfered. Diem destroyed the only democratic institution functioning in South Vietnam.

Diem then turned on the national elections that the Geneva Accords had guaranteed for 1956. CIA chief Allen Dulles sent a memo to President Eisenhower in 1956 predicting an overwhelming victory, in both North Vietnam and South Vietnam, by Ho Chi Minh. The Vietminh assumed that France would stay in South Vietnam, honor the accords, and supervise the elections. But the French were gone. South Vietnam was an independent nation wallowing in American money. The United States was the new Western power in Vietnam, and its entire foreign policy revolved around anticommunism. The United States wanted an anticommunist government in Saigon—democratic or not. In 1955 Diem canceled the scheduled elections. Ho Chi Minh denounced the decision, but there was little he could do about it since the United States had no intention of forcing Diem to keep an agreement he had never signed.

Diem ruled South Vietnam with an iron hand. But he was always worried, with good reason, about conspiracy, revolution, and assassination. He led a monklike existence inside the presidential palace, sleeping on a narrow cot, covered by a mosquito net, and cooled by a slow-moving ceiling fan. Diem got up around 6:00 A.M., went to pray in a private chapel near his room, and breakfasted on a noodles and pork soup. He visited with staff members after breakfast and then underwent a physical examination, every morning, by a doctor. On his desk was a crucifix and a picture of the Virgin Mary. Diem received visitors in the afternoon, but the Saigon diplomatic corps dreaded his summons, knowing that it meant listening to a monologue of anywhere from three to ten hours. He worked all day and much of the night, falling asleep at 1:00 or 2:00 A.M., with documents on his lap.

Since he could trust nobody outside his immediate family, Ngo Dinh Diem created a family dynasty. Ngo Dinh Thuc, the oldest surviving brother, was a relaxed man blessed with congeniality and a fine sense of humor. He entered the Roman Catholic seminary to study for the priesthood, and with great political skills as well as a genuinely spiritual nature, he rose steadily in the Roman Catholic hierarchy, becoming a monsignor during World War II and then bishop of Vinh Long. In 1957 Pope Pius XII named Thuc the archbishop of Hue, the Roman Catholic primate for all of Vietnam.

Diem's younger brother, Ngo Dinh Luyen, was international spokesman for the family. Born in Hue in 1909 and educated at the French lycée there, Luyen was bright and articulate. In 1956, Diem named Luyen ambassador to Great Britain and roving ambassador to the rest of the world. Luyen preached a single message: Survival of the Republic of Vietnam was essential to the future of Asia. The next youngest brother was Ngo Dinh Can. Unlike the others, Can was poorly educated and had never traveled abroad. He lived a simple, reclusive life in Hue with his mother, and although he held no official position in the Diem regime, he was warlord of central Vietnam, absolute ruler of the region between Phan Thiet Province and the seventeenth parallel. Protected by his own secret police and private army, Can was autonomous, the law in the northern half of South Vietnam. Diem deferred to him in all matters concerning that region.

Diem's youngest brother, Ngo Dinh Nhu, was his closest associate as well as the political boss of South Vietnam from Phan Thiet Province to the Ca Mau Peninsula. Nicknamed "Smiley" by Americans because of a permanent smile fixed on his face, Nhu was privately contemptuous of the United States. Americans had too much power, too much money, and too little humility. Nhu was short on humility himself. A devout Roman Catholic educated at the École de Chartres in Paris, Nhu hated the Buddhists and wanted to "put the monks in their places." He was commander of the Vietnamese Special Forces and transformed them into his own personal army of henchmen, hit men, and spies. A heavy opium user and a chain smoker, Nhu admired Adolf Hitler. Next to Diem, Nhu was the most powerful man in South Vietnam.

Because of Diem's vow of celibacy, it fell to Nhu's wife, Tran Le Xuan,

Ngo Dinh Diem (second row, left) poses with his family. Behind him are his brothers Ngo Dinh Nhu (top left) and Archbishop Thuc (top right). Standing next to Ngo Dinh Diem is his sister-in-law, Madame Nhu.

MICHIGAN STATE UNIVERSITY ARCHIVES & HISTORICAL COLLECTIONS

to serve as first lady or, in the words of her critics, the "Queen of Saigon." She was completely Gallicized. Educated at private Catholic schools in France, she was more comfortable speaking French than Vietnamese. Although she fancied herself a reincarnation of the ancient Trung sisters, Madame Nhu was closer to a reincarnation of Marie Antoinette. Arrogant, intolerant, insensitive, and prudish, she led public campaigns against card playing, adultery, blue movies, gambling, horse racing, fortune telling, boxing, divorce, prostitution, dancing, and beauty contests. She wanted to outlaw the use of "falsies" in women's bras but gave up on the idea when she realized it would be impossible to enforce. Using her own private police force, Madame Nhu had people arrested for wearing loud clothing and boots or bizarre hairstyles. Her father, Tran Van Chuong, was a major landowner and former foreign minister for the Japanese regime during World War II. He was minister of state for Diem and then ambassador to the United States.

Ensconced in power, the Ngo family then turned on its last real rival in South Vietnam—the Vietminh. Less than 10,000 Vietminh remained in South Vietnam after the Geneva Accords; the other 100,000 or so withdrew to North Vietnam to wait for the elections. Diem refused to call them Vietminh, preferring the derogatory term "Vietcong," or "Vietnamese Communist." Diem launched a violent campaign against the Vietcong late in 1955, using ARVN soldiers and village officials to expose them. His slogan was blunt: "Let us mercilessly wipe out the Vietcong, no longer considering them human beings."

And that is just what Diem tried to do. Between late 1955 and early 1960, ARVN soldiers arrested more than 100,000 people accused of being Vietminh, even though there were only 10,000 Vietminh, at the most, in South Vietnam. Executions took place near the homes of the accused, so their bodies could be found and the village would be intimidated. Somewhere between 20,000 and 75,000 South Vietnamese were killed and another 100,000 sent to concentration camps for "reeducation." Diem also desecrated Vietminh war memorials and cemeteries, an unforgivable insult in a culture practicing ancestor worship and family obedience. Although the terrorism successfully reduced the number of Vietminh in South Vietnam from 10,000 people in 1955 to only 3,000 people in 1958, it inspired surviving Vietminh leaders to conduct a dedicated guerrilla war against the Diem government. Because most of Diem's victims were simple peasants, the terrorism drove a greater wedge between the Vietnamese people and the government.

The Vietminh leader in South Vietnam was Le Duan. Born in Quang Tri Province in 1908, Duan became an anti-French nationalist as a student. He spent most of the years between 1931 and 1945 in the French prison on Con Son Island. After World War II, he stayed in southern Vietnam. Convinced that the French were just trying to preserve their empire, Duan opposed the Geneva Accords of 1954—better to destroy French troops in the south just as they had destroyed the French at Dienbienphu. Nicknamed the "Flame of the South" because of his commitment to reunification, Le Duan went along with Ho Chi Minh's decision to sign the Geneva Accords, but when Ho called the Vietminh back to North Vietnam in 1954, Duan stayed behind. Between 1954 and 1956, when reunification elections were supposed to take place, Vietcong activities had been primarily political—working in villages to win support from common peasants. The guerrillas spent their time working with peasants, helping plant and harvest crops, delivering rice to markets, improving community buildings and peasant homes, and providing drugs and basic medical care.

Diem's decision to cancel the elections precipitated a bitter debate in North Vietnam. Most party members in North Vietnam were cautious about reigniting the armed struggle in the south. They were busy consolidating their power, and they wanted to avoid a confrontation with the United States. But most Vietminh who pulled out of South Vietnam after the Geneva Accords were native southerners who resented the division of Vietnam. The old ethnic rivalry between northern and southern Vietnamese was revived within the Vietcong. Southerners accused northerners of abandoning them, of enjoying the fruits of power in the north while southerners suffered under the oppression of Ngo Dinh Diem. Although Le Duan was circumspect in his proposals, he represented that southern point of view. As early as 1956 Duan urged Ho Chi Minh to overthrow the Diem regime, but Ho was cautious, preferring political to military action. Duan was obedient and worked hard to keep southerners in line, but he knew their patience was running out. In December 1956 North Vietnamese leaders compromised, agreeing that consolidating the revolution in North Vietnam was their number-one priority but that southerners should work to destabilize the Diem regime politically and defend themselves if necessary.

Ho Chi Minh's instructions to the Vietcong were crystal clear: Do not engage in military operations; that will lead to defeat. Do not take land from a peasant. Emphasize nationalism rather than communism. Do not antagonize anyone if you can avoid it. Be selective in your violence. If an assassination is necessary, use a knife, not a rifle or grenade. It is too easy to kill innocent bystanders with guns and bombs, and accidental killings of the innocent will alienate peasants from the revolution. Once an assassination has taken place, make sure peasants know why the killing occurred.

Vietcong assassins went after the most corrupt village officials first, those who stole from the peasants or raped women. Regardless of political affiliation, peasants were glad to see those officials dead. Where Diem had appointed Roman Catholics to preside over Buddhist villages, the Vietcong assassinated the Catholics, earning silent praise from local monks. And to strike terror into village leaders, to let everyone know that nobody was safe, the Vietcong sometimes targeted the best, most efficient officials for assassination. The Vietcong often decapitated their victims. Vietnamese spiritualism held that people who lost their heads were destined to an eternity of restless wandering in the world of spirits. Ho Chi Minh also told the Vietcong that the quickest way to the heart of a peasant was land. The Vietcong seized the land from absentee landlords, gave it to poor farmers, and spread the word that the Vietcong robbed from the rich to give to the poor. In mid-1957 the Vietcong launched their campaign against Diem. In 1958 they assassinated more than 1,100 village officials in South Vietnam, and they increased that number in 1959.

Diem responded to the deteriorating political situation in the only way he knew how—increasing the use of force, which played into the hands of the Vietcong. To keep peasants from being converted by Vietcong propaganda, Diem launched the Agroville Program, relocating peasants into hastily constructed villages placed along Vietcong infiltration routes. The villages were heavily defended and surrounded by barbed wire. It was difficult for the Vietcong to get in, but to the peasants the "new villages" looked like prisons. People were rounded up into forced labor gangs to build the camps and then were forcibly moved there, far from ancestral villages. As Vietnamese peasants looked upon their family land with deep reverence, relocation was a spiritual and physical crisis. The resettlement enraged peasants.

Diem had the National Assembly pass Law 10/59 in May 1959. Designed to wipe out the Vietcong, it created special military tribunals to arrest any individual "who commits or intends to commit crimes . . . against the State." Equipped with portable guillotines, the tribunals rendered one of three verdicts: innocent, life in prison, and death. In the ensuing trials a kangaroo-court atmosphere prevailed. Nhu's secret police took part in the trials, sometimes carrying out the guillotining of convicted "traitors." The campaign was effective. Diem's terrorism was so widespread and capricious that innocent peasants were afraid even to be seen with suspected Vietcong. Large numbers of Vietcong either quit the party or were killed. Communist party membership in South Vietnam shrunk to 3,000 people in 1959. But the 10/59 campaign also terrorized thousands of innocent peasants who came to hate the Ngo family.

Finally, the regime corrupted the 1959 National Assembly elections. Although there were opposition candidates running, the government prohibited newspapers from publishing their names or printing campaign literature. Opposition posters were not allowed to be displayed, nor could candidates opposed to Diem speak to gatherings of more than five people. In the southern part of the country, Nhu's secret police worked as election officials, handing out ballots and watching how people voted. In the northern provinces, Can's secret police performed the same functions. When it appeared that large numbers of people might not vote, the government passed an ordinance requiring them to carry a voter identification card that had been punched at the polls. When the election turned out to be a resounding victory for the Ngo family, Diem proudly announced, "The people have spoken."

Diem's increasing consolidation of power, along with the decline of the Vietcong, brought about a change in Communist party policy. Recognizing that it would probably take an armed struggle to overthrow South Vietnam, the Central Committee in Hanoi made three important decisions in 1959. First, Ho Chi Minh gave in to Le Duan's urgings and began infiltrating cadres into South Vietnam. At first they were southern-born Vietminh who had relocated to North Vietnam. After five years away from his family, one Vietminh remarked, "I was joyous to learn of my assignment to go south. I was eager to see my home village, to see my family, to get in contact with my wife."

Second, North Vietnam prepared for a more protracted military struggle throughout Indochina. The decision raised the question of how to transport troops and supplies into South Vietnam. In May 1959 the North Vietnamese military established Group 559 to develop a means of moving people and supplies from North Vietnam to South Vietnam through Laos and Cambodia. Group 759, established in July, was to develop techniques for infiltrating South Vietnam by sea.

The third decision established Indochina as a single strategic entity. In order to bring about the reunification of North and South Vietnam, the communists had to prevent the United States from securing control of Laos and Cambodia. In 1958 and 1959, with United States assistance, right-wing forces in Laos ousted the neutral government of Prince Souvanna Phouma and consolidated their power. The Royal Army then attacked strongholds of the Pathet Lao, the Laotian communist guerrillas. The civil war in Laos worried North Vietnam. If the Royal Army succeeded in expelling the Pathet Lao from their mountain strongholds, Group 559 would be hard-pressed to get people and supplies into South Vietnam, since the Laotian mountains were the vital communication link. In September 1959 North Vietnam established Group 959 to provide supplies to Pathet Lao guerrillas and urged Vietnamese soldiers to join the fight. In 1960 North Vietnamese and Pathet Lao troops defeated the Royal Army along the border and secured the corridor Hanoi needed into South Vietnam. When the time was right, North Vietnam would begin moving large numbers of cadres, supplies, and eventually soldiers down that Laotian corridor into South Vietnam.

The United States and South Vietnam were preparing for a different type of invasion. The United States was trying to build ARVN into a reliable fighting force. American policymakers wanted to reduce it from a ragtag army of 250,000 poorly equipped, demoralized troops to a streamlined, state-of-the-art army of 150,000 "gung ho" soldiers. The United States also wanted a reliable, 40,000-man local militia. The training unit was the Military Assistance and Advisory Group (MAAG), commanded by General Samuel ("Hanging Sam") Williams. Fresh from duty in Korea, where he had witnessed the North Korean and Chinese invasions, Williams was convinced that the assault on South Vietnam would come by way of a large-scale invasion of North Vietnamese and perhaps Chinese troops across the seventeenth parallel. Along with seven hundred United States military advisers, Williams trained the South Vietnamese army in the art of conventional warfare—how to use artillery, air support, and armor to repel an invasion.

For Williams the key was military: train and equip ARVN to defeat the communists when the invasion began. He placed ARVN soldiers in static positions along the borders with Laos and North Vietnam. When ARVN troops moved, they depended on armored personnel carriers and trucks, and they rarely ventured off the main roads. Off the main roads was, of course, exactly where the Vietcong were operating. In what can only be considered an extraordinary example of naivete, Williams remarked in 1957: "We have exactly 342 men, the number allowed by the Geneva Armistice Conference. It would be a breeze if we had more."

It was not an easy task. Few people in South Vietnam had any sense of patriotic nationalism; their country was a diplomatic creation just a few years old. Asking men and women to die for their country is one thing; asking them to die for someone else's country is quite another. There was no identity between the army and the nation. The other problem MAAG faced was the traditional Vietnamese suspicion of foreigners. One American said that MAAG's greatest challenge was "assuring the Vietnamese that the United States is not a colonial power—an assurance that must be renewed on an individual basis by each new adviser." Still, the United States supplied $1.65 billion to South Vietnam between 1956 and 1961, and nearly 80 percent of the money went into military equipment and personnel. The United States and ARVN thought they were ready for the invasion.

But Le Duan was training the Vietcong for a very different kind of war. For them the real issue was political, not military. They wanted to secure the allegiance of the peasants and destroy the credibility of the Diem regime. With peasant support they would enjoy food, protection, and recruits, and through selective terrorism they would prove that Diem could not provide security. On a grand scale, Vo Nguyen Giap told the Vietcong: "Establish yourselves in the Central Highlands. Like the French before them, the Americans and their puppet Diem will stay in the cities. Then extend your influence into the lowland jungles and the villages of the Mekong Delta. Assault on the cities will be only the last stage of the conflict." Le Duan's instructions to the guerrillas were known as the Xuan Mai: "When the enemy masses we disperse. When the enemy passes we harass. When the enemy withdraws we advance. When the enemy disperses, we mass."

Instead of coming across the seventeenth parallel by the thousands, former Vietminh came a few at a time down the Ho Chi Minh Trail—through the jungles and mountains of the North Vietnam panhandle into Laos and then into South Vietnam. It was an arduous trip—one to two months of hard marching. When they arrived in South Vietnam, they joined up with Vietcong already there. They brought weapons with them or dug up weapons and ammunition they had buried in 1954.

The nature of the political uprising in South Vietnam has caused considerable debate in the United States. Antiwar activists claimed that it was spontaneous, purely a civil war and popular rebellion against a repressive government that North Vietnam ignored until American intervention forced them to react. At the other extreme, supporters of the war in the United States saw it purely in terms of communist aggression from North Vietnam against South Vietnam. The truth, of course, is in between. Historian William Duiker has argued that the rebellion was a "genuine revolt based in the South . . . organized and directed from the North." Diem created a wealth of hostility and resentment, which North Vietnam exploited through superb organization and extraordinary willpower.

Alienated from the government of Ngo Dinh Diem as well as frightened by the threat of Vietcong violence, South Vietnamese peasants vacillated for a while but eventually sided with the people in power at the local level. Whether they truly believed in the Vietcong cause or were simply intimidated matters little. When guerrillas controlled a region, the peasants went along. By late 1960, with reinforcements from North Vietnam and new recruits from South Vietnam, the number of armed Vietcong had increased to 10,000, and they were expanding out from their strongholds in the mountains of Quang Ngai Province, the U Minh Forest in Kien Giang and An Xuyen Provinces, the Plain of Reeds along the Cambodian border, and the swamps of southeastern Vietnam. They began to launch lightning guerrilla strikes against ARVN forces near the major cities.

Government soldiers, trained in conventional warfare, were no match for the guerrillas. Diem and Nhu packed the ARVN officer corps with Roman Catholics. Loyalty to the Ngo family, not leadership ability or tactical skill, was the prerequisite for appointment. Soldiers distrusted their superiors' abilities and resented their religion. Morale was poor and commitment weak, hardly the stuff of which successful resistance is built. Diem viewed ARVN as a military force whose primary responsibility was keeping the Ngo family in power, not destroying the communists. Diem and Nhu discouraged offensive operations for fear that heavy government casualties would lead to popular discontent and political uprisings.

In 1959 and 1960 the political situation deteriorated rapidly. The number of assassinations and kidnappings was up, as were terrorist assaults on government offices, military bases, American transport convoys, and hotels and bars catering to GI servicemen. On July 8, 1959, Vietcong commandos infiltrated the American base at Bien Hoa and killed two air force personnel—Major Dale Buis of Imperial Beach, California, and Sergeant Chester Ovnand of Copperas Cove, Texas. The Americans were amazed at the audacity of the Vietcong, or "Charlie" as they came to call them. Diem announced, "Vietnam is a nation at war." For American troops, a new saying became common: "The daytime is ours, but the night belongs to Charlie."

In 1960 there were nearly nine hundred American advisers in South Vietnam carrying out the "Hanging Sam" training program, but they could not undo the damage of Diem's regime. On November 11, 1960, just a week after John F. Kennedy defeated Vice President Richard Nixon for president, South Vietnamese paratroopers under the command of Colonel Vuong Van Dong launched a coup against Diem, surrounding the presidential palace in Saigon and demanding his resignation. The coup collapsed when loyal ARVN marines and infantry attacked the paratroopers, but the event sent chills throughout the Saigon diplomatic community. Diem arrested thousands of people.

The deteriorating political situation only fueled the communist drive for reunification. In September 1960 the Third Congress of the Lao Dong party, the political group that assumed power from the Vietminh in 1951 and became the ruling force in North Vietnam, called for the "liberation" of South Vietnam and reunification. Vietcong recruiting efforts were increasingly successful in the south, since Ngo Dinh Diem's regime was daily creating thousands of disaffected people. On December 20, 1960, at a secret location in South Vietnam, North Vietnam established the National Liberation Front to give political direction to the Vietcong guerrillas.

At that very moment, John F. Kennedy was meeting with Dwight Eisenhower, planning the transition to the new administration. International tensions were running high. South Vietnam did not have any priority in the transition meetings. A year later Kennedy ruefully recalled, "You know, Eisenhower never mentioned it, never uttered the word, Vietnam."

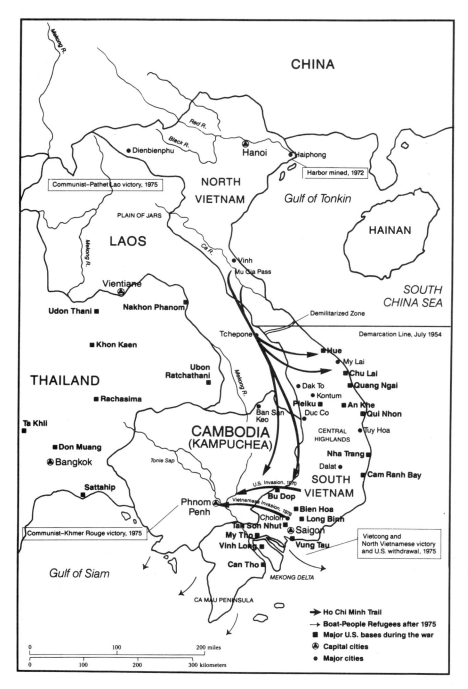

Vietnam, showing 1954 North/South division, and routes of invasions and evacuations, 1945 to 1975.

4

The New Frontier in Vietnam, 1961–1963

We are going to win in Vietnam. We will remain here until we do win.
— Robert F. Kennedy, 1962

When the 1960s dawned, the United States was ready to embark on the salvation of the world. The evil of communism was spreading everywhere, and the forces of democracy had to take a stand. The most popular late-1950s novel dealing with that stand criticized Americans not for being too idealistic but for their failure to be more idealistic. William J. Lederer and Eugene Burdick's *The Ugly American* (1958), written as a response to *The Quiet American*, stayed on the best-seller list for seventy-eight weeks and was made into a successful motion picture starring Marlon Brando. Set in Sarkhan, a fictionalized Vietnam, it details the failures of American policy. *The Ugly American* also has a character based on Colonel Lansdale. Unlike Greene's Pyle, however, Colonel Hillandale is an example of the type of American the country needs more of overseas. He moves among "the people" of Sarkhan, winning their trust and fighting communism.

The primary target of *The Ugly American* is the foreign service. The foreign service is unable to communicate in the language of its host country. Chosen too often for their "personal wealth, political loyalty, and the ability to stay out of trouble," America's ambassadors rarely have any language training. They hear only what their interpreters want them to hear and obtain from newspapers only what their readers want them to obtain. Isolated in the cities, they spend their days entertaining visiting American VIPs, socializing with other Western diplomats, and occasionally meeting with members of the local elite. They ignore the masses who live in rural poverty and speak only their own language. They have no knowledge of their enemy. They have not read the works of Mao Zedong, Karl Marx, or Vladimir Lenin. Instead they believe that American dollars will lead to victory.

In contrast, the communists speak the native languages and work closely with rural peasants, building loyalties and political support. In short, the novel argues, "We have been losing—not only in Asia, but everywhere." *The Ugly American* was a tale of woe but also a call for action. The United States was losing the fight against communism in the Third World, but it could still win. Time was slipping away, but enough time remained. The United States needed hard-working, well-trained professionals. "They must speak the language of the land of their assignment, and they must be more expert in its problems than are the natives." *The Ugly American* then ends with a challenge and a warning: "If the only price we are willing to pay is the dollar price, then we might as well pull out before we're thrown out. If we are not prepared to pay the human price, we had better retreat to our shores, build Fortress America, learn to live without international trade and communications, and accept the mediocrity, the low standard of living, and the loom of world Communism which would accompany such a move."

President John F. Kennedy was to become the embodiment of this call to action. At his inauguration in 1961, Kennedy elaborated on the themes that Lederer and Burdick had described: "Let the word go forth from this time and place, to friend and foe alike, that the torch has been passed to a new generation of Americans—born in this century, tempered by war, disciplined by a hard and bitter peace, proud of our ancient heritage." The words contained pride and arrogance, promise and warning: "Let every nation know, whether it wishes us well or ill, that we shall pay any price, bear any burden, meet any hardship, support any friend, oppose any foe to assure the survival and success of liberty." Kennedy talked about the need to help free nations and promised that his administration would never allow one form of colonialism to be replaced by another, for "those who foolishly sought power by riding the back of the tiger ended up inside." He asked for the commitment of all Americans, but he offered greatness in return: "In the long history of the world, only a few generations have been granted the role of defending freedom in its hour of maximum danger. I do not shrink from this responsibility—I welcome it. . . . The energy, the faith, the devotion which we bring to this endeavor will light our country and all who serve it—and the glow from that fire can truly light the world."

The speech was a tour de force. Only later—years later—did people ask what it meant. For any nation there were limits. No nation could pay, bear, meet, support, and oppose beyond those limits. Yet Kennedy promised just that; he pledged to remove limits, to go beyond the possible to achieve immortality for his nation. The address evokes a nation and a world at the brink of an abyss. Although America was enjoying almost a decade of peace and prosperity, the mood of the inaugural seemed deadly serious. Kennedy believed, as he had written in *Profiles in Courage* (1955), that "great crises produce great men." Coveting greatness, he was determined to produce at least the illusion of a crisis.

About John Kennedy there was an air of romance and courage, a hint that he was born for greatness. He was a sickly child reared in a family of great wealth. Joe Kennedy, his domineering father, expected his sons to show courage, drive, and manliness. They played sports, battled among each other, and competed for their father's love. Jack never used his physical troubles as an excuse; he played as hard as his brothers. The main difference between him and his brothers was that he loved to read. The tales of King Arthur, Scottish chiefs, James Fenimore Cooper, and Marlborough intrigued him. Tales of greatness and acts of courage molded his character.

Kennedy's education and military career strengthened his desire for greatness. If his father was rich, he was also Boston Irish and Catholic— determined that his sons would overcome the prejudices of the American establishment to win their place in that very establishment. Therefore he sent his sons not to Catholic institutions—to Holy Cross or Notre Dame—but to establishment schools and universities. Jack followed Joe, Jr., to Choate, an elite, Protestant prep school dedicated to producing Christian gentlemen who understood duty and obligation and believed that leadership was their rightful heritage. From Choate Jack went to Harvard, where he continued to mix and compete with the Protestant elite. The immigrant family's rage to succeed burned in him. But he learned to conceal the fire beneath a cool facade. Years later, when he was president, he twitted one of his aids for refusing to resign from a prestigious Washington, D.C., club that did not encourage Jewish or black membership. The aide remarked that Kennedy belonged to the equally elitist Links in New York, which was just as restrictive. "Jews and Negroes," Kennedy laughed. "Hell, they don't even allow Catholics!" But a Kennedy—Boston Irish, establishment-bred, wealthy, and Catholic—had quietly kicked down the door.

World War II allowed Joe, Jr., and Jack to show their father and their country their mettle. Jack enlisted in the navy, and on the night of August 1, 1943, in waters near the Solomon Islands, a Japanese destroyer cut his PT-109 in half. Two men died, and Kennedy saved the life of another badly burned crew member. It was all very courageous—the stuff of his childhood reading. And it was fully covered by the American press. Not to be outdone, Joe, Jr., volunteered for a near suicidal bombing mission. Just before his takeoff, he told a friend, "I'm about to go into my act, and if I don't come back tell my dad . . . that I love him very much." He did not come back. He was the one his father had groomed for politics. Now that Joe, Jr., was gone, Jack was the one. "He demanded it," Kennedy later said of his father's desire that he enter politics.

On 1946 Kennedy ran for Congress from Cambridge, Massachusetts. Running as a "fighting conservative," he was easily elected. In 1952 he won a United States Senate seat from Massachusetts and set his sight on the presidency, the ultimate prize. The Senate was just an advanced position from which to launch his final campaign. Between 1952 and 1960, he attacked tasks that enhanced his national reputation. Most important, in an era that was suspicious of ideology, Kennedy had a voting record that was certainly not liberal and not exactly conservative. He did not want to alienate potential presidential support with an unwise Senate vote.

If any philosophy guided Kennedy's actions, it was a belief in the need to demonstrate courage and manliness. He lived in pain. Addison's disease struck him in the late 1940s, and this adrenal deficiency made him susceptible to infections. In 1954 and again in 1955 he underwent serious spinal operations. There were also bouts with anemia, allergies, and various other illnesses. His brother Bobby later recalled, "At least one-half of the days that he spent on this earth were days of intense physical pain." But Jack seldom complained and tried not to allow a fragile body to circumscribe his life. In fact, he reacted to physical limitations by emphasizing the need to live a physically challenging life. To impress Kennedy, one associate remembered, you had to "show raw guts, fall on your face now and then. Smash into the house once in a while going after a pass. Laugh off twisted ankles or a big hole torn in your best suit." As president, Kennedy was determined to show raw guts. Robert Frost, the poet, described Kennedy as "young ambition eager to be tried."

Along with courage, Kennedy evinced a belief in a locker-room sense of manliness. He enjoyed the company of men, the talk of politics, power, and women. Women—like wars—were things to be won. Like his father, Kennedy regarded sexual conquests as a sign of manhood. During his Washington years he moved from one affair to the next. He did not even bother to learn the names of his one-night stands, referring to them by the generic names of "Kiddo" or "Sweetie." One woman remembered, "He was as compulsive as Mussolini. Up against the wall, Signora, if you have five minutes, that sort of thing. He was not a cozy, touching sort of man. In fact he'd been sick for so long that he was sort of touch-me-not." Another woman recalled that for Kennedy, "Sex was something to have done, not to be doing."

The people who came to Washington to join the administration personified the Kennedy mystique: money, power, courage, sensuality, and brains. The Kennedys were "lace-curtain Irish" who despised the origins of the Brahmin elite but aped its trappings. Critics quipped that if you cut them, the Kennedys would bleed "Irish green." What Joe Kennedy struggled for all his life was acceptance, and, with John in the White House, the family had it. The Kennedys surrounded themselves with glamorous, talented people—athletes and astronauts, Silver Star and Congressional Medal of Honor winners, Rhodes scholars, Nobel laureates, all-stars, and prizewinning writers. The Kennedys made winning—in bed, in battle, and in boardrooms—a way of life.

For secretary of state, Kennedy turned to David Dean Rusk. Cherokee County, Georgia, was a world away from the rocky beaches of Cape Cod. The Rusks were "redneck" dirt farmers. Dean was, in their own words, "quick"—smart but not a "smart-aleck," soft-spoken but blessed with the tenacity of a pit bull. They wanted him to go to school, perhaps to be a teacher or a country lawyer. Fate rescued Rusk. During his senior year at Davidson College in North Carolina he won a Rhodes scholarship to study at Oxford University in England. From the vantage point of the State Department, Rusk watched Hitler run over Europe and he vowed never to commit the sin of "appeasement." In 1942 Rusk joined the army and served under "Vinegar" Joe Stillwell in the China-Burma theater. With his combat experience in Asia and the prestige of the Rhodes scholarship, Rusk was named an assistant secretary of state in 1950, a post he kept until 1952, when he became president of the Rockefeller Foundation. With names like Rhodes, Stillwell, and Rockefeller on his résumé, Rusk attracted the attention of the Kennedys.

From the very beginning Rusk had no doubts about Ho Chi Minh or the war. It was part of a global communist conspiracy, not a civil war. Known as the "Buddha" because of his reticence to speak out in general meetings, Rusk was the hardest of the hard-liners, and even in retirement he was unrepentant. The American commitment in Vietnam had been "honorable and necessary. Our only mistake was withdrawing when we did."

Equally hard-line was Walt W. Rostow. A renowned economist at the Massachusetts Institute of Technology, Rostow began advising Kennedy on foreign affairs in 1958. Two years later his book *The Stages of Economic Growth* made him the premier expert on Third World modernization. The Kennedys doted on intellectuals with well-received books, and in 1961 the new president appointed Rostow as deputy special assistant for national security affairs. Rostow believed that modernization creates economic and social dislocations that can render a developing country vulnerable to communist insurgency. He suggested a two-stage approach to South Vietnam. First, the United States should use military force to cut off the Vietcong from their supply sources in North Vietnam, China, and the Soviet Union. He was an early advocate of large-scale bombing of North Vietnam. And at the same time, the United States should help accelerate modernization, to push South Vietnam through the stages of development until a modern economy emerged. Communism would then have no appeal.

Six years later Rostow was still in his ivory tower. At a 1967 briefing with John Paul Vann, a retired lieutenant colonel and Vietnam veteran who was heading up the army's pacification program, Rostow asked Vann if he agreed that the "war would be over in six months." Privately a critic of Rostow, Vann laughingly replied, "Oh hell no, Mr. Rostow. I'm a born optimist. I think we can hold out longer than that." Rostow was not amused. The briefing ended. For the rest of his life Rostow remained convinced that the United States failed in Vietnam only because not enough military firepower had been applied.

No less confident was Robert S. McNamara, Kennedy's secretary of defense. A Berkeley graduate with a Harvard MBA, McNamara was one of the famous "whiz kids" who rapidly moved through management ranks at Ford Motor Company, where he became president in 1960 at the age of forty-four. Possessing a keen, analytical mind and unbounded faith in technology, computers, and systems management, McNamara thought there was no way that a fourth-rate country like North Vietnam could stand up against the American miracle. On his first trip to South Vietnam in 1961, McNamara made up his mind quickly when he could not find a cold drink. Vietnam was a primitive, backward place. "North Vietnam will never beat us," he said. "They can't even make ice cubes."

McNamara assumed both logistical and operational control over the war, establishing strategic goals and objectives, selecting technologies, and, with an army of programmers, accountants, and statisticians, measuring progress. Death and victory were matters of calculus. McNamara did not have the ideological fervor of Rusk or the intellectual paraphernalia of Rostow, but he had their faith in American power—it was only a matter of time before the "superior system prevails." During that 1961 visit to Saigon, McNamara revealed his faith to Frederick Nolting, the American ambassador to South Vietnam. "Fred," he said, "anything you want in the way of instruments, gadgets, or material, we can provide. . . . Don't hesitate to ask for it."

The fourth key player was General Maxwell Taylor. A Missouri native who graduated from West Point in 1922, Taylor was the father of airborne warfare. He was with the Eighty-second Airborne Division in North Africa and Sicily and parachuted into France in command of the 101st Airborne Division on D-Day. Between 1945 and 1949 Taylor was the commandant of West Point, and when the Korean War broke out he took over the Eighth Army. He became chief of staff of the army and remained there until his retirement in 1959. But he was a frustrated chief of staff. The New Look military was good for the air force and navy, which could deliver nuclear warheads, but bad for the army, which became a military stepchild. The New Look, for Taylor at least, was pure folly, forcing the United States to resort to nuclear terror every time a political or military crisis developed somewhere in the world. Instead, Taylor pushed his "flexible-response" military policy. Nuclear weapons should be available for reacting to a nuclear attack, but a strong, well-equipped army and Marine Corps should be available for conventional threats. Finally, the president should have a counterinsurgency option to respond to guerrilla wars and political uprisings where conventional forces were inappropriate.

Taylor's flexible-response theory became a best-seller in his 1959 book *The Uncertain Trumpet*. Here was a general with a well-received book—perfect for the Kennedys. In 1961 the president appointed Taylor as his military adviser and in 1962 named him chairman of the Joint

President John F. Kennedy (right) meets with Secretary of State Dean Rusk (center) and Secretary of Defense Robert McNamara (left).
FRED WARD/BLACK STAR

Chiefs of Staff. The Kennedys found Taylor brilliant and reassuring, a fount of military wisdom who could be trusted to make wise, tough decisions. Attorney General Robert Kennedy named his second son Robert Maxwell Taylor Kennedy.

Finally, there was McGeorge Bundy. A descendant of the aristocratic Lowell family of Massachusetts on his mother's side, Bundy was born in Boston in 1919. Brilliant, caustic, and intolerant of lesser minds, Bundy graduated from Yale in 1940, and the Yale yearbook commented, "This week passed without Mahatma Bundy making a speech." After spending World War II in the army as a planner, Bundy returned to Harvard as a Junior Fellow. Without a Ph.D. or ever having taken a graduate-level political science course, Bundy was given tenure as a Harvard government professor. In 1953, at the age of thirty-four, he became the dean of arts and sciences at Harvard. Bundy was the lone Republican in his family, but he had earned Kennedy's respect in the late 1950s for his sheer brilliance. Of Bundy, Kennedy once said, "You can't beat brains." When Kennedy offered him the position of deputy undersecretary of state for administration, Bundy turned it down, refusing, he said, to leave Cambridge where he was a dean to go to Washington to be a dean. Bundy then turned down the appointment of assistant secretary of defense for international security affairs. Finally, the president asked Bundy to come to the White House as special assistant to the president for national security affairs. Bundy accepted.

The Kennedy administration was caught up in a post–World War II consensus that intoxicated American culture. Kennedy's advisers represented the essence of American power—the foundations, universities, corporations, and military. They had their first taste of leadership in World War II—the great triumph of American money, technology, organization, and will. They remembered the malaise of the Great Depression and contrasted it to the euphoria of the war, with its missionary zeal, national unity, unprecedented prosperity, and overpowering sense of virtue. During World War II the good guys fought the bad guys and the good guys won. The United States had become the premier economic and military force in the world. There seemed nothing that American power could not achieve. That conviction permeated American culture in the late 1940s and 1950s, coloring the way policymakers reacted to social and political change. Communists, not fascists, were the new embodiment of evil. America would provide the money, the leadership, and the technology to defeat the new threat.

Back in the late 1940s and early 1950s the United States had been drawn to Indochina by the fear of monolithic communism as well as by concrete economic needs to preserve Southeast Asia as a capitalist bastion. But during the Kennedy presidency those concrete economic and strategic interests acquired a new ideology of tough optimism. The administration accepted at face value the existence of an international communist conspiracy and the necessity of containment. There was one answer for world problems: Let American virtue define the moral issues and let American power resolve them. The real evil in Vietnam was communism. The United States should invest resources and apply power until the communists reached their breaking point, just as Hitler, Mussolini, and Tojo reached theirs.

Although Dwight Eisenhower never mentioned the word "Vietnam" to Kennedy, the debate started soon after the inauguration. Hard-liners wanted victory. General Lyman L. Lemnitzer, chairman of the Joint Chiefs of Staff in 1961, urged Kennedy to "grind up the Vietcong with 40,000 American ground troops . . . grab'em by the balls and their hearts and minds will follow." McGeorge Bundy was just as adamant. He urged Kennedy to attack the Vietcong—and if necessary North Vietnam—with an array of conventional weapons, including ground troops and strategic bombing. Rostow believed in Taylor's flexible-response idea and wanted to try it out: "It is somehow wrong to be developing these capabilities but not applying them in a crucial theater," he told Kennedy. "In Knute Rockne's old phrase, we are not saving them for the junior prom."

George Ball, on the other hand, counseled caution. The new undersecretary of state for economic affairs, Ball had undergraduate and law degrees from Northwestern. After spending World War II in the Lend-Lease Program, he became director of the U.S. Strategic Bombing Survey in London. Ball concluded that massive bombing of Germany had only marginally affected economic production while stiffening German resistance. In the early 1950s Ball was counsel to the French embassy in Washington, and he watched the French debate about Indochina. From the beginning of his tenure at the State Department, Ball argued that the Diem regime was corrupt, that a land war in Asia was not in the interests of the United States, and that the objective of creating a viable, democratic South Vietnam was impossible. Bundy could barely tolerate Ball, referring to him as the "Theologian." At a 1961 meeting with Kennedy, Ball predicted that the introduction of American troops would create its own momentum; within "five years there will be 300,000 American soldiers fighting in Vietnam." Kennedy laughed, "George, you're crazier than hell."

The president was caught in the middle. McGeorge Bundy described the first few months of the Kennedy administration: "At this point we were like the Harlem Globetrotters, passing forward, behind, sidewise, and underneath. But nobody has made a basket yet." In April the CIA invasion of Cuba at the Bay of Pigs ended in disaster, with Fidel Castro easily capturing the troops and enjoying a propaganda orgy. The incident sent Kennedy into a depression. What he feared more than anything else was appearing weak. Great presidents deal toughly with crises like wars and depressions; they do not conduct botched invasions. Kennedy was also afraid that the Soviets would misread the Bay of Pigs and decide that he could be bluffed. He needed more information about South Vietnam, but in the meantime Kennedy decided in May 1961 to send another five hundred American advisers. That brought the American contingent to 1,400 men.

But Kennedy also knew that five hundred more Americans in South Vietnam was not going to resolve the crisis. He decided to send Vice President Lyndon B. Johnson on a fact-finding mission. Johnson arrived in Saigon on May 10, 1961. Tall, loud, and gregarious, Johnson could not have been more different from the short, reserved, and soft-spoken Ngo Dinh Diem. While Johnson was raised in the democracy of central Texas, where politicians sold their souls for votes, Diem was a mandarin who expected deference from constituents. But the two men hit it off. Johnson stayed in Saigon four days and treated it like a Texas political campaign, full of official breakfasts, lunches, dinners, press conferences, meetings, speeches, and "pressing the flesh" events. The Vietnamese did not know what to make of Johnson. At six feet, four inches, he towered over them, and the muggy heat turned him into a fountain of sweat. In the back seat of the limousine, Johnson had three dozen pressed white shirts. He would come to a stop and plunge into the crowd, grabbing the "praying palms" of onlookers, who were using the traditional greeting of pressed palms and a bow. Johnson kept wanting to know, "Who the hell are they praying to?" By the time he finished shaking hands, he was drenched in sweat and would jump back into the limousine and change shirts, only to start all over again at the next stop.

Although this big sweaty American giant behaved oddly, the crowds warmed to him; they laughed when he hovered over them, dripping sweat and shaking their hands. Those who managed to shake his hand formed Shake the Hand of Lyndon Johnson Clubs. Johnson liked the Vietnamese, too, even though he had a hard time pronouncing their names. At a luncheon where Vietnamese guests were wearing name tags, Johnson kept mispronouncing the most common surname "Nguyen," calling people Mr. or Mrs. "Nu-gu-yen." When an aide told him the name was pronounced "Win," Johnson laughingly remarked, "We'll never lose the war. Everyone in the whole goddamn country is named 'win.' " At a farewell banquet, Johnson reiterated American support and remarked to Diem, "Your people, Mr. President, returned you to office for a second term with 91 percent of the votes. You are not only the George Washington, the Father of your country, but the Franklin D. Roosevelt as well." Privately, Johnson was much more pragmatic. To journalist Stanley Karnow he remarked, "Shit, man, he's the only boy we got out there." He told Kennedy that the United States should continue its military support and launch a "New Deal for South Vietnam" so that economic development could undercut the appeal of the Vietcong.

Johnson's trip to Saigon launched Kennedy on one of his most persistent and frustrating problems: the contradictory reports he received about South Vietnam. The Saigon press corps kept reporting a steady decline in support for Diem and steady increases in Vietcong strength. David Halberstam of the *New York Times*, Neil Sheehan of UPI, Nick Turner of Reuters, Peter Arnett of the Associated Press, Bernard Kalb and Peter Kalisher of CBS, James Robinson of NBC, Charles Mohr of *Time*, François Sully of *Newsweek*, Pepper Martin of *U.S. News & World Report*, and Stanley Karnow of *Time* consistently argued that the Diem regime was isolated and paranoid, that a stable democracy would never develop as long as the Ngo family held power. In short, the United States and South Vietnam were losing.

In June 1961 the Department of Defense sent Eugene Staley of Stanford University to Saigon to study the situation. In August, Staley told Kennedy that American policy must have three objectives: provide military protection from the Vietcong to peasants; convince Diem that "military operations will not achieve lasting results unless economic and social programs are continued and accelerated"; and create a self-sustaining economy in South Vietnam. Only then was the war winnable. But no sooner had Kennedy received Staley's report than Theodore H. White, a prominent journalist and fellow Bostonian, wrote from Saigon with a different story. White, a highly respected Asian expert who was then finishing his Pulitzer Prize–winning book *The Making of a President, 1960* (1961), which Kennedy had read in draft form and heartily enjoyed, claimed: "The situation gets steadily worse almost week by week. . . . Guerrillas now control almost all of the Southern delta—so much so that I could find no American who would drive me outside Saigon in his car even by day without military convoy. . . . What perplexes the hell out of me is that the Commies, on their side, seem to be able to find people willing to die for their cause."

For a straight answer, Kennedy sent Taylor and Rostow to South Vietnam in October. Rostow argued that to build a loyalty among South Vietnamese, the United States should finance the construction of an infrastructure of schools, hospitals, roads, bridges, land development, farm cooperatives, communications systems, and a stable currency. Rostow's ideas reflected his book on the stages of economic growth—which critics dubbed the "TV-in-every-thatched-hut" theory—and he wanted to push the country rapidly toward modernization.

At the same time Taylor's theories about flexible response were coming to fruition. He criticized the training efforts of the Eisenhower administration, which had focused on conventional tactics, how to fight a war of fixed battles and territorial acquisition in a country where the population was friendly. For Taylor, South Vietnam was not that place. It was a tropical jungle of hit-and-run guerrilla attacks where the local population was neutral at best. American training should teach ARVN how to fight a war of attrition against a guerrilla enemy—counterinsurgency. Finally, Rostow and Taylor called for the deployment of 8,000 regular United States ground troops and a 5,000-man combat engineering group. Between 1955 and 1961 the United States had poured $1.65 billion into South Vietnam, and ARVN troops were still not ready. While counterinsurgency was giving stability to Diem and training to ARVN to take over the war, Kennedy would have to increase the number of American troops until the Vietcong lost the will or the ability to fight. Rostow added that Kennedy should consider large-scale bombing of North Vietnam and the infiltration routes, earning him his new nickname, the "Air Marshal."

Kennedy was worried, however, about committing combat troops. He suspected that 13,000 soldiers would put up a good fight against the Vietcong, but he worried about what North Vietnam would do, how many troops could be sent south, and what role the Chinese communists would play. In a comment to Arthur M. Schlesinger, Jr., a Harvard historian and one of his advisers, Kennedy remarked: "They want a force of American troops. . . . But it will be just like Berlin. The troops will march in; the bands will play; the crowds will cheer; and in four days everyone will have forgotten. Then we will be told we have to send more troops. It's like taking a drink. The effect wears off, and you have to have another." Years later Taylor remarked that Kennedy "just didn't want to be convinced that this was the right thing to do. . . . It was really the President's personal conviction that U.S. ground troops shouldn't go in."

Kennedy found an ally in General Douglas MacArthur. Feeling heat from conservative Republicans complaining about softness on Asian communism, Kennedy sponsored a congressional luncheon with MacArthur as the guest speaker. The general did not disappoint him, proclaiming that "we would be foolish to fight on the Asiatic continent" and that "the future of Southeast Asia should be determined at the diplomatic table." Maxwell Taylor remembered that the speech "made a hell of an impression on the President . . . whenever he'd get this military advice . . . he'd say, 'Well, now, you gentlemen, you go back and convince General MacArthur, then I'll be convinced.' But none of us undertook the task."

For the time being Kennedy preferred a middle road—no ground troops but enough American expertise and firepower to get the job done. If Vietnam fell, Kennedy could expect political crucifixion at the hands of the China Lobby in the Republican party. Kennedy planned on running for reelection in 1964, and he was not anxious to give the Republicans a moralistic campaign issue. He told Rostow, "I can't take a 1954 defeat today," meaning that his campaign could not withstand a defeat like the one at Dienbienphu. But at the same time Kennedy did not want the war to get out of control. It was primarily a South Vietnamese affair; the United States should provide only technical advice and economic support. American pilots in South Vietnam were never to go up in the air without a Vietnamese trainee along (or, if no pilot trainee was available, at least some Vietnamese the pilot could pretend was a trainee). American advisers with ARVN were never to engage the Vietcong directly; and no American soldier wounded in action was allowed to receive a Purple Heart. In 1961 Kennedy was walking a political tightrope in Indochina.

John Kennedy was a pragmatist, a man comfortable with compromise. If people like George Ball were cautious, and others like Lemnitzer, Rostow, and Bundy wanted large-scale escalation, the middle ground was in between—a moderate, steady increase of economic and military resources, nothing dramatic and attention getting, but enough to do the job. The irony, of course, was that moderation meant escalation. When Kennedy took office in early 1961, there were nine hundred United States military advisers in South Vietnam. At the end of 1961 there were more than 3,200 advisers.

While the Kennedy administration debated the future of Vietnam, a crisis erupted in Laos. A mountainous country of 2 million people, Laos shared common experiences with Vietnam. In 1945 the French returned to Laos just as they had returned to Vietnam, and two half-brothers vied for control of the government. Prince Souphanouvong hated the French and had a passionate respect for Ho Chi Minh. In the 1950s he emerged as the leader of the Pathet Lao, a group of insurgent guerrillas bent on expelling the French and reforming Laotian society. Farther to the right was Souvanna Phouma, who rejected the revolutionary rhetoric of Souphanouvong but shared his passion for independence. After the Geneva Accords of 1954, which gave independence to Laos, the two formed a coalition government. But as the cold war intensified, John Foster Dulles became more opposed to the coalition and intent on ousting Souphanouvong and the Pathet Lao. Between 1954 and 1959 the CIA spent $300 million fighting the Pathet Lao in a secret war. The CIA spent enormous sums to see to it that General Phoumi Nosovan, a hopelessly corrupt right-winger and former lackey of the French, took control of Laos as head of the so-called Committee for the Defense of the National Interests.

By 1960 it looked as if the first domino in Indochina was about to fall. Souvanna Phouma and Souphanouvong joined forces in a guerrilla war against Phoumi Nosovan and the CIA. Just before he left office, Eisenhower made the American commitment clear: "We cannot let Laos fall to the Communists even if we have to fight," which meant propping up the Nosovan government. But Nosovan could not be saved. He was just too corrupt and too alienated from the Laotian people. Souvanna Phouma and Souphanouvong made steady headway. It seemed only a matter of time before Laos fell.

In March 1961 Kennedy stationed 5,000 American troops in eastern Thailand, hoping the show of force would provide some encouragement to Nosovan. But it was too late. The Defense Department offered a proposal for airlifting American troops into Laos, but Kennedy was skeptical. Laos was landlocked, and it would have been logistically impossible to support the troops. The Bay of Pigs mess had left Kennedy somewhat suspicious of his military and CIA advisers. The president decided on a diplomatic settlement. In May 1961 the United States participated in the Geneva Conference on Laos. W. Averell Harriman, heir to the great railroad fortune and former ambassador to the Soviet Union, headed the American delegation. The final agreement, signed in July 1962, created a neutral Laos with Souvanna Phouma at the head of a coalition government that included Souphanouvong and the Pathet Lao, called for an end to CIA activities in Laos, and insisted on the withdrawal of Vietminh troops from the northeastern border. The CIA, the Pathet Lao, and the Vietcong had no intention, of course, of keeping the agreement.

The CIA had already commissioned Air America, the CIA commercial airliner, to begin dropping supplies to Meo (Hmong) tribesmen, a 9,000-member Laotian mercenary army hired to fight the Pathet Lao and attack North Vietnam supply routes.

Although the Geneva Agreement gave Kennedy some breathing space on Laos, it rigidified his approach to South Vietnam. Harriman urged a diplomatic settlement for Vietnam, arguing that the Diem regime was "repressive, dictatorial and unpopular." Chester Bowles, an undersecretary of state, told the president that by committing support to Diem the United States was "headed full blast up a dead end street." Both advisers wanted the president to consider a comprehensive diplomatic settlement followed by an American withdrawal. But failing at the Bay of Pigs and then allowing the Pathet Lao some power in a neutralist Laotian government, Kennedy was worried about appearing weak. As a result, the administration did not take seriously proposals for a diplomatic solution, a coalition government in Saigon composed of the Vietcong and Diem supporters, or a unilateral withdrawal. Nikita Khrushchev, head of the Soviet Union, did not help much. In January 1961 he had publicly announced Soviet support for "wars of national liberation" around the globe, and Kennedy took that threat seriously. Instead of a negotiated settlement, the Kennedy administration opted for a political and military alternative—counterinsurgency.

Maxwell Taylor's counterinsurgency proposals seemed perfect for South Vietnam. Kennedy had been intrigued with the idea ever since reading *The Uncertain Trumpet*. What he needed was someone he could trust as a counterinsurgency adviser. Kennedy picked Victor ("Brute") Krulak. At five feet, four inches and 134 pounds, Krulak talked his way into the U.S. Naval Academy in 1930 when he was only sixteen. The other midshipmen called him "Brute," and the nickname stuck. But what Krulak lacked in size, he made up for in imagination. He graduated in 1934, went into the Marine Corps, and in 1937 designed the standard landing craft used in the Pacific during World War II. Eleven years later Krulak was ahead of his time in seeing the tactical advantages of the newly invented helicopter, and he wrote the Marine Corps manual describing helicopter tactics.

During World War II, Krulak won the Navy Cross in the Solomon Islands. During an amphibious raid on Choiseul in 1943, his landing craft hit a coral reef and began to sink under Japanese fire. John F. Kennedy pulled his PT boat beside the landing craft and rescued the marines. Krulak thanked Kennedy and promised him a bottle of fine scotch. In the confusion of battle, Krulak did not get the bottle sent, but in 1961 he remembered and shipped a bottle of Three Feathers to the White House. Kennedy remembered. In 1962 he named Krulak, then a major general, as counterinsurgency specialist to the Joint Chiefs of Staff.

Kennedy, Krulak, and Taylor did not have to create a counterinsurgency strategy. They brought to the task American experience fighting the Huk Rebellion in the Philippines and the successful British campaign against the Malayan communists. Soon after gaining independence in 1946, the Philippines faced a communist-led radical movement with more than a million followers on Luzon. The CIA sent Edward Lansdale to build a counterinsurgency movement, and Lansdale selected Ramon Magsaysay, secretary of defense for the Philippines, as the key leader. Together they reformed the Filipino army, improving pay and discipline and firing incompetent, politically appointed officers. Army treatment of civilians improved; election laws were enforced; and tenant farmers gained the right to sue landlords. Finally, Magsaysay and Lansdale offered amnesty or death to the Huk rebels. By 1953 the rebellion was over.

The British had similar success in Malaya. Early in the 1950s, communist insurgents threatened the British colony. British officials launched a large-scale counterinsurgency effort under the direction of Robert Thompson. Thompson concentrated on winning the "hearts and minds" of ordinary peasants by providing them with military security, land reform, and economic development. Although it took ten years to put down the insurgency, Malaya was secure by 1960.

United States officials felt they had two models of successful counterinsurgency programs against Asian communists. After putting down the Huk Rebellion, Edward Lansdale went to South Vietnam to head the CIA effort. In 1961 Thompson went to Saigon as head of the British liaison mission, where he could provide technical expertise to the counterinsurgency program. In Washington, D.C., two people began working on counterinsurgency. Roger Hilsman, a Texas native with a Yale Ph.D. in international relations, spent the 1950s with the CIA before becoming director of intelligence for the State Department in 1961. He warned repeatedly in 1961 and 1962 that military action alone could not solve guerrilla wars; popular support gained through economic development and political reform, proven in the Philippines and Malaya, was indispensable. Krulak, Hilsman, Lansdale, and Thompson hatched what became the Strategic Hamlet Program.

What none of these experts realized was that the model programs could not be transplanted from the Philippines and Malaya to South Vietnam. The situations were very different. In the Philippines the insurgents were not nationalist leaders. The United States granted the Philippines independence in 1946. Most Filipinos spoke English and lusted after the American consumer culture. The two countries were allies during World War II, and Douglas MacArthur was a Filipino hero. Filipino Independence Day was the Fourth of July. When Lansdale launched the CIA counterinsurgency program on Luzon, he represented a country and a culture widely admired by Filipinos.

In Malaya the British were still colonialists in the 1950s, but independence was palpable. Most Malayans expected the British to do what they had already done in India and Pakistan. Britain was the government in Malaya and did not have to work through client politicians and military officials. The British counterinsurgency effort was efficient and disciplined. Ethnic reality simplified the British task. The communists were ethnic Chinese, a minority group in Malaya greatly resented by the native population. There was little chance the communists could launch a broad-based peasant uprising. Few Malayans would die for Chinese revolutionaries.

Compared to South Vietnam, the Philippines and Malaya had been easy. Communism and nationalism fused in the minds of millions of Vietnamese, northern and southern, and Ho Chi Minh wore the mantle of independence. The Diem government was corrupt and isolated, its mandating Roman Catholicism alien in a Buddhist society. The Vietcong and the South Vietnamese were the same people ethnically and culturally, making it almost impossible to identify the enemy. The Military Assistance and Advisory Group (MAAG) spent eight years trying to prepare ARVN for conventional war, but the Vietcong were getting bolder and better. ARVN still needed more flexible military training. The United States would have to buy the time. On February 12, 1962, Kennedy made the first purchase when he established the Military Assistance Command, Vietnam (MACV), or "Macvee," to direct the United States military effort in South Vietnam. Maxwell Taylor personally selected "one of my boys" to command MACV—General Paul Harkins.

A 1929 graduate of West Point, Harkins earned the nickname "Ramrod" during World War II because of the ruthlessness with which he implemented every whim of General George S. Patton, whom he served as deputy chief of staff. When Patton died in 1945, Harkins attached himself to Taylor's rising star as chief of staff with the Eighth Army in Korea. Harkins knew that military careers are built on successful efficiency reports, and immediately after arriving in Saigon in February 1962 he started issuing a daily "Headway Report" showing the steady progress being made against the Vietcong. There was a common theme in all the Headway Reports: the war was going well, but Harkins needed the "3Ms—more men, more money, more matériel." It was not long before the Saigon press corps dubbed him "General Blimp" because of his inflated success reports. Among American younger officers, the phrase "pulling a Harkins" became synonymous with bonehead decisions and bureaucratic foul-ups. But Harkins got his "3Ms." At the end of 1962 there were 11,300 American military personnel in South Vietnam, and the United States was spending $500 million a year to keep the war going. By mid-1962 huge Globemaster transport planes arrived hourly at the Tan Son Nhut airbase delivering military equipment. François Sully, a veteran reporter on Indochina, had seen it all before when French troops poured into Indochina in 1953. He remarked to an

American journalist that it was *"déjà vu.* The American planes bringing American equipment and confident young soldiers dressed in American green fatigues. It looks like 1953 all over again."

As the buildup continued during the Kennedy administration, the number of American women in South Vietnam increased accordingly. With the number of military advisers exceeding 11,000, more and more troops came down with local diseases or suffered from accidents and combat wounds. To meet these medical needs, the army's Eighth Field Hospital deployed to Nha Trang in 1962; the unit included dozens of army nurses, most of whom were women. As the responsibilities of the U.S. embassy staff expanded during the Kennedy administration, several hundred female employees of the State Department were transferred to Saigon. All of the service branches, as well as the Central Intelligence Agency, had women employees in South Vietnam during the early 1960s. Finally, American women working with the United States Army, the Agency for International Development, and the Peace Corps found themselves working in South Vietnam during the Kennedy years.

Most of those 11,300 military personnel were soldiers. The United States was there to fight a war. In November 1962 General Earle Wheeler said that it "is fashionable in some quarters to say that the problems in Southeast Asia are primarily political and economic rather than military. I do not agree. The essence of the problem is military." Harkins agreed. He placed American officers and noncommissioned officers (NCOs) at every level in ARVN, where they planned and provided tactical advice for military operations. At the battalion level, advisers accompanied ARVN in the field.

The advisers hoped to convince the Diem regime to abandon its "fortress psychology" and go after the Vietcong. In February 1962 two Vietnamese pilots attacked the Norodom Palace in strafing runs trying to kill Diem. He became so paranoid that he kept the best ARVN units near Saigon, where they could quickly suppress any uprising. But that left the countryside to the Vietcong. Harkins wanted ARVN to "take the war to the enemy," but Diem was terrified that losing battles or sustaining heavy casualties would create political discontent and undermine his regime. Nor was he much more excited about victories, which produced popular generals who might pose a political threat. Not surprisingly, a contagious spirit of caution and conservatism infected ARVN at every level.

In addition to providing military advisers to South Vietnam, the Kennedy administration also provided air support. In April 1961 the air force created the 4400th Combat Crew Training Squadron, nicknamed "Jungle Jim." Crew members trained Vietnamese pilots in tactical air support, dropped propaganda leaflets over Vietcong territory, and supplied ARVN outposts along the Cambodian and Laotian borders. At first the American pilots were under strict orders to perform covertly, always flying with a Vietnamese pilot in Vietnamese aircraft. But when the

Vietnamese pilots proved less than aggressive, American pilots assumed greater initiative. By 1962 and 1963 they were flying combat missions on their own.

The navy and marines were not to be outdone by the army and the air force. In 1961 the Marine Corps launched Operation Shufly. From bases at Soc Trang in the Mekong Delta and Danang along the northern coast of South Vietnam, marine helicopters carried ARVN troops into battle, while marine advisers instructed ARVN in amphibious assault tactics. But the real entrance of the navy and Marine Corps to Vietnam began with Victor Krulak's brainchild—Operation Plan 34-A, Oplan 34-A in "Pentagonese."

For years the navy and marines conducted clandestine "DeSoto Missions" against the Soviet Union, China, and North Korea—covert intelligence gathering by commando teams and naval vessels. Krulak thought that North Vietnam, with its long coastline, was perfect for even more aggressive activities. He wanted PT boats to attack radar sites in North Vietnam while Vietnamese, Chinese, Korean, and Filipino mercenaries blew up highways, bridges, and ammunition dumps, before being quickly extracted. The plan struck Kennedy's fancy—PT boats, commandos, blackened faces, frogmen, secrets, passwords, adventure. He approved Oplan 34-A on November 20, 1963, three days before his assassination. By mid-1963 the number of American military personnel in South Vietnam was approaching 15,000 people.

The men, money, matériel, and training bore some fruit. By late 1962 ARVN forces totaled 210,000 troops augmented by 142,000 militia. Equipped with M-14 rifles and M113 armored personnel carriers, backed by tactical air support from Farmgate pilots, informed by good intelligence reports from the CIA and Special Forces, and enjoying MACV operational planning, some ARVN units—particularly the ARVN Airborne Division, the First Infantry, and the ARVN marines—began to attack the Vietcong. They even had some unexpected success in War Zone D north of Saigon, in the U Minh Forest on the Gulf of Thailand, and in the Plain of Reeds west of Saigon.

Harkins thought he was creating a killing machine, a mobile army force to do what George Patton's Third Army had done to the Germans in World War II. The word was "attrition"—wearing down the Vietcong to the point where they could not keep fighting. Harkins started adding up the numbers of combat operations, search-and-destroy missions, tactical air sorties (round-trip attacks run by one aircraft), bombing tonnages, weapons captured, ARVN troop increases, and weapons distributed to militia. By the end of 1962, the numbers looked good. Robert McNamara said in a press conference, "Every quantitative measurement we have shows we're winning this war." The most important statistic of all was the "body count," the number of Vietcong killed. General Lyman Lemnitzer, chairman of the Joint Chiefs of Staff in 1960–1961, viewed the U.S. mission as teaching ARVN "to kill Communists." One day in 1961 when Douglas Pike, a psychological operations officer with the United States Information Office in Saigon, remarked that the French had killed or wounded more than a million Vietminh, Lemnitzer had a simple answer: "Didn't kill enough then. We'll teach 'em to kill more."

Back home, few Americans had any idea of what was going on in Vietnam. Military themes in popular culture still revolved around traditional World War II themes. Television shows included *12 O'Clock High*, which told stories about an Air Force bomber group in England during World War II; *The Wackiest Ship in the Army*, a World War II comedy that took place in the South Pacific; *Combat!*, which told the story of a World War II army platoon; *Convoy*, which portrayed the navy during the battle of the Atlantic in World War II; *Mr. Roberts*, a television version of the successful Broadway play and movie showing another side of World War II; *McHale's Navy*, a slapstick comedy set in the South Pacific during World War II; and *Hogan's Heroes*, a comedy set in a German prisoner-of-war camp. All of these shows, even the comedies, were extremely promilitary. The screw-ups of *McHale's Navy* and *Hogan's Heroes* could still outfight and outthink the enemy, even if in some highly unorthodox ways.

Even comic books, the most basic form of popular culture, reflected a traditional point of view. Dell Publishing Company began producing its *Jungle War Stories* in July 1962. Set in South Vietnam, these stories featured U.S. Special Forces and tried to explain why the United States was in Vietnam. Communist forces, inspired by the Soviet Union and Red China, were undermining the government of South Vietnam as part of a global conspiracy to conquer the world. The Vietcong appeared to be bloodthirsty sadists who tortured and killed the innocent civilians of South Vietnam. In contrast, the Green Berets were portrayed as superior men of military prowess, humanitarianism, and leadership who helped the South Vietnamese defend themselves against the communist juggernaut.

Critics of the war were few and far between. A. J. Muste, one of America's veteran pacifists, headed the Fellowship of Reconciliation (FOR) during the 1950s and early 1960s. First established in 1914 during World War I, the FOR had long been the most influential pacifist group in Great Britain and the United States. Muste began warning Americans about the war late in 1962. The War Resisters League (WRL) was even more active. Founded in 1923 as a secular pacifist organization, the WRL had opposed American involvement in World War II and the Korean War. By early 1963, under the leadership of David Dellinger, the WRL focused its protests on the expanding American military advisement effort in Vietnam. Except for these isolated voices, the Kennedy administration's Vietnam policy was virtually unopposed.

Harkins also wanted to win the "hearts and minds" of the people, improve the morale of South Vietnamese peasants, strengthen their loyalty to Diem, and reduce their vulnerability to Vietcong recruiting. Coun-terinsurgency rested on two fundamental principles, both of which had evolved out of the experiences in the Philippines and Malaya and Rostow's theories about economic development. First, peasants needed security against Vietcong attack; they needed to be able to go to sleep at night in peace. And second, when they woke up in the morning, they needed land, jobs, and schools where they could build economic prosperity. People enjoying the good life would not fall prey to communistic rhetoric.

The American military arm of counterinsurgency in Vietnam was the Special Forces. During the 1950s the Michigan State University Advi-sory Group launched economic development projects in South Vietnam, and the CIA formed local militias—Civilian Irregular Defense Groups (CIDG)—among Montagnard tribesmen. First organized in 1952 to al-low the army to fight covertly behind enemy lines, the First Special Forces Group sent a few advisers into South Vietnam in 1957. But in 1961 they caught President Kennedy's fancy. An avid reader of Ian Fleming's "James Bond" novels, Kennedy was fascinated by the para-phernalia of espionage, covert action, double agents, and guerrilla war. Against the wishes of army brass, he authorized the Special Forces to wear the Green Beret in 1961. He increased them from 2,500 to 10,000 men and sent the Fifth and Seventh Special Forces Groups to Vietnam. Late in 1962 the Green Berets took over CIDG training from the CIA.

While the Special Forces were taking over the CIDGs, and MACV was trying to get ARVN to fight its own war, Roger Hilsman and Robert Thompson were putting in motion the Strategic Hamlet Program. It was a new version of the older Agroville program. "Strategic hamlets" were peasant villages surrounded by barbed wire and mine fields. Inside the strategic hamlets there would be schools, a community center, a small hospital and pharmacy, and homes for the peasants. American pilots could then open fire on the Vietcong, who by definition were all the people outside the hamlets. Unable to hide, the Vietcong would be crushed by the killing machine. MACV turned the job of building the strategic hamlets over to Diem, who just as promptly turned it over to Nhu, who went about the construction process with a vengeance. By the end of the summer of 1962, Nhu claimed to have built 3,225 hamlets and placed 4.3 million peasants behind the barbed wire. Robert Thompson was appalled by Nhu's slipshod approach. "No attention was paid to their purpose," Thompson said. "Their creation became the purpose itself."

Harkin's daily Headway Reports were not confirmed, however, by pessimistic reports from journalists in Saigon. For an independent look, Kennedy asked Senator Mike Mansfield of Montana to go to Saigon in December 1962. A devout Roman Catholic and former professor of Asian affairs, Mansfield had been an early supporter of Ngo Dinh Diem. But in Saigon he received alarming reports from the press corps, and he gave Kennedy a pessimistic report: "Vietnam, outside the cities, is still . . .

The so-called Strategic Hamlet Program herded Vietnamese peasants away from their ancestral villages and confined them to fenced, fortified compounds that were more like minimum-security prisons than real communities.
FRANÇOIS SULLY/BLACK STAR

run largely by the Vietcong. . . . Out of fear or indifference or hostility the peasants still withhold acquiescence, let alone approval of the [Saigon] government. . . . In short, it would be well to face the fact that we are once again at the beginning of the beginning." The report caught Kennedy off guard. He lashed out at Mansfield, accusing him of defeatism. When a reporter asked Kennedy if Mansfield's opinion did not justify a withdrawal, Kennedy acidly replied, "For us to withdraw would mean a collapse not only of South Vietnam but of Southeast Asia. So we are going to stay there." Mansfield was more pessimistic with his congressional colleagues, to whom he reported that the war "could involve an expenditure of American lives and resources on a scale which would bear little relationship to the interests of the United States or, indeed, to the interests of the people of Vietnam."

Kennedy was growing more and more frustrated. He wanted out of Vietnam but did not know how. In a comment to one of his aides, Kennedy said, "I got angry with Mike for disagreeing with our policy so completely, and I got angry with myself because I found myself agreeing with him." He did not want to appear weak; he dreaded anything resembling the defeat at the Bay of Pigs. But he did not want the war to become a large-scale conflict. That was why Mansfield's report had been such a blow. The war was already costing a fortune, and, according to someone Kennedy trusted, the investment made no difference at all.

Kennedy then asked Roger Hilsman and Michael Forrestal, a White House Far Eastern affairs adviser, to evaluate the situation. They returned from Saigon in January 1963 with an optimistic report. Two weeks later Kennedy sent General Earle Wheeler, the army chief of staff, and Victor Krulak to Saigon. They castigated Mansfield and predicted early victory. All the heavy brass worried Harkins, so he issued his most optimistic prediction of all: at the end of 1963 Kennedy could withdraw 1,000 troops from South Vietnam, and all the rest by the end of 1965.

But in 1963 the general's statistical cloth began to unravel. North Vietnam brought 4,500 infiltrators down the Ho Chi Minh Trail in 1959 and 1960, 6,300 in 1961, and nearly 13,000 in 1963, increasing the Main Force Vietcong from 3,000 people in 1960 to 10,000 in 1961, to 17,000 in 1962, and to 35,000 in 1963. Most were former Vietminh, native southerners regrouped to North Vietnam after 1954. They were highly motivated, well trained, and anxious "to go home." Secret intelligence reports indicated that the Vietcong were gaining strength, that they were fielding 600- to 700-man battalions supported by communications and engineering units, and that the Ninth Vietcong Infantry Division would soon be ready for full deployment.

And they were well armed. Homemade shotguns and World War II vintage rifles were a thing of the past. Between early 1962 and mid-1963, MACV distributed more than 250,000 weapons to CIA and Special Forces irregular troops—M-14 carbines, shotguns, submachine guns, mortars, recoilless rifles, radios, and grenades. Most of them ended up with the Vietcong. Some ARVN outposts were particularly notorious for losing weapons. Americans called them "Vietcong PXs." The American cornucopia of death was so reliable that in mid-1963 Vietcong commanders relayed messages north that it was easier to capture American weapons than bring Chinese and Soviet arms down the Ho Chi Minh Trail.

Nor were the Vietcong having any trouble finding recruits. The Strategic Hamlet Program was a bonanza for them. Within a matter of months the Diem regime herded millions of peasants into hastily constructed hamlets that were more like concentration camps than villages. Peasants were forced to build the new hamlets, dig the huge, water-filled moats around them, string the barbed wire, and knock down their old homes. Millions of peasants left ancestral villages at gunpoint for the confinement of the strategic hamlets. The Vietcong used a simple response: "When the Diem regime falls and the Americans leave, you will be able to go home again." The peasants listened. The Vietcong also infiltrated the Strategic Hamlet Program. Nhu gave control of the program to Colonel Pham Ngoc Thao, who ruthlessly implemented it. What

Nhu did not know was that Thao was a Vietcong agent. His instructions were to be brutal in building the strategic hamlets, to alienate as many peasants as possible. He was eminently successful. According to historian Larry Cable, "The United States had about as much effective control over the . . . Strategic Hamlet Program, as a heroin addict has over his habit."

No less successful in lining up peasants behind the Vietcong was American air power. Between early 1961 and the end of 1962 air force personnel in South Vietnam increased from 250 to 2,000, and the number of monthly bombing sorties from 50 to more than 1,000. By the middle of 1963 the air force was conducting 1,500 sorties a month, dropping napalm, rockets, and heavy bombs and strafing the Vietcong. The problem, of course, was that air power was indiscriminate. Guerrillas died, to be sure, but so did peasants. Between the bombing runs and the strategic hamlets, the Vietcong were able to recruit as many new soldiers as they could equip and supply. In 1960 main-force Vietcong soldiers were supported by only 3,000 village and regional self-defense troops, but that number increased to more than 65,000 in late 1963. At the end of the year the communists had more than 100,000 troops— main force and militia—at their disposal.

More than anything else, the battle of Ap Bac in January 1963 exposed the problems of the war. Late in December 1962, two hundred troops from the Vietcong 514th Battalion dug in along a mile-long canal at the edge of the Plain of Reeds in Dinh Tuong Province, near the village of Ap Bac. Hidden by trees, shrubs, and tall grass, they had a clear view of the surrounding rice fields. When intelligence reports revealed the Vietcong, MACV felt it finally had an opportunity to engage the elusive enemy in a set-piece battle. More than 2,000 troops from the ARVN Seventh Division, advised by Lieutenant Colonel John Paul Vann, went into battle.

The operational plan was simple. Two ARVN battalions would approach from the north and south, while a company of M113 armored personnel carriers came in from the west. The eastern approaches would be left unguarded, so that if the Vietcong tried to escape, they would be destroyed by tactical air strikes and heavy artillery. In previous battles, the Vietcong fled when they saw the M113s and CH-21 helicopters, but this time was different. They held their positions. With small-arms fire they brought down five helicopters and nearly destroyed nine more, and they methodically killed the machine gunners on the M113s. ARVN troops refused to attack, and the ARVN command refused to reinforce them. The Vietcong escaped with twelve casualties, leaving behind two hundred dead or wounded ARVN troops and three dead American advisers.

The battle of Ap Bac had immediate repercussions. Reporters like Neil Sheehan and David Halberstam knew they had a story; after a year of

Headway Reports, Ap Bac showed how the war was really going. The military tried, of course, to discredit the journalists. Admiral Harry Felt, commander of the United States Pacific fleet, went to Saigon after the battle and announced in a press conference: "I don't believe what I've been reading in the papers. As I understand it, it was a Vietnamese victory— not a defeat, as the papers say." Harkins nodded and agreed: "Yes, that's right. It was a Vietnamese victory. It certainly was." Robert McNamara confidently proclaimed, "We have definitely turned the corner toward victory." But the only people turning any corner were the Vietcong.

The Diem government was steadily deteriorating, not only because of its mandarin values and the Strategic Hamlet Program but also because of bizarre eccentricities and paranoia. Elder brother Ngo Dinh Thuc, archbishop of Hue, used his political clout to augment church property. One critic charged that his requests for contributions "read like tax notices." He bought farms, businesses, urban real estate, rental property, and rubber plantations, and he employed ARVN troops on timber and construction concessions. Ngo Dinh Can, the dictator of Hue, accumulated a fortune as head of a smuggling syndicate that shipped huge loads of rice to Hanoi and large volumes of opium throughout Asia. Ngo Dinh Luyen, the South Vietnamese ambassador in London, became a multimillionaire speculating in piasters and pounds using insider information gleaned from his brothers in Saigon. More bizarre still were the antics of Ngo Dinh Nhu. By 1963 Nhu was smoking opium every day. His ambition had long since turned into a megalomania symbolized by the Personalist Labor Revolutionary party, or Can Lao—secret police known for torture and assassination. Can Lao troops, complete with Nazi-like goose-step marches and stiff-armed salutes, enforced Nhu's will. Madame Nhu had her own stormtroopers, a group known as the Women's Solidarity Movement and Paramilitary Girls, which worked at stamping out evil, or at least what Madame Nhu considered evil— dancing, card playing, prostitution, divorce, and gambling. The Nhus amassed a fortune running numbers and lottery rackets, manipulating currency, and extorting money from Saigon businesses, promising "protection" in exchange for contributions. After reading a CIA report on the shenanigans, President Kennedy slammed the document down on his desk and shouted, "Those damned sons of bitches."

President Diem's peculiarities were fast becoming derangements. He was addicted to eighteen-hour work days and then left paperwork at the side of his cot to attend to when he woke up in the night to go to the bathroom. His need for privacy had become seclusion. Afraid to leave business to others, Diem assumed more and more duties, even personally approving all visa requests and deciding which streets got traffic lights. He gave military orders as well, not just to divisions and battalions but to companies, often not keeping their commanding officers informed of his decisions. In discussions with foreign journalists and American officials,

Diem offered incredible, mind-numbing monologues of five, six, even ten hours, with the visitors not able to get in a single comment. Charles Mohr saved his questions for when Diem was lighting another cigarette; those were the only occasions he stopped talking. Robert Shaplen of the *New Yorker* recalled that in those interviews Diem's "face seemed to be focused on something beyond me. . . . The result was an eerie feeling that I was listening to a monologue delivered at some other time and in some other place—perhaps by a character in an allegorical play." South Vietnam was a dictatorship: dissidents were imprisoned, tortured, or killed; elections were manipulated; the press, radio, and television were controlled; and universities were treated as vehicles for government propaganda.

The national holiday on October 26, 1962, celebrating the triumphant Diem elections in 1955, exposed the depth of Diem's isolation. He staged an elaborate military parade through Saigon. ARVN troops and armored personnel carriers left the field late in September to get ready for the parade, much to the dismay of American advisers fighting the Vietcong. Diem invited a few members of the press corps and some foreign diplomats to join him on the stand. The parade proceeded uneventfully, except for one bizarre fact: Diem sealed off the entire parade route and several city blocks from the public. The parade wound its way along the Saigon River with no spectators, only vacant sidewalks. ARVN troops and Nhu's secret police forced store owners to close up shop and leave their buildings. Diem wanted no contact with his people. For David Halberstam the parade was a surrealistic experience: "One felt as if he were watching a movie company filming a scene about an imaginary country."

What ultimately brought down Diem was the Buddhist crisis in the summer of 1963. There had long been a smoldering resentment among the Buddhists who had seen power, land, government jobs, and money flow to the Roman Catholics. The Buddhist political movement was led by Thich Tri Quang, an intensely nationalist monk who headed the militant United Buddhist church. Although he was not a communist, Quang had cooperated with the Vietminh in fighting the French and the Japanese. What Thich Tri Quang was able to exploit, in the name of civil liberties, was a widespread popular desire in many parts of South Vietnam to overthrow Diem, expel the United States, and restore Vietnam to its traditional moral values.

Pent-up feelings exploded on May 8, 1963, the 2,587th birthday of Gautama Buddha. Diem prohibited Buddhists from flying their religious flags during the holiday. More than 1,000 Buddhist protesters gathered at the radio station in Hue demanding revocation of the order. When they refused to disperse, ARVN troops opened fire, killing eight people and wounding dozens more. The next day 10,000 Buddhists showed up demanding an apology, repudiation of the antiflag regulation, and payments to the families of the wounded and the dead. Buddhist hunger strikes spread throughout the country, and demonstrators walked the streets in Saigon. Late in May, Ngo Dinh Can imposed martial law on Hue and patrolled the streets with armored personnel carriers, tanks, and ARVN troops. In Saigon, Ngo Dinh Nhu's police assaulted Buddhist crowds with attack dogs and tear gas.

Diem was incapable of compromise; madarin leaders expect obedience from the masses, not insurgency and protest. Nor was the Ngo family capable of any political sensitivity. On June 11, 1963, Thich Quang Duc, a seventy-three-year-old Buddhist monk, knelt on Pham Dinh Phung street in Saigon, surrounded by Buddhist monks, nuns, and invited journalists. A colleague doused him with five gallons of gasoline, and Duc lit a match and ignited himself, burning to death in protest of the Diem regime. The picture of his motionless body burning for ten minutes spread across the world wire services. A series of Buddhist torch suicides came in rapid succession. Madame Nhu remarked that she would be "willing to provide the gasoline for the next barbecue."

Throughout July, Ambassador Frederick Nolting pleaded with Diem to reach some accommodation with the Buddhists. Kennedy threatened to cut off economic and military assistance unless Diem acquiesced, but Diem, stiffened by Nhu's fanatical opposition to American pressure, became more intractable. Many noncommunist South Vietnamese resented the American presence in their country, and Diem had to be careful about appearing to cave in to American pressure. In Vietnamese history, appearing as a puppet to a foreign power was political suicide. If Diem backed down, he might lose what little political support he still had.

The assault on the Buddhists continued. Late in July, Nhu's goon squads, many of them dressed in ARVN uniforms, placed barbed wire around hundreds of Buddhist pagodas and arrested Buddhist leaders. Two weeks later they invaded the pagodas and dispersed all meetings there. In Hue they killed thirty worshipers and wounded two hundred more at the Dieu De Pagoda. Diem arrested children for carrying antigovernment signs and closed schools. By mid-August he had jailed more than a thousand adolescents. Finally, he imposed martial law throughout the country on August 20, 1963.

The madness precipitated an intense debate in Washington. Harkins and Nolting insisted that the war was going well, despite the political problems, and that victory was still within reach. Maxwell Taylor, Robert McNamara, Walt Rostow, and Dean Rusk agreed. Senator Mike Mansfield, on the other hand, argued that defeat, not victory, was just around the corner. At a meeting of the National Security Council on August 31, Paul Kattenburg, a State Department official who headed the Interdepartmental Working Group on Vietnam, suggested that the United States should "get out while the getting is good." Unfortunately for Kattenburg, his boss was at the meeting. "We will not," Dean Rusk insisted, "pull out until the war is won." Kattenburg kept his mouth shut, but his State Department career was over. Rusk posted him to Guyana.

It was clear to everyone in the administration, regardless of their feelings about the war, that it was time for a change. Frederick Nolting had to go. An aristocrat Virginian, Nolting sympathized with the Ngo family. But who would replace him? The new United States ambassador to South Vietnam needed Asian experience, but at the same time he had to be independent of the military. The inner circles at the White House discussed the matter at length during the summer of 1963, and Dean Rusk stunned everyone by suggesting Henry Cabot Lodge, Jr. The mere mention of Lodge's name was practically sacrilege. If the Kennedys bled "Irish green," Lodge was the "bluest of the blue bloods," a North Shore Yankee Republican whose ancestors occupied the Commonwealth of Massachusetts for three hundred years. The Kennedys had long resented Boston Brahmins who disdained the famine Irish immigrants. It was not that Kennedy had not already tasted some revenge. He defeated Lodge for the Senate seat in 1952, and in 1960 Lodge was Richard Nixon's running mate. On the night Lodge accepted the Republican vice-presidential nomination, Kennedy watched Nixon and Lodge raise their clenched hands on television. He remarked to Kenny O'Donnell, his close friend and aide: "That's the last Nixon will see of Lodge. If Nixon ever tries to visit the Lodges at Beverly, they won't let him in the door."

But the more Kennedy thought about Rusk's suggestion, the more he liked it. Fluent in French, Lodge had a Harvard education and a lifetime of experience. A three-time United States senator and former ambassador to the United Nations, Lodge would not kowtow to anyone. And because of his gilt-edged Republican credentials, Lodge might deflect some of the right-wing criticism of the administration. There was one final, mean little twist to the Lodge appointment. O'Donnell remembered that "the idea of getting Lodge mixed up in such a hopeless mess as the one in Vietnam was irresistible." It took Lodge a few days in Saigon to realize what a hopeless mess it was. In an August 28 cable to President Kennedy, Lodge said that the United States was "launched on a course from which there is no respectable turning back: the overthrow of the Diem government. . . . There is no possibility that the war can be won under a Diem administration. The chance of bringing off a generals' coup depends on them to some extent. . . . We should proceed to make an all-out effort to get the generals to move promptly." Lodge had thrown down the gauntlet.

Kennedy wanted an independent assessment of how the war was going. On September 6 he asked Victor Krulak to take another look. He also sent Joseph Mendenhall, a career diplomat who had spent three years in Saigon. Both men made whirlwind trips, returning to the White House at about the same time on September 10. Krulak had met with Harkins and

Lodge and a variety of MACV officials. Mendenhall spent his time with lower-echelon embassy officials and journalists. Krulak reported to Kennedy that the war was being won and that he could begin the promised withdrawal of 1,000 troops by the end of the year. Mendenhall said that the Vietcong were getting stronger, that a religious civil war between Buddhists and Catholics was imminent, that the Diem regime had lost even the little credibility it once enjoyed, and that a communist victory was certain. Incredulous, Kennedy remarked at the end of their joint briefing, "You two did visit the same country, didn't you?"

Still not satisfied, Kennedy sent Maxwell Taylor and Robert McNamara to Saigon two weeks later. By that time peasants were leaving the strategic hamlets in droves, and the Vietcong were cutting up the barbed wire and using it in mines. The Vietcong now fielded more than 35,000 troops and another 65,000 people in support services. Taylor and McNamara listened to Harkins and came back with the great promise "that the military campaign has made great progress and continues to progress" in spite of "serious political tensions in Saigon." By the end of 1965, they said, "It should be possible to withdraw the bulk of U.S. personnel."

But the war was being lost. When one of Kennedy's aides asked him how the administration could withdraw from Vietnam without being crucified politically, the president responded, "Easy. Put a government in there that will ask us to leave." When he was in Saigon, Maxwell Taylor arranged a tennis match with General Duong Van Minh to feel him out about the possibilities of a coup. Taylor tried delicately to broach the issue, but a suspicious Minh kept his own counsel, preferring to talk only about forehands and backhands. Lodge was more direct. He distanced himself from Diem and Nhu, and it did not take long for them to realize that the United States was seeking their removal. South Vietnamese military leaders were worried that a frustrated United States might cut off military aid. General Tran Van Don, ARVN chief of staff, was aware of Maxwell Taylor's approach to Duong Van Minh, and he let Lucien Conein know that coup plans were under way. French-born but American-raised, Conein spent World War II in France as an OSS agent. He was now a CIA agent in Saigon with powerful ARVN connections. He let Tran Van Don know that the United States wanted a new military government. The plotting started.

Diem and Nhu were not fools. They got wind of the plotting and hatched a scheme of their own. Known as Operation Bravo, it involved staging a fake revolt in Saigon, complete with demonstrations, assassinations of prominent politicians—including Minh, Tran, Conein, and Lodge—orchestrated "revolutionary broadcasts" over Saigon radio, and the flight of Diem and Nhu to secret headquarters in the countryside. Once the chaos seemed at its peak, they would reenter Saigon with a column of ARVN troops commanded by their trusted military adviser

General Ton That Dinh. They would then crush the "rebellion" and "save" South Vietnam. What they did not know was that Ton That Dinh was part of the conspiracy. On November 1, 1963, the two brothers realized that Operation Bravo was not to be, and they fled to Cholon. The brothers talked with several supporters and decided to surrender. Diem telephoned staff headquarters and said that he was ready to surrender with "military honors." The surrender, the rebel leaders informed him, would be unconditional, but they promised him safety.

Minh dispatched two jeeps and an armored personnel carrier. Among the men on the mission was Minh's bodyguard, Captain Nhung, a professional assassin who notched his pistol after each killing. As the convoy set off, Minh gave Nhung a prearranged signal. Diem and Nhu were not as safe as they thought. In office or out they were powerful men whose craftiness and base of support commanded respect and honest fear. Such men, several rebels agreed, were best dead. "To kill weeds," one of them said, "you must pull them out by their roots." And Captain Nhung was an expert at this sort of gardening. Diem and Nhu surrendered, and rebels put them in the personnel carrier. Both men's hands were tied behind their backs. The convoy then headed for the rebel headquarters. Captain Nhung rode with the brothers. When the vehicles arrived at Joint General Staff headquarters, Diem and Nhu were dead. Both had been shot. Nhu had also been stabbed several times. *"Mission accomplie,"* Nhung told Minh in French.

That was not the end of it. Archbishop Ngo Dinh Thuc fled to Rome. Ngo Dinh Can was arrested in Hue and executed in Saigon. Madame Nhu escaped the bloodbath only because she was in the United States. When news of the assassinations became public, celebrations erupted in the streets of Saigon. Although Lodge had not planned on the assassinations, he was not disturbed by them. The rebels told him that Nhu and Diem had died of "accidental suicide." To David Halberstam, Lodge remarked: "What would we have done with them had they lived? Every Colonel Blimp in the world would have made use of them." A few months later Minh said: "They had to be killed. Diem could not be allowed to live because he was too much respected among simple, gullible people in the countryside, especially the Catholics and the refugees. We had to kill Nhu because he was so widely feared—and he had created organizations that were arms of his personal power."

When Kennedy got the news, he was profoundly disappointed. During his administration the United States spent nearly $1 billion in South Vietnam, increased the number of American military advisers to more than 16,000, and had 108 United States soldiers killed there. But the Vietcong were stronger than ever. General Duong Van Minh argued a few weeks earlier that the Vietcong had "more of the population on their side than has the GVN [Diem regime]" and that the "heart of the Army is not in the war." Two weeks after the coup, Kennedy instructed Michael

Forrestal to begin a "complete and very profound review of how we got into this country, what we thought we were doing, and what we now think we can do. . . . I even want to think about whether or not we should be there." Kennedy never got a chance to see the report. On November 22, 1963, he was assassinated in Dallas. Lyndon Johnson became president. A few days after the funeral, Johnson sent a memo to all State Department officials: "Before you go to bed at night I want you to do one thing for me: ask yourself this one question . . . what have I done for Vietnam today?"

5

Planning a Tragedy, 1963–1965

It is fashionable in some quarters to say that the problems in Southeast Asia are primarily political and economic rather than military. I do not agree. The essence of the problem is military.
—General Earle G. Wheeler, 1962

Lyndon Baines Johnson was the Lon Chaney of American politics. Just as Chaney, the man with a thousand faces, could play any film role, Johnson could play any political role. He could be all things to all people. Few people could resist him face to face because of his chameleonic qualities. Always friendly, always ready to smile and flatter, never afraid to show affection or to express his love, Johnson was almost irresistible. He believed that the intellectuals who criticized him simply did not understand him. He said they

> never take the time to think about what really goes on in these one-to-one sessions because they've never been involved in persuading anyone to do anything. They're just like a pack of nuns who've convinced themselves that sex is dirty and ugly and low-downed and forced because *they* never have it. And because they never have it, they see it all as rape instead of seduction and they miss the elaborate preparation that goes on before the act is finally done.

But who was the real Lyndon Johnson? Was he the conservative oil-and-gas man? Certainly other conservative oil-and-gas men believed that Lyndon was their boy in Washington, and they provided the dollars that fueled his political career. Or was he a good Texas populist like his father had been? Or perhaps he was a New Deal liberal Democrat. Perhaps he himself was not sure who he was. All his life he seemed bent on creating a past for himself out of whole cloth. He lied about his birth, his parents, his grandparents, his education, and his loves. He claimed that his great-great-grandfather died defending the Alamo. When a reporter confronted him with the fact that none of his relatives fought at the Alamo, Johnson exclaimed: "God damn it, why must all those journalists be such sticklers for detail? Why, they'd hold you to an accurate description of the first time you ever made love, expecting you to remember the color of the room and the shape of the windows. . . . The fact is that my great-great-grandfather died at the Battle of San Jacinto, not the Alamo." But that ancestor—the one who had not died at the Alamo—had also not died at San Jacinto.

Johnson lied to create the person he wanted to be. He advised correspondents to burn his letters. He arranged to have information about his college years cut out of hundreds of copies of the Southwest State Teachers College yearbooks. As his biographer Robert A. Caro writes, "In a sense, Lyndon Johnson not only attempted to create, and leave for history, his own legend, but to ensure that it could never be disproven." The real Lyndon Johnson is a riddle. He was born in 1908 in the Texas Hill Country, a hot, dry, poor section of the state. His family was poor, but his mother came from a once-prosperous family that had been financially ruined by a bad investment. In her mind, at least, she remained above the world of dirty men and coarse women who populated the Hill Country. And she told Lyndon that he, too, was meant for better things, that unlike his father—who was very much at home among the unlettered folk of the Pedernales—he had culture in his blood. He grew up torn between the worlds of his mother and father. His father cussed and talked politics; his mother read and dreamed of a better life. Lyndon embraced his father's world. He mastered the crude Texas metaphors, drank alcohol, trafficked in power politics, and expressed distrust, if not outright contempt, for ideas, books, and lofty education.

At Southwest Texas State Teachers College, Johnson showed that to achieve power he was willing, even eager, to work tirelessly at the most thankless task. Quick to recognize who had power, he attached himself to that person, shamelessly flattered that person, made himself indispensable to that person. It was a formula that Johnson repeated endlessly during his life. At San Marcos, Johnson attached himself to the school's president, Cecil Evans. Within a year Johnson was determining who got campus jobs, the life-blood of many poor students. Control of campus jobs translated into power. And he used the power to control campus politics. Nicknamed "Bull" (short for "Bullshit") Johnson because he told so many lies, Lyndon nevertheless made the tiny school his fiefdom. The acquisition of power, he often said, was necessary before he could do "good works." Perhaps his ends were noble, but so often it seemed that Johnson's only end was more power.

After a brief stint as a teacher, Johnson went to Washington as a secretary to Congressman Richard Kleberg. It was 1931, a bleak year in the capital, but Johnson was euphoric. He moved into the Dodge Hotel, where seventy-five other legislative secretaries lived, and studied the conduits of power. He asked the older secretaries questions continually. He roamed the halls asking questions. He haunted the bathroom seeking knowledge. On his first night there he took four separate showers because he wanted to meet and talk to the other secretaries. The next morning he walked to the bathroom five times at ten-minute intervals so that he could meet more people. He extracted from each conversation knowledge about the workings of Washington that he mentally cataloged and filed away for future reference. Secretaries were not his only source of knowledge. He read the Washington newspapers as well as the *New York Times* and the *Wall Street Journal*. He talked with elevator operators, cooks, and janitors. And he courted the legislators. He was deferential, full of "Yes, sir" and "No, sir," and his flattery knew no bounds. One person called Johnson a "professional son." No father could wish for more respect and consideration and love from a son than Johnson *seemed* to give.

Johnson courted several power brokers on Capitol Hill. Most important, he snuggled in close to Sam Rayburn, whose sharp eyes seemed to see through everyone and whose power was unquestioned. Rayburn liked Lyndon—perhaps even understood him—and he became an unmatched patron. He helped Johnson get appointed as the Texas director of the National Youth Administration. He also aided Johnson's successful bid for a vacant congressional seat in 1937. No constituency was better served by an elected official. Johnson wrestled free the federal money needed to build great dams—dams that produced electricity. Because of Johnson, electric light replaced candles and prosperity overcame poverty in the Hill Country.

Politically, Johnson kept rising. Although he lost his first bid for the Senate, he won a seat in his second try in 1948. In 1951 he became the Democratic whip of the Senate; in 1953, the Senate minority leader; in 1955, the Senate majority leader. Each new position meant more power and new challenges. Each he mastered with the skill of a political artist. Nobody did it better. And, of course, he loved the power that came with success. One night in 1958, a bit tight and in a good mood, he put an arm around two Texas congressmen and boasted, "I'm one powerful sonofabitch." It was an understatement. He was *the* powerful sonofabitch, and everything he did demonstrated that power. This was true even to the smallest detail. The telephone, for example, had replaced the sword and the pen as the symbol of power, and Johnson made sure he was often photographed using the telephone. "No gunman," remarks one historian, "ever held a Colt .44 so easily" as Johnson handled a telephone.

Of his staff and cabinet Johnson demanded loyalty above honesty, sincerity, and good advice. Discussing the subject, Johnson once declared: "I don't want loyalty. I want *loyalty*. I want him to kiss my ass in Macy's window at high noon and tell me it smells like roses. I want his pecker in my pocket." For the sake of debate Johnson was willing to listen to the other side, but he listened with open ears and a closed mind. After the discussion ended, he expected everyone to agree with his previously formulated ideas. If after he flattered and reasoned and listened a person still did not agree with him, he exiled that person from the inner circle. In this matter Johnson domesticated dissent.

Raised in an area where the frontier was still visible, Johnson also tended to view life in a highly macho way. There were strong men and weak men, and in any contest the strong won. To show weakness was worse than cowardly—it was unmanly. Casting aspersions on the Kennedy crowd, Johnson said that they vacationed at that "female island"— Martha's Vineyard—and spoke with affected accents. His macho ethos extended to nations. No country could afford to be unmanly, especially in the face of a bully. Remembering Munich—and considering its "lesson" as a universal truth—Johnson remarked, "If you let a bully come into your front yard one day, the next day he will be up on your porch and the day after that he will rape your wife in your own bed." Again his choice of imagery is revealing. It is concrete and packed with sexual metaphors. It breathes an obsession with personal honor and bravery, the need to defend home and family.

The consummate politician, Johnson may have considered foreign affairs above politics. During the years when his power was the greatest in the Senate, he seldom opposed President Eisenhower on any foreign policy issue. In this area he believed fully in bipartisanship. "I want to make absolutely sure," Johnson said in 1953, "that the Communists don't play one branch of government against the other, or one party against the other as happened in the Korean War. . . . If you're in an airplane, and you're flying somewhere, you don't run to the cockpit and attack the pilot." When bipartisanship died in the Vietnam War, Johnson reacted with anger and pain. "Don't they [the American people] realize," he told an aide, "I'm the only President they've got." He could not explain to the people that he *was* their only pilot. Working in the small universe of the United States Senate, he learned everyone's likes and dislikes. This was impossible as the president. On a personal level he was warm, friendly, humorous, and very hard to resist. Before a large group or a television camera, Johnson lost his charm. His manner and language stiffened; his sense of humor and charm fled. But when John Kennedy died, Johnson—the master of backroom politics—stepped into the public light.

When he took the oath of office after Kennedy's assassination, Lyndon B. Johnson was a cold warrior. For Johnson the Truman Doctrine, the Marshall Plan, the Berlin Airlift, the fall of China, the Korean War, and the Cuban missile crisis were formative events in American history, signposts of a strong commitment to keep the rest of the world from taking the road to communism. He was a true believer. There really was a monolithic communist conspiracy stirring up aggression around the world. In South Vietnam the threat was the Vietcong, who were pawns in the hands of North Vietnam, a puppet of Moscow and Beijing. The United States was in Vietnam, he said, "to join in the defense and protection of freedom of a brave people who are under attack that is controlled . . . and directed from outside their country."

Most American policymakers shared a moral consensus about the war. The debate was about tactics, not morality, questions of how, not why. Those who saw the war in military terms argued about which weapons to use, whether to emphasize conventional or counterinsurgency tactics, how to use air power to the best advantage, or if the United States should destroy the dike system in North Vietnam. Others claimed that the war should be settled at the negotiating table. Still others advanced a political solution—winning the "hearts and minds" of the South Vietnamese people. But few questioned the basic mind-set of 1964, the prevailing American consensus about power, virtue, technology, and the domino theory. Even the most serious critics of United States policy in Vietnam were preoccupied with the conduct of military policy, not with its moral or intellectual foundations. While he was crucifying American military leaders for their conduct of the war, David Halberstam of the *New York Times* wrote early in 1965: "Vietnam is a strategic country in the area. It is perhaps one of only five or six nations that is truly vital to U.S. interests." A few months earlier his colleague Neil Sheehan had written, "The fall of Southeast Asia . . . would amount to strategic disaster." Somehow, some way, the United States had to take a stand in South Vietnam. Lyndon B. Johnson was not the only person convinced of that.

There was also the question of credibility. In the early 1960s most American policymakers saw the world divided between two camps— good and evil. The United States was the only "good guy" with the resources to make a difference. In order to maintain NATO, SEATO, CENTO, OAS, and ANZUS, the United States had to prove itself periodically, demonstrating its firm stand against aggression. To flee Vietnam would seriously undermine American credibility throughout the world. Credibility seemed especially important in 1964. Civil war was raging in Laos, and Cambodia Prince Norodom Sihanouk proclaimed his neutrality in the cold war. Chinese talk of fomenting wars of national liberation was as vitriolic as ever. Anti-American riots erupted in Panama, and Fidel Castro threatened to export revolution throughout the Western Hemisphere. If the United States was going to maintain its global commitment to anticommunism, South Vietnam had to be saved. According to Dean Rusk, if South Vietnam fell to the communists, "Our guarantees with regard to Berlin would lose their credibility." It was, he said, "part of the same struggle."

Despite those fears, Johnson remained cautious. There were political risks in rapid escalation. If the United States intervened on a massive scale in South Vietnam, there would be an outpouring of criticism abroad as well as the possibility of serious opposition at home. Johnson had an ambitious program of antipoverty and civil rights legislation planned, and he did not want to undermine his political base in Congress. There was another risk. If the United States entered the war on a large scale, ARVN forces might cease to fight altogether. Like John Kennedy before him, Lyndon Johnson sought a middle road. Slowly but surely the war escalated. By the summer of 1964 American military advisers in South Vietnam reached 20,000 men. On February 1, 1964, the navy implemented Oplan 34-A, Victor Krulak's plan for secret missions against North Vietnamese coastal installations. In case the time came to bomb or invade North Vietnam, the United States needed precise information about coastal radar, radio installations, and antiaircraft sites. Squads of South Vietnamese commandos in American-made patrol boats conducted covert raids along the coast in order to activate North Vietnamese radar. United States intelligence-gathering vessels in the South China Sea then collected the necessary information.

Operation Farmgate was also expanding. Because American pilots found the Vietnamese too cautious, they assumed more and more responsibility, even though their orders required a Vietnamese copilot on all sorties. By mid-1964 more than one hundred air force pilots were flying regular combat missions to support ARVN operations. Farmgate flights did not come to light until May 1964, when Captain Edwin G. Shank was shot down in his T-28 fighter. Before the flight that killed him, Shank wrote a letter to his wife, claiming: "They won't tell you people what we do over here. I'll bet you that anyone you talk to does not know that American pilots fight this war. . . . [The Vietnamese] are stupid, ignorant, sacrificial lambs, and I have no use for them. . . . They're a menace to have on board." Shank's wife released the letter to the press, and it was published nationwide through the wire services.

The air force was also building up its sortie count through Operation Ranch Hand. American advisers had long complained about the ability of the Vietcong to melt back into the jungles where they could not be located. As early as 1961, Walt Rostow and Robert McNamara learned that army chemists had developed new herbicides; the most powerful was Agent Orange. Here was a technological solution. If advisers and pilots could not locate the enemy because of the jungle, then eliminate the jungle. In January 1962 the Kennedy administration had Air Force C-123 aircraft dump defoliants on selected areas of the Ca Mau Peninsula. In 1964 Johnson increased the Ranch Hand sorties. Using the motto "Only you can prevent forests," Ranch Hand pilots turned more than 100,000 acres of jungle and rice paddies into mud.

By that time the debate between those who saw the war primarily in diplomatic or political terms and those who saw it in military terms was coming to an end in Washington, and the militarists had the upper hand. That new consensus reflected itself in a number of important personnel changes. Roger Hilsman was the first to go. At the time, he was an assistant secretary of state for Far Eastern affairs and an advocate of the political, "hearts-and-minds" war. President Johnson took an immediate disliking to Hilsman. Hilsman's close relationship with Robert F. Kennedy, whom Johnson loathed, was one strike against him, and strike two was his opposition to the hard-line approach of Maxwell Taylor and Walt Rostow. Strike three came at a dinner party when Johnson overheard Hilsman insult General Lyman Lemnitzer for losing control of the Vietnam situation in 1960 and 1961. When Hilsman got word that Johnson was about to fire him, he resigned. The president replaced Hilsman with William Bundy.

The president also exiled W. Averell Harriman. During the Kennedy administration the old diplomat had made himself useful, negotiating the Laotian settlement and shuttling back and forth with messages from Washington. Like everyone else, Harriman did not want to see South Vietnam fall to communism, but he did not think the solution was on the battlefield. The only permanent settlement was political and diplomatic, a position he advocated insistently, much to the anger of Rostow, Rusk, McNamara, and Taylor. Also, because of Harriman's close ties to the Kennedys, Johnson did not "trust him to take out my garbage." Early in 1964 the president relieved Harriman of his Asian duties and assigned him, in Harriman's own words, "to the oblivion of African affairs."

Hilsman and Harriman were gone, and Henry Cabot Lodge, Jr., joined them. By the spring of 1964 Lodge felt that he had completed his assignment in South Vietnam. Lodge was preoccupied with politics at home. A moderate Republican, he worried about the shrill voices of "Barry Goldwater and the Neanderthals" in the GOP's right wing. He wanted to get back home in time for the presidential primaries, in which he hoped to deny Goldwater the nomination. Lodge even flirted with the idea of a dark-horse candidacy of his own.

After some indecision, Johnson asked Maxwell Taylor to step down as chairman of the joint chiefs and take over the embassy in Saigon. Taylor preached escalation—enough American advisers, money, and air power to win the war once and for all. He was convinced that the United States must make the war too expensive for Hanoi to pursue and so bloody for the Vietcong that they could not replace their casualties. The North Vietnamese saw what was happening—the militarization of the war, the dispatching of a major American general to take control of a difficult situation. Vo Nguyen Giap wrote that the "appointment of Taylor to South Vietnam reminds us of such top French generals as De Tassigny and Navarre going to Indochina every time the French Expeditionary Corps was in serious difficulty. Our compatriots in the South and the heroic southern liberation troops . . . will certainly reserve for Taylor . . . the fate our people reserved for the former defeated French generals." History would repeat itself.

With Taylor in Saigon, Johnson appointed the army general Earle G. Wheeler chairman of the Joint Chiefs of Staff. Wheeler's career had been spent in planning and logistics rather than in infantry combat, but he was known as a superb organizer and manager. As deputy chief of the U.S. European command and then as army chief of staff in the early 1960s, Wheeler listened to the debate over the war, but he had few doubts. It was simply a matter of military strength. The United States should crush the Vietcong and the North Vietnamese.

When Taylor went to Saigon in 1964, Paul Harkins came home. He retired from the army when he realized that Wheeler was going to get the chairmanship of the joint chiefs. Johnson held a special ceremony at the White House for Harkins and decorated him, but the name "General Blimp" and the phrase "pulling a Harkins" followed him everywhere. He had proclaimed success too many times. Instead of victory, he left behind a quagmire of confusion and bitterness. Harkins's successor was General William C. Westmoreland. Born to a distinguished family in Spartanburg, South Carolina, Westmoreland looked every bit the southern gentleman-turned-soldier. He was six feet tall, but his ramrod posture, dark eyebrows, and white hair made him seem taller. A century earlier in Confederate gray, Westmoreland would have been a perfect compatriot for Stonewall Jackson or Robert E. Lee. Westmoreland punched all the right tickets—West Point graduation in 1936, World War II combat in North Africa, Sicily, France, and Germany, postwar command of the 101st Airborne Division, superintendent of West Point, and a tour as secretary to Maxwell Taylor and the joint chiefs.

At first Westmoreland disagreed with proposals to bomb North Vietnam unless policymakers were willing to introduce ground troops. Air bases needed protection from Vietcong attacks, and ARVN troops could not be trusted with the job. Also, if ARVN was tied up defending American air bases, they would not be in the field fighting the Vietcong. It was already hard enough to get them out there. The need for defensive perimeters around places like Bien Hoa and Danang would only give ARVN commanders another excuse for staying put. ARVN was so laced with corruption and incompetency that it would take years of serious training before it would be ready to take on the Vietcong. By that time the United States, with the application of enough firepower, could wipe out the Vietcong as a fighting force, leaving no enemy for ARVN to worry about. As for the "hearts and minds," Westmoreland looked with disdain on "rice paddy peasants" and believed they would gravitate naturally to whatever government exercised power. With the Vietcong gone, South Vietnam would have, by definition, a stable government.

What Westmoreland wanted was American ground troops, as many as 200,000 of them. For a year or so he planned to fight a defensive war until he built the infrastructure to support a major military effort. Once that infrastructure was in place, Westmoreland planned to unleash the American military on the communists. Through what Westmoreland called "search-and-destroy" missions, American infantry would aggres-

In February 1965, as final plans for the introduction of U.S. ground troops were underway, National Security Adviser McGeorge Bundy (left) met in Saigon with General William Westmoreland (right) and Maxwell Taylor (center), U.S. ambassador to South Vietnam.
UPI/BETTMANN

sively seek out the enemy. American infantry, artillery, armor, bombers, and gunships would cut the enemy to pieces. According to William DePuy, Westmoreland's chief of operations, "We are going to stomp them to death."

A major policy decision was imminent in Washington. ARVN desertions reached epidemic levels, exceeding 6,000 people a month in 1964. Politically the Vietcong controlled up to 40 percent of the territory of South Vietnam and more than 50 percent of the people. Early in 1963 the Vietcong had 23,000 troops organized into a hodgepodge of undermanned battalions, companies, platoons, and squads. They also had another 50,000 local self-defense militia troops. All that changed by late 1964. Those 23,000 soldiers became 60,000 men organized into seventy-three battalions of six hundred men each. Of those seventy-three battalions, sixty-six were full infantry units and seven were heavy weapons and antiaircraft machine gun battalions. The battalions were organized into regiments complete with communications and engineering units. And behind those 60,000 troops were 40,000 more people engaged in full-time support services. Another 100,000 village self-defense forces rounded out the communist order of battle. Vietminh veterans trained the Vietcong well, creating highly motivated soldiers, real "sledge hammer battalions" in the words of Neil Sheehan. Westmoreland was convinced that ARVN would be completely unable to deal with them. He argued: "The VC are destroying battalions faster than they were planned to be organized under the build-up program. . . . The only possible US response is the aggressive employment of US troops together with Vietnamese general reserve forces to react against strong VC/DRV [Vietcong and North Vietnam] attacks." Only the creation of the vaunted American killing machine could handle the Vietcong.

Most American policymakers believed the revolt in South Vietnam was directly connected to its support base in North Vietnam and that the United States would have to take the war to Hanoi to achieve a complete victory. Maxwell Taylor, along with Walt Rostow, McGeorge Bundy, and Robert McNamara, called for expansion of the war north of the seventeenth parallel through strategic bombing. The idea was simple: Raise the pain level to the point where North Vietnam could stand it no longer.

The Johnson administration's understanding of the connection between the war in South Vietnam and support in North Vietnam was quite accurate. Throughout the late 1950s and early 1960s politicians in North Vietnam debated the question of how much assistance to send south. The debate was inextricably connected to the larger Sino-Soviet split. The Soviets and Chinese were competing with one another for influence. Under Nikita Khrushchev, the Soviets preached the gospel of peaceful coexistence in the early 1960s. North Vietnamese politicians who wanted to focus on building up their own country, as well as military officials worried about a confrontation with the United States, used the Soviet ideology to advocate caution. Their leader was Truong Chinh, a moderate who served as the Marxist theorist in the Lao Dong party and always favored caution and negotiation.

But most of the North Vietnamese leadership were more militant. While the Soviet Union was prudent and careful, Mao Zedong and the Chinese were not, calling for wars of national liberation to overthrow United States influence in the Third World. The bitter anti-American posture of the Chinese encouraged people like Le Duan and General Tran Van Tra, commander of Vietcong military forces in South Vietnam. They wanted a total commitment to destruction of the South Vietnamese regime, expulsion of the United States, and reunification of the country, regardless of the cost.

When the Central Committee of the Lao Dong party met in Hanoi in December 1963 to evaluate the situation, the debate continued. If North Vietnam increased its support of the revolution in South Vietnam, it might alienate the Soviets and place itself in the Chinese camp, not something any Vietnamese politician wanted to do. But if North Vietnam did not support the Vietcong, it might never be able to get the United States out of Indochina. The debate continued into the next year. Finally, in a meeting on March 27–28, 1964, Ho Chi Minh called for a unified effort and whatever sacrifice was necessary to bring the revolution in South Vietnam to a successful conclusion. A week later North Vietnam began training northern-born Vietnamese for deployment south.

At the same time Johnson's advisers drafted plans for attacking North Vietnam. A leading figure in the development of those plans was William Bundy. William Bundy, McGeorge's older brother, was a graduate of Yale and the Harvard Law School who, after a stint with the CIA, became a deputy assistant secretary of defense in the Kennedy administration. On March 1, 1964, William Bundy proposed bombing North Vietnam and mining Haiphong harbor to both stop infiltration of supplies to the Vietcong and demonstrate that the United States possessed the will to win. Later in the month McGeorge Bundy produced what became known as National Security Adviser Memorandum (NSAM) 288, providing for gradually escalated bombing of military and economic targets in North Vietnam, particularly in response to Vietcong attacks in South Vietnam. NSAM 288 also committed the United States to the survival of an independent noncommunist government in Saigon. It argued that the United States would increase its level of military and economic assistance, but that South Vietnam would have to prepare for a full-scale war. McGeorge Bundy warned that such military measures "would normally require a declaration of war under the Constitution. But this seems a blunt instrument carrying heavy domestic overtones and above all not suited to the picture of punitive and selective action only." He urged the president to consider seeking a special congressional resolution supporting limited military action. Robert McNamara was convinced that "current trends . . . will lead to neutralization at best and more likely to a Communist-controlled state." He wanted a "tit-for-tat" policy in which the United States made Hanoi suffer for any damage done by the Vietcong. Privately, Johnson referred to the policy as the "titty program."

During April and May, the National Security Council, the Joint Chiefs of Staff, and MACV in Saigon developed what became known as Operations Plan 37-64. Its objective was "to conduct graduated operations to eliminate or reduce to negligible proportions DRV [Democratic Republic of Vietnam] support of VC [Vietcong] insurgency in the Republic of Vietnam." The plan involved three options: military action in Cambodia and Laos to eliminate Vietcong sanctuaries; increased levels of Oplan 34-A attacks on North Vietnamese coastal installations; and South Vietnamese and United States strategic bombing of ninety-eight preselected targets in North Vietnam. In his White House office, Walt Rostow, the "Air Marshall," taped a large map of North Vietnam on the wall, and, with the help of econometric models, selected targets for the bombing runs.

To deal with the problem on a political level, Johnson decided he wanted a joint congressional resolution "supporting United States policy in Southeast Asia." Such a resolution would give the administration carte blanche in Indochina, allowing aerial bombardment, intervention in Cambodia and Laos, or any other "tit-for-tat" response that would bring North Vietnam to the negotiating table. It was, in effect, a pre-dated declaration of war. William Bundy drafted the resolution, and the administration waited for the right time to submit it to Congress. It did not have to wait long.

On August 1, 1964, the USS *Maddox*, an American destroyer, was patrolling within a range of ten to twenty miles off the North Vietnamese coast, collecting electronic data on North Vietnamese radar signals and ship movements. The ship was also monitoring four South Vietnamese gunboats, which the night before had left Danang and attacked North Vietnamese coastal sites as part of Oplan 34-A. North Vietnamese patrol boats approached the *Maddox*. In just a few moments, the *Maddox* opened fire, and the patrol boats launched several torpedoes. Jets from the USS *Ticonderoga* attacked the North Vietnamese ships, damaging all of them. The next day the *Maddox* was joined by another destroyer, the USS *C. Turner Joy*. President Johnson ordered the ships to continue their patrols.

More South Vietnamese gunboats left Danang for Oplan 34-A attacks. On August 4 the *Maddox* and the *C. Turner Joy* picked up radio traffic from confused and enraged North Vietnamese naval vessels. Tension was running high on both the *Maddox* and the *Turner Joy*. Men on both ships saw blips on the radar they believed represented PT boats, and the sonar man on the *Maddox* reported underwater noises that he believed to be the sounds of incoming torpedoes. Both ships commenced evasive actions and began firing into the dark at the direction of the radar blips, although they made no visual sightings of North Vietnamese patrol boats. Several hours later, Captain John Herrick, head of the DeSoto Mission on board the *Maddox*, concluded that there probably had been no attack, that rough seas and atmospheric conditions generated spurious radar blips, and that the evasive movements of the ships had created torpedolike sonar sounds. In a cable to the Pentagon, Herrick reported that conclusion. By the time Herrick sent the cable it was too late. The Pentagon and White House were like hornets' nests, and Admiral Ulysses S. Grant Sharp, Jr., the commander of American naval forces in the Pacific, confirmed to Robert McNamara that a "bona fide ambush has occurred." The evidence at the time as to whether an attack had really occurred was contradictory, but the Johnson administration decided nonetheless to retaliate. Late that afternoon, the USS *Ticonderoga* and the USS *Constellation* sent aircraft to attack torpedo boat bases and oil storage facilities in

North Vietnam. While the attack was going on, Johnson spoke live over all three television networks: "Aggression by terror against peaceful villages of South Vietnam," he said, "has now been joined by open aggression on the high seas against the United States of America." He then reassured the country: "We know, although others appear to forget, the risks of spreading conflict. We seek no wider war."

The next day Johnson met with congressional leaders to explain the air strike and seek their support for the joint resolution Bundy had drafted. At the meeting Senator Mike Mansfield reminded Johnson of his long-standing opposition to American military involvement in Indochina. Johnson asked Senator William Fulbright, an Arkansas Democrat, to serve as floor manager for the resolution. An old friend and veteran of many Senate battles, Fulbright agreed. Senator George Aiken, a Republican from Vermont, did not like the resolution, telling Johnson, "By the time you send it up, there won't be anything for us to do but support you." He saw the resolution as open-ended permission for Johnson to wage war without a formal declaration. But Johnson gave Mansfield and Aiken what other senators called the "full Johnson"—the arm tightly around their shoulders, his face nose-to-nose with theirs, and his voice pleading, cajoling, begging, whining, promising, and threatening. Before the meeting ended, they agreed to support the resolution.

At a joint session of the Senate Armed Services and Foreign Relations committees, Senator Wayne Morse, the renegade Democrat from Oregon, wanted to know if the United States had provoked the North Vietnamese patrol boat attack. Robert McNamara assured him that the "navy played absolutely no part in, was not associated with, was not aware of any South Vietnamese actions, if there were any. . . . This is the fact." It was, of course, a bald-faced lie. On August 7 the administration submitted to Congress the resolution William Bundy had written. Its wording was simple and direct, with enormous potential consequences:

> The congress . . . supports the determination of the President . . . to take all necessary measures to repel any armed attack against the armed forces of the United States and to prevent further aggression. . . . The United States is, therefore, prepared, as the President determines, to take all necessary steps, including the use of armed force, to assist any member or protocol state of the Southeast Asia Collective Defense treaty requesting assistance in defense of its freedom.

The House of Representatives passed the resolution by voice vote, but a debate developed in the Senate. Senator George McGovern of South Dakota stated that he did not wish his vote for the resolution "to be interpreted as an endorsement of our long-standing and apparently growing military involvement in Vietnam." Daniel Brewster of Maryland worried that the resolution might "authorize or recommend or approve the landing of American armies in Vietnam or in China."

The strongest opposition came from Senators Ernest Gruening of Alaska and Wayne Morse of Oregon. Back in 1954, when John Foster Dulles tried to drum up support for the French, Morse resisted, asking: "What is it we are going to fight for and to defend? I am a Senator and I don't know." Gruening was a liberal Democrat. In March 1964 he had claimed on the Senate floor: "All Vietnam is not worth the life of a single American boy. . . . [The United States] is seeking vainly in this remote jungle to shore up self-serving corrupt dynasties or their self-imposed successors, and a people that has demonstrated that it has no will to save itself." Gruening called the resolution "a predated declaration of war" that he would not be able to support.

Before the floor debate someone in the Pentagon tipped Morse off that DeSoto Missions and Oplan 34-A operations probably inspired the first attack and that the alleged second attack might not have even occurred. Morse opposed the resolution, arguing that the place to settle the issue "is not by way of the proposed predated declaration of war, giving to the President the power to make war without a declaration of war." But a chorus of approval drowned Morse and Gruening. The Senate passed the resolution eighty-eight to two. Later that day Morse predicted, "History will record that we have made a great mistake." When he heard that Congress passed the resolution, Johnson laughed and told an aide that the wording of the resolution "was like Grandma's nightshirt. It covers everything."

The Gulf of Tonkin Resolution, in the short run at least, was a stroke of political genius. The president's standing in public opinion polls soared. More than anything else, the president wanted to be elected in his own right, to occupy the White House on his own merits, not on John F. Kennedy's. With the election of 1964 coming up, he wanted to project the image of a wise, thoughtful, and decisive leader, a balance between toughness and moderation. The bombing raids on North Vietnam, followed by the president's stated willingness to go to the negotiating table, seemed tough but reasonable to most Americans. Later, when doubts mounted about what had actually happened in the Gulf of Tonkin on August 4, 1964, Johnson remarked to an associate, "Those dumb stupid sailors were probably shooting at flying fish."

Three weeks before the Gulf of Tonkin incident, the Republicans nominated Senator Barry Goldwater of Arizona for president. In his acceptance speech, Goldwater said that America should no longer "cringe before the bullying of Communism. . . . Failures cement the wall of shame in Berlin. Failures blot the sands of shame at the Bay of Pigs. Failures mark the slow death of freedom in Laos. Failures infest the jungles of Vietnam." Johnson's decision to bomb North Vietnam, however, stole Goldwater's thunder, transforming a foreign policy liability for Johnson into a political asset.

Goldwater was a man of strong opinions and brutal honesty. Convinced that the United States was soft on communism abroad and drifting down the road to socialism at home, he preached against the welfare state, Social Security, the Nuclear Test Ban Treaty of 1963, the Laotian settlement of 1962, and any rapprochement with the Soviet Union and China. Johnson, on the other hand, instinctively understood that most Americans had vivid memories of the Great Depression and the New Deal and, in 1964 at least, resented neither the welfare state nor Social Security. In fact, they overwhelmingly supported both. He also realized that most Americans had an instinctive fear of nuclear weapons and that Goldwater's saber rattling scared them.

In the election of 1964, Johnson went after Goldwater's most vulnerable points. Proclaiming the coming of the "Great Society," the president campaigned for expansion of Social Security and Medicare, creation of job-training programs, a "War on Poverty," and civil rights legislation. Johnson's message was simple: Every American deserved to be treated equally and to enjoy basic economic opportunity. Goldwater criticized government spending, large deficits, high taxes, and bureaucratic waste, but most Americans were not interested. On foreign policy, the Democrats ruthlessly attacked Goldwater, portraying Johnson as a wise, temperate leader and Goldwater as an extremist, an "unguided missile," a dangerous man. The Johnson campaign produced several nasty television commercials. The "Daisy Girl" spot showed a little girl plucking flower petals and counting them until a deep male voice drowned out hers with a missile countdown, followed by detonation and the nuclear mushroom cloud, all of this with a promise that President Lyndon Johnson would not get the country involved in a nuclear war. The Democrats transformed Goldwater's slogan "In your heart you know he's right," to "In your heart you know he might."

In his foreign policy speeches, Johnson appeared calm and in control, not prepared to start a larger war in Vietnam but not ready to "turn tail and run" either. In late September he told a campaign rally in Eufaula, Oklahoma: "We don't want our American boys to do the fighting for Asian boys. . . . But we are not about to start another war and we're not about to run away from where we are." The speech was well received; most Americans wanted to pursue a moderate position.

But three developments propelled the United States toward war: the instability of the South Vietnamese government, the increasing aggressiveness of the Vietcong, and the dramatic escalation of North Vietnamese transfers of troops and supplies into South Vietnam. Duong Van ("Big") Minh, nicknamed because of his unusual six-foot height, took control of the government after overseeing the assassination of Ngo Dinh Diem and Ngo Dinh Nhu. He had been trained in the French colonial army and had been responsible for crushing the Binh Xuyen in 1955. Minh replaced the Diem government with a Military Revolutionary Council, of which he served as chairman. He repealed Madame Nhu's morality legislation and released most of Diem's political prisoners incarcerated at Poulo Condore.

But the relaxed political atmosphere only led to more unrest. Buddhist factions struggled for power, and hostility between Catholics and Buddhists grew worse. Student protest groups hit the streets demanding political and economic reform. Minh's reign began an unprecedented period of political instability in Saigon, a revolving door of new governments every few months. The people who replaced Diem came from middle-class families with French educations, and they were members of the old anticommunist South Vietnamese elite. They were hardly different from Diem. Minh stayed in power only three months. His closest associates on the council were Tran Van Don and Le Van Kim. Tran Van Don was born in France in 1917, served with the French army in World War II, and joined the Vietnamese National Army in 1951. He rose to become a commander of I Corps, the northern military district of South Vietnam. Le Van Kim, commandant of the National Military Academy, spent years in Paris with the French police and came back home to join the Vietnamese National Army. Don and Kim were French citizens, and like Duong Van Minh they were Roman Catholics. From the very beginning, Minh, Don, and Kim faced repeated plots to overthrow them, some coming from their own military subordinates and others from the Buddhist majority.

The conspirators succeeded on January 29, 1964. Nguyen Khanh, a thirty-six-year-old ARVN officer whose baby fat appearance was belied by a tiny goatee, carried out a bloodless coup that pleased Americans. They hoped Khanh's strong-arm, one-man rule would be more decisive than Minh's rule-by-committee style, just as they hoped Khanh's Buddhist faith would mute the antigovernment movement among the Buddhist clergy. Lyndon Johnson called Khanh "my American boy." Cursed with a paranoia matched only by that of Diem, Khanh was more inclined toward intrigue than government. More than once he called for a "March to the North," a farfetched mass popular invasion of North Vietnam. When American bombers attacked North Vietnam after the Gulf of Tonkin incidents, Khanh was euphoric. Anticipating war, he declared martial law on August 7 and banned freedom of speech, press, and assembly. Two weeks later Khanh issued the infamous Vung Tau Charter, a constitution he wrote overnight declaring himself president and dictator of the Republic of Vietnam. The reaction was swift. Buddhists and students took to the streets protesting Khanh's government. At one point an enraged mob surrounded Khanh on a Saigon street and forced him to climb up on a tank and shout "Down with dictatorships!" At the end of the month he backed down, losing face and credibility among the people he needed the most—his own generals.

The scheming and plotting commenced once again, and early in September, Khanh brought Big Minh back into power, along with Tran Thien Kheim, ARVN chief of staff. Together they ruled Vietnam as a triumvirate for two weeks until General Lam Van Phat overthrew Khanh. The United States managed to restore the triumvirate to power a few days later. At the end of October, Khanh established the High National Council, representing a variety of political groups, to draft a new constitution. It was ready on October 20, 1964, and Khanh voluntarily stepped down in favor of a civilian government headed by Phan Khac Suu, a devout Cao Daist who had opposed the French, the Vietminh, and Diem. Suu appointed Tran Van Huong, a former schoolteacher and Vietminh soldier, as prime minister. Maxwell Taylor said he was "glad to get rid of that troublemaker Khanh."

The new civilian government was no more successful than its military predecessors. Plotting and conspiracies were endemic, and Nguyen Khanh yearned for power again. In December 1964, supported by a number of young military officers including Nguyen Cao Ky and Nguyen Van Thieu, Khanh dissolved the High National Council and replaced it with the Armed Forces Council. Three weeks later the Armed Forces Council dissolved the civilian government, ousted Tran Van Huong, and ordered Khanh to form a new civilian government. Khanh kept Phan Khac Suu as chief of state and named Nguyen Xuan Oanh as prime minister. George Ball called it the "Government of the Week Sideshow" in Saigon. The president was, as usual, the most blunt, telling anyone who would listen, "I'm sick and tired of this coup shit."

Vietcong tactics propelling the United States toward war, however, made Johnson more sick. Although some American advisers had been killed, their deaths usually occurred in combat operations where the Vietcong fired at ARVN soldiers and the Americans. Far more common were Vietcong tricks at American installations, where guerrillas infiltrated a military outpost at night and left behind Vietcong flags or printed messages on the wall, letting the Americans know that they were not safe. Still hoping that the United States would eventually see their side of the war, the Vietcong had been loath to alienate American policymakers by killing United States soldiers. But after the Gulf of Tonkin and the American bombing raids on North Vietnam, Vietcong tactics changed. Intentional attacks on Americans increased dramatically. On November 1, 1964, several sampans moved up a stream near the American air base at Bien Hoa and dropped off mortar-carrying guerrillas. They set up several 81-mm mortars and shelled the base, killing four Americans, wounding seventy-two more, and destroying or damaging thirteen B-57 light bombers. Almost as soon as the attack started it was over. The Vietcong got back on the sampans and drifted away downstream.

Maxwell Taylor recognized the attack for what it was—a dramatic shift in Vietcong tactics, which, he believed, had occurred only under orders from Ho Chi Minh. Taylor cabled Johnson that the attack "is a deliberate act of escalation and a change in the ground rules. . . . It should be met promptly by an appropriate act of reprisal against a DRV target. . . . The ultimate objective should be to convince Hanoi to cease aid to the VC (and not merely lay off us)." But with the presidential election just two days away, Johnson was being careful. He asked William Bundy to draft a policy response. On November 3, 1964, Johnson defeated Goldwater by a landslide, taking 61 percent of the popular vote and 486 of the 540 electoral votes. That same day Bundy offered three options to Johnson, including widespread bombing of North Vietnam, but the president ultimately decided to continue the existing policy of "tit-for-tat" reactions to Vietcong and North Vietnamese attacks in South Vietnam.

Most Americans had not noticed the increased number of American military advisers being deployed to South Vietnam. Opposition to the war was still muted, confined to vocal elements of the peace movement. David Dellinger and A. J. Muste, leaders of the War Resisters League (WRL), had been calling for de-escalation of the war in Vietnam since early 1963. In the pages of *Liberation*, an influential radical magazine supported by the WRL, they asked the American people to take a careful look at what was happening in Southeast Asia. Membership in the War Resisters League totaled only 3,000 people in 1964, but they were true believers committed to peace. In the spring of 1964, when President Johnson dispatched several thousand more military advisers to South Vietnam and modestly increased draft calls, the WRL began to organize a formal protest movement against the war. On May 16, 1964, they sponsored a demonstration in New York City in which twelve young men burned their draft cards. The demonstration received widespread coverage in newspapers and the television news. The War Resisters League was highly skeptical of the administration's account of what happened in the Tonkin Gulf on July 31–August 1, 1964, and vigorously opposed the subsequent bombing of North Vietnam. In December 1964, the WRL sponsored the first nationwide demonstrations against the Vietnam War. President Johnson disregarded them, comparing the War Registers League to "summer gnats in the hill country. They fly around a lot but never bite."

Some of Johnson's closest advisers suggested that only a sustained bombing of North Vietnam and Laos could stop the infiltration and demoralize the enemy. George Ball still opposed the scheme. He did not think bombing would break Hanoi's will, and he feared raising the ire of the Soviets or the Chinese. "Once on the tiger's back," he said, "we cannot be sure of picking the place to dismount." But Ball was a minority of one in the inner circle. Early in January 1965 Maxwell Taylor cabled Johnson from Saigon: "We are faced here with a seriously deteriorating situation characterized by continued political turmoil, irresponsibility and division within the armed forces, lethargy in the pacification programs . . . and deepening discouragement and loss of morale. . . . The situation will

Burning Selective Service (draft) cards was one of the earliest forms of symbolic opposition to the war in Vietnam.
HIROJI KUBOTA/MAGNUM PHOTOS

continue to go downhill toward some form of political collapse unless new . . . elements can be introduced." For Taylor, Westmoreland, Rusk, the Bundys, Rostow, and McNamara, "new elements" meant massive bombing of North Vietnam and/or commitment of American troops. ARVN did little to stem the growing power of the Vietcong, and the United States was not prepared to take over the war. Bombing North Vietnam became increasingly attractive. What stopped Johnson late in 1964 from adopting the proposal for large-scale bombing of North Vietnam was fear about reprisals. If the communists escalated the war, he did not think South Vietnam would be able to handle it. Johnson later recalled, "The political base in the South . . . was probably too shaky to withstand a major assault."

When Johnson asked about bombing Vietcong targets in retaliation for the attack on Bien Hoa, the joint chiefs passed the question on to General Westmoreland in Saigon. Westmoreland found himself in a quandary. For months he had been requesting the deployment of more aircraft and pilots to MACV, but now he had to tell General Earle Wheeler that because of heavy jungle cover, the problem of differentiating guerrillas from civilians, and the mobility of the enemy, he could not locate suitable Vietcong targets.

The Vietcong were not about to make the president wait long for another opportunity. On Christmas Eve in Saigon, a Vietcong agent drove a car bomb into the basement parking lot of the Brinks Hotel, bachelor quarters for many American officers. The bomb exploded and blew out the entire bottom floor of the hotel, killing two Americans and wounding fifty-eight. Once again the president's advisers called for a retaliatory air strike against North Vietnam, but Johnson overruled them. Such a reaction during Christmas might be misinterpreted at home, and a massive air strike would be a disproportionately hostile response to the Brinks Hotel incident.

Johnson's cautiousness disturbed his advisers, especially Robert McNamara and McGeorge Bundy. In a memo to the president on January 5, 1965, they wrote that they were utterly certain "that our current policy can lead only to a disastrous defeat. . . . What we are doing now, essentially, is to wait and hope for a stable government . . . but there is no real hope of success in this area unless and until our own policies and priorities change." They argued that American indecisiveness was undermining the anticommunist effort in South Vietnam. "The Vietnamese see the enormous power of the United States withheld and they get little sense of firm and active U.S. policy." To bludgeon North Vietnam into submission and stabilize South Vietnamese politics, the United States should begin a concerted air war above the seventeenth parallel. Still Johnson hesitated.

Westmoreland's claim that MACV could locate no Vietcong targets worthy of air attack assumed incredible dimensions on January 2, 1965, when Vietcong troops destroyed two companies of ARVN Rangers and tanks near Binh Gia, a village outside Saigon. More than two hundred ARVN troops died in the engagement, and five American helicopter pilots were wounded. One American officer, after praising the enemy's fighting abilities, said that the "big question for me is how its troops, a thousand or more of them, could wander around the countryside so close to Saigon without being discovered." The Vietcong had the equivalent of three full divisions in the field, but MACV operational planners could not pick any bombing targets where they could hurt the guerrillas.

Five weeks later the Vietcong struck again, this time at Camp Holloway outside of Pleiku, where the Fifty-second Combat Aviation Battalion was stationed. In the middle of the night on February 7, 1965, they rained mortar shells on the base and attacked a camp of 180 United States advisers about four miles away. In fifteen minutes seven Americans were dead and another hundred wounded. McGeorge Bundy was in Saigon on a fact-finding mission, and the next day he toured Camp Holloway with Westmoreland and Taylor. Deeply affected by the wounded men, Bundy wanted blood, prompting Westmoreland to think that, like so many civilians in positions of authority, Bundy "smelled a little gunpowder and . . . developed a field marshal psychosis." Still they urged Johnson to retaliate. "Old Mac's really got himself stirred up," Johnson told George Ball. "Those poor wounded boys in the hospital sure as hell got to him."

Bundy was not the only person affected. The attack on Pleiku stirred Johnson to action: "They're killing our men while they sleep in the night. I can't ask our American soldiers to continue to fight with one hand tied behind their back." On February 8, Johnson ordered American aircraft carriers to attack guerrilla bases in Dong Hoi, above the seventeenth parallel, while South Vietnamese pilots attacked similar sites at Vinh Linh and Chap Le. The air strike was known as Flaming Dart I. Johnson also ordered the evacuation of 1,800 United States dependents from South Vietnam.

Three days later the Vietcong struck again, attacking the Viet Cuoung Hotel in Qui Nhon, which served as quarters for the American 104th Maintenance Detachment. While staging a brief firefight, the guerrillas planted two hundred pounds of plastic explosives around the foundation of the four-story hotel. When they were detonated, the building collapsed in rubble, burying forty-three American soldiers, only twenty-two of whom were dug out alive. President Johnson unleashed another air strike—Flaming Dart II. Within the next several days, the United States began Operation Rolling Thunder, the sustained bombing of North Vietnam that lasted, off and on, until the end of 1968. When Vice President Hubert Humphrey wrote a memo opposing the raids, the president banned him from Vietnam planning sessions. Johnson's need for consensus, especially with the situation deteriorating, was becoming an obsession.

The sustained bombing of North Vietnam had been more than two months in the making, and the Vietcong attack on Pleiku gave the Johnson administration the opportunity to implement the plans. "To take no action now," Maxwell Taylor argued, "is to accept defeat in the fairly near future." The decision was an important turning point in the war. The "tit-for-tat" approach was abandoned in favor of a long-term bombing campaign. The United States had escalated the war. At first the president kept tight control of the bombing, bragging that the pilots "can't even bomb an outhouse without my approval." But in the early spring he relaxed that control, authorized the use of napalm, allowed pilots to drop their bomb loads on alternate targets without prior approval, and increased the frequency of the attacks. In April 1965 American and South Vietnamese pilots flew 3,600 sorties against North Vietnam,

Later in February another coup shook South Vietnam. Buddhist monks organized hunger strikes, protest marches, and immolations; rumors of plots and coups were constant; and late in January 5,000 students destroyed the library of the United States Information Agency in Hue. Military confidence in Nguyen Khanh declined, especially among a group of younger officers on the Armed Forces Council. Led by Nguyen Van Thieu, the forty-one-year-old commander of the ARVN Fifth Division, and Nguyen Cao Ky, a thirty-four-year-old general in the Vietnamese Air Force, the "Young Turks" drove Khanh into peaceful exile as "roving ambassador." In fourteen months, the government of South Vietnam had changed hands seven times.

Along with the changes in the South Vietnamese government came ominous news from the CIA and from MACV intelligence sources. The bombing strikes were supposed to convince North Vietnam that its attempt to seize control of South Vietnam would be too expensive. But those assumptions came from a cold war mentality, the conviction that the war in Vietnam was just another example of communist aggression, and that if the United States brought its power to bear—economic and military—the communists would back down. It had worked with the Truman Doctrine, the Marshall Plan, and the Korean War. From the American perspective, the struggle in Indochina was simply a case of external communist aggression. But from the perspective of the Vietcong and the North Vietnamese, it was a war to end foreign domination and reunite the two Vietnams. For most Americans, the war was a military struggle to be decided on a battlefield, but for Ho Chi Minh, it was a political struggle to be decided in the minds of the Vietnamese peasants. For the United States, Vietnam was a limited war to be escalated in carefully orchestrated stages until the communists' breaking point was reached. For Ho Chi Minh, it was a total war, the culmination of centuries of struggle, a cause to die for, a cause worthy of risking complete annihilation. In a 1962 interview with the French journalist Bernard Fall, Ho Chi Minh stated that it "took us eight years of bitter fighting to defeat you French in Indochina. . . . The Americans are stronger than the French. It might take ten years, but . . . I think the Americans greatly underestimate the determination of the Vietnamese people. The Vietnamese people have always shown great determination when faced with an invader."

Instead of intimidating or frightening the North Vietnamese, the American bombing raids of 1964 and early 1965 stiffened their resolve, convincing them that the United States was intent on their destruction. Whatever political opposition Ho Chi Minh faced at home disappeared. The flow of supplies and personnel into South Vietnam increased. Until the fall of 1964 the Vietcong were an independent unit in South Vietnam, composed primarily of Vietminh regroupees born in the south and recruits from recently alienated peasants. They armed themselves with American weapons stolen or purchased from ARVN. By the end of 1964 North Vietnam was shipping Soviet and Chinese weapons down the Ho Chi Minh Trail, along with weapons specialists, trainers, and logistical experts from the People's Army of Vietnam (regular North Vietnamese troops). Hanoi had dispatched the first northern-born regulars in August 1964. Instead of dispersing them among the Vietcong as they had done with the regroupees, Hanoi let them operate as the independent

808th Battalion. The Ninety-fifth Regiment reached South Vietnam in December, and by the spring of 1965 three more regiments were there—a total of 65,000 northern-born regular troops. The refrain "born in the North to die in the South" began to be heard in North Vietnam.

The entire American military strategy in Vietnam rested on a foundation of political quicksand. Escalation frightened neither North Vietnam nor the Vietcong; they were in for the duration. Early in 1965 the CIA reported that the Vietcong were stronger than ever before and were on the eve of a military victory in South Vietnam. The CIA and MACV also informed Johnson that the Vietcong posed a serious threat to American air bases. To make sure that South Vietnamese pilots participated in the air strikes, Maxwell Taylor insisted that the air force pilots from Danang, not navy pilots from carriers, conduct the strikes against North Vietnam. That meant a dramatic increase in the number of air force personnel, aircraft, and munitions. The buildup made Danang a primary Vietcong target, the perfect place to humiliate the American war machine. ARVN troops could not be trusted to defend Danang adequately.

On February 21, 1965, General Westmoreland asked for two marine battalions to protect Danang. He estimated that there were at least twelve Vietcong battalions with 6,000 troops in the area. The marines would improve security and permit ARVN troops to go out into the jungles after the Vietcong. Westmoreland routed his request through Maxwell Taylor, but the ambassador opposed the introduction of American ground troops. In a cable to President Johnson, Taylor argued: "Intervention with ground forces would at best buy time and would lead to ever increasing commitments until, like the French, we would be occupying an essentially hostile foreign country. . . . The white faced soldier . . . is not a suitable guerrilla fighter. . . . The French tried to adapt their forces to this mission and failed. I doubt that the U.S. forces could do much better." But Johnson was afraid of another Bien Hoa or Pleiku. American airmen at Danang needed security, and on February 26, 1965, he approved the request for two marine battalions.

Johnson's decisions stirred the souls of the Marine Corps. Out in Hawaii, where he had assumed command of the Fleet Marine Force, Pacific Command, General Victor Krulak ordered the Ninth Marine Expeditionary Brigade to Danang. Plans were already under way to change the unit's name to the III Marine Amphibious Force. To avoid any comparisons with the French Expeditionary Corps, Krulak and Westmoreland wanted the word "Expeditionary" expurgated. On March 8, as if it were Iwo Jima or Tarawa all over again, 3,500 troops stormed the beaches in full battle regalia, complete with M-14 rifles, landing craft, naval air support, amphibious tractors, helicopters, 105-mm howitzers, M48 tanks, and 106-mm recoilless rifles. But instead of a firefight, they encountered young South Vietnamese women waiting on the beaches with flowered leis to put around their necks. The smiling mayor of Danang welcomed the troops to his city. The marines clambered into trucks for the ride to the airbase, and all along the way waved at thousands of schoolchildren lining the highway and welcoming them.

When the news of the successful deployment of the marines reached Lyndon Johnson, he smiled broadly and remarked to an associate, "Now I have Ho Chi Minh's pecker in my pocket." William Bundy remembered that the arrival of the marines created a mood of "disaster avoided or postponed. . . . But on the whole it was a period when no move seemed right, and the outcome remained wholly murky." George Ball, still playing devil's advocate, opposed the move, writing that the presence of ground troops would make the United States' position "approach that of France in the 1950s. We would incur the opposition of elements in Viet-Nam otherwise friendly to us. Finally, we would find ourselves in *la guerre sale* with consequent heavy loss of American lives on the rice paddies and [in the] jungles." Events would soon vindicate George Ball.

6

Into the Abyss, 1965–1966

*When the day comes for me to meet my Maker . . . the thing I
would be most humbly proud of was the fact that I fought
against . . . the carry-out of some . . . tactical schemes which
would have cost the lives of thousands of men. To that list of
tragic accidents that fortunately never happened I would
add the Indochina intervention.*
—General Matthew Ridgway, 1956

Maxwell Taylor's prediction that "it will be very difficult to hold the
line" came true sooner than he thought. The marines in Danang were
there only three weeks when General William Westmoreland decided to
establish another air base at Phu Bai south of Hue. In mid-April two
more battalions arrived to establish and defend Phu Bai. That brought
the marine contingent in I Corps to more than 8,600 troops. Deployed
around Phu Bai and Danang, sitting in stationary placements, they
itched for a fight. It was not going to be difficult to find one. The Vietcong were steadily gaining power. By the spring of 1965 no American
could venture more than a few miles outside any major city without an
armed convoy. The Vietcong were everywhere. When Nguyen Cao Ky
called for an invasion of North Vietnam in 1965, John Paul Vann wrote,
"The goddamn little fool can't even drive a mile outside Saigon without
an armed convoy and he wants to liberate the North! How damned
ridiculous can you get?"

Few Americans harbored any real hope of transforming ARVN into a
reliable fighting force. ARVN suffered from desertion, absenteeism,
cronyism, and nepotism. Too many officers were promoted because of
political connections, not tactical abilities. Those officers capable of fighting a war were often immobilized by fear of failure, which meant taking
too many casualties, and by fear of success, which posed a political threat
to their superiors. Doing nothing was the surest way to promotion. Corruption was rampant. In some ARVN units half the roster consisted of
"potted-tree soldiers," men who never appeared for service because they
paid bribes to retain civilian status. They were safe behind the lines, like
a plant in its own pot. The government still sent monthly pay and allow-
ance checks in their names, which ARVN officers pocketed. Peasant
soldiers—underpaid, far from home, and commanded by officers on the

take—deserted in record numbers. ARVN troop levels increased from 243,000 in late 1963 to 514,000 a year later, but they were paper troops. The desertion rate of 6,000 a month in 1964 increased to 11,000 a month in 1965. The desertion rate at ARVN draft induction centers reached 50 percent. Creating a disciplined, highly motivated army takes a generation, not a year. The United States had such an army, and so did the Vietcong and the North Vietnamese. South Vietnam did not.

Behind ARVN was a government weakened by corruption, assassination, fraudulent elections, and constant political intrigue. The February 1965 coup of the Young Turks brought Nguyen Cao Ky and Nguyen Van Thieu to power.

Nguyen Cao Ky was born in Son Tay, a city near Hanoi, in 1930. When he was twenty, France drafted him into the Vietnamese National Army, and three years later the army sent him to pilot training. Ky rose quickly in the ranks, one of the few promoted because of ability rather than corruption. His personality was perfectly consistent with the stereotype of a jet pilot. Ky liked fancy jumpsuits and purple scarves, and he carried two pearl-handled revolvers in holsters. In 1961, when he was "just a colonel," Ky wanted to prove his flying skills to William Colby, the CIA station chief in Saigon. Ky got Colby into the cockpit and took him on a roller-coaster, mountain-hopping, wave-skimming flight from the Central Highlands to the South China Sea. Ky later laughed to another Vietnamese pilot that Colby was going to "have to go and clean the shit out of his pants."

Ngo Dinh Diem awarded Ky his general's star in 1962. Ky hated Nguyen Khanh. At one point in 1964, during a flight from Bien Hoa, Ky almost carried out an incendiary raid on Khanh's headquarters. Along with Nguyen Van Thieu, Ky ousted Khanh in February 1965. He was a member of the ruling ten-man National Leadership Committee and wielded executive power. He showed up at his first meeting with Maxwell Taylor wearing a white sharkskin dress jacket, tight silk black pants, bright red socks, and a purple scarf, prompting an American official to describe him as a "saxophone player in a second-rate night club." Ky was thoroughly Westernized. A well-trimmed mustache gave him an American look, and he walked with a swagger, imitating John Wayne, drinking Budweiser beer, and watching reruns of *Gunsmoke* and *Have Gun Will Travel* on armed forces television. William Bundy remembered the administration's initial reaction to Ky—it "seemed to all of us the bottom of the barrel, absolutely the bottom of the barrel."

The chairman of the National Leadership Committee and the chief of state was Nguyen Van Thieu. Born in Ninh Thuan Province in 1923, Thieu graduated from the Vietnamese Military Academy in 1949 and distinguished himself fighting the Vietminh. After graduating from United States Command and General Staff College in 1957, Thieu commanded the ARVN Twenty-first, First, and Fifth Infantry Divisions. During the 1963 coup against Diem, Thieu led a brigade against the presidential guard. He was one of the Young Turks on the Armed Forces Council in 1964 and, along with Nguyen Cao Ky, staged the overthrow of Nguyen Khanh in 1965.

Except for his lust for power, Thieu was different from Ky. American military leaders appreciated Thieu's conservatism, proper dress, and political caution. Thieu seemed more astute than Ky, with little of Ky's hostility for Buddhism. And Thieu was ready to forge a political and military alliance with the Americans in order to defeat the communists. The Americans also found Thieu more circumspect. While Ky was talking about building luxury hotels along the coast once the Vietcong were destroyed, Thieu focused on more immediate problems—how to locate and attack the Vietcong, undermine their control over rural peasants, and intimidate the North Vietnamese.

But like Ky, Thieu was part of the corruption of Saigonese politics. American money created new opportunities for graft at every level— sales of weapons, marketing of opium and heroin, kickbacks on military construction projects, licensing fees for American businesses operating in Saigon, and payments from thousands of potted-tree soldiers. Americans knew about the corruption. Between 1965 and 1972 the United States ambassador or MACV commander questioned Thieu more than one hundred times about official corruption in his government, but each time, after a warning, they let him off. It was Ky's impulsiveness that really bothered Americans. They wanted to maneuver Thieu into the role of chief executive, with Ky switched to military czar, where his impetuousness could be controlled.

The corrupt, illegitimate government of South Vietnam, with its incompetent, ineffectual military, could not handle the Vietcong. The choice Lyndon Johnson faced was simple: Escalate American involvement and rescue Saigon or get out before the collapse. After a White House breakfast early in March 1965, the president told General Harold K. Johnson, "You get things bubbling, General." The general toured Vietnam a few days later and learned just how desperate the situation was. Two marine battalions guarding Danang were not going to make much difference. Westmoreland asked for two full divisions of American combat troops, one to go to the Central Highlands and the second for Saigon. In what the press corps regarded as the understatement of the year, General Johnson argued that "what the situation requires may exceed what the Vietnamese can . . . do."

On March 15 General Johnson recommended deploying an international force near the Demilitarized Zone (DMZ).* To stop the infiltration

---

*Established at Geneva in 1954, the DMZ was a five-mile-wide buffer zone dividing North Vietnam from South Vietnam. It extended from the South China Sea to the village of Bo Hu Su along the Ben Hai River, and from there due west to Laos along the seventeenth parallel.

of troops and supplies from North Vietnam, he also proposed bringing engineering and logistical battalions so they could prepare for the arrival of large numbers of American ground troops. Finally, General Johnson wanted a full infantry division to defend United States installations. Maxwell Taylor demurred. He worried that American troops were inadequately prepared for guerrilla warfare in Vietnamese jungles, that ARVN might do even less with more American soldiers around, and that even a few infantry troops would dramatically alter the American mission in Vietnam.

But Vietcong attacks undercut Taylor's cautiousness. As if to confirm American fears, two Vietcong agents drove a gray Renault up to the United States embassy in Saigon on March 30, 1965. When an embassy guard approached the car, another Vietcong agent on a motor scooter shot and killed him. In the trunk of the Renault were 300 pounds of plastic explosives connected to an American-made brass detonator. At 11:00 A.M. the bomb exploded, gutting the embassy's first three floors and wounding 52 Americans. The blast killed 20 Vietnamese and wounded 130 others in the street. President Johnson was at a dinner party when he heard the news. The next morning at an impromptu press briefing he said, "Outrages like this will only reinforce the determination of the American people . . . to strengthen their assistance and support for the people and government of Vietnam."

Johnson lied when he reassured the reporters that he knew of "no far-reaching strategy that is being suggested or promulgated." Before the attack Johnson called Maxwell Taylor home for consultation. In meetings on April 1 and 2, the administration developed what became known as National Security Adviser Memorandum (NSAM) 328 authorizing deployment of 20,000 engineering and logistical troops to South Vietnam and the beginning of offensive operations against the Vietcong. John McCone, head of the CIA, reacted strongly to NSAM 328. Intelligence reports indicated that the Rolling Thunder air strikes "have not caused a change in the North Vietnamese policy of directing Viet Cong insurgency, infiltrating cadres and supplying material. If anything, the strikes to date have hardened their attitude." McCone believed that American ground troops, without a significant escalation of the air war over North Vietnam, would fail: "We will find ourselves mired down in combat in the jungle in a military effort that we cannot win. . . . If we are to change the mission of the ground forces, we must also change the ground rules for strikes against North Vietnam. We must hit them harder, more frequently, and inflict greater damage." Operation Rolling Thunder had to be escalated.

The president still hoped for another way out. On April 7, 1965, in a speech at Johns Hopkins University, Johnson extended the olive branch, offering to hold "unconditional discussions" to end the conflict. He also

When navy pilot Commander George Jacobsen, Jr., flew his first sortie over North Vietnam in the summer of 1965, America had high hopes for air power. The bombing campaigns, however, failed to deter North Vietnam.
UPI/BETTMAN

offered billions of dollars of United States assistance to develop the Mekong River Delta once peace had been achieved. Johnson viewed the offer as his trump card. "George Meany [the American labor leader] would jump at that offer in a minute," he told McGeorge Bundy. Early in May, Johnson launched Operation Mayflower by suspending the bombing raids over North Vietnam to see if Ho Chi Minh was ready for talks, warning that if "this pause should be misunderstood . . . it would be necessary to demonstrate more clearly than ever, after the pause ended, that the United States is determined not to accept aggression without reply in Vietnam."

The bombing pause did not provoke the desired response. Ho Chi Minh insisted that peace would come only after all American troops left South Vietnam, the National Liberation Front (NLF) participated fully in the government of South Vietnam, all bombing raids over North Vietnam stopped, and the two countries enjoyed a "peaceful reunification . . . without any foreign interference." The United States wanted a peace settlement based on the withdrawal of North Vietnamese forces from South Vietnam as well as the elimination of the National Liberation Front in South Vietnam. The impasse had not changed. Pham Van Dong had been through it all before: "We entered into negotiations with the French colonialists on many occasions, and concluded with them several agreements in an effort to preserve peace. To them, however, the signing of agreements was only designed to gain time to prepare . . . for further aggression. . . . This is a clear lesson of history . . . which our people will never forget."

Both sides were prisoners of history. For American policymakers, the recollections of Munich—of Britain and France's giving in to Hitler's demands only to see him take over much of Europe—were overpowering. American policymakers saw Ho Chi Minh as just another bully, not a national hero, who would back down in the face of brute power. But the North Vietnamese were in some ways just as blind. They saw the Americans as just another foreign power, a contemporary version of the Chinese and the French, intent on colonizing Vietnam. Nothing the Americans said could be trusted. There could be no negotiations. On May 18, 1965, the president ended Operation Mayflower and resumed the bombing.

A few weeks earlier, Johnson had dispatched Robert McNamara, Earle Wheeler, William Bundy, and Maxwell Taylor to Honolulu to meet with Admiral Ulysses S. Grant Sharp, commander in chief of the United States Forces in the Pacific (CINCPAC), and General Victor Krulak. They agreed to send another 40,000 marines and army infantry to South Vietnam. But they also decided to keep American troops out of the Central Highlands, confining most of them to the northern coast of I Corps. Johnson approved the decision. Early in May the 173d Airborne Brigade, the first army combat troops, arrived to protect the Bien Hoa air base. Another marine battalion went to Chu Lai. By the end of May 1965 there were nearly 50,000 American troops in South Vietnam.

But Johnson wanted the middle road, and he refused to give Westmoreland full rein. The decision to move beyond a few thousand marines in defensive positions precipitated an intense debate about how to prosecute the war. Retired army general James Gavin proposed the "enclave strategy." A 1929 West Point graduate, Gavin won a Silver Star during World War II. Before his retirement in 1960, he earned his third star as a lieutenant general. John Kennedy appointed Gavin ambassador to France in 1961. The French let Gavin know that the Vietnamese were a relentlessly militaristic people, that the United States would bog down in the jungles just as the French had. When he returned to the United States in 1964, Gavin preached the enclave strategy. He believed that if American ground troops were going to be introduced to South Vietnam, they should only be used to defend "coastal enclaves"—major cities along the South China Sea. Securing all of South Vietnam would take a million troops and an entire decade. Casualties would be severe, as would political criticism. Better to use fewer soldiers to hold coastal enclaves. Such a strategy would prove to North Vietnam that the United States was willing to stay indefinitely in South Vietnam. If Ho Chi Minh knew that the United States would be there for the long term, he would be more willing to settle the dispute diplomatically. The enclave strategy would also minimize American casualties, leaving the real bloodletting to the ARVN. The American people were willing to tolerate large contingents of American troops stationed indefinitely overseas—twenty years in West Germany and fifteen years in South Korea had proved that. What they would not tolerate was a long-term commitment with mounting casualties. The war would lose political support at home.

President Johnson adopted the enclave strategy. American combat troops were confined to the major American bases but could patrol to a fifty-mile radius. The president hoped that such an approach would stop short of a full-scale ground war while buying time for the South Vietnamese government to stabilize and for the bombing raids to push North Vietnam toward the negotiating table. Still worried about the political fallout over a serious escalation, that "that bitch of a war" might destroy "the woman I really loved—the Great Society," Johnson did not truthfully explain his decision to the public. He said the troops were in South Vietnam to protect the bases. It was the perfect time to go to Congress to ask for more money. The GIs were already in the field, and the president insisted that they were there for self-defense. On May 4, 1965, Johnson asked Congress for another $700 million to support those troops, and the legislators quietly agreed. For the next three years President Johnson argued that in the Gulf of Tonkin Resolution of 1964 and the May 1965 funding vote, Congress consented to the Vietnam War.

At this point the president tried to do what President Harry Truman did in Korea—put together a multinational, "free world fighting force." But Vietnam was not Korea. British Prime Minister Harold Wilson argued that the war was a dead end and that Johnson should stop the bombing and seek a negotiated settlement. Charles de Gaulle of France was more blunt. "The United States," he said, "cannot win this war. No matter how far they push it in the future, they will lose it." Australia, New Zealand, and the Philippines sent small contingents, and the South Koreans sent their vaunted Capital Division and a Marine Brigade to II Corps in October 1965 and the White Horse Division in September 1966. But that was all. It was going to be an American war.

Westmoreland came back with requests for more troops. The 23,000 military advisers, the 8,600 marines, the 20,000 engineering and logistical troops, and the promised 40,000 new combat troops would not be enough. In his memoirs General Westmoreland remembered that the "enemy was destroying [ARVN] battalions faster than they could be reconstituted." General Earle Wheeler echoed that opinion, arguing that "the ground forces situation requires a substantial . . . build-up of U.S. and Allied forces in the RVN [Republic of Vietnam], at the most rapid rate feasible." The generals wanted an end to the enclave strategy and the beginning of full-scale offensive operations. Wheeler insisted that the United States "must take the fight to the enemy. No one ever won a battle sitting on his ass."

Westmoreland and Wheeler told Johnson in June 1965 that they needed another 150,000 troops. Dean Rusk was stunned by the request. Just a month before, the administration had been heatedly discussing whether or not to send 3,500 marines to protect Danang. Rusk asked Westmoreland whether there really was "a serious danger of complete military collapse within a relatively short period of time." Westmoreland was brutally honest. ARVN "cannot stand up to this pressure without substantial US combat support on the ground. . . . The only possible response is the aggressive deployment of US troops." As far as Westmoreland was concerned, it was time to get on with the war.

Not everyone was convinced. Johnson was frustrated that a "raggedy-ass, fourth-rate country like North Vietnam [could] be causing so much trouble," and he worried that the war might get out of control. Westmoreland and Wheeler assured him that with the introduction of more ground troops the war would be won. George Ball thought differently. He wanted Johnson to stop listening to the generals, limit American ground troops to 100,000, and withdraw if South Vietnam proved unable to carry its fair share. Johnson saw the problem in simpler terms. Years later in his memoirs he wrote that the situation "reached the desperate point. . . . We had tried everything . . . to get . . . to the peace table . . . from November 1963 to 1965. And we had not succeeded. And we either had to run in or run out."

Johnson's handling of the revolution in the Dominican Republic in the last week of April 1965 strengthened his resolve. A rebel movement led by Juan Bosch overthrew the Dominican military government, and the CIA said communists were at work. Johnson sent 21,000 marines to seize control of the country, stabilize the government, and establish a pro-American regime. The decision was popular with most Americans. Success in the Dominican Republic reassured Johnson and raised his hopes that enough soldiers could achieve similar success in South Vietnam.

But in Vietnam, enough was never enough. General Earle Wheeler recalled later that by the summer of 1965 "it became amply clear that it wasn't a matter of whether the North Vietnamese were going to win the war; it was a question of when." At the same time Nguyen Cao Ky told Maxwell Taylor that more American ground troops were necessary if the country was going to survive the monsoon season. Johnson faced a critical choice that summer. He had approved a troop level of 95,000 in June, but Westmoreland and Wheeler wanted more. In fact, they wanted Johnson to send forty-four infantry battalions to South Vietnam—another 100,000 troops. John McCone and Walt Rostow wanted a dramatic escalation of the Rolling Thunder bombing raids.

George Ball, on the other hand, wanted Johnson to find a way to get out before it was too late. On July 1, 1965, with his usual eloquence, Ball told Johnson he was facing a "protracted war involving an open-ended commitment of U.S. forces, mounting U.S. casualties, no assurances of a satisfactory solution, and a serious danger of escalation at the end of the road. . . . Once we suffer large casualties, we will have started a well-nigh irreversible process. Our involvement will be so great that we cannot—without national humiliation—stop short of achieving our complete objectives." Senate Majority Leader Mike Mansfield told Johnson, "There is not a government to speak of in Saigon." Maxwell Taylor, skeptical of what ground troops would be able to achieve, wanted Johnson to limit the troops to 95,000 men and stick to the enclave strategy.

Johnson sought the advice of Robert McNamara, whom he called "the smartest man I ever met." McNamara presented his analysis early in July. He told Johnson that there appeared to be three options. The first, advocated by George Ball and Mike Mansfield, involved an early withdrawal from the war with as few casualties as possible. A second alternative, the one favored by Maxwell Taylor, limited American forces in Vietnam to 95,000 men fighting an enclave war and preparing ARVN to take over. If that did not work, then the United States should get out. Finally, the president could side with Westmoreland, Wheeler, McCone, and Rostow—expand the military effort against the Vietcong and North Vietnam until they had to negotiate or be destroyed.

McNamara told Johnson that the third option was the only way of saving Southeast Asia. He proposed giving Westmoreland his forty-four battalions, mining Haiphong harbor, sealing off North Vietnam from all external commerce, and bombing to destroy munitions, fuel supplies, railroads, bridges, airfields, surface-to-missile sites, and war industries. He wanted to call up 225,000 army reservists to active duty. Short of nuclear weapons, McNamara wanted to bring every ounce of American firepower to bear.

The proposal was so far reaching and involved such a dramatic alteration in the nature of American policy that McGeorge Bundy took exception, counseling Johnson to be careful. The commitment was too open ended, the outcome too blurred, to justify such an investment. "If we need 200,000 men now for these quite limited missions," Bundy wrote to McNamara at the end of June, "may we not need 400,000 later? Is this a rational course of action? . . . If US casualties go up sharply, what further actions do we propose to take or not to take?" What if the Chinese or Soviets intervened? What if the bombing did not bring North Vietnamese diplomats to the table? What if the war went on for years without resolution? The terrible "ifs" multiplied.

Johnson turned for advice to the "Wise Men," a group of elder statesmen who represented the American foreign policy establishment. If the

United States ever had an aristocracy, it was these men—Ivy Leaguers with a wealth of experience wielding power. Included in the group were Dean Acheson; Robert Lovett, a Wall Street investment banker and former secretary of defense; and John McCloy, former head of the World Bank. Johnson called them to the White House on July 10 to evaluate McNamara's proposal. In a letter to Harry Truman after the meeting, Acheson recalled listening to Johnson "complain about how mean everyone was to him . . . (every course of action was wrong; he had no support from anyone at home or abroad; it interfered with all his programs, etc., etc.). . . . I blew my top and told him he was wholly right on Vietnam, that he had no choice except to press on. . . . With this lead my colleagues came thundering in like the charge of the Scots Grey at Waterloo."

Johnson decided on a middle course. For political reasons withdrawal was out of the question, but so was McNamara's omnibus proposal. Right-wing politicians would crucify Johnson politically if he withdrew and South Vietnam fell to communism, but McNamara's plan placed the United States in a state of war emergency. Johnson accepted most of McNamara's proposal, except for the all-out bombing campaign over North Vietnam and the calling up of reserves. Johnson listened to Dean Rusk, who argued that the United States "should deny to Hanoi success in South Vietnam without taking action on our side which would force the other side [China, Soviet Union] to move to higher levels of conflict." Rusk wanted to keep limits on Rolling Thunder. Johnson agreed. Although he increased the number of sorties from 3,600 in April to 4,800 in June, the president kept them below the twentieth parallel. At the end of July, in a low-key speech, he announced the deployment of another 50,000 troops. It was a lie, or at least a half-truth. He had decided to send another 150,000 and to abandon the enclave strategy.

Johnson took liberty with the truth because he felt he had no choice. With civil rights legislation and the Medicare bill already before Congress, he did not want to alienate any of his support. He was still confident that he could win the war and secure the Great Society, but in order to do so he had to lie. The most vociferous critics of the war—people like Senators Mike Mansfield or Wayne Morse—also tended to be the most liberal on domestic issues. Johnson did not want to alienate them, so he kept promising sincere attempts to negotiate a settlement and kept denying that he had implemented any fundamental change in policy. While misleading the American public, Lyndon Johnson had decided to engage in a land war in Asia.

Few American presidents have made such colossal miscalculations. The Vietnam War was a quagmire in strategic thinking. The Johnson administration, like its predecessors, had a difficult time precisely defining the real enemy in Vietnam. At times policymakers talked vaguely of communism, while at other times they identified the Chinese, the North Vietnamese, or the South Vietnamese guerrillas as the real culprits.

The first rule in strategic thinking is political, not military: Those who make war must be certain of the nature of their enemy; only then can they apply the proper level of force and know just what constitutes a victory.

The second rule of strategic thinking is also political: Those who make war must maintain support for the war at home so people will make the necessary sacrifices. But here, too, Johnson faced a dilemma. Withdrawal was not an option, especially for a Democratic president familiar with the criticism directed at Truman in 1949 for the fall of China. Johnson was certain that the "loss" of Vietnam would precipitate "a mean and explosive debate" that would "shatter my Presidency, kill my administration, and damage our democracy." The international repercussions would be even worse. If the United States did not finish the job in Vietnam, American credibility around the world would be compromised and communists would launch more "wars of national liberation."

But at the same time, the United States could not engage in total war either. Although the Sino-Soviet split and, beginning in 1966, the Cultural Revolution in China, probably precluded direct Soviet or Chinese intervention, the Johnson administration worried constantly about the prospects of another Korea. By definition, then, the Vietnam War was going to be a limited war, one in which political issues dictated military constraints. That did not bother Johnson, at least not at first. He promised Senator George McGovern of South Dakota, "I'm going up old Ho Chi Minh's leg an inch at a time." Because he believed North Vietnam would cave in quickly to American firepower, the president thought the people would tolerate heavy casualties in the short term if they saw victory and peace on the horizon. But when the North Vietnamese proved to be intransigent and long suffering, limited war became a horrendous political liability. The longer it went on, the more political support Johnson lost at home.

The Johnson administration also violated the third rule of strategic thinking: Those who make war must remember that war is ultimately a political event. The military, like diplomacy, is simply a tool for achieving political objectives. The political objective was establishing a stable, democratic, noncommunist government in South Vietnam, but the United States was never able to correlate the use of military hardware with nation building. Saigonese politics were inherently undemocratic in the first place, and as the United States escalated the war and the volume of firepower, the war's sheer destructiveness inevitably alienated more and more people in South Vietnam. Even a clear military victory over North Vietnam would not necessarily translate into the creation of a stable democratic regime in South Vietnam.

Within that strategic fog, William Westmoreland tried to fight a war. He was convinced that the United States should focus on destroying the enemy—just what the Allies had done to Germany and Japan during

World War II. The United States economy was unmatched in its ability to produce and deliver military firepower, and Westmoreland planned to build, in the words of journalist Neil Sheehan, a "killing machine," a huge army backed by the latest in technology and organization. Westmoreland would fight the communists in three stages. In 1965 and early 1966 he would build the infrastructure to support a large, modern army. He estimated it would take one soldier in a logistical support role to maintain each soldier in the field.

The second stage would begin in late 1966. Westmoreland planned to establish a system of fortified firebases in South Vietnam, each with the capability of covering a large area in artillery fire. From those bases infantry patrols would go on search-and-destroy missions to locate the enemy. GIs would use the old technologies—aircraft surveillance and tracking dogs—as well as the latest—hand-carried radar, infrared spotting scopes, and urine-detection "people-sniffer" devices. IBM 1430 computers back in Saigon consumed huge amounts of CIA and MACV data, developed probability curves, and tried to predict when and where the enemy would attack. Operation Ranch Hand would be expanded. Rather than fight the enemy head-on, Westmoreland wanted to rely mostly on tactical firepower, directing artillery, helicopter gunships, fixed-wing gunships, and B-52 bombers on the enemy. The third stage involved ARVN's moving into the area for "clearing operations"—killing any enemy troops who survived the bombardment—and local militia would then maintain security.

The weak link in the strategy was ARVN and the Regional Forces and Popular Forces, which American troops derisively termed "Ruff-Puffs." But even if they did not do their job of clearing and securing behind the killing machine, Westmoreland was confident that the enemy could not long stand the heavy losses they would incur. "We'll just go on bleeding them," Westmoreland said, "until Hanoi wakes up to the fact that they have bled their country to the point of national disaster for generations." Sooner or later the Vietcong would no longer exist, and the North Vietnamese would no longer be able to put fighting men in the field.

Operation Starlight, for Westmoreland at least, proved his point. On August 18 at the Batangan Peninsula in northern South Vietnam, the Third Battalion of the Third Marine Division came ashore while the Second Battalion of the Fourth Marine Division flew into landing zones to the west, chasing the First Vietcong Regiment. Fighting was heavy, and the marines called in artillery, naval bombardment, and tactical air support. More than 6,000 marines participated. Operation Starlight was the first large battle with Main Force Vietcong. When the battle of Chu Lai, as the marines called it, was over, the United States claimed 573 Vietcong dead, compared to 46 dead marines and another 204 wounded. Westmoreland's "boys" inflicted death at the rate of twelve to one. The math was self-evident. How long could the enemy hold out? Westmoreland intended to go after the enemy with a vengeance, to slaughter them at record rates while the air force was reducing to rubble North Vietnam's military bases, industrial plants, roads, and bridges. The enemy would have to capitulate. Westmoreland truly believed that the United States could win a war of attrition.

Although Westmoreland wanted to unleash American forces in big-unit operations, Washington restricted his actions. To stop the infiltration of supplies into South Vietnam, Westmoreland wanted to invade across the seventeenth parallel and hold territory there, bringing the ground war home to North Vietnam. But at the White House memories of Korea, of crossing the thirty-eighth parallel only to be attacked by hordes of Chinese soldiers, were still vivid. It was too risky. Johnson did not want to wake up the slumbering giant. He confined American troops south of the seventeenth parallel. Westmoreland also wanted to invade Laos south of the seventeenth parallel to stop the infiltration along the Ho Chi Minh Trail, as well as Cambodia to attack enemy staging areas along the border. The United States should routinely bomb the staging areas, even if Laos and Cambodia opposed such actions. But Johnson remained cautious and prudent, too prudent and too cautious for Westmoreland.

Logistical planners and strategic bombing experts told Westmoreland that cutting off the flow of supplies by bombing raids and military occupations of large amounts of territory would stretch American resources without achieving acceptable results. A much easier approach was to mine or blockade Haiphong harbor, the depot where most of the Soviet and Chinese supplies entered North Vietnam. Johnson balked because it increased the probability of a confrontation with the Soviets. Rather than take that risk, Johnson vetoed the proposal. In his memoirs, Westmoreland said that "Washington's phobia that . . . mining the harbor would trigger Chinese Communist or Russian intervention was chimerical."

In addition to political limitations on military operations, Westmoreland faced obstacles in the command structure. MACV was a "subordinate unified command." Although Westmoreland eventually directed 543,000 American troops fighting a land war in Asia, real authority over the war was in Honolulu with CINCPAC. During Westmoreland's four years with MACV, CINCPAC was Admiral Ulysses S. Grant Sharp. To get requests to and decisions from the president and the joint chiefs, Westmoreland had to go through CINCPAC. Command of air operations was even more complicated. Westmoreland controlled the air force sorties inside South Vietnam and on the southern parts of the Ho Chi Minh Trail in Laos, but CINCPAC controlled naval air strikes over North Vietnam and northern Laos. To say the least, the command and control structure often prevented a unified battle plan.

Westmoreland's real problem was the lack of a coherent American strategy. He gave tactical questions careful thought and devised a regimen of infantry patrols with artillery and aerial bombardment. The United States won almost every battle through tactical firepower. But war is not just a tactical exercise. Strategic thinking incorporates economic, cultural, and political reality. Westmoreland wrestled with an impossible mission—winning a war without being able to define just what victory meant. He expected to fight a conventional war—to kill so many enemy troops that communists would not continue the fight. But he had no idea about the depth of their will to fight or about how many people they were willing to lose.

Although politicians confused the issue, Westmoreland was unwilling to adapt to the strategic constraints given him. Trained to command infantry in battle and successful enough in military politics to rise to the top, Westmoreland now had his war, and he wanted to be able to do what he had seen Douglas MacArthur, George Patton, Jr., Dwight D. Eisenhower, and Maxwell Taylor do—mobilize the killing machine and annihilate the enemy. He did not want to fight a limited war with complicated political constraints. Throughout his tour of duty, Westmoreland pressed the Johnson administration for more troops, more firepower, and fewer rules.

The Marine Corps had a different idea. Although the deployment of two battalions to Danang in March 1965 finally put them in the war, the marines had misgivings. Trained as assault troops, the marines at Danang found themselves holding static positions and defending territory. That had never been part of their historical mission. Their purpose was to overrun the enemy, take heavy casualties, and evacuate, leaving army infantry to hold the positions. Premier among the critics was Victor Krulak, one of the few senior military officers convinced that the key to victory was political, not military. For Krulak the big engagements between United States, ARVN, Main Force Vietcong, and the North Vietnamese "could move to another planet today, and we would still not have won the war because the Vietnamese people are the prize."

The Marine Corps was more capable than the army at pacification. For decades before World War II, marine detachments occupied several Central American and Caribbean countries, where they worked with local governments and emphasized pacification. The marines had been through this before—in Cuba, Haiti, the Dominican Republic, Nicaragua, and Panama. Krulak wanted American troops in Vietnam—marines as well as army infantry—to fight small-unit actions while investing most of their energies in pacification. Krulak proposed placing a marine rifle squad with a South Vietnamese Regional Forces (local militia) company in what he called a combined action platoon (CAP). The CAPs would provide security while pacification programs—

health, education, economic development, and land reform—would win over the peasants. But Westmoreland vetoed the plan; he was just going to solve the problem militarily.

Although muddled strategic thinking bedeviled the American effort in Southeast Asia, North Vietnam had a simple political goal that enjoyed clear strategic expression: Expel the American military from Indochina, conquer South Vietnam, and reunify the two countries. The North Vietnamese knew they could not match American firepower. The war would be won or lost, Ho Chi Minh repeated over and over again, in the minds of the typical American citizen and the typical South Vietnamese peasant. Once Americans brought in large numbers of troops, traditional Vietnamese resentments of foreigners festered. When the Americans employed their firepower—massive artillery bombardment and air strikes— civilian casualties mounted. So did peasant resentment. Women, children, and old people died, homes were destroyed, and refugee camps filled. Ho Chi Minh was certain that South Vietnam would never generate loyalty among the peasants. Saigonese Catholics were too arrogant, too materialistic, and too corrupt to gain peasant trust and rule with legitimate authority.

Vo Nguyen Giap looked on the American buildup with incredulity— amazement at the wealth and technology but disbelief that such resources would be invested so poorly. In 1969, looking back on the first four years of the war, he remarked, "The United States has a strategy based on arithmetic. They question the computers, add and subtract, extract square roots, and then go into action. But arithmetical strategy doesn't work here. . . . If it did, they'd already have exterminated us. . . . When a whole people rises up, nothing can be done." Giap was right. Westmoreland measured progress by adding up the dead, the "body count," as well as the numbers of prisoners taken, weapons captured, tonnages exploded, sorties flown, and "battalion days in the field," a way of gauging infantry activity. But those statistics did not measure commitment. Even the American bombing of North Vietnam, originally designed to break the people's will, only made them more angry and resentful, more willing to sacrifice everything on Ho Chi Minh's bold course.

But the Vietnamese people were not the only strategic objectives. Just as critical were the American people. Vietnam had already waged one war against Westerners. The French tired of the war and imposed increasing pressure on their government to withdraw. Ho Chi Minh expected Americans to be no different. Vietnam was a little place a long way from Main Street. Once the boys started coming home in body bags, the American people would insist on a settlement. While Westmoreland planned a war of military attrition, Ho Chi Minh waged a war of political attrition. When his generals pushed for more aggressiveness, Ho Chi Minh reassured them: "Don't worry. I've been to America. I know Americans. They are an impatient people. They will leave."

The key was staying in the war until the Americans gave up. It might take a long time. Westmoreland expected North Vietnam to give up once American forces destroyed tens of thousands, and then hundreds of thousands, of communist soldiers. But Ho Chi Minh estimated that rural South Vietnam and all of North Vietnam could produce 250,000 to 300,000 new military recruits a year. For a war of attrition to erode Vietnam's ability to stay with the war, Westmoreland would have to kill that many people every year. From their perspective of a limited war, American leaders could not imagine Vietnam making such a sacrifice. But Ho Chi Minh was willing.

By that time Vo Nguyen Giap, although still an influential member of the Politburo in Hanoi, no longer controlled war strategy. Those decisions were firmly in the hands of Le Duan, the militant advocate of reunification who was now general secretary of the Lao Dong party. Late in 1964 Duan named Nguyen Chi Thanh head of the Central Office for South Vietnam (COSVN), which controlled the Vietcong effort in South Vietnam. Born in Thua Thien Province in 1914, Thanh taught school until 1946, when he joined the Vietminh after French troops shot his father. Unlike Giap, Thanh argued that the North Vietnamese should engage the United States in big-unit, conventional battles before American firepower reached its peak. If the North Vietnamese inflicted heavy losses on the American army early in the war, Lyndon Johnson would stop the buildup. Giap took exception, countering that the North Vietnamese should not get into a slugging match with the American heavyweight. For a brief period, Thanh had the upper hand.

The battle of the Batangan Peninsula in August 1965 intensified the debate. To Thanh, despite the heavy losses, the battle was proof that "the Southern Liberation Army is fully capable of defeating U.S. troops under any circumstance, even though they [U.S. troops] have absolute superiority of . . . firepower." Thanh also pointed out that the Americans had withdrawn from the peninsula soon after the battle, and the Vietcong returned in force. Thanh answered Giap's charge that casualties were too high by arguing that the Americans had suffered 250 dead and wounded soldiers and that the United States would be politically unwilling to accept such casualties. Thanh remained convinced that big-unit confrontation was the only way to go. Giap preferred smaller scale battles and guerrilla warfare. Le Duan sided with Thanh, until the battle of the Ia Drang Valley.

The First Air Cavalry Division, deployed to Vietnam in September 1965, was the latest in tactical innovation. The helicopter was to airborne warfare what the tank had been to armored cavalry—a new tactical development providing mobility and firepower. The "air cav" deployed to II Corps in the Central Highlands to stop any enemy attempt to cut South Vietnam in half by driving to the South China Sea. Late in October, North Vietnamese troops attacked a United States Special

Forces camp at Plei Me. Westmoreland sent in the air cav. But in mid-November, when 400 American troops went through what they thought was the unoccupied Ia Drang Valley southwest of Plei Me, the North Vietnamese Sixty-sixth Regiment surprised them. Four days of fighting followed before the enemy withdrew. In the three weeks since the attack on Plei Me, American firepower buried the enemy in exploding shells: nearly 35,000 artillery rounds, more than 7,000 rounds of aerial rockets, and more than 50,000 helicopter sorties. For the first time in the war, B-52 bombers flew in tactical support. When the battle ended, nearly 1,800 North Vietnamese were confirmed dead, with probably that same number wounded or soon to die. "Only" 240 Americans were dead.

But for both sides the casualties changed the nature of the war. In Hanoi the heavy losses gave Vo Nguyen Giap the upper hand in his debate with Nguyen Chi Thanh. Le Duan also thought the casualties were too high. The North Vietnamese lost nearly half a division in one battle. Although Duan and Thanh were not ready to abandon conventional warfare in favor of guerrilla actions, they were willing to return to small-unit operations and to change tactics. To limit the effectiveness of American artillery and air power, they developed a tactic termed "clinging to the belt," engaging the Americans at close quarters under heavy jungle cover—short-range firefights, ambushes, and hand-to-hand combat—and forcing officers to call in artillery and air strikes close to or even on their own positions. The North Vietnamese had to keep the tactical initiative by staying out of the way of American search-and-destroy operations. While Westmoreland expected the North Vietnamese to move into what Mao Zedong called the "third phase of revolutionary warfare"—large-scale conventional battles at the battalion, regimental, and division levels—North Vietnam prepared to be more flexible.

Ho Chi Minh and Vo Nguyen Giap realized that time, not big battles, was their best tactic. From July to September 1965, the United States inflicted forty deaths for every American death. That was clearly too heavy, and by determining when and where to fight, North Vietnam reduced those figures to fifteen to one by the end of the year. The longer the communists held out, the more likely the United States would tire of the struggle. If the United States kept up the fight long enough, the "number of dead American boys will steadily increase," Giap said. "Their mothers will want to know why. The war will not long survive their questions."

In Saigon, Westmoreland used Ia Drang to boost his troop requests up to 375,000 men, with the option of asking for 200,000 more. Robert McNamara was visibly shaken by the deaths of 240 Americans in one battle. He told Johnson that "U.S. killed-in-action can be expected to reach 1,000 a month and the odds are even that we will be faced in early 1967 with a 'no decision' at an even higher level." That would soon pose a colossal political problem. The war was becoming the central theme of the

Johnson administration, eclipsing the Great Society domestic programs. Anticipating a hostile political reaction at home and abroad to more troop requests, McNamara suggested, "We must lay a foundation in the minds of the American public and world opinion for such an enlarged phase of the war and . . . we should give NVN [North Vietnam] a face-saving chance to stop the aggression." Johnson accepted McNamara's proposal for another pause in Rolling Thunder. On Christmas Eve 1965 the bombing stopped. But Ho Chi Minh still insisted on the unconditional withdrawal of all American troops and participation of the National Liberation Front in the South Vietnamese government. On January 31, 1966, Johnson resumed the raids.

While Johnson offered peace, the battle of the Ia Drang Valley boosted Westmoreland's morale. The deaths of 240 Americans did not startle him; he viewed those deaths in the context of a military victory. The boys died nobly, giving the enemy a real thrashing. The enemy lost nearly half a division; attrition was working. "The death of even one man is lamentable," Westmoreland said of the Ia Drang Valley, "and those were serious losses, yet I could take comfort in the fact that in the Highlands . . . the American fighting man . . . performed without the setbacks that had sometimes marked first performances in other wars." Westmoreland then pursued the troop buildup with a vengeance. Throughout the last half of 1965 and most of 1966 he built the infrastructure he needed. In addition to the jet air bases at Tan Son Nhut, Bien Hoa, and Danang, Westmoreland added four more, along with six new deep-water ports, four central supply and maintenance depots, twenty-six permanent base camps, seventy-five new tactical airstrips, and twenty-six hospitals—more than 16 million square feet of construction. He built 2,500 miles of paved roads and installed the Southeast Asia Automatic Telephone System (SAATS), complete with 220 communications centers and 14,000 circuits. To supply electricity needs, he brought in 1,300 commercial generators and dozens of World War II tankers converted to floating generator barges.

Westmoreland made the permanent base camps high-quality wooden barracks built on concrete slabs with hot showers. High-ranking officers enjoyed air-conditioned quarters in mobile trailers. Foremost Dairy and Meadowgold Dairies built fresh milk and ice cream plants at Qui Nhon and Cam Ranh Bay, and to supply troops in remote locations with fresh ice cream, Westmoreland built forty army ice cream plants. To make sure that the soldiers got three meals a day of fresh fruit, vegetables, meat, and dairy products, he built thousands of cold storage lockers throughout South Vietnam. To amuse the troops, he built the famous PXs—air-conditioned movie theaters, bowling alleys, and service clubs full of beer, Cokes, hot dogs, hamburgers, french fries, malts, sundaes, candy, and ice. No army in the history of the world had more of the amenities of home.

The escalation of the United States military effort in South Vietnam also brought about an increase in the number of women assigned to Indochina. Approximately 11,000 of the women serving in Vietnam were nurses. President Johnson's decision to send ground troops to South Vietnam meant a dramatic increase in casualties. To deal with cases of sick and wounded soldiers, the Pentagon began to deploy army medical detachments in the spring of 1965. The Third Field Hospital went to Tan Son Nhut in April 1965, and the Fifty-eighth Medical Battalion reached Long Binh in May. The Ninth Field Hospital was stationed in Nha Trang in July, and it was followed by the Eighty-fifth Evacuation Hospital in August, the Forty-third Medical Group and the 523d Field Hospital in September, and the First Medical Battalion, Second Surgical Hospital, Fifty-first Field Hospital, and Ninety-third Evacuation Hospital in November. Eventually, the army assigned forty-seven medical units to South Vietnam. Navy nurses worked on the USS *Repose* and the USS *Sanctuary*, hospital ships that sailed between the Demilitarized Zone and Danang off the coast of Vietnam in the South China Sea. Air force nurses worked on medevac aircraft evacuating the wounded to Japan, Okinawa, the Philippines, and the United States. There were no Marine Corps nurses.

In many ways, nursing was the most emotionally hazardous duty of the entire war. During the course of a tour of duty, day after day for an entire year, nurses were exposed constantly to sick and wounded young men. They frequently encountered men and boys younger than they who were suffering from massive, almost unbelievable wounds. The combination of helicopters and field hospitals allowed some soldiers to survive wounds that in any previous war would have been fatal. Sarah McGoran, an army nurse, remembered wounds "so big you could put both your arms into them." Napalm and white phosphorous bombs created a new definition of burns—"fourth degree." A navy nurse told Kathryn Marshall, who wrote *In the Combat Zone* (1987), that many of the burn victims were "essentially denuded. We used to talk about fourth-degree burns—you know, burns are labeled first, second, and third degree, but we had people who were burnt all the way through." That same nurse remembered some wounds so horrific that medical terminology did not exist to describe them. "Horriblectomies were when they'd had so much taken out or removed. Horridzoma meant the initial grotesque injury but also the repercussions of the injury." Rachel Smith remembered the process of numbing herself "to the screams of teenaged boys whose bodies had been blown to bits, moaning for their mothers, begging for relief, praying for death. Pretty soon it just became another day's work for me. Otherwise, I would've gone nuts." Later in the war, the nurses found themselves treating soldier-addicts, young men using marijuana, opium, amphetamines, cocaine, and heroin to block out the war. "Nobody told me," an army nurse recalled, "I

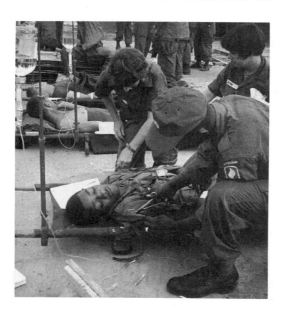

Combat nurses in Vietnam, working in trying circumstances and treating unprecedented types of injuries, provided crucial support and care to U.S. soldiers.

UPI/BETTMANN

was going to be taking care of so many strung-out motherfuckers. I mean, this was supposed to be a *war*."

In addition to the nurses, another 1,300 military women performed nonmedical jobs in Vietnam. Usually assigned to the Women's Army Corps, they worked as secretaries at MACV. Others were in the Army Signal Corps. Military women also worked as air traffic controllers, intelligence officers, decoders, and cartographers. For the most part, they were assigned to Saigon and the major bases in South Vietnam.

Ten of thousands of civilian women also had jobs in South Vietnam during the war. The American Red Cross sent women to Vietnam, as did such other service groups and relief organizations as the American Friends Service Committee, the Mennonite Central Committee, the Agency for International Development, Army Special Services, the USO, Supplemental Recreational Activities Overseas, Catholic Relief Services, and the Christian Missionary Alliance. Civilian women worked with the CIA's Air America and World Airways. Women came to South Vietnam with the international construction firms that had secured billions of dollars in government contracts. Among those construction firms were Brown and Root, Bechtel, Martin Marietta, and a host of others. Eventually, more than 50,000 American women served there in military and civilian capacities. Eight of them made the ultimate sacrifice. Seven military women died of accidents and disease; Lieutenant Sharon M. Lanz of the Army Nurse Corps died on June 8, 1969, when North Vietnamese rockets hit Chu Lai.

Although the escalation of the ground war and bombing campaigns made infiltration of supplies from North Vietnam more difficult, they did not stop it. By the early summer of 1966, 8,000 North Vietnamese Army (NVA) troops a month were coming into South Vietnam. The communist troop contingent in South Vietnam reached 435,000 people: 46,300 North Vietnamese regulars, 114,000 Main Force Vietcong, 112,000 guerrillas, and more than 160,000 local militia. They did not need ice cream and bowling alleys, so the logistical requirements were simple. By 1966 they needed eight tons of supplies a day. They lived off the land and the peasants.

The supplies the communists could not get from South Vietnamese peasants came from the Soviet Union and China. During the early 1960s, when Nikita Khrushchev preached peaceful coexistence with the West, North Vietnam gravitated toward the Chinese. But Khrushchev was ousted in 1964, and the new regime, headed by Leonid Brezhnev, was more interested in assisting North Vietnam. The Soviet Union and China were competing for leadership of the communist world, and neither could ignore the fact that the United States was conducting a major war against their tiny ally. The Soviets saw the American decision to escalate the war as an opportunity to diminish Chinese influence in Southeast Asia and augment their own. China supplied Hanoi with rice, trucks, AK-47 rifles, and 50,000 laborers, but the Soviets had sophisticated military technology—fighter aircraft, tanks, and surface-to-air missiles. North Vietnam exploited the Sino-Soviet split, and between 1965 and 1968 received more than $2 billion in assistance from the two powers.

The war's escalation undermined Johnson's political position and threatened his Great Society. At the end of 1965 there were 184,300 American troops in South Vietnam, with another 200,000 scheduled to arrive. Since 1959, 636 United States soldiers had died and another 6,400 had been wounded, most of them in the previous two months. Opposition to the war surfaced among liberal Democrats, those people Johnson especially needed to pass the civil rights and antipoverty legislation. In the spring of 1965 Senator Frank Church of Idaho warned Johnson, "There are limits to what we can do in helping any government surmount a Communist uprising. If the people themselves will not support the government in power, we cannot save it."

The White House press corps added to Johnson's troubles. The journalists questioned everything. Throughout the 1964 election campaign Johnson promised to avoid a land war in Asia, but the discrepancies between his 1964 promises and his 1965 actions were not the main reason for the growing hostility. Politicians rarely live up to election rhetoric. It was the lies that alienated reporters. On May 23, 1965, David Wise of the *New York Herald Tribune* coined the term "credibility gap," and a few days later Murray Marder of the *Washington Post* amplified it. Desperate to keep the war from gutting his Great Society, Johnson intentionally misled the press. He lied in the summer of 1964 about the incidents in the Gulf of Tonkin; he lied in April 1965 by denying that NSAM 328 authorized offensive operations by United States ground troops; and he lied repeatedly about the number of ground troops he had approved for combat in South Vietnam.

Johnson's lies and his calls for more troops disrupted the lives of American youths. They were the "baby boomers," born in the wake of the "good war" and reared in prosperity. They were better fed, better housed, and better educated than any previous generation. They *believed* that anything was possible. They assumed that America's problems—racial injustice, pockets of poverty, the cold war—would be solved. Optimism was their birthright. By the late 1960s they constituted 20 percent of the population. Johnson's war in Vietnam had no place in their world view. As the draft calls went out and the lies multiplied, they responded with anger and frustration. As the war lengthened, they rebelled. Rebellion was not new. During the late 1950s and early 1960s a certain amount of discontent was a rite of passage. "Rock 'n' rollers" rebelled against the music and the clothes of their parents; "beats" rebelled against materialism; college students rebelled against racism.

Theological and social liberals in the mainstream Protestant denominations were not comfortable with Johnson's decision to escalate. They reacted immediately to the escalation, forming Clergy and Laymen Concerned About Vietnam (CALCAV) to mobilize the religious community to take an ecumenical stand against the war. It attracted some conservatives and radicals and functioned as one of the first important channels for Jewish and Catholic peace activism. Originating in New York in 1965, CALCAV served as a protest vehicle for clergy and laity from churches that were silent on the war issue. Established to help defend the right to dissent, CALCAV, which was clearly in the mainstream of American life, argued that nothing was accomplished by escalating the war and advocated a negotiated settlement. Adopting a moderate tone and asserting its patriotic motivation in opposing the Vietnam War, CALCAV combined moral and pragmatic arguments in voicing its condemnation of the war. Always careful to avoid extreme arguments and tactics, CALCAV expressed its opposition in ways that kept it on good terms with its basically white, middle-class, religiously motivated constituency, which proved to be the source of a great deal of its success.

The decision to Americanize and militarize the conflict in Vietnam jump-started the antiwar movement in the United States, broadening its narrow base to include new elements in American society. Student groups, New Leftists, and civil rights activists took a critical look at the war. More than thirty other antiwar organizations sprouted in 1965, and they were represented by the National Coordinating Committee to End the War in Vietnam, an umbrella organization established in August in Madison, Wisconsin.

American universities proved to be fertile ground for the antiwar movement. The intellectual left, which had been inactive in the Eisenhower era, was generally unable to function as an early critic of war policy because of its connection with the liberal bipartisanship of diplomacy in the period after World War II. In the early 1960s, few of them spoke out about the war, even though the seed of all the principal arguments that were used later in the Johnson administration existed while Kennedy was president. A symbiotic relationship existed between the Kennedy administration and the intelligentsia, and Johnson began his presidency with noticeable attempts to court the intellectual community. That changed when Johnson ordered 3,000 marines into Danang on March 10, 1965. They were the first contingent of regular combat troops sent to Vietnam. At the University of Michigan in Ann Arbor, several faculty members organized a "teach-in"—patterned after the famous 1960 civil rights "sit-ins"—for March 24, 1965. More than 3,500 students attended the teach-in, where faculty members discussed the nature of the war. Similar teach-ins occurred at campuses across the country in the spring of 1965, culminating with the "National Teach-In" at 122 colleges and universities on May 15, 1965.

The protests soon spread beyond the campuses, confirming the youth counterculture's sense of alienation and betrayal. Until the escalation of the war, the public antiwar movement had largely been confined to the Old Left, but by the summer of 1965, New Left groups also became active in the opposition to the Vietnam conflict. The most prominent of those organizations was the Students for a Democratic Society (SDS). SDS was founded in January 1960 by a group of students who had been politically associated with the Socialist party. Tom Hayden emerged as its first leader, and SDS was active in the civil rights movement. By 1964, especially after the Gulf of Tonkin incident, SDS began to organize campus demonstrations and teach-ins against the war and circulated "We Won't Go" petitions among draft-age men. On April 17, 1965, SDS sponsored a demonstration in Washington, D.C., which brought more than 20,000 protesters to the city. SDS membership grew from 2,000 to nearly 30,000 members during the next year. Other New Left groups— such as the Catholic Peace Fellowship, the Emergency Citizens' Group Concerned About Vietnam, the "Another Mother for Peace" organization, and the National Emergency Committee of Clergy Concerned About Vietnam—also became active in opposing the war.

Other students ventured beyond talk. Some turned in their draft cards, others burned theirs. They played "tit-for-tat" with the government. As Johnson escalated the war, they escalated theirs. Berkeley students formed a draft resistance movement. "To cooperate with conscription is to perpetuate its existence, without which the government could not wage war," announced an antiwar leader. Even more concretely, activist Dennis Sweeney wrote, "I choose to refuse to cooperate with the selective service because it is the only honest, whole, and human response I can make to a military institution which demands the allegiance of my life." Johnson was a president facing two wars—both undeclared and both tearing at the heart of his domestic programs.

Hostility from the press, the antiwar movement, and mounting casualties made the front-page news every day. To keep it from getting worse, Johnson decided not to call up the reserves, not to declare a national emergency, not to declare war, and not to tell the truth. When the time came to pay for the war, he chose not to raise taxes. Gordon Ackley, chairman of the Council of Economic Advisers, told Johnson that the war was going to cost $3 billion a month in 1966. Either Johnson had to reduce the war effort, postpone Great Society domestic programs, or raise taxes. Hoping the war would be over by the end of the year, Johnson ignored the advice, financing the war and the Great Society with budget deficits.

Criticism also intensified in Congress. The leading critic was Senator J. William Fulbright of Arkansas. A Rhodes scholar and a former president of the University of Arkansas, Fulbright was the quintessential cerebral southerner, soft-spoken yet eloquent, politically astute but willing to take moral stands. Elected to the Senate in 1944, Fulbright was a close friend and ally of Lyndon Johnson. But by 1965 he was alarmed about the war. Determined to expose it to public scrutiny, Fulbright convened the Senate Foreign Relations Committee for special hearings on the war in February 1966. Forever after Johnson referred to Fulbright as "Halfbright," a nickname Harry Truman had coined for him. Hoping to upstage the hearings, Johnson convened another conference in Honolulu on February 6–8, 1966, where he met with Nguyen Van Thieu, Nguyen Cao Ky, Henry Cabot Lodge (who had replaced Maxwell Taylor as ambassador), Maxwell Taylor, and William Westmoreland.

The Honolulu Conference did not overshadow Fulbright's hearings. Dean Rusk testified for hours spouting the administration line about external communist aggression and saving Southeast Asia. Fulbright countered that the war had really started out as "a war of liberation from colonial rule . . . [which] became a civil war between the Diem government and the Vietcong. . . . I think it is an oversimplification . . . to say that this is a clear-cut aggression by North Vietnam." Fulbright brought in James Gavin, who opposed escalation and called for the enclave strategy instead of offensive operations. Fulbright's trump card was George Kennan, the former ambassador to the Soviet Union who was architect of the post–World War II containment policy. Kennan testified that Vietnam was far away, only tangential to American strategic interests, and that the United States "should liquidate the involvement just as soon as possible."

The hearings changed few minds. Wayne Morse pushed a bill to repeal the Gulf of Tonkin Resolution, but it was voted down ninety-two to five. The Senate approved another $12 billion for the war. Westmoreland launched search-and-destroy missions in all four corps zones. More than 1,700 American troops died in the first three months of 1966, but they killed 15,000 enemy troops. Ho Chi Minh replaced each one, deploying the NVA 324B and 324C Divisions into South Vietnam. The death tolls steadily mounted in 1966, and at midyear Westmoreland asked for 100,000 more troops, hoping to have 480,000 in the field by mid-1967 and as many as 680,000 by early 1968. The joint chiefs urged Johnson to expand the Rolling Thunder raids to include petroleum storage facilities in Hanoi and Haiphong. The raids took place at the end of June 1966.

By that time the war was taking its toll on the administration. George Ball, a longtime critic, finally resigned as undersecretary of state. McGeorge Bundy, the national security adviser, decided the troop buildup had assumed ridiculous proportions. He left the White House in 1966 to head the Ford Foundation. Johnson replaced him with Walt Rostow, who still preached military victory over North Vietnam and the modernization of South Vietnam. Westmoreland reported victory after victory to Johnson. But Lyndon Johnson was frustrated and confused. He had a sinking feeling that he was losing control of the war. One night in June 1966 he could not get to sleep. Pacing the floor and cursing, he woke up Lady Bird and complained that "victory after victory doesn't really mean victory. I can't get out. I can't finish it with what I have got. So what the hell do I do?"

7

The Mirage of Progress, 1966–1967

It lies within our grasp—the enemy's hopes are bankrupt.
With your support we will give you a success that will im-
pact not only on South Vietnam, but on every emerging
nation in the world.
     —William Westmoreland, November 1967

For the first time in history a battlefield commander, in the middle of a war, addressed a joint session of Congress. President Johnson summoned Westmoreland home to discuss the latest requests for more ground troops. On April 28, 1967, his starched uniform tattooed with medals and ribbons from other wars, the general stood ramrod straight and begged for time and support. The greatest problem American boys faced in Vietnam was not enemy troops, he argued, but the will to continue at home: "These men believe in what they are doing. . . . Backed at home by resolve, confidence, patience, determination, and continued support, we will prevail in Vietnam over the Communist aggressor." The thunderous applause reminded many of Douglas MacArthur's "old soldiers never die" speech. Pivoting in a crisp about-face, Westmoreland saluted Vice President Hubert Humphrey and Speaker of the House John McCormack, about-faced again and saluted the entire Congress, and then marched out of the House. It was great theater, "a good speech" in the words of Senator J. William Fulbright. "From the military standpoint it was fine," he said. "The point is the policy that put our boys over there."

Whatever Westmoreland was saying publicly, his private comments had frightened people at the White House. In response to a question from Robert McNamara about how long it would take to achieve victory, Westmoreland said that it could be five years. The enemy was far more determined than anyone had anticipated. Enemy supplies were getting through in ever-increasing volumes. The bombing campaigns over the Ho Chi Minh Trail did not succeed in cutting off the Vietcong and North Vietnamese troops in South Vietnam from their supply bases above the seventeenth parallel. They just intensified communist efforts to keep the supplies flowing by constantly improving the transportation system into South Vietnam. In 1963 the Ho Chi Minh Trail was primitive,

In spite of the most intensive bombing campaign in history, U.S. Air Force and Navy pilots never succeeded in destroying, or even temporarily closing, the Ho Chi Minh Trail. The flow of troops and supplies from North Vietnam into South Vietnam went on virtually uninterrupted.

MARC RIBOUD/MAGNUM PHOTOS

requiring a physically demanding, month-long march of eighteen-hour days to reach the south. But by the spring of 1964, the North Vietnamese began dramatic improvements in the trail. They put nearly 500,000 peasants to work full and part time, building and repairing roads. In one year the peasants built hundreds of miles of all-weather roads complete with underground fuel storage tanks, hospitals, and supply warehouses. They built ten separate roads for every main transportation route. By the time the war ended, the Ho Chi Minh Trail had 12,500 miles of high-quality roads, complete with pontoon bridges that could be removed by day and reinstalled at night and miles of bamboo trellises covering the roads and hiding the trucks.

Despite the most intense aerial pounding in history, the Ho Chi Minh Trail served continuously as the communist lifeline. As early as mid-1965 the North Vietnamese could move 5,000 men and 400 tons of supplies into South Vietnam every month. Robert McNamara estimated that by mid-1967 more than 12,000 trucks were winding their way up and down the trail. By 1974 the North Vietnamese had even managed to build 3,125 miles of fuel pipelines down the trail to keep their army functioning in South Vietnam. Three of the pipelines came all the way out of Laos and deep into South Vietnam without being detected.

North Vietnam had an agricultural economy with few industries vital to the war effort. Anticipating an escalation of the bombing, the North Vietnamese built enough underground tanks and dispersed them widely enough to have a survival level of gasoline, diesel fuel, and oil lubricants. In 1965 and 1966 North Vietnam began evacuating nonessential people from cities and relocating industries—machine shops, textile mills, and other businesses—to the mountains, jungles, and caves. Home manufacturing filled the modest need for consumer goods. By late 1967 Hanoi's population had dropped from 1 million to 250,000 people. A little planning had robbed the American pilots of their effectiveness.

The air war was doomed. The only targets that mattered were bridges, roads, and transportation centers, and almost as soon as they were bombed the North Vietnamese repaired them. They replaced steel bridges with ferries and easily repairable pontoon bridges. A long history of fighting the drought and flooding in the Red River Valley had created a cooperative spirit among the North Vietnamese that served them well. Political teams organized people to repair roads, help troops and supplies get across rivers, and build air-raid shelters, bunkers, tunnels, and trenches. American pilots found themselves returning to the same places again and again to bomb the same targets.

The bombing was, to be sure, devastating. During the war the United States dropped 1 million tons of explosives on North Vietnam and 1.5 million tons on the Ho Chi Minh Trail. In 1967 the bombing raids killed or wounded 2,800 people in North Vietnam each month. The bombers destroyed every industrial, transportation, and communications facility built in North Vietnam since 1954, badly damaged three major cities and twelve provincial capitals, reduced agricultural output, and set the economy back a decade. Malnutrition was widespread in North Vietnam in 1967. But because North Vietnam was overwhelmingly agricultural—and subsistence agriculture at that—the bombing did not have the devastating economic effect it would have had on a centralized, industrial economy. Moreover, the Soviet Union and China gave North Vietnam a blank check, willingly replacing whatever the United States bombers destroyed.

Weather and problems of distance also limited the air war. In 1967 the United States could keep about 300 aircraft over North Vietnam or Laos for about thirty minutes each day. It was mathematically impossible to stop the infiltration over the thousands of miles of roads of the Ho Chi Minh Trail, especially with hundreds of thousands of Vietnamese repairing damage on a moment's notice. Torrential rains, thick cloud cover, and heavy fogs also hampered the bombing. Trucks from North Vietnam could move when the aircraft from the carriers in the South China Sea could not.

Throughout the war North Vietnam steadily improved its air defense system until they had the most elaborate air defenses in the history of the world. They built 200 Soviet SA-2 surface-to-air missile sites, trained pilots to fly MiG-17s and MiG-21s, deployed 7,000 antiaircraft batteries, and distributed automatic and semiautomatic weapons to millions of people with instructions to shoot at American aircraft. The North Vietnamese air defense system hampered the air war in three ways. First, American pilots had to fly at higher altitudes, and that reduced their accuracy. Second, they were busy dodging missiles, and that consumed "time over target" and reduced the effectiveness of each individual sortie. Finally, they spent much of their time firing at missile installations and antiaircraft guns instead of supply lines. The air war did not bludgeon North Vietnam into submission; it did not even keep food out of Vietcong mouths, bullets out of NVA rifles, or North Vietnamese troops out of South Vietnam. In 1967 alone North Vietnam moved more than 90,000 troops into South Vietnam in spite of the heaviest air bombardment in history.

The diplomatic dimension of the bombing assumed more importance as the war progressed. The North Vietnamese shot down more than 900 American aircraft, and hundreds of pilots were taken prisoner after ejecting from their crippled planes. Those prisoners of war (POWs) became diplomatic hostages, pawns in the war. The North Vietnamese knew how badly the United States wanted to bring those POWs home, and they eventually used them as diplomatic bargaining chips. The Jason Study, commissioned by Robert McNamara in 1966, initially confirmed the effectiveness of the bombing campaigns, which only encouraged administration officials in their convictions that U.S. air power could bludgeon North Vietnam into submission.

The reaction to the report was predictable. Dean Rusk and Walt Rostow believed that the answer was more bombing. Until May 1965, American bombing raids were confined to targets south of the twentieth parallel. After May 1965 Johnson lifted several restrictions, although he still ordered American pilots to hit no targets within thirty miles of Hanoi or the Chinese border or within ten miles of Haiphong. In April 1966 the operational area was expanded to all of North Vietnam, and by the end of June the list of targets included petroleum storage facilities in Hanoi and Haiphong. Rolling Thunder attacks expanded in February 1967 to include Hanoi-area factories, railroad yards, power plants, and airfields. The United States flew 25,000 sorties over North Vietnam in 1965, but that number increased to 79,000 in 1966 and 108,000 in 1967. The United States stayed with the bombing campaign because it was cheaper, in dollars and lives, than ground combat and therefore more acceptable at home.

Robert McNamara was ready to try another technological tool. The only sure way of stopping infiltration across the Demilitarized Zone from North Vietnam was to station huge numbers of troops just south of the seventeenth parallel. Instead, McNamara proposed construction of an electronic barrier. Critics dubbed it "McNamara's Wall." Against their better judgment, the Third Marine Division agreed to construct the barrier—a twenty-five-mile bulldozed strip of jungle complete with acoustic sensors, land mines, infrared intrusion detectors, booby traps, and electronic wires along the northern border of South Vietnam to detect NVA infiltration. The marines constructed a bulldozed strip of land 660 yards wide and 8.2 miles long from Con Thien to the sea, but the whole project never really got off the ground, a victim of its own ambitious technology and opposition from the military. The marines felt it would tie too many troops down in static positions waiting for the NVA troops to penetrate the electronic barrier. They also assumed that even if it worked, the North Vietnamese would just go around it through Laos. The whole idea struck the North Vietnamese as silly. "What is the use of barbed wire fences and electronic barriers," said General Tran Do, "when we can penetrate even Tan Son Nhut air base outside Saigon?"

It was that kind of war. For most American combat soldiers, the Vietnam experience proved to be a combination of surrealistic incongruity, boredom, suffering, and danger. At the beginning of the buildup in 1965 and early 1966, most troops arrived in South Vietnam by ship after long voyages from the United States. Their journey to war was not unlike that of their fathers, who had gone to Europe and the Pacific in large, crowded troop transports. By the end of 1966, however, most of the major military units had deployed to Vietnam, and replacement troops arrived by commercial jet. With more than 1 million American soldiers arriving or leaving the country each year, the military did not possess enough planes or ships to carry the load, so they contracted the job out to commercial airlines. Soldiers went to war in air-conditioned jets, drinking cocktails and beer along the way and ogling the short-skirted stewardesses. Recalling his own trip to South Vietnam via Braniff Airlines, Rob Riggan wrote in *Free Fire Zone:* "We might have been over Gary, Indiana. . . . Stewardesses with polished legs and miniskirts took our pillows away from us. As we trooped out the door, they said: 'Good luck! See you in 365 days.' "

At the sixth-month point in a soldier's tour of duty, he was back on the jetliner, drinking highballs and staring at the stewardesses, now known as beautiful "round eyes from the world." The planes took the troops on "R and R"—Rest and Recreation—since the military provided a paid vacation for its men, jetting them to Honolulu, Hong Kong, Tokyo, Bangkok, Manila, Singapore, Taipei, Penang, Kuala Lumpur, and Australia, putting them up in luxury hotels and letting them do whatever they wanted. Many of the men spent the week with their wives, who were flown in, while others dissipated the time with booze and prostitutes. But at the end of the week, they left the air-conditioned hotels, climbed aboard the commercial jets, and returned to the combat zone, hoping to stay alive for six more months and to return to the world of round-eyed stewardesses.

Most of the jets landed at such large American bases as Bien Hoa and Danang. When the troops deplaned, pungent odors of burning excrement assaulted their noses. Base outhouses covered 55-gallon drums that collected the wastes. When the barrels filled, rear-echelon soldiers poured in kerosene and set them on fire, filling the air with a distinctive smell most troops would never forget. One soldier remembered that Vietnam smelled like "sweat, shit, jet fuel, and fish sauce all mixed together." In the moist humidity, the odors seemed to hang permanently in the air.

After several days of orientation at the big bases, the soldiers in combat groups made their way—via jeeps, trucks, or helicopters—out to their respective military units. More than 60 percent of the land that greeted them consisted of heavily forested mountains, hills, slopes, plateaus, and valleys, stretching from the seventeenth parallel south to within fifty miles of Saigon. Sparsely populated, the uplands provided perfect cover and staging areas for North Vietnamese regulars. The remainder of South Vietnam consisted of heavily populated lowlands where Vietcong guerrillas enjoyed the protection of local villages.

From base camps, combat soldiers went after enemy troops in "search-and-destroy" operations. They would often be "inserted" into an area by helicopter and then patrol for anywhere from two or three days to a month at a time. Troops often hacked their way through thick uplands vegetation, tall elephant grass, or flooded rice paddies, loaded down by 80-pound packs, heavy, armor-lined flak-jacket vests, rifles, mortars, ammunition, and canteens. Infantrymen called the patrols "humping the boonies." During the monsoon season, rain fell constantly, and soldiers had to put up with perpetually wet feet and sometimes "immersion foot"—swollen, blistered, and decaying flesh. If they marched through standing water, leaches burrowed into the skin of their legs and groin. The ninety-degree-plus heat and humidity sapped their strength, and many troops were unable to carry enough water to keep themselves from becoming dehydrated. In heavy, canopied jungles, the air resembled a sauna. During Operation Virginia Ridge near the Demilitarized Zone in May 1969, Bravo Company of the First Battalion of the Third Marine Regiment lost 65 of its 147 men during the first three days of the operation, even though there was no contact with enemy troops. Heat exhaustion forced the evacuation of nearly half the company.

Land mines posed the greatest threat to patrolling American combat troops. The Vietcong placed land mines everywhere, always making sure to let local villagers know where they were. Knowing that accidental peasant casualties would diminish Vietcong influence among the people, they taught villagers how to identify mine locations. Villagers

The search-and-destroy patrols by U.S. soldiers involved days of fatiguing movement through rice paddies and jungle trails, battling insects, leeches, heat, and monsoons and, periodically, bloody firefights with an elusive enemy.
UPI/BETTMANN

often helped the Vietcong manufacture the land mines out of unexploded American ordnance and artillery shell casings. American soldiers were convinced that rural peasants supported the Vietcong because so few peasants, and so many GIs, stepped on the mines. Land mines caused as many as one-third of all American casualties during the war.

Despite all this effort, American soldiers had trouble locating communist troops. The tactical initiative remained with the enemy. North Vietnam's strategy was based on choosing when and where to fight. If United States military pressure became too intense, the communists simply melted back into the jungles or into sanctuaries in Cambodia, Laos, and North Vietnam. Many of Westmoreland's larger operations did not find the enemy in concentrated numbers. Worried that enemy forces were preparing to attack the major cities, Westmoreland launched Operation Attleboro in mid-September 1966. Troops probed the "Iron Triangle," or War Zone D, a sixty-square-mile area of rice paddies, dense jungle, rubber plantations, and underground tunnels twenty miles northwest of Saigon. Since late in the 1940s the Iron Triangle had been a communist stronghold. American troops encountered the Vietcong Ninth Division and the NVA 101st Regiment. When the battle was over in mid-

November, Westmoreland claimed 1,106 enemy casualties, but he had not trapped and destroyed the communists.

In January 1967 the First and Twenty-fifth Infantry Divisions, the 173d Airborne Brigade, the Eleventh Armored Cavalry, and several ARVN units—a total of more than 35,000 troops—moved into the Iron Triangle again. They spent several weeks removing civilians before going after the Vietcong. Designating the campaign Operation Cedar Falls, they laid waste to the whole region, including the village of Ben Suc, which gained notoriety in the American press after being completely leveled. When the dust settled, another 720 Vietcong were dead and most of their tunnels, elaborately constructed over the previous twenty years, were destroyed. But given the size of the operation, the body count disappointed Westmoreland. More frustrating was its aftermath. Even as American troops were leaving the Iron Triangle, they saw Vietcong with AK-47 rifles walking back into the area. Journalist Malcolm Browne decided that Westmoreland's strategy was "like a sledgehammer on a floating cork. Somehow the cork refused to stay down."

Westmoreland followed up Operation Cedar Falls with Operation Junction City, an assault on War Zone C in Tay Ninh Province near the Cambodian border. More than 45,000 American and ARVN troops attacked in late February 1967. The operation lasted nearly three months before the Vietcong Ninth Division escaped across the border. By that time the division had suffered more than 2,700 casualties. But even that number seemed paltry compared to the investment. The American attack had been unable to trap Vietcong main units. Still, the deputy MACV commander, William DePuy, claimed that Junction City delivered "a blow from which the VC in this area may never recover."

Official MACV studies indicated that only 1 percent of all army and Marine Corps search-and-destroy sweeps into the countryside ever resulted in contact with the enemy, and that in 85 percent of all firefights the first shot was fired by enemy troops. The difficulty American soldiers had in finding enemy troops and seizing the tactical initiative led to extraordinary, and ultimately counterproductive, attempts to apply firepower to the problem. Looking back on the war, Robert Komer, the American pacification expert and a deputy to General William Westmoreland, said: "One of our greatest military frustrations in Vietnam was . . . pinning down an elusive enemy. . . . Hanoi was able to control the rate of its own losses by hit-and-run tactics, evasion and use of sanctuaries, which led to military stalemate."

Difficulty in finding enemy troops was not an accident. The communists tried to fight only when they had the advantage—a regiment against a battalion or a battalion against a company. Long before the battle, they rehearsed in scale-model exercises, hid supplies of rice, ammunition, and medicine, and camouflaged bunkers and tunnels. They moved to the battle site in small groups and then assembled for action. They preselected several withdrawal routes; the goal was always to engage the Americans and then break away before the artillery and aerial bombardment began. Soon after the battle started, they began a withdrawal that would not stop until after twelve hours of hard marching in the jungle. More often than not the Americans would be unable to find them.

To deal with that frustration, American policymakers let their faith in technology reach absurd levels. As the fighting escalated in 1966 and 1967, so did the urgency of locating enemy troops. Westmoreland expanded Operation Ranch Hand. C-123 transport planes carrying several chemical agents, particularly dioxin-laced Agent Orange, sprayed suspected enemy strongholds with the herbicides. Eventually, Operation Ranch Hand dumped 19 million gallons of chemical poison on nearly 6 million acres, more than 20 percent of the entire land area of South Vietnam.

Westmoreland also wanted to find some way of separating peasants from communist troops. The creation of "free fire zones" was the answer. Labeled "specified strike zones" after 1965, "free fire zones" were described by the Pentagon as "known enemy strongholds virtually uninhabited by noncombatants. They are areas which have been cleared by responsible local Vietnamese authority for firing on specific military targets." The creation of free fire zones was an attempt to design the war along conventional military lines, with enemy forces and friendly forces occupying separate areas. The conveniently labeled "enemy areas" were then subjected to the full application of American firepower.

A badly flawed logic lay behind the free fire zones. Isolation of enemy forces was accomplished not by combat and territorial acquisition but by computer definition. Traditional Vietcong strongholds were defined as being free of noncombatants. Anyone living there was the enemy. In places not identified as Vietcong strongholds, American and ARVN troops relocated civilians. Loudspeakers, aerial leaflet drops, and infantry unit sweeps warned inhabitants to evacuate before the killing machine arrived. Once inhabitants had been warned and evacuation attempts made, MACV declared the region a free fire zone and opened up. By 1967 the free fire zone map at Westmoreland's headquarters was so filled with designated areas outlined in red that the whole country seemed a strike zone.

When American troops went on search-and-destroy missions, they often destroyed villages suspected of harboring enemy troops. Early in August 1965, for example, marines pursued Vietcong troops into the village of Cam Ne in I Corps. Unable to find the guerrillas, the frustrated marines, using Zippo lighters, burned 150 village huts in their futile search. Morley Safer of CBS News filmed the entire event, and Walter Cronkite broadcast it on the evening news. "Zippo squads" were common during the war. Civilians who lost their homes were relocated to refugee camps.

Occasionally, the hunt for enemy troops assumed surrealistic proportions. During Operation Cedar Falls, the villagers of Ben Suc got a taste of the killing machine. A known Vietcong refuge, Ben Suc was doomed. American troops evacuated 6,100 people—no doubt Vietcong as well as civilians—and relocated them to a refugee camp at Phu Loi. A huge sign greeted them: "Welcome to the reception center for refugees fleeing communism." Engineers from the First Infantry Division brought in heavy equipment, including huge Rome plows, and leveled the village. They destroyed every hut, every building, every piece of vegetation. They left behind twenty acres of dust and 6,100 bitter peasants.

One of the most sensational incidents occurred at Ben Tre, the capital city of Kien Hoa Province. In February 1968 Vietcong troops overran the city and dug in against an awesome display of American firepower. After massive air strikes and naval bombardments, American and ARVN troops recaptured Ben Tre, but by that time the town did not exist anymore. More than 600 civilians were dead, 1,500 seriously wounded, and 4,000 homeless. Journalist Peter Arnett asked an American major about such indiscriminate use of explosives. His answer was the most famous quotation of the war: "It became necessary to destroy the town in order to save it."

The collective impact of such enormous firepower was catastrophic. Arc Light campaigns—B-52 raids inside South Vietnam—brought a level of destruction similar to tactical nuclear weapons. Six B-52s flying in formation at 30,000 feet could drop a bomb load that would pulverize almost everything within an area of about 1.5 square miles. Often Vietnamese peasants and enemy troops did not even know the B-52s were coming. They called B-52 strikes "whispering death." The combined effect of naval shelling, B-52 Arc Light raids, 300 daily fighter-bomber sorties, helicopter gunships, howitzers, and mortars equaled the detonation of 3.5 million pounds of explosives in South Vietnam each day of the war. General William DePuy summed the strategy up perfectly in the spring of 1966: "The solution in Vietnam is more bombs, more shells, more napalm . . . until the other side cracks and gives up."

But civilian peasants, not the Vietcong and North Vietnamese, cracked first. Americans failed to understand that the village was the soul of Vietnamese culture, the key to the "hearts and minds" of the people. The village was where they were born, where the bones of their ancestors were buried, where mud and water produced the rice that fed their children. Peasants expected to spend all their lives in their villages. American forces destroyed the peasants' way of life. By the end of 1966 more than 2 million South Vietnamese had lost their homes in accidental bombardments or been moved out of free fire zones before soldiers intentionally destroyed their homes. The number of homeless reached 3 million in 1967 and almost 4 million in 1968.

And that was not the worst of it. Between 1965 and 1972 more than 400,000 civilians died in South Vietnam and another 1 million were wounded, most from the "friendly fire" of American forces. One-third of the South Vietnamese population, and nearly 50 percent of the rural population, either lost their homes or were killed or wounded by the United States firepower. South Vietnamese civilian casualties reached almost two-thirds the number of Vietcong and North Vietnamese killed. In Quang Ngai Province of I Corps in 1967, the artillery and aerial bombardment was so intense that by year's end more than 300 of the province's 450 villages had been completely obliterated and the number of peasants killed or wounded from indiscriminate shelling was averaging 1,000 people a week. When journalist Neil Sheehan asked Westmoreland if the civilian casualties bothered him, the general replied, "Yes, Neil, it is a problem, but it does deprive the enemy of the population, doesn't it?"

In more subtle ways the American presence disrupted the social fabric of traditional Vietnamese society. The destructiveness of the war drove millions of South Vietnamese into the cities, but so did the billions of dollars being pumped into the country. The entire urban Vietnamese economy revolved around providing services to Americans. By 1967 most Vietnamese workers were either Vietcong, ARVN soldiers, or service workers for Americans. So Vietnamese employees of the United States government would have something to spend their money on, the United States brought in a cornucopia of consumer goods—transistor radios, televisions, motor scooters, and watches. Indigenous Vietnamese industries shriveled up and died; inflation skyrocketed; and corruption was rampant.

The idea of winning the "hearts and minds" of these peasants through pacification was absurd given this level of destruction and social change. Pacification became a bureaucratic backwater of the war, a hodgepodge of programs to which the United States paid lip service only. The most prominent civilian pacification program was the Agency for International Development's $500 million-a-year effort to build schools, health clinics, and agricultural stations. At the same time the CIA had its own pacification program—political action teams of trained South Vietnamese cadres whose mission was to find and eliminate the Vietcong infrastructure. Army Special Forces conducted pacification programs among Montagnard peoples. And in response to American pressure, South Vietnam launched its own pacification effort. The New Life Hamlet Program, successor to the defunct Strategic Hamlet Program, was just as unsuccessful because it forcibly relocated peasants to secure areas. ARVN troops brutally carried out the relocations. In 1966 the New Life Hamlet Program gave way to the Ap Doi Moi Program, which translated as "Really New Life Hamlets." Like its predecessors, it was riddled with official corruption and angered peasants who did not want to leave their ancestral homelands.

Westmoreland chafed at the numbers of civilians, CIA agents, and ARVN troops engaged in such disjointed pacification efforts, and he yearned to bring them all under the MACV umbrella. In November 1966 Ambassador Henry Cabot Lodge created the Office of Civil Operations to coordinate pacification, but Westmoreland kept up his demands and in May 1967 President Johnson finally gave in. He established a new agency—Civil Operations and Revolutionary Development Support (CORDS)—to control all pacification efforts. Placing CORDS under the direct control of Westmoreland and MACV militarized the pacification effort.

Johnson named Robert Komer as director of CORDS and deputy commander to William Westmoreland. Born in Chicago in 1922, Komer was a CIA veteran with a Harvard MBA who arrived at the National Security Council in 1961 preaching the gospel of pacification. He was self-confident, pushy, and abrasive, nicknamed the "Blowtorch." According to one of Henry Cabot Lodge's aides, Komer was "a Guildenstern at the court of Lyndon I—willing to please his President at all costs." By 1966 Komer was a special assistant to Johnson. He insisted that South Vietnam would have to win peasant loyalty before a long-term political settlement was possible.

Komer whipped CORDS into shape and launched into pacification. Soon there were 8,000 Americans directly engaged in pacification, and within months Komer claimed progress in winning "hearts and minds." To prove his point Komer established the Hamlet Evaluation Survey, an elaborate, computerized system for measuring the number of South Vietnamese peasants living in areas "controlled" by the Saigon government. Using eighteen political, economic, and military variables, the survey classified villages into one of five categories, depending on the depth of loyalty to Saigon. At the end of 1967 Komer confidently told Johnson that approximately 67 percent of the South Vietnamese were loyal to their government. Although Komer was proud of his report, antiwar critics were suspicious. In 1963 General Paul Harkins had also declared 67 percent of the peasants loyal to Saigon. Years later, Komer reflected on how completely American policy failed to perceive reality in South Vietnam: "Politically, we failed to give due weight to the popular appeal of the Viet Cong . . . or the depth of factionalism among traditional South Vietnamese elites. We only grasped belatedly the significance of the steady attrition of GVN authority . . . in the countryside . . . which was directly linked to how the Viet Cong conducted the war."

All the pacification efforts foundered on the strategic reality of the war. For every American dollar spent on pacification, nearly one hundred were spent on military operations. For every American worker engaged in land reform, health care, and education, sixty soldiers were busy blowing the country up. Neither the United States nor South Vietnam could provide villagers security from the Vietcong. During the last seven months of 1966, the Vietcong murdered or kidnapped more than 3,000 Revolutionary Development personnel. Whatever good the pacification programs achieved was undone by the indiscriminate bombardment. Four million peasants were driven from their ancestral villages. Nothing could compensate for that.

The South Vietnamese government continued to frustrate Americans. Nguyen Cao Ky and Nguyen Van Thieu consolidated their power in Saigon, but they had rivals farther north. Buddhists, especially in their northern strongholds around Hue, resented Ky and Thieu. Both were Roman Catholics with deep ties to the French; both were critical of Buddhist values; both were military officers. Led by Thich Tri Quang, the premier Buddhist monk in the country, northern Buddhists wanted a civilian government sympathetic to Buddhist culture and Vietnamese independence. From the day they took power in 1965, Nguyen Cao Ky and Nguyen Van Thieu faced political rivals in the north.

The most prominent was Nguyen Chanh Thi, the "Warlord of the North." A Buddhist with close ties to Thich Tri Quang, Thi hated Ky. Thi had risen through ARVN ranks to become commander of I Corps in 1965. American marines in I Corps respected Thi for his courage and aggressiveness. In March 1966 Ky traveled to Hue for some military conferences, but Thi snubbed him, calling Ky "my little brother" and ridiculing him in public. Ky returned to Saigon seething with anger; he relieved Nguyen Chanh Thi of his command and put him under house arrest. It was just the signal the Buddhists had been waiting for. Thich Tri Quang organized widespread protest demonstrations throughout the northern regions of South Vietnam, claiming that the military government was capricious and dictatorial and calling for creation of a civilian, constitutional democracy. At the end of March, protesters seized the radio stations in Hue and Danang. Promising to "liberate Hue and Danang from the communists," Ky led two marine battalions into Danang and waited for the protests to die out. When they did not die out, he attacked Danang and found himself fighting his way through ARVN troops still loyal to Thi. The battle lasted more than a week and included house-to-house combat in Danang. In Hue demonstrators attacked the United States Consulate, and Ky had to take military control of the city early in June.

The civil war in Danang and Hue in 1966 raised more doubts in the United States about Nguyen Cao Ky. Although he had broken the back of the Buddhist political movement, it had been expensive, especially in terms of American public opinion. American troop levels were approaching 300,000 people, and casualties were mounting. The images broadcast on television of South Vietnamese fighting South Vietnamese did little to strengthen American support for the war.

The paltry numbers of ARVN casualties created similar results. By the end of 1965 there were supposedly 514,000 men serving in the South Vietnamese armed forces along with 184,000 Americans. In 1966 more than 6,000 American soldiers died in Vietnam, as did nearly 12,000 South Vietnamese soldiers. But in 1967, as the pace of the war quickened, the statistics changed. American troop levels climbed to 485,000 men at the end of 1967, and ARVN forces went up to just under 800,000 soldiers. But that year nearly 10,000 Americans died, compared to 12,716 South Vietnamese. In the election campaign of 1964 President Johnson had promised that "American boys shouldn't die in a war Asian boys should be fighting," but that was exactly what was happening.

The Buddhist crisis of 1966 and the inability of ARVN to fight at an acceptable level convinced American leaders that Nguyen Cao Ky had to go. He was too unpredictable, and he had failed to get ARVN into sustained combat. Ambassador Henry Cabot Lodge recommended replacing Ky, and Westmoreland concurred. Nguyen Van Thieu decided to run for president in 1967. The decision caught Ky off guard. He viewed Thieu as a rival. He liked to irritate Thieu by arriving at meetings early and parking his helicopter on the pad Thieu intended to use. The prospects of both of them running for president frightened American leaders, who had nightmares of a divided military, a civil war, or a weak civilian candidate emerging to take control. They convinced Ky to accept the vice presidency.

The Thieu-Ky ticket won the presidential elections of 1967, but it was hardly a showcase for democracy. They arrested Buddhist leaders during the campaign and denied serious rivals positions on the ballot. The election was marked by voter coercion, multiple voting by ARVN troops, fraudulent vote counts, and widespread stuffing of ballot boxes. With all that, Thieu and Ky managed to secure only 35 percent of the vote and win, while a virtually unknown Buddhist peace candidate, Truong Dinh Dzu, came in second with 17 percent. Johnson praised the elections as the "birth of democracy in Southeast Asia," but network broadcasts carried another message: The sideshow of South Vietnamese politics had concluded another performance. Most South Vietnamese observers came to the same conclusion. Vietnamese tradition held that political authority was a mandate from heaven. Legitimate political leaders should have overwhelming support from the people, and 35 percent was hardly a heavenly mandate.

Although few people outside Hanoi realized it, the war was reaching a turning point at the end of 1967. American military officials in Saigon believed the Vietcong and North Vietnamese were approaching the long-awaited "crossover point" at which they could not put troops in the field fast enough to replace their dead. By the end of 1967 Westmoreland estimated that more than 220,000 enemy troops were dead. Robert Komer said, "Wastefully, expensively, but nonetheless indisputedly, we are winning the war. . . . We are grinding the enemy down by sheer weight and mass."

In the first half of 1967 the body count was up to 7,316 Vietcong and North Vietnamese a month. MACV's attrition charts, which did not include local enemy militia, showed that the number of enemy troops had declined from 275,000 men in late 1966 to 242,000 in mid-1967. In response to a question about the crossover point, Westmoreland answered in August 1967, "Enemy armed strength is falling, not spectacularly and not mathematically provable, but every indication suggests this. . . . There is evidence that we may have reached the crossover point." Victor Krulak was unimpressed. He remembered that in 1963 General Paul Harkins made a similar claim, describing a decline in Vietcong from 124,000 men to 102,000. No such decline had taken place.

Krulak realized that by 1967 the war had become a stalemate. The United States was spending $2 billion per month on the war, and although the communists had taken severe casualties, the United States had come nowhere near killing the 250,000 troops a year necessary to slow down the enemy. In Hanoi, Ho Chi Minh knew, however, that stalemate meant victory for them and defeat for the United States. They were willing to stay with the fight indefinitely—years or even decades if necessary—but the United States was not. An endless war in Vietnam was politically intolerable.

But the data convinced Westmoreland and Komer. They also saw proof in the growing success of the Chieu Hoi, or Open Arms Program. Launched in 1963 by Robert Thompson, Chieu Hoi offered amnesty to Vietcong and attracted thousands of deserters by 1967—Komer claimed more than 40,000. By the end of the war in 1973, supposedly 159,741 Vietcong deserters changed sides. Critics called the program "R and R [rest and recreation] for Communists." Most genuine defectors were low-level Vietcong who had never been enthusiastic about their commitment; the others were Vietcong plants trying to infiltrate the program. Some changed sides as many as five times during the war. William E. Colby, the pacification leader and later CIA chief, estimated that in 1969 and 1970 only 17,000 of the reported 79,000 Chieu Hoi converts were sincere. But Westmoreland and Komer were true believers.

There was other evidence as well, good enough at least for true believers. The Vietcong were having trouble by 1967 getting new recruits, primarily because so many millions of South Vietnamese were in refugee camps. The population of Saigon had swelled from 1.4 million in 1962 to 4 million in 1967, and it was also more difficult for the Vietcong to get new recruits out of the cities. Intelligence reports also indicated that Main Force Vietcong battalions were no longer at peak strength of

600–700 troops. Westmoreland took comfort in that, even though Hanoi replaced the Vietcong with regular North Vietnamese troops in numbers sufficient to augment total communist strength.

On March 20–21, 1967, Westmoreland met with President Johnson and several other administration officials at Guam to discuss the war. The previous June, Johnson had agreed to increase American ground troops to 430,000 by mid-1967, but at Guam, Westmoreland asked for more. A week later he suggested 542,000, calling it a "Minimum Essential Force." He also let Johnson know that what he really needed was an "Optimum Force" of 678,000, which would finish off the enemy in about three years. Johnson could not give Westmoreland 678,000 troops without calling up the reserves and raising draft calls to 60,000 men a month, both of which would raise the ire of Congress and inspire more vehement antiwar protests. Westmoreland would have to make do with 542,000 men. The Vietnam War was already bigger than Korea.

But when he got back to Saigon, Westmoreland learned that MACV intelligence estimated that Vietcong–North Vietnamese troop strength, including paramilitary and local self-defense troops, exceeded 500,000 people. The general was visibly shaken and wondered, "What am I going to tell the press? What am I going to tell Congress? What is the press going to do with this? What am I going to tell the president?" Still confident of victory, Westmoreland decided on a simple solution: Don't count the paramilitary and self-defense troops. He did not believe they had much impact on the war anyway, but more important than that, "The people in Washington were not sophisticated enough to understand and evaluate this thing and neither was the media."

Although Westmoreland's confidence in military victory continued to inspire Johnson, Rusk, and Rostow, there were growing defections. Throughout late 1966 and early 1967 Henry Cabot Lodge grew skeptical of Westmoreland. The undisciplined application of artillery and air power was wreaking havoc throughout South Vietnam. One American officer said, "It was as if we were trying to build a house with a bulldozer and wrecking crane." Lodge decided that Westmoreland was applying World War II tactics to a modern guerrilla war and that he was incapable of incorporating political variables into his strategic thinking. In April 1967 Lodge retired to Boston.

Lodge's replacement was Ellsworth Bunker. Heir to the National Sugar Refining Company fortune, Bunker was a multimillionaire who became a Democrat during the 1930s. During the 1950s and early 1960s, he filled ambassadorial posts in India, Argentina, and Italy. A New Englander with an obsessive taste for maple syrup (he had it flown fresh to Saigon) and all the reserve of his Yankee forefathers, Bunker earned the title of "Mr. Refrigerator" from the Vietnamese in Saigon. In May 1967 Bunker was prepared to give his entire support to William

Westmoreland and the war effort. With Lodge's departure, Johnson lost his only independent point of view in Saigon.

Sir Robert Thompson, the British expert on counterinsurgency, lost faith as well. Ever since 1961 he had warned against a military solution to the political problem in Vietnam, and when he saw William Westmoreland unleash the killing machine, Thompson knew immediately that the United States was doomed. "American policy in South Vietnam," Thompson warned Henry Cabot Lodge, "is stupid. It doubles the firepower and squares the error. Every artillery shell the United States fires into South Vietnam might kill a Vietcong but will surely alienate a Vietnamese peasant."

Johnson also lost Robert McNamara in 1967. Slowly but surely in 1966 and 1967 McNamara experienced the sickening sensation that he had been wrong, horribly wrong, and that hundreds of thousands of people were dead because of his decisions. The United States could not stop the flow of men and supplies from North Vietnam, not unless America was willing to unload strategic nuclear weapons on North Vietnam and Laos. In October 1966 McNamara wrote a memo warning the president that to "bomb the North sufficiently to make a radical impact on Hanoi's political, economic and social structure would require an effort which we could make but which could not be stomached either by our own people or by world opinion." As far as he was concerned, the United States had played the trump card of air power and lost. More than 11,000 Americans were already dead and another 250 a week were dying. The joint chiefs rejected McNamara's opinion and urged Johnson to stay the course. At the end of October 1966 Johnson flew to Manila to meet with American military officials and the heads of state of South Vietnam, Australia, Thailand, South Korea, and the Philippines. At the end of the conference he issued the Manila Declaration calling for peace in Southeast Asia and cooperative efforts to conquer hunger, disease, and illiteracy, and provide freedom and security for everyone.

On an impulse, Johnson flew from the Philippines to the huge American base at Cam Ranh Bay, South Vietnam, where he waded into GIs shaking hands as if it were an election for county commissioner. The troops received him with so much enthusiasm that Johnson left with a renewed dedication to the war. When he walked back aboard *Air Force One*, Johnson urged the GIs to keep fighting until they had "nailed the coonskin to the wall." But Johnson really did not want to continue the "coon hunt." Throughout 1966 he sent prominent American diplomats around the world with the message that he was ready to discuss "any proposals—four points or fourteen or forty; we will work for a cease-fire now or once discussions have begun." But Ho Chi Minh's position had not changed: End the bombing, withdraw American troops, remove Thieu and Ky from office, and establish a coalition government in South Vietnam that included the National Liberation Front. Johnson remarked to Dean Rusk, " I keep trying to get Ho to the negotiating table. I try writing him, calling him, going through the Russians and the Chinese, and all I hear back is 'Fuck you, Lyndon.' "

Of course Johnson's diplomatic posture had not changed either. The United States still insisted that first North Vietnam had to withdraw its troops from the South and stop supplying the Vietcong. Nor was Johnson willing to accept any political role for the National Liberation Front in South Vietnam. Vice President Hubert Humphrey said it "would be like putting the fox in the chicken coop." All the mediation attempts failed.

Disturbed about the military and diplomatic stalemate, McNamara asked Johnson in May 1967 to stop the air war over North Vietnam, put a cap on troop levels, and seek a diplomatic settlement. The "picture of the world's greatest superpower," he told him, "killing or seriously injuring 1,000 noncombatants a week, while trying to pound a tiny backward nation into submission on an issue whose merits are hotly disputed, is not a pretty one." McNamara was now skeptical of the attrition strategy and Westmoreland's talk of the crossover point. He later recalled: "The point is that it didn't add up. If you took the strength figures and the body count, the defections, the infiltration and what was happening to us, the whole thing . . . didn't add up. . . . How the hell the war went on year after year when we stopped the infiltration or shrunk it and when we had a very high body count. . . . It didn't add up." In the words of the historian Larry Berman, "Hanoi could prolong the war indefinitely by strategically controlling the rate of their losses." Plagued by personal doubts, McNamara commissioned a top-secret study in June 1967. He asked Leslie H. Gelb of Harvard to write a history of American involvement in Vietnam. Morton Halperin, deputy assistant secretary of defense, assisted Gelb. Within a few years their work would become known as the "Pentagon Papers." But at the moment McNamara was asking Gelb to get the study under way, Johnson decided to get McNamara out of his administration. By the end of the summer Johnson managed to position McNamara for the presidency of the World Bank. In November 1967 Robert McNamara resigned.

The disagreement between Westmoreland and McNamara reflected a larger division in Washington politics. On one side were the hard-liners, men like Senators John C. Stennis of Mississippi, Henry Jackson of Washington, Stuart Symington of Missouri, Gale McGee of Wyoming, and Russell Long of Louisiana, all of whom had strong ties to the military. Long lashed out at all those "who encourage the Communists to prolong the war. I swell with pride when I see Old Glory flying from the Capitol. . . . My prayer is that there may never be a white flag of surrender up there." The joint chiefs threatened to resign in mass if Johnson adopted McNamara's proposal for deescalation. In August 1967 Stennis, who chaired the Senate Armed Services Committee, convened hearings on the war. After listening to a parade of military officials, the committee concluded that "civilians had consistently overruled the unanimous recommendations of military commanders and the joint chiefs of staff." Admiral Ulysses S. Grant Sharp later wrote: "We could have flattened every war-making facility in North Vietnam. But the handwringers had center stage. . . . The most powerful country in the world did not have the willpower needed to meet the situation."

While people like Stennis, Jackson, McGee, Symington, Long, and Sharp wanted to lift all the restrictions, Westmoreland and Walt Rostow worked out specific plans. In particular, they wanted to implement heavy American bombing of Vietcong and North Vietnamese sanctuaries in Laos and Cambodia. They also wanted to invade Laos and Cambodia and cut the North Vietnamese supply lines along the Ho Chi Minh Trail. Both men urged Johnson to permit Westmoreland's "hook north of the DMZ" to trap the assembled North Vietnamese troops and stop their operations in I Corps. Finally, they wanted a massive bombing campaign against every military and industrial target in North Vietnam. Withdrawal was unacceptable. Johnson was frustrated with their aggressiveness. To General Earle Wheeler's demand for escalation in the Rolling Thunder raids, Johnson said, "Bomb, bomb, bomb, that's all you know." To Westmoreland's requests for more troops, Johnson said, "When we add divisions, can't the enemy add divisions? If so, where does it all end?"

But increasing numbers of people in the Washington establishment criticized Johnson from the other direction. Senators Wayne Morse of Oregon and Ernest Gruening of Alaska had been early critics, but other prominent legislators joined their ranks in 1966 and 1967. Senator J. William Fulbright of Arkansas was among the first, and he was soon followed by Senators Eugene McCarthy of Minnesota, Robert Kennedy of New York, George McGovern of South Dakota, George Aiken of Vermont, Edward Kennedy of Massachusetts, Frank Church of Idaho, and Mark Hatfield of Oregon. They proposed everything from a bombing halt to a troop withdrawal to peace negotiations—anything but escalation. Several retired military officers also declared their opposition to the war. David Shoup, winner of the Congressional Medal of Honor at Tarawa during World II and commandant of the Marine Corps under Dwight Eisenhower and John Kennedy, told a college audience in May 1966, "I don't think the whole of Southeast Asia, as related to the present and future safety and freedom of the people of this country, is worth the life or limb of a single American." James Gavin spread the opinions he had shared with the Senate Foreign Relations Committee in 1966, that the United States should shift to an enclave strategy because a "free, neutral and independent Vietnam can be established, with guarantees of stability from an international body." Johnson wanted nothing of enclaves, arguing that "we can't hunker down like a jackass in a hailstorm." Former general Matthew Ridgway called for a bombing halt, arguing, "There is nothing in the present situation or in our code that requires us to bomb a small Asian nation back into the stone age."

The conflict over the war was not confined to official Washington. In early 1965 White House Social Secretary Bess Abell suggested to Eric F. Goldman, the resident intellectual in the Johnson administration, that it would be nice to do something "cultural" during the spring social season. It was the sort of thing that the Kennedys did so well. There had been the dinner for Nobel Prize winners and a Pablo Casals concert. Jack and Jackie had been at their witty best, fashionable, charming. Abell did not want to copy the Kennedys, but she did want something along the same lines that would have the same results. Goldman thought it was an outstanding idea. He then suggested a White House Festival of the Arts. Abell harbored a few reservations—"writers and artists. These people can be troublesome"—but she went along. Johnson also liked the idea. Without thinking too much about it, he felt that it would be a "nice thing" to do.

Invitations were sent to leading artists in painting, sculpture, litera- ture, music, dance, cinema, and photography. Goldman made certain that "no attention was given to politics, ideology, opinions or personal habits of the people chosen." The list included a former communist, a number of radicals, and a liberal sprinkling of drunks. Almost every- one who was invited accepted, and a large number of people who were not invited tried to wangle an invitation. The trouble started when one person who was invited decided that he could not in good conscience attend. Poet Robert Lowell, after considerable thought, reached the conclusion that art and politics were inseparable, and that his atten- dance might serve as a form of quiet support for Johnson's actions in Vietnam. In an open letter to Johnson published in the *New York Times,* Lowell wrote: "We are in danger of imperceptibly becoming an explosive and suddenly chauvinistic nation, and may even be drifting on our way to the last nuclear ruin. . . . I feel that I am serving you and our country best by not taking part in the White House Festival of the Arts."

For Johnson—who after all was simply trying to do a "nice thing"—it was proof that "those" people did not like him. He believed they cer- tainly would not have treated Jack Kennedy in such a fashion. And that the *Times* gave front-page treatment to the letter was proof that the entire eastern establishment was opposed to him. Although Johnson's division between "them" and "us" was an oversimplification—most art- ists and intellectuals gladly accepted their invitations—it did contain a germ of truth. For "them" Johnson was the hick from the Hill Country of Texas, the cowboy who picked up puppies by the ears, proudly displayed his gall bladder scar, and held conferences while sitting on the john. The *New York Review of Books* editor Robert B. Silvers and the poet Stanley J. Kunitz drafted a public telegram to Johnson supporting Lowell's position, and eventually more than twenty influential artists, writers, and critics signed the telegram. Vietnam, not the arts, had become the issue.

Feeling betrayed, Johnson threatened not to attend the affair, but in the end he showed up for a few minutes. The event turned into a nasty political get-together. John Hersey read from his book *Hiroshima* (1946) and prefaced his reading by stating, "We can not for a moment forget the truly terminal dangers, in these times, of miscalculation, of arrogance, of accident, of reliance not on moral strength but on mere military power. Wars have a way of getting out of hand." Cultural critic Dwight Macdonald treated the festival as if it were a political rally. He offensively criticized his host, verbally assaulted guests, and worked to get signatures on a pro-Lowell petition. When he got into an argument with actor Charlton Heston, the Hollywood star said, "Having convictions doesn't mean that you have to lack elementary manners. Are you really accustomed to signing petitions against your host in his own home?" Although Johnson was gone before the fireworks started, he knew what was going on. Loud enough for the press to hear, he said, "Some of them insult me by staying away and some of them insult me by coming." At least, he added later to a friend, "nobody pissed in the punchbowl."

By 1967 the alienation was spreading. On college campuses the years of rage had commenced. No longer were antiwar students silently listening to administration spokesmen. It was their time to speak, and if the Johnson administration was not prepared to listen, they were prepared to allow their actions to express their hostility. Protesters followed government officials, obstructing their movements and interrupting speeches. In October 1966, for example, the Socialist party leader Norman Thomas, frail and nearly blind, spoke out at Harvard against the war. "If I die before this *terrible* war is ended," he said, "I will feel that my whole life's work for decency has been a failure." Students lashed out at symbols of the power establishment. They campaigned to abolish Reserve Officer Training Corps (ROTC) programs. They chased military recruiters and companies with war contracts off campus. And not all the disruption occurred at the "radical" universities. By early 1967 even traditionally conservative Stanford had been pulled into the antiwar movement. When good-natured Vice President Hubert Humphrey spoke at Stanford, hundreds of students, in an orchestrated protest, stood up and left the auditorium halfway through his talk. Others later chanted, "Shame! Shame!" at Humphrey.

The protests swept beyond the campuses. They became part of the youth counterculture, confirming feelings of alienation and betrayal. Quick to respond to changes in the popular mood, folksingers wrote and performed songs with antiwar messages. Phil Ochs, a handsome, angry folksinger who emerged from the same Greenwich Village clubs as Bob Dylan, sang at protests across the country. As he sang, he talked—about the need to end the war and the country's reactionary government. Introducing one song, he noted, "Now, for a change of pace, here's a protest song. . . . A protest song is a song that's so specific that you cannot mistake it for bullshit. . . . Good word, bullshit . . . ought to be used more often . . . especially in Washington. . . . Speaking of bullshit . . . I'd like to dedicate this song to McGeorge Bundy." In 1967 Ochs helped to organize several "War Is Over" rallies. The songs of Phil Ochs, Joan Baez, and other troubadours of the antiwar movement combined with the voices of frustrated students. The resulting wail echoed across the country. It called for an immediate end to the war.

The stalemate in Vietnam also undermined what the historian William Turley calls "the reflexive patriotism of ordinary citizens." Some Americans opposed the war on fundamental, moral grounds, while others felt Johnson was not fighting it properly. Whatever their explanations, most Americans were discouraged about Vietnam. In the summer of 1967 support for the war dropped under 50 percent for the first time. When Johnson went to Congress in August for a 10 percent income tax surcharge to pay for the war, it dropped even more. By October only 28 percent of the public said they supported Johnson. At the end of the month, more than 100,000 people gathered in Washington to protest the war; 35,000 of them showed up at the Pentagon entrance.

But it was hardly a unified movement. Dyed-in-the-wool pacifists like A. J. Muste and David Dellinger opposed all wars on moral grounds. New Left radicals like SDS leader Tom Hayden hoped to use the Vietnam War protest movement to also destroy racism and capitalism and build a new society. Liberal critics like Senator J. William Fulbright, the historian Arthur M. Schlesinger, Jr., and the economist John Kenneth Galbraith felt that the United States was backing a corrupt regime and fighting an impossible war in a country unrelated to American national security. Although most Americans did not identify with antiwar activists, they were nevertheless tired of the war. What the antiwar movement managed to do was keep Johnson's Vietnam policies at the forefront of public debate—week after week, month after month, year after year.

President Johnson responded to those who opposed the war in three ways. First, he launched Operation Chaos, a CIA domestic surveillance campaign to spy on antiwar leaders and prove that they were communists. Eventually Operation Chaos developed files on more than 7,000 Americans and accused them, without real evidence, of being communists or communist stooges directed by Hanoi. Several years later the Nixon administration would add more information to those files.

Second, Johnson set in motion a public relations blitz to rebuild public support for the war. The program included formation of the Committee for Peace and Freedom in Vietnam, a group dedicated to inspiring the "silent center," or what Richard Nixon would later call the "silent majority." Speakers went out around the country trying to prove the war was being won. The president also decided on an encore performance by General Westmoreland. The April appearance before Congress had played to such good reviews. On November 21, 1967, Westmoreland spoke before the National Press Club, claiming, "We are making progress. . . . The enemy's hopes are bankrupt."

Finally, the president tried to prove his willingness to negotiate in a speech in San Antonio, Texas, on September 29, 1967. For the first time he slightly modified American demands. Instead of insisting on an immediate withdrawal of all North Vietnamese troops, he offered to stop bombing North Vietnam if Ho Chi Minh agreed to serious negotiations and promised not to use the bombing halt to increase infiltration into South Vietnam. Johnson even hinted at allowing the National Liberation Front to participate in the South Vietnamese government. Journalists quickly dubbed the proposal the "San Antonio Formula," but North Vietnam made no response, except to say that the United States should stop all bombing of North Vietnam, withdraw all troops from Indochina, remove Thieu and Ky from office, and permit a coalition government in Saigon that included the National Liberation Front. It was the same message North Vietnam had been sending for years.

But in addition to the debate among policymakers in Washington and the large controversy over the war in the society as a whole, a struggle between army and marine officials was raging in Saigon and Washington. The most effective of the American pacification programs involved the marine combined action platoons, but Westmoreland all but destroyed it by 1967. Since 1965 the marines argued that attrition was not working. Victor Krulak wrote to Robert McNamara in 1966 that the "raw figure of VC killed . . . can be a dubious index of success since, if their killing is accompanied by devastation of friendly areas, we may end up having done more harm than good." To Westmoreland's constant litany that the United States was winning the war militarily, Krulak retorted, "You have to win totally, or you are not winning at all."

The marines thought they had the answer. The northern five provinces of South Vietnam were thick with rain forests and rugged mountains, except along a twenty-five-mile strip between the South China Sea and the mountains, where 98 percent of the people lived. From bases at Chu Lai, Phu Bai, and Danang, the marines wanted to mix with the population, fighting the Vietcong when necessary but conducting pacification programs among peasants with combined action platoons. Campaigning in the mountains, where 2 percent of the population lived, was irrelevant because, as Krulak said, "there is nothing of value there."

Westmoreland disagreed. There were Main Force Vietcong and North Vietnamese in those mountains, and he wanted the marines to kill them. By mid-1967 there were already 55,000 marines in I Corps, commanded by General Lewis Walt. Twice a winner of the Navy Cross in World War II, Walt grew up on a Kansas ranch before playing football at the Colorado School of Mines and joining the Marine Corps. He had the discipline of an offensive lineman, but in I Corps he found himself in an impossible situation. On the one hand General Victor Krulak wanted him to continue the combined action platoons and wait for the Vietcong to venture down to the coast, where the killing machine could cut them to pieces. On the other hand, he was under the operational command of William Westmoreland, who ordered him to head into the Annamese mountains and kill the enemy.

Walt could not do both. The marine contingent would peak at 70,000 troops at the end of the year, but it was not enough. He could not send battalions into the mountains on search-and-destroy missions while other battalions were down on the coast providing land reform, health care, education, and police security. Vo Nguyen Giap understood the problem. "The marines are being stretched as taut as a bowstring," he said. Marine commandant Wallace Greene tried to make the case to the joint chiefs, but they sided with Westmoreland.

Ho Chi Minh had been watching American politics with great interest. It did not look much different from the political battles in Paris thirteen years before. He knew that Lyndon Johnson's political base was eroding just at the moment that American military might in South Vietnam was reaching its peak. A year later Vo Nguyen Giap remarked in an interview that the "Americans will lose the war on the day when their military might is at its maximum and the great machine they've put together can't move any more. . . . We'll beat them at the moment when they have the most men, the most arms, and the greatest hope of winning."

What North Vietnam was planning was a great military uprising throughout South Vietnam early in 1968. But to achieve that the communists had to draw American forces out of the major cities and bases. Giap argued there was an "acute contradiction on which American strategy flounders. Is it necessary to disperse their troops in search of an enemy which is everywhere—without finding any part to strike? Is it necessary to regroup their forces, to abandon vast territory to the adversary?" The United States faced the same dilemma as had the French. The very debate between Westmoreland and the marines over whether to spread out into the northern mountains in search of the enemy or hold to the coastal plain in pacification programs had a familiar ring to it.

Throughout 1967 the United States and North Vietnam fought a series of "border battles" near the Demilitarized Zone in I Corps, along the Laotian and Cambodian borders in the Central Highlands of II Corps, and in the rubber plantations and jungles in III Corps northwest of Saigon. Since 1966 the NVA 324B Division had been pushing across the Demilitarized Zone, trying to draw the marines into the jungles and hills of I Corps. Westmoreland wanted the marines to go after them, but the North Vietnamese then pulled back across the DMZ, only to come back again and again over the next several months. By October the debate over strategy between Walt and Westmoreland was finished. Walt pulled the Third Marine Division out of Danang and established a series of fixed positions south of the DMZ at Gio Linh and Con Thien in the east, and along Route 9 to Khe Sanh, where they could fight North Vietnamese coming across the DMZ or in from Laos. That left the First Marine Division stretched out from Chu Lai in the south to Danang in the north. To reinforce them Westmoreland deployed Task Force Oregon to I Corps. It was a composite unit of the Eleventh Infantry Brigade, the 196th Light Infantry Brigade, and the 198th Infantry Brigade. They concentrated their efforts in Quang Nam, Quang Tin, and Quang Ngai provinces. Westmoreland was ready to make war in I Corps. Marine pacification was over. It was time to search and destroy.

The first of the border battles of late 1967 took place at Con Thien. Known as the "Hill of Angels," Con Thien was actually three hills south of the DMZ in eastern Quang Tri Province. Troops from the Third Marine Division assumed a defensive position at Con Thien, as part of McNamara's electronic barrier, hoping to interrupt NVA troop movements across the DMZ. Early in September, North Vietnamese troops, equipped with Soviet artillery, began shelling the marine positions. Convinced the enemy was setting the stage for a conventional battle, Westmoreland thought he would finally have an opportunity to take the NVA 324B and 324C Divisions head-on. He launched Operation Neutralize to relieve the marines at Con Thien, and during the next month more than 4,000 B-52s and fighter-bomber sorties, along with heavy naval bombardment, struck the NVA positions. By the last week of October the United States had dumped 40,000 tons of explosives on Con Thien, and the North Vietnamese suddenly broke off the engagement, leaving behind 2,000 dead.

No sooner had the siege of Con Thien been lifted than the Vietcong and North Vietnamese struck again, far to the south near the Cambodian border. On October 27, the Eighty-eighth NVA Regiment attacked Song Be in Phuoc Long Province, and two days later the Vietcong attacked at the rubber plantations of Loc Ninh in Binh Long Province. For ten days the Vietcong 273d Regiment assaulted American positions defended by the First Infantry Division. When the battle was over, the First Infantry had lost 50 men while the Vietcong sustained 2,000 casualties, half of them combat deaths. The Vietcong disengaged early in November and retreated into Cambodia. Westmoreland proclaimed another great victory.

But in November the North Vietnamese staged a series of skirmishes near Dak To in Kontum Province, including an attack on the Special Forces camp there. Hoping to cut off infiltration through Laos into II Corps and relieve the attack on Dak To, Westmoreland dispatched portions of the Fourth Infantry Division and the 173d Airborne Brigade to defend Dak To and search out the enemy. They were hunting for the Twenty-fourth NVA Regiment. Throughout most of November the American troops assaulted fortified NVA positions, complete with tunnels and bunkers, along the ridge lines in the area. By November 20 the center of battle was focused on Hill 875, about twelve miles west of Dak To at the Cambodian border. Westmoreland hit the NVA positions at Hill 875 with 300 B-52 sorties and 2,000 fighter-bomber sorties before American troops went up the hill. Before they arrived at the top, the North Vietnamese had already left. It was Thanksgiving Day. More than 1,200 North Vietnamese were dead, but so were 289 Americans. Helicopters flew in hot turkey and stuffing, mashed potatoes with gravy, candied yams, cranberry sauce, hot rolls and butter, and lots of beer, Cokes, and ice cream. Westmoreland argued, "We had soundly defeated the enemy without unduly sacrificing operations in other areas." An American journalist at Hill 875 remarked, "With victories like this, who needs defeats?"

But Westmoreland was never more certain that victory was at hand. By the end of 1967, although 16,021 GIs were dead, the enemy death toll was more than fifteen times that. Nearly half of all the enemy battalions, Westmoreland claimed, were no longer combat-effective. The border battles were proof of American superiority. Enemy supply lines had been so decimated by American firepower that enemy troops had to keep close to the Laotian and Cambodian borders and the Demilitarized Zone. The communists were no longer capable, Westmoreland was convinced, of bringing the war to the heart of South Vietnam.

Lyndon B. Johnson needed advice. Like Eisenhower and Kennedy before him, he listened to those who wanted more war and those who wanted less, and he charted a middle course, hoping to secure the political integrity of South Vietnam without triggering a Soviet or Chinese intervention. Yet, that middle course led inexorably to steady escalation until he found himself in the middle of the dreaded Asian quagmire. But the advice he was getting was still the same: Some said fight a bigger war and others said negotiate a way out. For another opinion, Johnson turned to the Wise Men.

On November 1, 1967, they assembled at the White House, the "best and the brightest" of two generations. Dean Acheson was there, as were McGeorge Bundy, Maxwell Taylor, Henry Cabot Lodge, W. Averell Harriman, and George Ball. The other five were General Omar Bradley, World War II hero and chairman of the Joint Chiefs of Staff during the Korean War; Supreme Court Justice Abe Fortas, one of Johnson's closest advisers; Clark Clifford, another intimate of Johnson who had been a trusted Truman aide and head of the Foreign Intelligence Advisory Board during the Kennedy administration; Douglas Dillon, former secretary of the treasury under Kennedy; and Robert Murphy, a prominent career diplomat.

Johnson asked them if he was on the right course, and the Wise Men responded as he expected. Acheson told the group, "We certainly should not get out of Vietnam." McGeorge Bundy concurred, arguing that "getting out of Vietnam is as impossible as it is undesirable." While he listened to the Wise Men, Walt Rostow became exultant, urging Johnson "to have a full leadership meeting of this kind, introduced by yourself, after which you could put the whole thing on television." They all told Johnson what he wanted to hear, all except one. Former Undersecretary of State George Ball suddenly stood up and shouted: "I've been watching you across the table. You're like a flock of buzzards sitting on a fence, sending the young men off to be killed. You ought to be ashamed of yourselves."

Ball's point of view was a minority of one. Withdrawal was still out of the question, especially without some change in the political climate in South Vietnam, without some hope for the survival of a noncommunist government there. Nor would Johnson's personality permit it. He was too proud, too committed to presidential greatness to give up. McGeorge Bundy suggested abandoning the big-unit sweeps that brought such heavy casualties. Smaller unit operations, designed to reduce American casualties, should be tied to a concerted effort to transfer major combat responsibilities to ARVN. That way the American people would tolerate politically an effort that might take five or ten years to accomplish. For the first time in years, Johnson began seriously to reconsider his commitment to Westmoreland's strategy of attrition.

With the debate over, the war swirling around him, and the presidential elections looming ahead, Lyndon B. Johnson was desperate for good news. The antiwar movement was capturing headlines, as were the racial rebellions in America's major cities. He needed a victory to salvage his administration, something akin to what the battle of Antietam did for Abraham Lincoln in 1862 or the Normandy invasion did for Franklin D. Roosevelt in 1944. Johnson looked toward Khe Sanh. Military intelligence indicated that North Vietnam had massed nearly 40,000 troops around Khe Sanh in western Quang Tri Province, eighteen miles south of the DMZ and eight miles east of Laos. Westmoreland thought Khe Sanh had great strategic significance. It could be used for covert operations into Laos, reconnaissance flights over the Ho Chi Minh Trail, or as a base to cut off infiltration along Highway 9. Johnson saw it as a great disaster or a great opportunity. "We must try very hard to be ready," he said to Walt Rostow. "We face dark days ahead."

Late in 1967, when the buildup began and infiltration down the Ho Chi Minh Trail increased, Westmoreland decided that North Vietnam was at long last planning the conventional invasion and that Khe Sanh would be its focal point. The North Vietnamese 325C Division was northwest of Khe Sanh; the 304th Division was to the southwest; and elements of the 320th and 324th Divisions were ready for reinforcement. Westmoreland sent in another 6,000 marines and launched Operation

Niagara to pulverize the enemy. Johnson had a scale model of Khe Sanh built in the White House situation room so he could follow the battle day-by-day and eventually hour-by-hour. The press called Khe Sanh "another Dienbienphu."

For the next two months Westmoreland sent more than 5,000 aircraft sorties against the North Vietnamese positions, detonating more than 100,000 tons—200 million pounds—of explosives on less than five square miles. On January 21, 1968, the North Vietnamese artillery bombardment began. It was just what Westmoreland expected. At Dienbienphu the Vietnamese preceded the infantry assault with intense artillery bombardment. The marines dug in and waited. Westmoreland waited. Lyndon Johnson waited. But the attack never came. Instead, tens of thousands of Vietcong were sneaking into the cities and provincial capitals of South Vietnam. In the early morning hours of January 31, while Americans waited for the attack on Khe Sanh, the Tet offensive began.

8

Tet and the Year
of the Monkey, 1968

*If this is a failure, I hope the Viet Cong never have a major
success.*
—Senator George Aiken, February 1968

It was January 24, 1968, and in Saigon, Robert Komer offered an assessment of the war at the "five o'clock follies," when the press gathered to hear the latest "General Blimp" reports. Komer was at his optimistic best: "We begin 1968 in a better position than we have ever been." At the White House, Lyndon Johnson was in his bathrobe, unable to sleep, pacing the floor as he read the cables on Khe Sanh. A Pentagon photographic analyst was on hand waiting for one of the president's requests to explain something in an aerial photograph. A table model of Khe Sanh, with small flags posted on the periphery, indicated the presence of several NVA divisions. In the middle, poised on the plateau, were the insignias of marine battalions. Khe Sanh was Johnson's obsession. "I don't want any damn Dinbinphoo," he told Earle Wheeler.

William Westmoreland was no less obsessed. The border battles of late 1967 and early 1968 at Con Thien, Loc Ninh, Dak To, and Khe Sanh convinced him that the enemy shift to conventional warfare was at hand; the invasion would begin just south of the Demilitarized Zone. For two months Westmoreland transferred combat units north. By early January 1968 more than half of all American combat units were in I Corps. MACV headquarters buzzed with talk of Dienbienphu, but Westmoreland would have none of it. "We are not, repeat not, going to be defeated at Khe Sanh. I will tolerate no talking or even thinking to the contrary."

The real target was not Khe Sanh; it was all of South Vietnam. In mid-1967 North Vietnam contemplated a major attack. American firepower had inflicted massive casualties on communist troops, and the Thieu-Ky government seemed to be stable. North Vietnam was weary of the bombing and yearned for peace. United States troops controlled the cities and, because of Vietnam's narrow width, could attack in the countryside indefinitely. Hanoi also worried about a possible United States invasion of North Vietnam. Rapid urbanization in South Vietnam was shrinking the number of people available in the countryside for Vietcong recruitment. The communists wanted a dramatic military event, one that would undermine the Saigon regime and force the United States out.

The nature of that event was intensely debated. Nguyen Chi Thanh went to Hanoi in June 1967 to call for a massive attack on the cities of South Vietnam using local Vietcong guerrillas, Main Force Vietcong, and NVA regulars. He predicted tactical as well as strategic success. Thanh felt sure the communists could inspire a peasant uprising in South Vietnam, undermine the Thieu-Ky regime, force an ARVN surrender, secure a military foothold in the major cities and provincial capitals, and inflict enormous casualties on Americans. Thanh also wanted to bring the war home to the South Vietnamese cities.

In the Politburo, Le Duan supported Thanh, but Vo Nguyen Giap opposed him. The United States was at the height of its power. If the massive attack failed and Main Force Vietcong and NVA units were destroyed, the revolution would be set back years. Giap offered an alternative. NVA troops would create diversions in border areas, drawing American combat units out of the cities, while Vietcong guerrillas, with some Main Force support, launched the general offensive. Thanh retorted that Giap was sacrificing the Vietcong, who were mostly southerners, while North Vietnamese regulars were safe in diversionary activities. The debate was intense until July 6, 1967, when Thanh died suddenly. Giap's view prevailed.

North Vietnam also devised a series of diplomatic diversions. In the fall the National Liberation Front initiated secret contacts with the United States embassy and mentioned the possibility of peace talks. In December 1967 Pham Van Dong announced Hanoi's intention to sit down and talk about the war once the United States stopped the bombing. The North Vietnamese were trying to create political havoc—to drive a wedge between the United States and South Vietnam, which did not want peace talks of any kind, and to raise hopes in America that a negotiated settlement was near.

Late in July the Politburo voted to launch the attack early in 1968. By September the North Vietnamese were infiltrating huge volumes of supplies and hiding them near provincial capitals and major cities. More than 84,000 Vietcong troops, most of whom were southern-born guerrillas, moved into position while NVA troops distracted Westmoreland with the border battles. As the end of the year approached they appealed to ARVN and MACV for a cease-fire during the Tet holiday so that Vietnamese could celebrate the new year. Tran Van Tra headed Vietcong forces in South Vietnam. Tra first assumed command of Main Force Vietcong in 1963, but Nguyen Chi Thanh took over in 1964. When Thanh died, Tra was back in power. As operational planner of the offensive, Tra selected Tran Do, a commander beloved by his troops because of his willingness to live in the field with them.

Although American intelligence realized that more supplies than ever were moving down the Ho Chi Minh Trail, they were convinced the attack would come at Khe Sanh. General John Chaisson, a Westmoreland aide, told reporters three days after the beginning of the Tet offensive: "Well . . . the intelligence did not indicate that we were going to have any such massive attacks as this. . . . We were quite confident that something would happen around . . . Tet . . . but . . . intelligence at least never unfolded to me any panorama of attacks such as happened this week." The Vietcong had managed to move 84,000 troops and thousands of tons of supplies without being detected. South Vietnam took the Tet cease-fire at face value. Half of ARVN troops went home on holiday. Saigon dramatized the problems. Seventeen ARVN battalions and 17,000 national police defended the city, which was surrounded by major American airfields, command centers, and bases, housing thousands of American troops. The Vietcong infiltrated five armed battalions into Saigon. In the week before Tet they drifted into the city on foot, bicycles, and mopeds. Before the fighting started, they established a central command post and a field hospital at the Phu Tho racetrack in Cholon.

Just after midnight on January 30, 1968, the Vietcong attacks began. In addition to assaults on thirty-six of the forty-four provincial capitals and five of six major cities, they attacked the United States embassy, Tan Son Nhut air base, the presidential palace, and the South Vietnamese general staff headquarters. In I Corps they hit Quang Tri City and Tam Ky, seized Hue, raising the National Liberation Front flag over the Citadel, and attacked the marines at Chu Lai and Phu Bai. II Corps was involved in assaults on Tuy Hoa and Phan Thiet as well as the American bases at Bong Son and An Khe. In III Corps the Vietcong went after ARVN headquarters at Bien Hoa and United States Field Force headquarters at Long Binh. The attacks in IV Corps—the Mekong Delta—were fierce. The Vietcong hit other provincial and district capitals.

The most spectacular attack was on the American embassy. At 1:30 A.M. on January 31, the Vietcong blew a hole in the embassy wall and poured through carrying explosives and automatic weapons. All night long a battle raged between guerrillas and the troops from the 101st Airborne, who helicoptered onto the embassy roof. By 9:00 A.M. the embassy was secure. Bodies littered the compound. Bloody footprints marched up the external stairway. Reporters were everywhere, prompting Kate Webb of the UPI to describe the scene as "a butcher shop in Eden." Westmoreland marched into the compound at 9:20 A.M. and claimed an American victory, arguing that the communists were being slaughtered throughout the country and the attack on Saigon was only a diversion before the main attack near Khe Sanh. The journalists were dumbfounded. How could he claim a victory when the Vietcong got into the embassy compound, supposedly the single most secure place in South Vietnam?

The other most enduring image of the Tet offensive occurred the next day. General Nguyen Ngoc Loan, head of the South Vietnamese police, saw ARVN troops escorting a Vietcong soldier down the street. Loan walked up to him, placed a revolver to his temple, and blew his brains out. Eddie Adams, an Associated Press photographer, and a Vietnamese cameraman for NBC News filmed the whole incident. That night millions of Americans watched the killing in their living rooms or read about it the next morning. Those two pictures—Westmoreland on the embassy grounds and Loan shooting the Vietcong—became symbols of the Tet offensive.

The battle to drive the Vietcong out of Saigon was bloody. More than 10,000 ARVN troops moved into Cholon in a house-to-house search. On February 3 MACV declared much of Cholon a free fire zone and told civilians to get out. The next day American and South Vietnamese aircraft conducted a massive bombing of Cholon to dislodge the enemy. After six days of bombardment, the 199th Light Infantry Brigade moved into Cholon, attacked the Phu Tho racetrack, and wiped out the rest of the Vietcong. Much of Cholon lay in rubble.

The bloodiest fighting occurred in Hue, where 7,500 communist troops, most of them NVA regulars, attacked the city. Formerly the imperial capital of Vietnam, the center of Vietnamese cultural life, Hue was the premier symbol of Vietnamese nationalism. It was cosmopolitan and exotic, famous for its wide boulevards and pagodas. It was also difficult to defend. Isolated by the Annamese mountains and bordered by Laos to the west and the Demilitarized Zone to the north, Hue had no access to a major port.

North Vietnamese artillery began blasting away just before 4:00 A.M. on January 30. The NVA Sixth Regiment attacked MACV headquarters in Hue and the field offices of the ARVN First Division. Other NVA troops blocked Highway 1 north and south of Hue. When dawn broke, the gold-starred flag of the National Liberation Front was waving above the Citadel, the centuries-old home of the Vietnamese imperial family. Hue had fallen. The bloodbath began immediately. The communists rounded up 2,800 citizens of Hue—intellectuals, government officials, random civilians, and religious leaders—and systematically slaughtered them. Instead of leaving the bodies on public display, as they had always done in the past with political assassinations, they buried the victims in shallow graves. Another 2,000 people were never seen again. Local Vietcong cadres, not NVA regulars, carried out the massacre. There was an ideological dimension to the killings—liquidation of entire groups of people—which had not been seen before. Most victims had connections to the South Vietnamese army or government or worked for the American military.

Westmoreland reacted quickly. Within hours elements of the First Air Cavalry Division, the 101st Airborne Division, the ARVN First Divi-

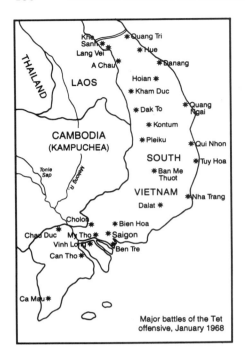

Major battles of the Tet
offensive, January 1968

sion, the First Marine Division, and ARVN rangers and marines began a house-to-house assault on Hue. For more than three weeks the artillery barrage continued, reducing Hue to rubble. On February 24, 1968, Westmoreland declared victory. By that time there was not much left. More than 10,000 civilians were dead, killed by enemy terrorism or random American bombardment. Half the buildings in the city were destroyed, and 116,000 of the city's 140,000 people were homeless. The communists suffered 5,000 combat deaths, to 216 for the United States and 384 for ARVN.

After the recapture of Hue, the Tet offensive stuttered and declined. The Vietcong started a new series of attacks beginning February 18, but they were primarily rocket and mortar bombardment. They launched "Tet II" in May and a smaller offensive in August, but American and ARVN forces easily beat them back. Giap was right. The American military proved far more responsive than Nguyen Chi Thanh ever thought possible. When the Tet offensive was over, as many as 40,000 Vietcong were dead, compared to 1,100 Americans and approximately 2,300 South Vietnamese. The civilian toll was even worse. Up to 45,000 South Vietnamese were dead or wounded, and more than 1 million people had lost their homes.

The Tet offensive was a tactical disaster for the communists. They achieved none of their major objectives. The South Vietnamese did not rise up and welcome them as liberators; the government of South Vietnam did not collapse; ARVN soldiers did not surrender; and the cities did not fall under communist control. When Tet started, ARVN troops left the countryside to fight in the cities, and when they withdrew from villages, Vietcong political cadres headed into the vacuum to recruit peasants. But ARVN and American forces quickly returned to the villages, and Vietcong agents were exposed and often arrested. That process, as well as their horrendous battlefield casualties, badly debilitated the Vietcong. In fact, they never again fielded full battalions. After the Tet offensive, NVA regulars assumed a far greater role in the fighting. For South Vietnamese communists, it was about time. They resented the fact that Giap had not committed the NVA divisions to the campaign. Had Nguyen Chi Thanh lived, they believed, the offensive would have been a different story.

But tactical disaster did not mean strategic defeat. In fact, Tet was an overwhelming, if unintentional, strategic victory for the communists. General Tran Do remembered, "We didn't achieve our main objective, which was to spur uprisings throughout the south. . . . As for making an impact in the United States, it had not been our intention—but it turned out to be a fortunate result." Americans were in no mood for more talk about victories. Although Lyndon Johnson claimed at a press conference on February 2 that "we have known for some time that this offensive was planned by the enemy," most people were not convinced. Senator Robert Kennedy claimed that Tet "has finally shattered the mask of official illusion with which we have concealed our true circumstances, even from ourselves." For Senator Mike Mansfield, Tet was the disaster he had been anticipating. "From the outset," he said, the war "was not an American responsibility, and it is not now an American responsibility, to win a victory for any particular Vietnamese group, or to defeat any particular Vietnamese group." Senator George Aiken of Vermont said, "If this is a failure, I hope the Viet Cong never have a major success."

The usually conservative *Wall Street Journal* argued that "the American people should be getting ready to accept . . . the prospect that the whole Vietnam effort may be doomed." The *St. Louis Post-Dispatch* said that Tet exposed "the hollowness of the Saigon government's pretensions to sovereignty . . . the fraud of our government's claims of imminent victory, and the basic untenability of the American military position." Art Buchwald parodied Westmoreland's claims of victory, titling his column, "We Have the Enemy on the Run, Says General Custer." Describing an interview with General George Armstrong Custer, Buchwald wrote, "The battle of Little Big Horn has just turned the corner and the Sioux are on the run."

The greatest defection was Walter Cronkite, the dean of American broadcast journalists and anchor of the CBS Evening News. When he started getting news reports of Tet, he said, "What the hell is going on? I thought we were winning the war." After a few days, Cronkite went to Vietnam for his own look. When he returned he issued on the evening broadcast of February 27 his personal opinion: "We have been too often disappointed by the optimism of the American leaders to have faith any longer in the silver linings they find in the darkest clouds. The bloody experience of Vietnam is to end in a stalemate." There would be no military victory. Cronkite wanted peace negotiations. The president was watching the broadcast. "If I have lost Walter Cronkite," Johnson said, "I have lost Mr. Average Citizen."

All the negative reactions forced Lyndon Johnson into a depression, but he also had to deal with Earle Wheeler and William Westmoreland, both of whom wanted to remove all restrictions on the killing machine and bring in another 206,000 American troops. Wheeler cabled Westmoreland on February 9 with the message that the "United States is not prepared to accept a defeat in South Vietnam. In summary, if you need more troops, ask for them." Westmoreland came back with a request for 206,000 troops. He also asked Johnson to mobilize the reserves, permit an invasion of Laos, Cambodia, and North Vietnam, and expand the air war. His new proposal was Operation Complete Victory.

Johnson found himself dealing with the old question—whether to widen the war and raise American troop levels. At a special meeting of his top advisers on February 9, Johnson listened to them talk about Westmoreland's proposals. Earle Wheeler, who played no small part in Westmoreland's troop requests, knew the war was stretching American military resources to the limit. He wanted a national mobilization, a call-up of reserves, and a declaration of war. Dean Rusk opposed such an escalation. Opposition to the war, which had prevented Johnson from even raising taxes a few years before, was more severe than ever.

By this time the new secretary of defense, Clark Clifford, was on the scene. A Kansas native and a graduate of the Washington University Law School, Clifford had been special counsel to Harry Truman in 1946 and became Truman's most trusted adviser. Tactful but tough, he headed the Foreign Intelligence Advisory Board in 1961, serving as the official watchdog over the CIA. He had a special ability to sniff out exaggeration, hyperbole, and bureaucratic dissembling. Clifford directed Lyndon Johnson's election campaign in 1964 and for several years was a leading "hawk," a supporter of the war. Early in 1968 Clifford replaced Robert McNamara as secretary of defense, and within weeks he heard "Blimpies" coming out of Saigon. In the middle of Earle Wheeler's plea for more troops and fewer restrictions, Clifford voiced his concern: "There is a very strange contradiction in what we are saying. . . . I think we should give some very serious thought to how we explain saying on one hand that the enemy did not take a victory and yet [we] are in need of many more troops and possibly an emergency call-up." Johnson was quick to see Clifford's shrewdness. The press would have a field day with the rhetoric of victory and the deployment of 206,000 more troops. All Johnson immediately agreed to was the deployment of another 12,000 troops.

The irony of it all was that Tet had been a tactical victory for the United States. But the American press portrayed it as a tactical defeat. Johnson and Westmoreland were victims of their own rhetoric. Ever since 1962 American leaders had predicted an enemy collapse and an imminent military victory. Victory, they had said repeatedly, was just around the corner; they could see "the light at the end of the tunnel." When the Tet offensive exposed the rhetoric, reporters had a story, comparing the strength of the enemy with MACV's descriptions of its weakness. In a matter of days, tactical victory became strategic defeat.

Johnson asked Clifford to review the proposals and "give me the lesser of two evils." Clifford insisted that Westmoreland specifically describe what he would do with the 206,000 troops, what results he would achieve, and when he would achieve them. He asked Alain Enthoven, a senior assistant and systems analyst in the Defense Department, to evaluate United States strategy. Enthoven presented a scathing attack a few weeks later. The troop requests would not shorten the war, and 206,000 new troops promised "no early end to the conflict, nor any success in attriting the enemy or eroding Hanoi's will to fight." He also claimed that such a troop buildup would completely Americanize the war and create a tremendous political backlash at home.

Enthoven proposed a new strategy. Military victory was out of the question. Westmoreland was never going to reach the crossover point. Instead Enthoven wanted to deploy American troops in areas where they could provide "population security," stop any major communist attacks, and keep the enemy off balance with limited offensive operations. In the meantime, ARVN must take the offensive and reverse the Americanization of the conflict. The proposal became known as "Vietnamization." It was actually little different from what the Eisenhower and Kennedy administrations had tried to accomplish years before. The United States would then seek a negotiated political settlement and withdraw, leaving South Vietnam to its own destiny.

Those were the choices Johnson faced, and none of them was really palatable. The sum total of Westmoreland's tactical victories between 1965 and 1968 was zero. Pentagon assurances that the Vietcong had suffered a major defeat convinced nobody. Senator Eugene McCarthy of Minnesota, with the Democratic presidential primary in New Hampshire a few weeks ahead, said, "If capturing a section of the American embassy and several large cities constitutes complete failure, I suppose by this logic that if the Viet Cong captured the entire country, the administration would be claiming their total collapse." Eugene McCarthy taught school and worked as a professor of English before being elected to Congress in 1948. Ten years later he won a seat in the United States Senate. Hardly a typical politician, McCarthy was a mystic who was far more comfortable sitting in coffee shops discussing philosophy than working the halls of Congress. The journalist Theodore White claimed that McCarthy might "have love in his heart—but it is an abstract love, a love for youth, a love for beauty, a love for vistas and hills and song. . . . All through the year [1968] one's admiration of the man grew, but one's affection lessened." Early in 1967 McCarthy called for an end to the war. On November 30, 1967, he decided to take on Johnson in the upcoming presidential primaries. Few paid any attention until Tet. By February thousands of college students, freshly shaved, trimmed, and dressed in shirts and ties—part of a "Get Clean for Gene" campaign—walked door-to-door in New Hampshire garnering votes for McCarthy in the March 12 primary. The results were astonishing. McCarthy took 42 percent of the vote to Johnson's 48 percent.

Four days later Senator Robert Kennedy of New York declared for the nomination. McCarthy's supporters were outraged. Kennedy seemed a rank opportunist willing to enter the fray only after the shift in the political wind. Johnson was just as outraged. He hated Robert Kennedy. The Kennedy administration had taken the first major step in escalating the conflict in Vietnam, and Robert Kennedy had promised in 1962 that the United States "would remain there until we win." Now Kennedy wanted an end to the war. McCarthy and Kennedy both opposed Lyndon Johnson on the ballot of the April 2 presidential primary in Wisconsin.

Lyndon Johnson was a larger-than-life figure who personalized everything around him. On one occasion an aide tried to direct him to one of several helicopters, saying "Mr. President, that's not your helicopter." "Son, they're all my helicopters," Johnson replied. Vietnam was *his* war. He brooded about it all the time. One observer described Johnson's role:

> He made appointments, approved promotions, reviewed troop requests, determined deployments, selected bombing targets, and restricted aircraft sorties. Night after night, wearing a dressing gown and carrying a flashlight, he would descend into the White House basement "situation room" to monitor the conduct of the conflict. . . . Often, too, he would doze by his bedside telephone, waiting to hear the outcome of a mission to rescue one of "my pilots" shot down over Haiphong or Vinh or Thai Nguyen. It was his war.

But if it was "his war," Johnson did not want to be alone. Obsessed with consensus, he wanted agreement from everyone. Johnson was a great giver of gifts, especially presidential gifts—lighters, tie clasps, bowls, cuff links, electric toothbrushes, waterproof watches, and silk scarves, all with the presidential seal. If a person traveled with Johnson aboard

Air Force One or a presidential helicopter, he received a certificate commemorating the event. To show his appreciation for his staff, Johnson gave "CARE" boxes filled with favorite candies. He gave and gave. Some people's gifts come with strings attached; Johnson's came with steel chains. In return he demanded gratitude, love, and, most of all, loyalty. If his gifts were not paid with the proper emotional interest, he was deeply hurt. Now, with so many people turned against him, Johnson angrily asked a friend, "How is it possible that all these people could be so ungrateful to me after I have given them so much?"

That need for consensus doomed the Vietnam policy. Like other Democrats, Johnson was petrified by fear of anticommunist conservatives who would crucify him politically if he abandoned Vietnam. But in order to keep his contacts with the liberal establishment, Johnson would not give in to military requests for dramatic escalation. At each juncture when he had to make a decision, Johnson chose neither victory nor withdrawal. Instead, he decided to prevent defeat, which was essentially a strategy of stalemate. And for the United States, stalemate meant defeat.

A political fire storm was raging around him. On March 10 the *New York Times* released the news that Westmoreland wanted another 206,000 troops. Senator J. William Fulbright opened new hearings by the Senate Foreign Relations Committee, and 139 members of the House signed a petition asking Johnson to reevaluate Vietnam policy. On the NBC Evening News, reporter Frank McGee told the nation that 206,000 more troops would only result in more destruction, not peace and victory. "We must decide whether it is futile," McGee said, "to destroy Vietnam in an effort to save it." By mid-March the public opinion polls indicated that only one-quarter of Americans supported Johnson's conduct of the war.

Johnson had to make a decision. Westmoreland was not going to get the 206,000 troops, but Johnson had to decide whether to endorse the strategic proposals of Alain Enthoven and Clark Clifford. Once again he turned to the Wise Men. Just four months before, back in November 1967, all of them except George Ball told him to stay with it and force North Vietnam to the negotiating table while turning more of the war over to ARVN. They reminded him of the United States' role as protector of the Free World and told him not to lose faith. He wanted to hear from them again, hoping they could see a way out of the quagmire, a "peace with honor." State Department officials had used the phrase for years, laughingly referring to "peace with honor" as the "number of days between the departure of the last Marine and the rape of the first nun."

The Wise Men gathered at the State Department on March 25, 1968. It was their swan song. The elaborate network of military bases, regional alliances, and global commitments they created after World War II was stretched to the breaking point. The Tet offensive had exposed the vulnerability of the Pax Americana. Perhaps the United States was just not capable of stopping aggression anywhere in the world. The North Koreans had helped prove that point. On January 23, 1968, while Johnson and Westmoreland watched Khe Sanh, North Korean naval forces seized the USS *Pueblo,* a highly sophisticated intelligence-gathering ship plying the waters off the coast of North Korea. In the attack one American died and the ship and crew were taken captive. Johnson sent 350 aircraft to bases in South Korea as a show of force, but Vietnam had stretched his resources too thin. The *Pueblo* crew languished in a North Korean prison for nearly a year.

There were limits to American power, and the Wise Men were gathered to evaluate them. It was the same group that had supported Johnson back in November: Dean Acheson, Clark Clifford, Abe Fortas, McGeorge Bundy, Maxwell Taylor, Omar Bradley, Robert Murphy, Henry Cabot Lodge, Douglas Dillon, and George Ball. The retired army general Matthew Ridgway was there, as was Cyrus Vance, a former deputy secretary of defense and adviser to Johnson. They spent the first part of the afternoon and evening with Dean Rusk, Walt Rostow, United Nations Ambassador Arthur Goldberg, and CIA director Richard Helms listening to Generals Earle Wheeler and William DePuy, and Philip Habib of the State Department. When DePuy claimed that 80,000 Vietcong had died during Tet, Goldberg raised his eyebrows. He asked DePuy what the typical killed-to-wounded ratio was for the Vietcong. When DePuy said "about 3 to 1," Goldberg wanted to know how many Vietcong were still left in the field. When DePuy claimed there were 230,000 left, Goldberg started doing a little arithmetic. "I am not a great mathematician," he said, "but with 80,000 killed and with a wounded ratio of three to one, or 240,000, for a total of 320,000, who the hell are we fighting?" When General Earle Wheeler argued that the United States should not seek a negotiated settlement because "this is the worst time to negotiate," Henry Cabot Lodge leaned over to Dean Acheson and said, "Yes, because we are in worse shape militarily than we have ever been." When Wheeler said that it might take five to ten years to win the war, Douglas Dillon remembered thinking: "In November, we were told that it would take us a year to win. Now it looked like five or ten years, if that. I knew the country wouldn't stand for it."

The next morning the Wise Men met alone with Johnson. Wheeler was there at the beginning of the meeting, claiming that the Pentagon was not seeking a "classic military victory in Vietnam," which prompted an incredulous Dean Acheson to ask, "Then what in the name of God do we have five hundred thousand troops out there for? Chasing girls?" Johnson waved Wheeler out of the meeting and went around the table. He received a lot of counsel but no reassurance. McGeorge Bundy then presented their collective wisdom: "The majority feeling is that we can no longer do the job we set out to do in the time we have left. . . . We must begin to take steps to disengage. When we last met we saw reasons for hope. We hoped then there would be slow but steady progress. Last night and today the picture is not so hopeful." On that note Walt Rostow felt that he had "smelled a rat . . . a put-up job. . . . I thought to myself that what began in the spring of 1940 when Henry Stimson came to Washington ended tonight. The American Establishment is dead." So was Operation Complete Victory. Westmoreland would get neither his 206,000 new troops nor his invasions of Laos, Cambodia, and North Vietnam. When the meeting was over, Johnson said, "The establishment bastards have bailed out."

Dean Rusk had also wavered, although he would never do it publicly. His sense of loyalty ran too deep. He pushed the war for seven years, always with the conviction that it was necessary to save the world from "a billion Chinese armed with nuclear weapons." Johnson had a deep-seated trust for Rusk, a trust born of shared rural beginnings. When Rusk urged Johnson to consider a partial bombing halt over North Vietnam as a first step in launching a new peace initiative, Johnson listened, even though he remained skeptical. But if there was even a glimmer of hope that Ho Chi Minh would respond, he wanted to try. "Even a blind hog," the president said, "sometimes finds the chestnut."

Lyndon Johnson was a broken man. In his memoirs he remembered that moment clearly: "They were intelligent, experienced men. I had always regarded the majority of them as very steady and balanced. If they had been so deeply influenced by the reports of the Tet offensive, what must the average citizen be thinking?" All his life, Johnson had viewed himself as a "can-do" politician who made life better for his constituents. He prided himself on his ability to forge a consensus, to secure the support of most people for his ideas. Johnson needed consensus; he hated dissension and disapproval. But suddenly he saw himself as a hated man. The near defeat at the hands of Eugene McCarthy in New Hampshire, the entrance of Senator Robert Kennedy into the presidential race, and his own private polls indicating defeat in the upcoming Wisconsin primary convinced him that he had to take another look at Vietnam as well as his own political career. Johnson was feeling old in the spring of 1968, tired and finished.

Johnson's health was a recurring anxiety. It was not uncommon for him to undergo physical examinations every week or call in a physician to look at him every day. His 1955 heart attack still frightened him. He had abdominal and throat surgery in 1965 and 1966, and during the course of his presidency more than forty precancerous lesions and one small malignant tumor were removed from his skin. Johnson was convinced he would not live out a second term. He even had a secret actuarial study predict his longevity: "The men in the Johnson family," he said, "have a history of dying young. . . . I figure with my history of heart trouble I'd never live . . . another four years. The American people have had enough of presidents dying in office."

Long before the Tet offensive, Johnson was giving serious consideration to retiring. Tet confirmed what his own body told him. At the end of March, the president reached two momentous decisions. The war was a cancer consuming his health, his political career, and his beloved Great Society. The idea of running again for president, of facing hostile crowds shouting obscenities for a whole year, was unthinkable. Like few other presidents in American history, Johnson always had his nose to the political winds, and the spreading stink was undeniable. To avoid a divisive political campaign and prove his sincerity in seeking an end to the war, Johnson delivered a speech on the evening of March 31, 1968, that stunned the whole country. He told the American people that he was "reducing . . . the present level of hostilities. . . . I have concluded that I should not permit the Presidency to become involved in partisan divisions that are developing. . . . Accordingly, I will not seek, and I will not accept, the nomination of my party for . . . President."

Hanoi's leaders shouted for joy at the news. The war was over, if not militarily then certainly politically. Ho Chi Minh's prediction that the United States would not sustain the war politically came true. In an interview with a French journalist in 1968, Giap said: "This is the most tragic defeat for the Americans. The Tet offensive marked a turning point in this war. . . . It burst like a soap bubble the artificial optimism built up by the Pentagon. . . . Gone, and gone for good, is the hope of annihilating the Liberation forces. . . . Gone are the pacification projects. They would have to start all over from scratch." On April 1, 1968, Lyndon Johnson stopped all Rolling Thunder raids north of the nineteenth parallel, and two days later the North Vietnamese accepted the invitation to discuss the war. They were not serious, of course, any more than they had been in 1954 when they had offered to talk to the French about Dienbienphu. Diplomacy was simply another tool in bringing about the final expulsion of the United States from Indochina. Johnson picked W. Averell Harriman to head the American delegation.

But Johnson's announcements did not constitute a real change in strategy, just tactical adjustments. Along with Walt Rostow, William Westmoreland, and Earle Wheeler, he still wanted to achieve the original goal of establishing a stable, noncommunist government in Saigon. The thrashing Westmoreland had given the communists at Tet was proof of American military superiority, and, even more encouraging, ARVN had fought its Tet battles with courage and discipline. The weak link in the strategy was politics at home, Johnson believed. By withdrawing from the presidential race, rejecting the requests for more troops, and limiting the bombing of North Vietnam, Johnson hoped to buy political time for his basic policies to succeed.

Lyndon B. Johnson was not the only political victim of Tet. William Westmoreland also had to go. No less than his predecessor General Paul Harkins, Westmoreland succumbed to the "General Blimp" rhetoric—

tactical victories amid strategic defeat. Johnson brought Westmoreland home in April 1968 and named him army chief of staff. Before he left Vietnam, Westmoreland said that the "war cannot be won in the classic sense, because of our national policy of not expanding the war . . . [but we] denied to the enemy a battlefield victory . . . and arrested the spread of communism." He returned to Washington unreconstructed. Johnson replaced him with General Creighton ("Fighting Abe") Abrams.

Even though Johnson limited the air war over North Vietnam and prepared the way for negotiations in Paris, he was doing everything possible to shore up the political and military situation in Saigon. At first the center of attention was the A Shau Valley, actually a series of several valleys and mountains in Thua Thien Province. By 1968 the A Shau Valley had become one of the principal entry points into South Vietnam from the Ho Chi Minh Trail and the staging area for most enemy attacks in I Corps. More than 6,000 NVA troops were in the valley, and Westmoreland and Abrams worried that they were ready for a second offensive. Designating the attack on the A Shau Operation Delaware, Westmoreland had B-52s pound the valley for a week in mid-April before sending in elements of the First Cavalry (Airmobile) Division, the 101st Airborne Division, the 196th Light Infantry Brigade, and the ARVN First Division to attack the troops, supply caches, and bunkers. The battle raged for three weeks, costing the United States more than sixty helicopters. But they killed 850 North Vietnamese troops, compared to 139 of their own dead, drove them out of a region they had controlled for years, and captured an unprecedented number of weapons.

By the time Operation Delaware was winding down in the north, Tet II was under way farther south. With the peace talks just weeks away, enemy troops jockeyed for position. On May 5, 1968, the communists launched 119 attacks on provincial and district capitals throughout South Vietnam. They attacked Saigon and Tan Son Nhut air base and got two regiments into the northern suburbs of Saigon and back into Cholon. They also fired 122-mm rockets into Saigon for several days. The U.S. Twenty-fifth Infantry Division fought back, and tactical air strikes eventually dislodged the enemy. When the fighting ended, 160,000 more civilians were homeless.

That spring Khe Sanh was a problem again. The Tet offensive distracted American attention from Khe Sanh, but Westmoreland predicted that it was the real communist objective. He anxiously waited for an attack that never came. The North Vietnamese began to withdraw in March. American troops were there without an enemy to fight. Creighton Abrams wanted to get them out of Khe Sanh for use in other battles, but in Washington there was concern about the political fallout of withdrawing from Khe Sanh. Clark Clifford, sensing the mood of the nation, wondered about "all the hoopla last year, the talk of Dienbienphu, of Khe Sanh as the western anchor of American defenses in I Corps, the doorway to the Ho Chi Minh Trail. How's it going to look when we pull out?" Vo Nguyen Giap understood the dilemma: "As long as they [the Americans] stayed in Khe Sanh to defend their prestige, they said Khe Sanh was important; when they abandoned Khe Sanh, they said Khe Sanh had never been important." Abrams needed the men. The marines and air cav troops left Khe Sanh on June 13, 1968. General Rathvan Tompkins described what was left of Khe Sanh after 22,000 American bombing sorties: "Khe Sanh was absolutely denuded. The trees were gone . . . everything was gone. Pock-marked and ruined and burnt . . . like the surface of the moon."

Throughout 1968 the United States tried to take advantage of the communists' post-Tet weaknesses. To Vietnamize the war, Johnson insisted that South Vietnam assume more responsibility. ARVN went from 798,000 to 850,000 troops, and Creighton Abrams conducted increasing numbers of joint United States–ARVN military operations. ARVN troops received crash training programs in the latest military technology and equipment. It was not an easy task, since the South Vietnamese did not mind having the United States doing the fighting. A frustrated Clark Clifford, after a July 1968 visit to South Vietnam, complained that it was still largely an American war and that "the South Vietnamese leaders seemed content to have it that way."

The pacification programs were also expanded. The Vietcong suffered terribly during Tet and were vulnerable to military as well as political action. Robert Komer wanted to destroy them before the peace negotiations reached a settlement. His computerized Hamlet Evaluation Survey indicated that 1,200 villages were still under Vietcong control. Komer left South Vietnam later in 1968 to become ambassador to Turkey and was replaced by William E. Colby. As head of the Civil Operations and Revolutionary Development Support office, Colby designed the Accelerated Pacification Campaign and the Phoenix Program in 1968.

Born in St. Paul, Minnesota, in 1920, Colby graduated from Princeton in 1940 and spent World War II in the Office of Strategic Services fighting with the French resistance. After the war he earned a law degree at Columbia and joined the CIA in 1950. Colby became CIA station chief in Saigon in 1959. After three years there he returned to Washington to head the CIA's Far East Division. Late in 1968 he replaced Komer as deputy MACV commander in charge of pacification. A devout Roman Catholic, Colby saw life as a constant struggle between good and evil. Neil Sheehan said that if Colby had been born in the sixteenth century, he would have been perfect as a soldier for Christ in the Jesuit order. The post–World War II embodiment of evil was communism, and Colby viewed himself as an anticommunist crusader, a civilian soldier fighting for a free world.

Under the Phoenix Program, Colby planned to destroy the Vietcong infrastructure. With CIA and CORDS assistance, he charged South Vietnam with eliminating the Vietcong leadership through arrest, conversion, or assassination. The South Vietnamese implemented the program aggressively, but it proved to be laced with corruption and political infighting. Some South Vietnamese politicians identified political enemies as Vietcong and sent Phoenix hit men after them. The pressure to identify Vietcong led to a quota system that incorrectly labeled many innocent people as the enemy. By 1972 as many as 20,000 people, many of them Vietcong, had been assassinated. Although Phoenix undoubtedly hurt the Vietcong, it was nothing compared to the decimation of Tet and the post–Tet military campaigns MACV waged against them.

With the Phoenix Program eliminating the Vietcong infrastructure, Colby launched the Accelerated Pacification Campaign to win over the loyalties of the 1,200 Vietcong-controlled villages. Using local anti-Vietcong militia to provide security and differentiate between Vietcong and nonpolitical families, the Accelerated Pacification Campaign set out to win the "hearts and minds" of peasants through economic development—clearing roads, repairing bridges, building schools, and increasing rice production—and land reform. The program lasted until early 1970. By that time the Accelerated Pacification Campaign redistributed more than 2.5 million acres of land to peasants and armed more than 500,000 local militia to protect villages from Vietcong attack. Those were no minor achievements, but they failed to counterbalance the destruction and dislocation that the killing machine was bringing to South Vietnamese peasants.

Back home the war was also taking its toll on American politics. With Lyndon Johnson out of the presidential race, Vice President Hubert Humphrey entered the contest. Born in South Dakota in 1911, Humphrey became mayor of Minneapolis in 1944. He gained a national profile at the 1948 Democratic convention when he campaigned for a strong civil rights position in the party platform. Humphrey won a seat in the United States Senate in 1948 and was reelected in 1954 and 1960. He was a Roosevelt liberal, an advocate of civil rights, Medicare, and prolabor legislation. He made an unsuccessful bid for the Democratic presidential nomination in 1960 and in 1964 accepted the vice presidential spot.

Those were the worst four years of Humphrey's life. Johnson was contemptuous of Humphrey, calling him a "little boy who cries too much." Shortly after the inauguration in 1965, Winston Churchill died, and instead of sending Humphrey to the funeral, Johnson asked Chief Justice Earl Warren to go. Humphrey never forgot the insult. Humphrey worried about escalating the war, and in retaliation Johnson froze him out of policy-making discussions.

When Johnson withdrew from the race, Humphrey made a quick decision to go for the nomination. His dilemma was obvious. For three years,

despite private misgivings, Humphrey had publicly supported administration policies in Vietnam. If he continued to back the idea of military
victory, he would not enjoy any support from insurgent Democrats ready
to split the party in two. But if he made public his personal opposition to
escalation, he risked Lyndon Johnson's wrath. Johnson no longer had
the power to designate his successor, but he could veto Humphrey.

The peace negotiations complicated Humphrey's troubles. The talks
began in Paris on May 13, 1968. W. Averell Harriman represented the
United States. North Vietnam sent Xuan Thuy. Thuy was one of the
earliest anti-French Vietnamese nationalists, and he had spent years in
French prisons. Between 1963 and 1965 he served as foreign minister of
North Vietnam. Nguyen Thi Binh represented the National Liberation
Front, the political arm of the Vietcong. Born in Saigon in 1927, she was
a strident student nationalist, opposed to French rule, and imprisoned
between 1951 and 1954 for anti-French activities. She joined the National Liberation Front in 1960 and was soon traveling the world promoting Vietcong goals. South Vietnam sent Vice President Nguyen Cao Ky
to head its delegation.

South Vietnam was in no mood to compromise. Any accommodation
with the communists, the South Vietnamese knew, would eventually
doom its leaders to labor camps or worse. The United States approached
the talks believing it held the advantage in Vietnam, while the North
Vietnamese were just as certain that the United States had suffered a
strategic defeat. From the beginning Johnson insisted that Harriman
take the hard line: Leave the Thieu-Ky government in place, deny representation for the National Liberation Front, implement mutual withdrawal of all North Vietnamese and American troops, and exchange
prisoners of war. Xuan Thuy, just as adamantly, articulated the North
Vietnamese position: Cease all bombing raids over North Vietnam, withdraw all American troops from South Vietnam, remove the Thieu-Ky
government, and create a coalition government in Saigon that included
the National Liberation Front.

The American delegation spent the first few weeks quartered in the
plush fifth floor of the Crillon Hotel, but after a few meetings with Xuan
Thuy, they moved down to the cheaper first floor and brought their wives
from Washington. It was going to be a long stay. Throughout 1968 the
impasse found expression in a debate over the size and shape of the negotiating table. Ky refused to sit at the same table with Nguyen Thi Binh,
especially if her place indicated equal status with him. Binh, of course,
insisted on equal status. Harriman found himself trying to think of a
table design that would satisfy them both. The world press corps de-
scended on Paris to report the talks but ended up taking pictures again
and again of the table. Art Buchwald noted that once they had finished
the six-month debate over the shape of the table, the diplomats would
have all of 1969 to decide on "butcher block, Formica, or wood finish."

Harriman considered Nguyen Cao Ky an impossible, petulant hack who made the communists look like paragons of virtue. One member of the American delegation drew a laugh out of Harriman when he suggested that they solve the problem of the size and shape of the table by using "different size chairs, with the baby's high chair reserved for Ky." More than one observer noted that during debate about the table, 8,000 Americans died along with 50,000 North Vietnamese and perhaps another 50,000 South Vietnamese civilians. Throughout 1968 the Johnson administration did not waver from its position, and the Paris peace talks bogged down into an endless series of procedural arguments, deepening the cynicism with which Americans viewed the war.

The presidential candidates running against the war made the most of the stalled negotiations. Humphrey's strongest opposition came from Senator Robert Kennedy. Born in Boston in 1925, Kennedy graduated from Harvard and then from the University of Virginia Law School. He masterminded his brother's successful 1960 bid for the presidency and then became attorney general. Robert Kennedy was a man of intense passion and brutal honesty. Tact was not his strong suit. Joseph Kennedy, the patriarch of the family, felt that John was too forgiving of other people, too willing to let bygones be bygones. But Bobby was different. "When he hates you," the old man said, "you stay hated." After his brother's assassination, Kennedy served as attorney general for a few more months, but his dislike for Lyndon Johnson was matched only by Johnson's hatred for him. Although both agreed about the need for civil rights, education, and antipoverty legislation, their personalities were too different. They could never bridge the gap between the lace-curtain riches of Massachusetts and earthy poverty of the Hill Country. Kennedy left the Justice Department in 1964 and won a United States Senate seat from New York.

Robert Kennedy was a different man after the assassination. He lost his cocksure attitude and became introspective, reading deeply on philosophy, tragedy, and religion. He questioned the existence of God in a world that killed the innocent. He became enamored of Albert Camus, and from Camus, Kennedy wrote in his notebook, "Perhaps we cannot prevent this world from being a world in which children are tortured, but we can reduce the number of tortured children." By 1966 he concluded that the war was out of control, that the United States was seeking a military solution to a political problem. When he announced for the presidency on March 16, 1968, he said, "I have tried in vain to alter our course in Vietnam before it further saps our spirit and our manpower, further raises the risks of a wider war, and further destroys the country and the people it was meant to save." His campaign was an immediate success. The Kennedy mystique was a powerful force in 1968, as were Kennedy money and ties to the party machine. Eugene McCarthy commanded the respect of the antiwar movement, but its heart was with Kennedy. Kennedy defeated Humphrey in the California primary in June, but on the night of his victory he was assassinated in Los Angeles. His death put the nomination in Humphrey's hands. The Democrats then headed for their national convention in Chicago.

The Republican campaign was also revolving around the war. Nelson Rockefeller, heir to the Standard Oil fortune and governor of New York, was hoping for the GOP nomination. But Republican conservatives hated him, not only for his moderate liberalism but because of his tepid support of Barry Goldwater in the election of 1964. Michigan governor George Romney, a former president of American Motors, was another liberal Republican. Although GOP conservatives did not agree with many of Romney's positions, they did not detest him as they did Rockefeller. But Romney was a victim of his own rhetoric. He visited Vietnam early in 1968 and was suspicious of MACV propaganda. During the New Hampshire primary campaign in late February, Romney mentioned that he felt that MACV "brainwashed" him about the war's progress. Most Americans associated the word "brainwashed" with what the Chinese and North Koreans had done to American prisoners during the Korean War. The remark alienated large numbers of voters, and Romney lost the New Hampshire primary.

Richard M. Nixon won. Between 1953 and 1961 Nixon had served as vice president under Dwight D. Eisenhower, but he lost the 1960 presidential election to John F. Kennedy. After losing the 1962 California gubernatorial election, Nixon practiced law and spoke on behalf of Republican candidates, building up a long list of political IOUs that he called in during the 1968 election. In the vaguest terms, Nixon criticized Johnson's conduct of the war and promised that he could do better. On the eve of the New Hampshire primary he said, "I pledge to you that new leadership will end the war and win the peace in the Pacific." When Humphrey demanded that he spell out his peace plan, Nixon responded, "No one with this responsibility who is seeking office should give away any of his bargaining position in advance. . . . Under no circumstances should a man say what he would do next January." If Democrats were skeptical, Republicans were not. Nixon easily won the nomination.

Neither Nixon's vague peace plans nor Humphrey's equally vague promises satisfied frustrated American youths. For three years their calls for an end to the war had increased in stridency. Government officials and agents had ignored their demands, infiltrated their organizations, and criticized their actions. For a brief time some saw a glimmer of hope in Eugene McCarthy and Bobby Kennedy. But McCarthy's philosophical temperament alienated too many people, and Kennedy was dead. At his funeral, Tom Hayden, a leader of SDS, wept. Across the country other students shared those emotions. Michael Harrington, whose writings had brought poverty to the attention of Americans, later noted, "As I look back on the 60s [Robert Kennedy] was the man who actually could have changed the course of American history."

With Kennedy gone, young protesters lost their only powerful political voice. He might have been elected president. He might have made a difference. The remaining politicians were establishment figures who cared little for the dreams of the young. To register their protests—to voice their disenchantment with the political process that excluded them—members of various student organizations decided to go to the National Democratic Convention in Chicago. Some represented factions of the New Left. Many were committed Marxists, wedded to revolutionary change. Others were apostles of the counterculture whose politics were as nebulous as their religious beliefs. The only conviction they shared was the notion that liberal politics were moribund.

The establishment Democrats should have known what was in store. When Martin Luther King, Jr., was assassinated in April 1968, there were widespread racial rebellions throughout the country, including New York City. Late in April, when Columbia University president Grayson Kirk held a memorial service for King, the local SDS disrupted the gathering, accusing Columbia of being insensitive to the needs of black people and of supporting the Vietnam War through its contracts with the Institute for Defense Analysis. Eventually, a mob of students occupied several buildings on campus, including Kirk's office, and pictures of them smoking his cigars and drinking his sherry made all the wire services. The dispute went on for three weeks before New York City police forcibly cleared the campus.

The protest movement then shifted to Chicago. Orthodox politicians cared little for the creeds of the New Left and the politically outrageous. Chicago's Mayor Richard Daley mobilized 12,000 police and prepared to call out national guardsmen. He denied demonstrators the right to protest or march. Short, barrel-chested, and with the jowls of a big city boss, Daley promised that he would not allow any "long-haired punks" to dirty the city where he attended mass every day and where "decent" people lived. Novelist Norman Mailer caught Daley's disdain for the eastern press and the counterculture: "No interlopers for any network of Jew-Wasp media men were going to dominate the streets of his parochial city, nor none of their crypto-accomplices with long hair, sexual liberty, drug license and unbridled mouths."

Given Daley's attitude and the determination of the protesters, violence was certain. The Youth International party, or Yippies, led by Abbie Hoffman and Jerry Rubin, urged people to "vote Pig in '68." They nominated their own candidate—"Pigasus," a fat pig they paraded through the streets. They demanded legalization of marijuana and "all other psychedelic drugs," an "end to all censorship," total disarmament of all people "beginning with the police," and abolition of money and

In August 1968, as Democrats met to nominate a presidential candidate, the streets of Chicago erupted into violent antiwar demonstrations and police riots.
UPI/BETTMANN

work. "We believe," Point 15 of their manifesto stated, "that people should fuck all the time, anytime, whomever they wish." Such appeals were not part of Mayor Daley's vision for a better America.

Police repeatedly clashed with the demonstrators. They fired tear gas into groups of protesters. Caught in one attack, Sol Lerner of the *Village Voice* recalled, "We walked along, hands outstretched, bumping into people and trees, tears dripping from our eyes and mucus smeared across our faces." The police, armed with clubs, waded into the demonstrators. One person remembered, "I saw a cop hit a guy over the head and the club break. I turned to the left and saw another cop jab the guy right in the kidneys." Demonstrators fought back, threw rocks, overturned cars, set trash cans on fire. Reporters and photographers became victims of what was later termed a "police riot." Nicholas von Hoffman of the *Washington Post* reported that the police went after news photographers: "Pictures are unanswerable evidence in court. [The police had] taken off their badges, their name plates, even the unit patches on their shoulders to become a mob of identical, unidentifiable club swingers." But the television cameras did not blink, and the violence became entertainment in millions of homes. Disgusted by the police actions, Walter Cronkite told his prime-time viewers, "I want to pack my bags and get out of this city."

The violence in the streets spilled into the convention center. Several delegates were assaulted outside the convention hall. When Mike Wallace of CBS questioned the suppression of dissent, a cop slugged him on the jaw. Speaking from the podium, Senator Abraham Ribicoff of Connecticut condemned the "Gestapo tactics" of the Chicago police. His remarks brought Daley to his feet, shaking his fist and calling Ribicoff a "motherfucker." In this atmosphere Hubert Humphrey—whose theme was "The Politics of Joy"—received the nomination for president.

The debacle in Chicago doomed Humphrey's chances for the election. He was also hurt by the candidacy of Governor George Wallace of Alabama. Born to poor sharecroppers, Wallace was a populist who opposed civil rights legislation and called for a military victory in Vietnam. When he received no support from the regular Democratic party, Wallace created the American party. He drew substantial support in the Deep South and among some white ethnic workers in the North. Humphrey needed both groups to win. For his vice presidential running mate, Wallace selected retired air force general Curtis LeMay, whose opinion on the Vietnam War was quite simple. In 1967 he argued that the United States "must be willing to continue our bombing until we have destroyed every work of man in North Vietnam if this is what it takes to win the war." At the press conference when he accepted the nomination, he was even more blunt. In response to a question about how to end the war, LeMay instantly said that he "would bomb North Vietnam back into the stone age."

Throughout most of the fall, Humphrey tried to rid himself of the Vietnam millstone without alienating Johnson. Richard Nixon kept promising a "secret plan." Not until late October did Humphrey openly call for a negotiated settlement, and on October 31, 1968, hoping to breathe some life into the peace negotiations, President Johnson ended all Rolling Thunder bombing raids. He had little choice. Nguyen Van Thieu, suspecting that he might get better treatment from Richard Nixon as president than from Hubert Humphrey, refused to engage in serious talks in Paris, raising suspicions in the United States about whether the talks would ever amount to anything. Johnson hoped the bombing halt would boost Humphrey's chances. But it was too little and too late. Nixon won by a narrow margin. He received 43.4 percent of the popular vote and 302 electoral votes to 42.7 percent and 191 electoral votes for Humphrey and 13.5 percent and 45 electoral votes for Wallace.

Politics was not the only arena where American discontent with the war manifested itself. Popular culture reflected the malaise as well. By the 1966–1967 season, pro-military television programs were losing their appeal. Americans could watch a real war every night on the six o'clock news. During 1964–1965, the Nielsen ratings had *Combat!* as the tenth most popular television show in the country. Although its ratings slipped modestly in the next two seasons, the show still garnered a profitable share of the television audience. But *Combat!* was still canceled at the end of the 1966 season. Several of the series' stars, including Vic Morrow, attributed its demise to the growing criticism of the war in Vietnam. *Combat!* was not the only military program to fade from the airways during the late 1960s. By 1966, *Mona McCluskey, Convoy, McHale's Navy,* and *Wackiest Ship in the Army* were gone, and *Combat!* and *Twelve O' Clock High* disappeared the next season. When the 1968 fall season opened, only *Gomer Pyle* and *Hogan's Heroes* survived.

Overt antiwar themes made their way into television. In the early years of the war, references to Johnson's policies occasionally appeared on the controversial *That Was the Week That Was,* which aired from January 1964 until May 1965. Other shows offered antiwar sentiments in more subtle forms, including one concerning a real-life frontier American. *Daniel Boone* aired from September 1964 through the spring of 1970. Barry Rosenzweig supervised its writers, and he instructed them to portray the Revolutionary War by "making it Vietnam, with the colonials as the Vietcong and the English as the Americans." *Star Trek* consistently aired story lines condemning war and insisting that star fleet captains avoid interfering with the internal affairs of new civilizations they encountered. Even *Mission: Impossible* stopped overthrowing foreign governments and switched to more domestic missions, such as dealing with organized crime, for the government.

Other programs were not so subtle. The Smothers Brothers were a singing-comedy team who gained national fame during the popularity explosion of folk music in the early 1960s. In a midseason attempt to steal viewers from NBC's *Bonanza,* CBS gave them their own weekly variety program on Sunday nights. Tommy and Dick Smothers soon became folk heroes to antiwar activists. In September 1967, they invited folk singer Pete Seeger to appear on the show. He was scheduled to perform his sarcastic antiwar song "Waist Deep in the Big Muddy," but the network cut the segment when Seeger, backed by the Smothers Brothers, refused to cut the most controversial verse. In February 1968, after a long battle with CBS, Tommy Smothers once again introduced Seeger on the show, and this time Seeger was allowed to perform the song in its entirety. The Smothers Brothers continued to battle the network and its censors, but CBS finally canceled them in 1969, even though their ratings were excellent, after they featured an interview with Joan Baez, who made a reference to her husband's prison term for draft evasion.

Opposition to the war also found expression in a number of popular novels published in the mid-1960s. Most of the fiction portrayed Indochina as an alien place for Americans, a region of the world where they ought not be involved. John Sack's *M* (1967) was one of the first of the

Some critics called Vietnam a "living-room war" because
of the pervasive influence of television. Television
correspondents and cameramen roamed the countryside
looking for stories, and the networks subjected viewers to
a daily bombardment of Vietnam War news.
OFFICIAL U.S. MARINE CORPS PHOTO

antiwar novels. It focuses on M Company, a training unit of American
soldiers, and it follows them from basic training at Fort Dix, New Jersey,
through several months of combat in Vietnam. Sack juxtaposes Specialist 4 Demirgian, a "gung-ho" American soldier committed to the philosophical rationale of the war, with the corruption of ARVN troops, the
inability to distinguish between Vietcong and civilians, and the unbe-
lievably poor morale among United States soldiers. The novel climaxes
in a tragic killing of a Vietnamese girl by an American grenade lobbed
into a shelter to kill Vietcong.

David Halberstam's *One Very Hot Day* (1967) revolves around several
American advisers who are trying to train the South Vietnamese army.
The central character is a Captain Beaupré, who views the whole country as a worthless hellhole. A veteran of World War II and Korea, he has
no illusions about the Vietnam War, and his only objective is to stay
alive in the hot, sticky, despair-ridden environment. But Beaupré's
second-in-command—the young, idealistic Lieutenant Anderson—has
high hopes for successfully training the South Vietnamese soldiers and
winning the war against communism. In the end, the South Vietnamese
troops fail to fight, Beaupré manages to survive, but Anderson dies in a
firefight. Beaupré is unable to find any reason for his death, any meaning for an American to be dead in a nowhere-place called Ap Than Thoi.

Incident at Muc Wa was the title of Daniel Ford's 1967 novel about the Vietnam War. The book centers on Corporal Stephen Courcey, a demolitions expert who has just arrived in Vietnam. Along with several other American soldiers, he establishes an outpost at Muc Wa. The novel proceeds to expose the absurdities of the war through tragicomedy. Courcey's girlfriend from the States shows up at Muc Wa as a war correspondent, but she is unable to meet him because he is off in the jungles with a visiting general and army captain who are trying to earn their Combat Infantry Badges. The novel provides a caricature of stupid officers fighting a war for the wrong reasons. In the end, the troops at Muc Wa fight off a Vietcong attack, and the Vietcong, in Ford's words, "exfiltrate" the area. In the end, Courcey is killed in action.

Norman Mailer's *Why Are We in Vietnam?* (1967) is not actually set in Indochina. Placed in Texas, New York City, and the Brooks Range of Alaska, it is an antiwar story without ever being in Vietnam. A cast of characters—D. J. Jellicoe, Rusty Jellicoe, Alice Lee Jellicoe, Medium Asshole Pete, Medium Asshole Bill, and Tex Hude—end up in the Brooks Range of Alaska on a hunting trip. There, in a pristine and naturally savage environment, they use all the hunting technology they can muster and literally slaughter wolves, caribou, bighorn sheep, and bears. The carnage is extraordinary and, for Norman Mailer, symbolic of what American military technology was doing to the life and habitat of Southeast Asia.

James Crumley's novel *One Count to Cadence* (1969) and William Eastlake's *The Bamboo Red* (1969) were both written in the immediate wake of the Tet offensive. *One Count to Cadence* centers on a ten-man communications detachment stationed first at Clark Air Base in the Philippines and then in Vietnam during the early stages of the war. A Sergeant "Slag" Krummel is the narrator, and his foil is Joe Morning, a self-destructive loser. The novel exposes the gratuitous violence of military life—bars, brothels, fights, and profanity—as well as the futility of the war in Vietnam. The sergeant eventually betrays a best friend and buddy, and the team is decimated. The novel ends with the unit returning to the Philippines, where Joe Morning joins the communist-inspired Huk Rebellion there. *The Bamboo Red,* a surrealistic condemnation of the war, begins with the suicide of a Madame Dieudonne after she hears of the death of her American Ranger lover Captain Clancy. Eastlake tries to describe the absurdity of the war with implausible fantasy images: peace-loving hippie flower children wandering aimlessly through the Indochinese jungles; helicopter pilots having sex with medevac nurses while airborne; American Rangers topped with Roman helmets and accompanied by drummer boys airlifted into French-Vietnamese villas. The war in Vietnam makes no sense at all, just as the strange images of *The Bamboo Red* cannot fit into any rational world.

Even comic books reflected the increasing depth of antiwar sentiment in American popular culture. Comic book readers had become too sophisticated about the Vietnam War to accept the traditional stereotypes about the domino theory. Dell Comics' *Jungle War Stories,* which featured Vietnam War themes, had failed commercially in 1966, proving that the war was going to be difficult to sell to the American people. *Tales of the Green Beret* was dropped by most newspapers in 1967. In 1968 Marvel Comics abandoned cold war and Vietnam themes altogether, shifting the focus of Iron Man's exploits to such domestic issues as race relations, environmental problems, and crime. America was getting tired of Vietnam.

How times had changed from the confident naivete of 1965! The treatment of the Green Berets in American popular culture symbolized the changing public mood. During the Kennedy years, the Green Berets were perceived as missionaries with muscles. They received training that conformed to the prescription in *The Ugly American.* In theory, to be considered for the Green Berets, a volunteer had to be both ranger- and airborne-qualified, physically fit, and able to speak at least one foreign language. Once accepted into the outfit, the Green Beret was then trained to proficiency in "skills such as demolition, communications and field medicine . . . unarmed combat, SCUBA diving and mountaineering, and . . . all kinds of weapons." In addition, he had to know his enemy. At their training center at Fort Bragg, Green Berets read the works of Mao Zedong and Vo Nguyen Giap as well as prepared their bodies to meet the enemy in battle. Describing the Green Berets in his *The Best and the Brightest* (1972), David Halberstam wrote, "They were all uncommon men, extraordinary physical specimens and intellectual Ph.D.s, swinging through trees, speaking Russian and Chinese, eating snake meat and other fauna, springing counter-ambushes at night on unwary Asian ambushers who had read Mao and Giap, but not Hilsman and Rostow."

In Robin Moore's *The Green Berets* the "ugly American" is transformed into a bright and shining knight, a warrior for democracy. The novel was a huge financial success. Published in 1965, it rocketed onto the *New York Times* best-seller list. Although Moore upset government officials by portraying Green Berets taking part in forays into North Vietnam, his attitude toward the war echoed the official line. When asked why he is in Vietnam, a Green Beret replies, "First, I am a professional soldier and I take orders and do what I am told. Second, I don't want my children fighting the Communists at home." Once again the vision of toppling dominoes is conjured. And between Indochina and California, Moore posits the Green Berets, "a potent new weapon against the Communists."

But three years later John Wayne translated the novel onto the silver screen. In 1965 he bought the film rights for *The Green Berets* and consciously set about making a propaganda movie. Although he was an active and outspoken Republican, he strongly supported the Democratic policy in Vietnam. He wrote President Johnson that he believed it was "extremely important that not only the people of the United States but those all over the world should know why it is necessary for us to be there." Recalling the role of the film industry during World War II, Wayne suggested that he could "tell the story of our fighting men in Vietnam with reason, emotion, characterization and action. We want to do it in a manner that will inspire a patriotic attitude on the part of fellow-Americans—a feeling which we have always had in this country in the past during stress and trouble." Johnson's aide Jack Valenti advised the president that Wayne would be "saying the things we want said," and with this assurance Wayne received administration support for his project. Much of the film was shot at Fort Benning, and the army supported the effort with Huey helicopters and technical advisers.

The result was a controversial film that faithfully presented the administration's position. The central focus of the film is the awakening of a "liberal" journalist—played by David Janssen—to the real nature of American involvement. At first the journalist is skeptical; he doubts the domino theory, the threat of communism, and the viability of the government in South Vietnam. But after following the activities of the Green Beret lieutenant colonel Michael Kirby—played by John Wayne—he reverses his earlier opinions. Nevertheless, even the journalist realizes that it will be difficult to tell the true story of the war in Vietnam because of the liberal bias of the American press. "If I say what I feel," he informs Kirby, "I may be out of a job." In the end the film suggests that the United States' biggest fight is not against the North Vietnamese but rather against the liberal establishment that threatens the war effort by its opposition.

In most respects *The Green Berets* is a typical John Wayne war movie. It could have been set in the Pacific during World War II or in the West during the Indian wars. There are good guys and bad guys, with the former badly outnumbered by the latter. Yet despite every material disadvantage, good triumphs. The Vietnamese in the film even speak the pidgin English of the Indians in Wayne's Westerns. At one point a South Vietnamese tells Kirby, "We build many camps, clobber many V.C." *The Green Berets* simply updates the Western, replacing stagecoaches and horses with helicopters and changing the skin color of the enemy. But the mentality remains the same.

Unfortunately for Wayne, by the time the film was released in the summer of 1968 most Americans no longer believed the official administration line. Critics received *The Green Berets* in the same spirit of profound skepticism. Renata Adler in the *New York Times* wrote:

> *The Green Berets* is a film so unspeakable, so stupid, so rotten and false . . .
> that it passes through being fun, through being funny, through being camp,

through everything and becomes an invitation to grieve, not for our soldiers in Vietnam or for Vietnam (the film could not be more false or do a greater disservice to either of them) but for what has happened to the fantasy-making apparatus. . . . Simplicities of the right, simplicities of the left, but this one is beyond the possible. It is vile and insane.

Even trade journals criticized the film. *The Hollywood Reporter* called it "a cliché-ridden throw-back to the battlefield potboilers of World War II, its artifice readily exposed by the nightly actuality of TV news coverage."

There were good reasons for the public alienation. At the end of 1968 there were 536,000 American troops in Vietnam, along with another 65,000 troops from South Korea, Australia, and New Zealand. ARVN troops totaled 850,000. More than 30,000 Americans were dead. The communists staked their future on a stalemate with the United States. Convinced that they would always enjoy the tactical initiative and could decide when and where to engage American troops, the North Vietnamese were waiting for the American people to tire of the war. It was time for Richard Nixon to deliver on his "secret plan."

9

The Beginning of the End, 1969–1970

*We have to stop it with victory, or it will start all over again
in a few years.*
                                        —Richard Nixon, 1968

As a congressman and as vice president, Richard Nixon took pride in his reputation as the fastest dresser in the capital. It took him two and one-half minutes to put on a regular suit; formal wear took eight minutes. He was fast because there was so much to do. Other politicians may have been brighter than Nixon. Others certainly were better educated, better connected, and better liked. But few were better organized or willing to work as hard. For most of his career he carried a list of things to do in his suit pocket. And with an eye for the smallest detail, he did what was on the list. It was his saving grace, making up for the other graces he lacked. Unlike establishment politicians whom he hated, Nixon lacked a sense of humor, smooth social skills, and a glib style. But they lacked his drive, his willingness to do whatever it took to get the job done.

Given his background, Nixon's rise to power was swift. Born in Yorba Linda, California, in 1913, Nixon was raised in a poor family that, if not the embodiment of the American Dream, still believed in it. His parents were hard-working people, outspoken supporters of the "little man" and critics of big business. When Nixon was nine, his father moved the family to Whittier and bought a small grocery store. He devoted his life to the small business and eventually made a success of it. Nixon also worked—in school and after school. During the early 1930s Nixon attended Whittier College on an academic scholarship. But he continued to work at the store—waking at 4 A.M., driving into Los Angeles to pick up vegetables, setting up displays, attending classes, and studying until past midnight. Nixon also kept the books for the store and at Whittier played football, served as president of his class and several other organizations, worked as a reporter for the school newspaper, starred in school plays, and excelled on the debating team. In a letter of recommendation for Nixon to Duke Law School, Whittier president Walter Dexter wrote, "I cannot recommend him too highly because I believe that Nixon will become one of America's important, if not great leaders."

But Nixon was a bundle of contradictions. Outwardly he was confident to the point of arrogance, but beneath the surface was a shy, insecure person. As his biographer Stephen E. Ambrose noted, "He was sympathetic and solicitous to [a] woman who was stealing from the family store, but outraged and eager to punish those who spoke against the Constitution. He knew everyone . . . but had no real friends. He was a student leader . . . but shy around people." In every respect Nixon was a young man of action and shadow.

From Whittier College, Nixon went to Duke Law School, where he received outstanding grades but no invitations to join prestigious eastern law firms. He returned to Whittier, practiced law, married, enlisted in the navy after Pearl Harbor, and served with distinction. In 1945 a leading Republican banker in Whittier asked Nixon if he would be interested in opposing Democratic incumbent Jerry Voorhis in the 1946 congressional elections. Nixon was. True to form, he ran a hard race, working long hours and always planning. Aided by the conservative mood of the country—and exploiting that mood by accusing Voorhis of having communist support—Nixon won the election and then walked smack into history. A first-term congressman, he was appointed to the House Un-American Activities Committee (HUAC). A high-profile committee, HUAC took its investigations on the road, conducting sensational sessions in Hollywood and other media centers. Nixon's picture appeared frequently in the press. Within eighteen months he earned a reputation as a hard-working, careful congressman.

Then came the Hiss-Chambers case. Whittaker Chambers—overweight, rumpled, outspoken ex-communist—testified before HUAC that Alger Hiss was a communist. Hiss was a democrat of impeccable breeding—Johns Hopkins, Harvard Law, clerk for Oliver Wendell Holmes, counsel for the Senate investigation of the arms industry, a member of the Yalta Conference team, a leader in the organization of the United Nations, and president of the Carnegie Endowment for International Peace. To accuse such a man of being a communist agent was difficult even for the conservative anti-New Dealers on HUAC to stomach. If Chambers were lying—something he was known for—it would embarrass HUAC. It was Nixon who sensed that Hiss was lying and Chambers was telling the truth. It was Nixon who would not allow the case to die. And in the end, it was Nixon who was right and who received the fame for uncovering the "New Deal" spy.

After the Hiss case, Nixon moved rapidly up the political ladder. He won a Senate seat in 1950. In 1952 he was elected vice president of the United States. In 1960 he ran for president. It was then that his luck went south. Nixon faced another wealthy, Ivy League-educated, handsome easterner—John Kennedy. Nixon had more experience than Kennedy, and on paper he appeared better qualified. But Kennedy had something that could not be measured and that Nixon could not duplicate. He had confidence—a deeply rooted, intrinsic confidence. Nixon's campaign went badly. He banged his kneecap into an automobile door in Greensboro, North Carolina, and when the injury became infected he spent several weeks in Walter Reed Hospital—his leg in traction, his head on a pillow, and the nation speeding toward an election. After he checked out of Walter Reed, he caught a bad chest cold. Then—tired, worried, and looking both—he had to debate a fresh, tanned Kennedy in Chicago before television cameras. He lost both the debate and the election. It was a crushing defeat.

As Nixon would later truthfully say, he was no quitter. One lost election did not end a political career. In 1962 he ran for governor of California. Again he lost. Angry, frustrated, and most of all hurt, he told the press, "As I leave you I want you to know—just think how much you're going to be missing. You won't have Nixon to kick around anymore, because, gentlemen, this is my last press conference." After the press conference Nixon exited, as one reporter commented, "snarling." It appeared that his political career was over.

Of course it was not. Nixon traversed the country, speaking out on the important issues and cultivating political contacts. And as the war in Vietnam destroyed the Johnson administration, Nixon set his sights on 1968. Soon there was talk of a "new" Nixon, a more mature, more secure, more confident Nixon. But reporter Tom Wicker wrote in 1962: "He is, if anything, more reserved and inward, as difficult as ever to know, driven still by deep inner compulsion toward power and personal vindication, painfully conscious of slights and failures, a man who had imposed upon himself a self-control so rigid as to be all but visible." But in 1968 the public need to reject Lyndon Johnson was so great that it ushered Richard Nixon into the White House.

As national security adviser, Nixon selected Henry Kissinger, a man whose rotund body and craggy face were a cartoonist's delight. Heinz Alfred Kissinger was born in 1923 in Fürth, Germany, to a Jewish family. They fled Nazi persecution in 1938 and settled in New York City. Drafted into the army in 1943, Kissinger ended up in Germany serving as an interpreter. After the war he became one of Harvard's most brilliant undergraduates and then went on to earn his Ph.D. in 1954. By that time he was widely acknowledged, by students and professors, as a leading intellect on the campus. He joined the faculty, taking over the international relations course McGeorge Bundy had taught. Kissinger was a consultant to both the Kennedy and Johnson administrations and a foreign policy adviser to Nelson Rockefeller between 1964 and 1968. Nixon took notice of him during the 1968 presidential campaign.

Kissinger possessed several powerful convictions about international politics. In his 1957 book *Nuclear War and Foreign Policy,* he advocated use of tactical nuclear weapons in a total defense strategy. The filmmaker Stanley Kubrick used him as the role model for the Nazisaluting, German-accented megalomaniac in his 1964 dark comedy *Dr. Strangelove*. In his doctoral dissertation, a study of the Congress of Vienna of 1815, Kissinger had argued that diplomacy was a complicated, interrelated balancing act between the major powers. Any significant event in the life of one power automatically affected every other major power. The achievement of absolute superiority by one power imposed absolute insecurity on every other power and destabilized international politics. Every nation on earth had the right to legitimacy and security.

Kissinger had a strong disdain for moralistic assumptions. Woodrow Wilson's moral diplomacy undermined the Treaty of Versailles and indirectly contributed to World War II. The irrational fears of McCarthyism in the 1950s were another case. Moralistic images replaced rational calculations and prevented the United States, the Soviet Union, and China from dealing successfully with one another. Regardless of institutional differences, the major powers had to respect their rights to govern themselves internally without external, ideological interference.

As far as Vietnam was concerned, Kissinger considered it the height of folly. The United States should never have become bogged down in such a war. At best, Indochina was tangential to United States' national security. Mindless fears and moralistic assumptions about stopping global communism back in the 1950s and early 1960s pushed the United States into an untenable situation. Kissinger believed that a military victory in South Vietnam was out of the question unless the United States was willing to increase its combat strength to as many as 1.3 million men, something which Tet made politically impossible. For Kissinger, the United States had no choice but disengagement. How to do that was the question. Just before Nixon's inauguration, Kissinger wrote that the United States was "so powerful that Hanoi is simply unable to defeat us militarily. . . . It must negotiate about it. Unfortunately our military strength has no political corollary; we have been unable so far to create a political structure that could survive military opposition from Hanoi." Kennedy and Johnson gave South Vietnam more strategic importance than it deserved, but it was too late to withdraw. "The commitment of 500,000 Americans has settled the issue of the importance of Vietnam. For what is involved now is the confidence of American promises."

Secretary of State Dean Rusk returned to the University of Georgia to teach, and Nixon appointed William P. Rogers to replace him. A graduate of Colgate and the Cornell University Law School, Rogers had enjoyed a distinguished career. He joined Richard Nixon's staff working on the Alger Hiss case in 1950, and in 1957 President Eisenhower appointed him attorney general. In 1969 President Richard Nixon named him secretary of state. Nixon tended to be distrustful of the "Ivy League types" at the State Department whose roots were deep in the eastern establishment. He viewed Rogers as one of them. And Kissinger, propelled by a giant ego and convinced that the State Department bureaucracy was inherently conservative, insisted on making foreign policy at the White House. William Rogers found himself explaining and defending policies before Congress and the press that Nixon and Kissinger had formulated with little or no input from the State Department.

To replace Clark Clifford as secretary of defense, Nixon turned to the Republican congressman Melvin R. Laird. A Wisconsin native, Laird won a seat in Congress in 1952 and served there for the next seventeen years, earning a reputation as a tough but fair leader, a social moderate but a fiscal conservative. He was a big man, an imposing figure with a bald head and piercing eyes. Nixon selected Laird for the Pentagon because he was highly respected, by Republicans as well as Democrats, on Capitol Hill.

Laird was anxious to end the war. His opposition to further escalation was based more on political reality than on strong strategic or personal opinions. Laird knew the Congress; Nixon's honeymoon would be short-lived. Opposition to the war was endemic on Capitol Hill. The narrowly defined rules of engagement disgusted conservatives. Barry Goldwater, reelected to the Senate in 1968, best represented that point of view: "If we're not going to even try to win the damn thing, then let's get the hell out. Good men are dying for nothing." Liberals were no more satisfied. Vietnam was the wrong war in the wrong place at the wrong time for the wrong reason. During the campaign Nixon promised that he had a "secret plan" to end the war. There was no plan. Before the inauguration Nixon told Laird, "I've come to the conclusion that there's no way to win the war. But we can't say that, of course." Laird felt that if Nixon hesitated, what little political capital he had in Congress would disappear overnight. Within the administration, Laird became the voice for deescalation.

As Richard Nixon prepared for his inauguration in January 1969, W. Averell Harriman packed up and left the Paris hotel suite where he had spent six months arguing about the shape of the negotiating table. He tried in vain to get friends in the Soviet Union to put pressure on Ho Chi Minh and learned belatedly that nobody put pressure on Ho. Harriman returned to New York tired and disgusted. Nixon replaced him with Henry Cabot Lodge. Lodge had seen enough of Vietnam to know that Ho Chi Minh could not be bullied. The communists had the tactical advantage in military operations and realized that political support for the war in the United States was disappearing. It was just a matter of time before the United States quit altogether.

In Saigon, General Creighton ("Fighting Abe") Abrams had replaced William Westmoreland back in 1968. At fifty-three, Abrams was everything Westmoreland was not. Shorter, rounder, and coarser, and able to curse with the lowliest private, Abrams was a hard-drinking, cigar-chomping former tank commander who had earned a reputation as one of the great combat officers of World War II with George Patton's Third

Army. *Time* magazine claimed that Abrams could "inspire aggression from a begonia." Paradoxically, Abrams was a devotee of classical music and liked to retreat into the solitude of eighteenth- and nineteenth-century concertos and sonatas. He admitted that Tet had been a psychological and political, and therefore, strategic disaster for the United States. Abrams knew that he was working under new strategic assumptions. In 1968, 14,589 Americans died in South Vietnam. Similar casualty levels were out of the question. Abrams would not get any more troops, except for the 12,000 already scheduled to arrive. Westmoreland had tried to win the war; Abrams knew that his mission was to reduce American casualties, keep the Vietcong and North Vietnamese off guard, and get out of the country with some hope that South Vietnam was prepared to defend itself. But he did want "to kill as many of the bastards as he could."

During the last half of 1968 Abrams developed a tactical approach to fit the new strategic reality. Instead of continuing with Westmoreland's broad search-and-destroy missions, Abrams advocated smaller unit action on a more continuous basis. He liked musical analogies: "Sometimes you need to play the *1812 Overture* and now and then you have to let the violins play." It was time for the violins. Given the nature of the war and the problems American units had in maintaining the secrecy of operations, the Vietcong and North Vietnamese usually found out about large-unit actions before they were even launched. Explaining his approach to journalists in 1969, Abrams remarked, "We work in small patrols because that's how the enemy moves—in groups of four or five. When he fights in squad size, so do we. When he cuts to half squad, so do we." Between May 1967 and May 1968, Westmoreland launched more than 1,200 battalion-size operations. In 1969 Abrams reduced that number to about 700 battalion operations.

Abrams's tactical innovations fit perfectly with Nixon's decision to begin withdrawing American troops. In late 1968 Secretary of Defense Clark Clifford sanctioned Abrams's two-stage process for modernizing South Vietnamese military forces and gradually turning the war over to them. Melvin Laird resurrected Clifford's proposal and called it "Vietnamization." The idea was hardly new. In 1951 the French called it *jaunissement,* or "yellowing." France established the Vietnamese National Army, and central to the ill-fated Navarre Plan of 1953–1954 had been the assumption that the Vietnamese would assume greater responsibility for combat against the Vietminh. René Mayer, the French premier, remarked in 1953 that France "was trying to develop the national Vietnam army in order that we may one day bring back to Europe the greater part of the French Expeditionary Force."

The United States picked up where the French left off. Vice President Richard Nixon perfectly summed up American opinion about South Vietnam in April 1954 when he argued, "The Vietnamese lack the ability to conduct a war by themselves or govern themselves." J. Lawton Collins claimed that "the American mission will soon take charge of instructing the Vietnam army. . . . The aim will be . . . to build a completely autonomous Vietnamese army."

During the Kennedy administration, American advisers concentrated on training ARVN officers. In October 1963 General Charles J. Timmes proudly announced, "We have completed the job of training South Vietnam's armed forces." Yet two years later the major rationale for committing United States ground forces was to buy time to build an effective South Vietnamese army and turn the fighting over to it. In a letter to Duong Van Minh on January 1, 1964, Lyndon Johnson promised that as "the forces of your government become increasingly capable of dealing with this aggression, American military personnel in South Vietnam can be progressively withdrawn." Westmoreland and the joint chiefs lost sight of that objective in their naive assumption that the killing machine would make short work of the enemy, but even then Vietnamization was in the back of their minds. In his November 1967 speech to the National Press Club, Westmoreland announced that in two years "we will be able to phase down . . . our military effort, withdraw some of our troops, with the understanding that the Vietnamese will be prepared to take over those functions that are being now performed by our troops."

Vietnamization had been French and American policy for twenty years. The only difference in 1969 was that Richard Nixon had little choice *but* to turn the war over to South Vietnam and begin withdrawing American troops. Vietnamization was his only option. The antiwar movement was gaining momentum, in Congress as well as in the streets.

The reaction to Vietnamization was mixed. John Paul Vann enraged General Creighton Abrams when he said: "The first 100,000 Americans to leave would be for free. They are the clerks, the laundrymen, the engineer battalions building officers' clubs throughout the country. So many extraneous things are soaking up people not essential." Others had heard it all before. Senator John C. Stennis of Mississippi argued that the United States "would be badly mistaken if we think we can depend too much upon this South Vietnamese army winning this war. . . . I don't believe they will be able to do it and I believe Hanoi knows this better than we do. . . . We'll have to stay there for ten years at best."

But Nixon did not have years. He had months. On February 22, 1969, the North Vietnamese launched the Tet 1969 offensive, and although they achieved none of the surprise of a year before, 1,140 American soldiers died in three weeks of fighting. In April the number of United States troops in South Vietnam peaked at 543,400 men, and in mid-May Nixon offered a new peace plan. But like all of the earlier proposals, the new proposal was primarily a military document, a cease-fire, rather than a comprehensive political settlement. Nixon wanted mutual, simultaneous withdrawal of all American and North Vietnamese troops from South Vietnam, release of all prisoners of war, and establishment of an international body to supervise the cease-fire.

Pham Van Dong and Nguyen Van Thieu dashed Nixon's hopes for peace. In Hanoi, Pham Van Dong said that peace would come to Vietnam only after the complete withdrawal of all United States soldiers, the removal of Nguyen Van Thieu and Nguyen Cao Ky from office, and the participation of the National Liberation Front in the government of South Vietnam. Thieu reiterated what he called his "Four No's": "One, coalition government. Not negotiable. Two, territorial integrity. Not negotiable. Three, the Communist party in the Republic of South Vietnam. Not negotiable. Four, neutralism. Not negotiable." There was nothing to negotiate.

Fighting in the A Shau Valley also brought Nixon more political problems in May 1969. The North Vietnamese considered the A Shau critical to their logistical effort. Throughout 1967 and 1968 American forces conducted search-and-destroy sweeps of the area, and in May 1969 Creighton Abrams decided to attack. Between May 10 and June 7, 1969, the Ninth Marine Regiment and elements of the 101st Airborne Division (Airmobile) carried out Operation Apache Snow. The battle captured the attention of the American press when a protracted struggle developed on Ap Bia mountain in the A Shau Valley. The North Vietnamese had elaborate bunker complexes on the mountain. Abrams called in B-52 strikes and heavy artillery bombardment to pulverize the mountain before the American assault, but just before the troops attacked on May 18, a torrential rain fell. The bombardment denuded the top of the mountain, and the mud made the attack difficult. American troops went up the mountain twelve separate times. Before taking the summit on May 20, fifty-six Americans died and hundreds more were wounded. They found 630 dead North Vietnamese troops in the bunkers. The marines dubbed the killing field of Ap Bia "Hamburger Hill." The press loved the description and splashed it all over American newspapers and televisions at the end of May. Eventually, 241 Americans died in Operation Apache Snow.

The fact that Hamburger Hill was a tactical success in keeping the NVA off balance mattered little to the public. When Abrams abandoned Ap Bia on May 27, just a week after the battle, a hue and cry went up. Senator Edward Kennedy charged that "President Nixon has told us, without question, that we seek no military victory, that we seek only peace. How then can we justify sending our boys against a hill a dozen times, finally taking it, and then withdrawing a week later?" Combined with the stalled peace talks in Paris, Hamburger Hill seemed like more of the same—more firepower, more carnage, more for nothing.

Melvin Laird was right. Nixon's influence in Congress corresponded directly with what was happening in South Vietnam. If he appeared to be moving quickly on his promise to turn the war over to the South Vietnamese, most legislators were willing to let the administration gradually disengage from the conflict. They agreed with what Senator Richard Russell of Georgia had said back in 1964: "We either have to get out or take some action to help the Vietnamese. They won't help themselves. We made a big mistake going in there, but I can't figure out any way to get out without scaring the rest of the world."

As the first phase of Vietnamization, MACV upgraded ARVN firepower. During 1969 ARVN units received 700,000 M-16 rifles, 12,000 M-60 machine guns, 6,000 M-79 grenade launchers, 500,000 jeeps and trucks, 1,200 armored vehicles, and 1,000 pieces of artillery. The Vietnamese Air Force received F-5 fighters as well as 400 aircraft and 100 helicopters. The total value of American arms transfers to South Vietnam was $725 million in 1968, $925 million in 1969, and another $925 million in 1970. On June 8, 1969, Nixon flew to Midway Island for a summit meeting with Nguyen Van Thieu on Vietnamization, and at the end of the day they jointly announced the American troop withdrawals. In the communiqué Nixon said: "I have decided to order the immediate redeployment from Vietnam of the divisional equivalent of approximately 25,000 men." On August 27, 1969, the United States Ninth Infantry went home.

There was other progress in Vietnamization as well. The plan to get ARVN to assume more responsibility for offensive operations began to yield fruit late in 1969 and 1970. During that year, the enemy troops killed in action by ARVN increased from 20 to 32 percent. Nguyen Van Thieu removed a major peasant complaint against his government in 1969 by restoring the village elections and autonomy that Ngo Dinh Diem eliminated a decade earlier. Thieu also accelerated a land reform program and recognized titles to land given to the peasants by the Vietminh and Vietcong.

But Vietnamization gave the administration a new dilemma. Intelligence estimates confirmed that enemy troops had not recovered from the Tet offensive. Communist troops in South Vietnam had dropped from 242,000 in mid-1967 to 225,000 in 1969. The presence of 543,000 American and nearly 1 million ARVN troops, the Accelerated Pacification Campaign, and the Phoenix Program prevented the Vietcong from recovering from the Tet offensive. Tran Van Tra remembered having to break up the Vietcong 320th Regiment into platoons and squads to restore the Vietcong political infrastructure. "Sending a concentrated main force unit to operate in such a dispersed manner," he said, "was something we did reluctantly, but there was no alternative." The situation was serious enough that North Vietnam even flirted with the hope that the Chinese might send combat troops into the war. They already had 60,000 people in North Vietnam, most of them railway maintenance workers, storage personnel, and antiaircraft crews. But the Chinese were very cautious; they wanted to help North Vietnam, but they did not want to get into another Korea. In fact, the $525-million worth of goods North Vietnam received from China and the Soviet Union in 1968 dropped to only $200 million in 1970.

Despite enemy weaknesses, few people believed the South Vietnamese were ready to go it alone. Nixon had already scheduled the troop withdrawals. The Third Marine Division was to leave in late November and the Third Brigade of the Eighty-second Airborne Division two weeks later. By the end of 1969 Nixon and Kissinger wanted to reduce American troop levels to 470,000 people, but unless they agreed to some tactical innovations, the North Vietnamese would take over just as soon as the last American troops left. The only substitute for American troops was increases in American firepower and a widening of the war.

The increase in firepower involved dramatic increases in tactical and strategic strikes by B-52 bombers. Arc Light raids of B-52s over South Vietnam began in 1965, but in the battle of Khe Sanh army and marine infantry commanders discovered just how much damage the super-bombers could do. To maximize his strength, Abrams called in saturation B-52 raids on suspected enemy strongholds before sending in his soldiers. Critics said using B-52s in such a manner was like "swatting flies with a sledgehammer," but Abrams felt he had no choice. The only way he could keep enemy troops from overrunning the country while Americans pulled out was through increased bombardment.

Lifting conventional restraints was another consequence of Vietnamization. Since 1965 American military officials had requested authority to invade Laos and Cambodia in pursuit of the enemy, to cross the DMZ into North Vietnam, and to mine Haiphong harbor. During the Kennedy and Johnson administrations, policymakers avoided those alternatives for fear of triggering a Korean-like response from the Chinese. But the Cultural Revolution that disrupted China in the mid-1960s made response much less likely. Nixon and Kissinger listened to Wheeler and Westmoreland and asked them to draw up contingency plans for each proposal. They knew they had to do something. Nixon told H. R. Haldeman, his chief of staff, that he was "not going to end up like LBJ, holed up in the White House afraid to show my face on the street. I'm going to stop that war. Fast."

In March 1969 Nixon authorized Operation Menu. Abrams claimed on February 9, 1969, that MACV intelligence had located the Central Office for South Vietnam (COSVN) five miles across the border in Cambodia. There were also supply dumps and staging areas all along the border. Abrams wanted to destroy them with B-52 raids. Nixon wanted to limit enemy use of those sanctuaries, but he also wanted to use his "madman strategy." In 1953 Dwight Eisenhower sent secret messages to

China and North Korea that unless they ended the war, he would use nuclear weapons. Nixon believed the threat had brought the North Koreans to the negotiating table. Nixon wanted to convince North Vietnam's leaders that he had none of Lyndon Johnson's reservations, that he was "tougher," willing to escalate the war if necessary. Large-scale bombing of Cambodia would send a signal to Hanoi that there was a "new kid on the block who wouldn't put up with the old bullshit." Nixon wanted the North Vietnamese "to believe I've reached the point where I might do anything to stop the war. We'll just slip the word . . . that 'for God's sake, you know Nixon is obsessed about communists. We can't restrain him when he's angry—and he has his hand on the nuclear button'—and Ho Chi Minh . . . will be in Paris in two days begging for peace."

Nixon wanted the North Vietnamese to think that he was a bit deranged, an unstable personality who, in a moment of extreme frustration, might act capriciously, ordering in the B-52s with H-bombs. Ironically, in his worst moods, Nixon had exactly that streak in his personality. When he was under intense criticism, his lifelong demons—insecurity, resentment, and paranoia—took over, leaving him angry and often incoherent. During the last days of his administration, when the pressures of Watergate became unbearable, Nixon ended up like Johnson, a prisoner of the White House given to wandering the halls in the middle of the night. James Schlesinger, the secretary of defense, became so alarmed about Nixon's mental condition that he issued global instructions in July 1974 to all military commanders to disregard any orders from the president that did not bear his countersignature.

But those days were still five years away on March 18, 1969, when Nixon launched the B-52 raids over Cambodia. They were shrouded in secrecy. When the press picked up rumors of the bombing raids, the administration self-righteously denied them. To maintain the charade, the administration falsified military records to cover up the raids. On May 9, 1969, however, the *New York Times* broke the story. Nixon denied it, but he was enraged at what he considered the leaking of highly classified information and authorized illegal wiretaps on the telephones of journalists and suspected collaborators. Operation Menu continued until 1973, by which time 16,527 sorties of aircraft dropped 383,851 tons of explosives on Cambodia.

Later in 1969 the administration escalated the bombing of Laos, which had begun in 1965. Communist guerrillas—the Pathet Lao—controlled most of northern Laos, receiving substantial aid from North Vietnam. Bombing raids over the Plain of Jars were designed to assist Royal Laotian forces. The United States and South Vietnamese did not have the personnel to intervene directly in the conflict, but Nixon was intent on making life more difficult for communists in northern Laos.

Events in Hanoi created more problems. Congestive heart failure weakened Ho Chi Minh throughout 1969. He lost weight, energy, and

Ho Chi Minh (left) and Pham Van Dong (right) meet to discuss the war in the summer of 1969, just a few months before Ho Chi Minh's death.
MARC RIBOUD/MAGNUM PHOTOS

appetite. When he died on September 2, 1969, North Vietnam was grief stricken. Tens of thousands of mourners packed Ba Ding public square in Hanoi on September 9 for the funeral ceremony. Ho insisted in his will that neither time nor money be wasted on an elaborate funeral, and the entire proceeding took only thirty-five minutes. Sitting on a raised platform, Pham Van Dong and Vo Nguyen Giap wept openly. Westerners were accustomed to seeing unemotional, inscrutable communist leaders standing on the Kremlin balcony or in Tiananmen Square in Beijing. It dawned on many observers at that moment that Ho was beloved by his people.

The death of Ho Chi Minh had immediate political consequences. Ever since 1954 there had been no doubts about the center of power in Hanoi. But his death complicated the governing process. One-man rule gave way to collective leadership. Three men in particular—Pham Van Dong, Le Duan, and Vo Nguyen Giap—dominated the Politburo. As head of the Lao Dong party, Duan presided over domestic affairs. Pham Van Dong continued to exert leadership over foreign policy, and Vo Nguyen Giap oversaw defense matters. All matters of state policy needed approval by the triumvirate, a system guaranteed to be inflexible. Added to that was their commitment to see the war to its end. They elevated Ho Chi Minh to martyrdom.

An intense debate raged in Hanoi throughout the summer over how best to accomplish that mission. Truong Chinh, a close friend of Ho Chi Minh and chief theoretician for the Lao Dong party, argued that time was on their side and that they should be very cautious. Political reality was forcing deescalation on the United States, and North Vietnam must avoid any military action that might give Nixon a battlefield victory. Instead North Vietnam should maintain the tactical initiative and prepare for a "long-drawn-out fight." Vo Nguyen Giap, anxious to deliver a deathblow to South Vietnam, was willing to go along with Truong Chinh's argument for a while, but within a year he would call for a new offensive against South Vietnam, one that Truong Chinh would consider grossly premature.

But in Washington, Nixon found himself without a policy. The madman strategy was not working because North Vietnam kept insisting on its old demands: withdrawal of all American troops, removal of Nguyen Van Thieu and Nguyen Cao Ky from office, and participation of southern communists in a coalition government. Nixon and Kissinger hoped that the Soviet Union would bring pressure to bear on Hanoi. The Soviets were anxious for a strategic arms limitation treaty, and after 1968 they started to lose interest in Vietnam; problems in Asia, the Middle East, and Europe seemed more compelling. But even as late as 1970 the United States still did not appreciate the independence of Hanoi. In 1968 the Soviets just did not have as much influence over Hanoi as Nixon and Kissinger assumed.

And the antiwar movement was gaining momentum. The trial of the "Chicago Eight" began in September 1969. The government charged them with conspiracy to riot and obstruct justice during the Democratic National Convention the year before. The trial quickly turned into a media circus. Bobby Seale, the black activist, kept up a steady series of outbursts until Judge Julius Hoffman had him gagged and chained to his seat. The Yippie leader Abbie Hoffman petitioned to have his name changed so nobody "will think I am related to this fascist judge." Jerry Rubin of the Yippies and Tom Hayden, head of the Students for a Democratic Society, draped a Vietcong and an American flag across their defense tables. The trial lasted five months. In mid-February the jury acquitted them all of conspiracy charges, and later an appellate court overturned the convictions for contempt and rioting.

During the fall of 1969, the Vietnam Moratorium Committee and the New Mobilization Committee to End the War in Vietnam prepared a series of mass demonstrations. They developed a grass-roots organization, secured endorsements from leading antiwar politicians, and placed advertisements in the major metropolitan dailies. Millions participated in the October 15, 1969, moratorium. In Vietnam tens of thousands of soldiers donned black armbands in support of the moratorium. More than 100,000 people gathered on the Boston Common and 250,000 marched in Washington.

President Nixon reacted at once, releasing to the press a telegram from Pham Van Dong supporting the moratorium. Then, in a television speech on November 3, 1969, Nixon made a patriotic appeal to those he called the "silent majority" who he believed supported the war effort. Madame Nhu first coined the phrase back in 1963 when she argued that the "government of Ngo Dinh Diem is popular with a silent majority and is criticized only by a noisy minority of the population." Six years later Nixon made a similar argument: "Let historians not record that when America was the most powerful nation in the world we . . . allowed the last hopes for peace and freedom . . . to be suffocated by . . . totalitarianism. . . . Tonight—to you, the great silent majority of my fellow Americans—I ask for your support." The silent majority remained silent, but the antiwar activists did not. On November 15, 1969, the Vietnam Moratorium Committee staged a march that brought 500,000 people to Washington, D.C., the largest demonstration in United States history.

The antiwar movement triggered a clash of cultures in the United States. At its roots, the controversy was based on class distinctions. Most antiwar protesters were middle- and upper-class college students who had managed to avoid the draft. The deployment of American combat troops to South Vietnam in 1965 led to dramatic increases in the number of draft calls. But selective service still operated on World War II logic, when men working in strategic industries were exempted from military service. During the heaviest years of fighting in Vietnam, college students received draft deferments. Those deferments continued indefinitely if they went on to graduate school after receiving their degrees. Occupational deferments were awarded for engineers, scientists, teachers, and a variety of other professions. Some men also knew how to exploit the system, joining the National Guard, securing medical exemptions, getting married, even having children to take advantage of the range of selective service options. Instead of relying on the routine and often perfunctory physicals performed at army induction centers, for example, middle- and upper-class young men often received private physicals and showed up at induction centers with certifiable proof of disqualifying ailments. And when middle- and upper-class young men were drafted, their education levels often secured them jobs in the rear areas of the military bureaucracy. Typing skills or a few business classes were often enough to keep them out of harm's way.

As historian Christian G. Appy has written, Vietnam was a "working-class war." The men who fought and died in South Vietnam during the years of the war came overwhelmingly from the bottom half of the social structure. Young men from working-class or poverty-level families were four times more likely than middle-class young men to die in Vietnam.

Poor boys from small towns, farms, and urban centers did the fighting and dying in Vietnam, not young men from the suburbs. Economic class proved to be far more important than race or ethnicity in determining the social composition of the military during the Vietnam era. The system was hopelessly biased in favor of the privileged and against the poor and the working classes.

The discrimination against their own sons left many working-class Americans with painfully ambivalent feelings about the war and their country. They hated the war, loved their boys, and despised the antiwar movement. Their visceral resentment exploded into the "hard hat riot" of May 8, 1970, in New York City. Construction workers had learned a few days earlier that antiwar demonstrators from New York University and Hunter College were planning a rally in the financial district. About two hundred construction workers, wearing yellow hard hats, showed up at the rally and attacked the students, chanting "All the Way USA." They then marched to city hall and demanded that Mayor John Lindsay raise the flag, which had been at half-staff to mourn the dead students at Kent State, to the top of the pole. The workers sang the national anthem as the flag was raised. Seeing an antiwar banner over at Pace College, they broke into a building and beat up several students. The media dubbed May 8 "Bloody Friday."

Two weeks later, the Building and Trades Council of Greater New York sponsored a peaceful march that attracted more than 100,000 workers. They waved flags, expressed love for the United States, and praised the young men in the military who were putting their lives on the line. *Time* magazine described the event: "For three hours, 100,000 members of New York's brawniest unions marched and shouted . . . in a massive display of gleeful patriotism and muscular pride. [It was] a kind of workers' Woodstock." Ralph Cole, a firefighter who lost his son in Vietnam, recalled, "You bet your goddam dollar I'm bitter. It's people like us who give up our sons for the country. The business people, they run the country and make money from it. The college types, the professors, they go to Washington and tell the government what to do. . . . But their sons, they don't end up in the swamps over there, in Vietnam. Let's face it: if you have a lot of money, or if you have the right connections, you don't end up on a firing line in the jungle." Cole's wife felt the same way: "I'm against this war, too—the way a mother is, whose sons are in the army, who has lost a son fighting in it. The world doesn't hear me, and it doesn't hear a single person I know."

Richard Nixon and Henry Kissinger had more to worry about than the antiwar movement and other demonstrations. The My Lai massacre became the new focal point in the debate over the war. Journalist Seymour Hersh broke the story. *Life* magazine published grisly color photographs taken at the massacre—twisted bodies, bloodied black pajamas, naked, mutilated babies. Civilian casualties were hardly new, particu-

In May 1970, New York City construction workers staged the so-called hard hat rally, a prowar demonstration involving more than 100,000 people.
UPI/BETTMANN

larly in Quang Ngai Province. Ever since 1967, when Task Force Oregon deployed to I Corps, the killing machine had done its job well. Throughout 1967 and again in 1968, 50,000 civilians were killed or wounded in Quang Ngai, the vast majority of them victims of indiscriminate artillery bombardment, B-52 strikes, fighter-bomber napalm raids, and gunship attacks. But the deaths at My Lai seemed different, at least to most Americans. Indiscriminate bombardment could at least be explained away as accidental; the killing at My Lai could not. American soldiers massacred men, women, children, and babies in cold blood.

My Lai was a rural hamlet of approximately 700 people. On the morning of March 16, 1968, Lieutenant William Calley led an infantry platoon into My Lai. With helicopter gunships circling at 1,000 feet monitoring the operation, Calley ordered his men to round up all the civilians. Tensions ran high. The troops were frustrated with their inability to distinguish civilians from the Vietcong. Calley suddenly opened fire and ordered his men to shoot as well. They plowed through the village shooting anything that moved. When it was over, nearly 500 people were dead. Not one of them appeared to be a Vietcong. They even killed the babies. Calley's men spent the day in an orgy of sexual violence— sodomy, rape, and rape-murder.

Such high-ranking officers as Major General Samuel Koster, commander of the Americal Division, apparently knew of the killings but made no report and attempted no investigation. For more than a year the cover-up was successful until Ronald Ridenhour, a former infantryman with the Americal Division, wrote a letter to Congress describing the massacre. "I do not know for certain," he wrote, "but I am convinced that it was something very black indeed." The army convened a board of inquiry and decided that war crimes had occurred. The board reduced Major General Koster in rank to brigadier general; censured his assistant, Brigadier General George Young; and charged Colonel Oran K. Henderson, commander of the Eleventh Infantry Brigade, along with thirteen other officers and enlisted men, with war crimes.

On March 29, 1971, a military tribunal convicted William Calley of the premeditated murder of at least twenty-two civilians. Two days later he was sentenced to life in prison at hard labor. The army dropped charges against all the other defendants. The conviction provoked an intense debate throughout the country. Many Americans felt Calley was being made a scapegoat for the army. Governors Jimmy Carter of Georgia and George Wallace of Alabama insisted that Calley was the tip of the iceberg and should not be singled out for punishment. Richard Nixon reviewed the case personally before the sentence was carried out. He had Calley released from a military stockade and placed under house arrest in an apartment. In August 1971 Nixon reduced the sentence to twenty years, and then to ten years. William Calley was paroled in March 1974. General William Peers, who headed the army investigation of My Lai, summed up the absurdity of the event: "To think that out of all those men, only one, Lieutenant William Calley, was brought to justice. And now, he's practically a hero. It's a tragedy."

The troop withdrawals, the antiwar movement, and the My Lai massacre exposed serious problems in the killing machine and further undermined public support for the war. The morale of American troops was deeply eroded. Once Nixon announced the troop withdrawals, everyone realized it was only a matter of time before the United States was out and the Vietnamese would have to fight the war themselves. In his memoirs, William Westmoreland recalled that after 1969 "serious morale and disciplinary problems arose. That was to be expected. Men began to doubt the American purpose. Why die when the United States was pulling out?"

The war had always been confusing. Unlike soldiers in World War II, who averaged twenty-six years of age, the GIs in Vietnam averaged only nineteen. They knew relatively little about life or the world. Fresh out of high school, they went to war with John Wayne on their minds, hoping to protect freedom as Duke had done in *Flying Leathernecks, Back to Bataan,* and *The Sands of Iwo Jima.* They had grown up listening to the World War II recollections of their fathers, of being welcomed by the people of Europe, the Philippines, and China, whom they had come to liberate from Axis oppressors, vanquishing an evil enemy, and then being received as conquering heroes when they returned home. Vietnam would be to them what World War I had been to their grandfathers and World War II to their fathers.

But it was not to be. It did not take more than a few hours in South Vietnam for most troops to come to the conclusion that the Vietnamese, while loving the dollar bills in GI pockets, despised them as human beings. The Vietnamese smiled when they hustled the GIs for money and handouts, or when they worked for the military or an American company, but most Vietnamese kept their peace, looking at the soldiers with silent scorn and contemptuous stares. John Ketwig, in his book *And a Hard Rain Fell,* remembered a bus ride from Tan Son Nhut to Long Binh in which Vietnamese lined the road, threw garbage at the troop bus, and shouted "Go home, GI" and "Fuck you, GI." Enraged, one of the soldiers shouted back, "Hey, you fuckin' gooks. We're supposed to be here to save your fuckin' puny asses!"

Few soldiers believed they were fighting in South Vietnam to help the South Vietnamese. It was all but impossible to distinguish Vietcong troops from simple peasants, and even the peasants wanted the Americans out. Until 1969, however, most of the young troops believed in the domino theory. They were under no illusions about preserving democracy in South Vietnam from communist assault, but they were willing to die in the jungles of Southeast Asia to protect capitalism and freedom on the other side of the world. Stopping the spread of communism seemed a legitimate objective to most of the young men arriving in South Vietnam, even though their reception from the Vietnamese left much to be desired.

But when Richard Nixon began withdrawing troops from South Vietnam in 1969, even the domino theory lost much of its relevancy. The United States was getting out, whether or not South Vietnam was ready to go it alone. GIs had long since realized that they were not fighting for the South Vietnamese; now it seemed they were not even fighting to destroy Indochinese communism and protect America from falling dominoes. Uncertain about the American mission in Vietnam and confused about their own role in the conflict, many combat soldiers lost faith. Survival replaced victory as the focus of their lives. They might be willing to die to protect a buddy, but there was no longer any nobility in dying for democracy. Morale plummeted.

The tour of duty reinforced the sense of frustration. Unlike World War II, when soldiers stayed away from home for years, the tour of duty in Vietnam was twelve months for army troops and thirteen for marines. Every few days new, "green" troops arrived in the field full of news about the alienation back home. Soldiers found themselves fighting in a war that did not matter, dying for a cause that few believed in. Michael Herr asked, "How do you feel when a nineteen-year-old kid tells you from the bottom of his heart that he has gotten too old for this kind of shit?" Every six months a soldier also got a "Rest and Recreation"—"R and R"—leave, a week's vacation at a resort hotel in Hong Kong, Bangkok, or Honolulu. Among the troops the vacation was called "I and I"— "intoxication and intercourse." During those few days they were exposed to criticism about the war.

Soldiers lost faith in their officers. The commitment of troops to South Vietnam was so enormous that a shortage of qualified officers resulted. In addition, the phenomenon of "ticket punching"—where career officers insisted on a combat tour in Vietnam in order to beef up their personnel file—created an average six-month assignment with an individual unit before a new officer appeared. Six months was just not enough time for an officer to secure the loyalty of his troops or acquaint himself with the tactical situation.

The crisis in morale manifested itself in a number of ways. Desertion and absent-without-leave (AWOL) rates skyrocketed. The army desertion rate in 1966 had been 14.9 men per thousand. It quadrupled to 73.5 in 1971—three times higher than the worst desertion rates of the Korean War. The desertion rate for all military branches jumped from 8.43 men per thousand in 1966 to 33.9 in 1971. The AWOL rates were just as bad. In 1966 there were 57.2 AWOL incidents per thousand in the army, but that number jumped to 176.9 in 1971. Even the vaunted marines had problems. In 1967 the Marine Corps discharged 13.7 men per thousand for unfitness and misconduct; the figure jumped to 112.4 in 1971.

There were worse things than desertion, AWOL, and bad conduct. The military faced epidemics of "fragging" and drug abuse. "Fragging" was a term soldiers used to describe the assassination of overzealous officers and noncommissioned officers by their own troops. It first appeared in the Mekong Delta in 1967 when several American platoons were known for pooling their money to pay an individual for killing a hated officer or NCO, usually by throwing a fragmentation grenade into a tent, destroying the victim along with the weapon and leaving no evidence. To warn an officer who was too "gung ho," troops might leave a grenade pin on his pillow or throw a smoke grenade into his tent. If he persisted, one of his men would "frag" him. During the Vietnam War, the army claimed that 1,011 officers and NCOs were killed or wounded at the hands of their own men. There were 96 documented cases in 1969, 209 in 1970, and 333 confirmed and another 158 suspected incidents in 1971. In 1970 and 1971 American combat deaths in South Vietnam totaled 5,602 people, and the number of confirmed fraggings was 542. After the battle of Hamburger Hill in 1969, one underground GI newspaper carried an ad offering a $10,000 reward for fragging the officers who ordered the men up the hill.

But fragging was not the only sign of an army in crisis. Drug abuse reached epidemic proportions. From the "Golden Triangle" of Laos, Burma, and Thailand, a river of heroin, marijuana, and opium flowed into South Vietnam. A steady supply of amphetamines came from the United States and from makeshift labs in Saigon. Drugs were everywhere, like candy and ice cream on the street. Inefficient and ineffective in war, South Vietnamese government officials proved to be efficient and effective drug suppliers. A heroin addiction requiring $150 a day on the South Side of Chicago could be maintained in Saigon for $2 a day. The Pentagon estimated at the end of 1969 that nearly two of every three American soldiers in South Vietnam were using marijuana and an astonishing one out of every three or four had tried heroin. Tens of thousands of GIs returned home to America with the "monkey on their backs"—a full-blown heroin addiction. Late in 1970 CBS News brought the story home to the American people by broadcasting a "smoke-in" at a First Air Cavalry fire base, in which GIs smoked marijuana through the barrel of a combat rifle.

Fragging and drug abuse were so severe that Pentagon officials began to worry about the possibility of a military rebellion or collapse. Westmoreland told the joint chiefs that "an army without discipline, morale, and pride is a menace to the country that it is sworn to defend." Reports of field units bordering on mutiny in their refusal to carry out combat operations became increasingly frequent. McGeorge Bundy recommended to the administration that "extrication from Vietnam is now the necessary precondition for the renewal of the Army as an institution." The June 1971 issue of the *Armed Forces Journal* described "The Collapse of the Armed Forces." The killing machine was turning on itself. Creighton Abrams could not believe what was happening: "What the hell is going on. I've got white shirts all over the place—psychologists, drug counselors, detox specialists, rehab people, social workers, and psychiatrists. Is this a goddamned army or a mental hospital? Officers are afraid to lead their men into battle, and the men won't follow. Jesus Christ! What happened?"

By the beginning of 1970, at least for critics of the war, the Vietnamization policy was bankrupt. Kissinger and Nixon had been running the war for a year, and although troop levels had been reduced to 475,200 people at the end of 1969, another 9,415 Americans went home dead. Bipartisan opposition to the war widened in Congress. Senate Republican whip Hugh Scott of Pennsylvania called for "a withdrawal of American combat troops as soon as is physically possible." In full-page advertisements placed in newspapers around the country, a group of United States senators led by George McGovern, Harold Hughes, and Mark Hatfield described Vietnamization as "an invisible program to end an undeclared war backed by a silent majority."

Inside the administration a fierce debate boiled over the war. The Paris negotiations remained stalled, with Henry Cabot Lodge spending every day bickering with the North Vietnamese and the South Vietnamese over procedural details. Henry Kissinger began meeting secretly with Le Duc Tho, who had succeeded Xuan Thuy as the head of the North Vietnamese delegation, on February 21, 1970, but Tho remained resolute in his demand that Nixon withdraw all American troops from South Vietnam, remove Thieu and Ky from power, and permit the Provisional Revolutionary Government of South Vietnam, which had superseded the National Liberation Front in 1969, to participate in the government of South Vietnam. When Kissinger suggested that the communists were experiencing setback after setback in South Vietnam, Tho replied, "Before, there were over a million U.S. and puppet troops, and you failed. How can you succeed when you let the puppet troops do the fighting now?" Thieu was just as stubborn. He would not even talk to representatives of the Provisional Revolutionary Government.

Kissinger believed that as long as American troop withdrawals proceeded as scheduled, the enemy had no reason to compromise. The Twenty-sixth Marine Regiment, First Infantry Division, Ninth Infantry Division, Fourth Infantry Division, and Twenty-fifth Infantry Division were all scheduled for redeployment to the United States in 1970. American troop strength would drop to 335,000 by year's end. Kissinger wanted to slow down the reductions, renew massive bombing of North Vietnam, and consider a joint American–South Vietnamese invasion of North Vietnam, all in the hope of forcing the enemy into serious negotiations. Melvin Laird criticized the proposal, telling Nixon that "such tactics have not worked in Vietnam for the last twenty years and won't work now. Moreover, Congress will not tolerate such an expansion of the war."

In January 1970 the Politburo in Hanoi had already decided to broaden the war in Indochina. They had little choice. Since early in the 1960s the CIA-financed Hmong army in Laos, led by Vang Pao, had steadily grown in strength and mobility. Along with as many as twenty-five battalions of troops supplied by Thailand and Royal Laotian soldiers, the Hmong had begun to threaten the Ho Chi Minh Trail by 1969. In February 1970 NVA regular troops joined with Pathet Lao guerrillas and attacked the Hmong-Lao-Thai troops, driving them far to the west, away from the trail and off the Plain of Jars. That military operation secured North Vietnam's supply line to the south.

For the time being, President Nixon listened to Laird. He visited Saigon in February 1970 and listened to Creighton Abrams's plea for an invasion of the sanctuaries in Cambodia and Laos but remained unconvinced. That same month the bombing of Laos became public, and the political attacks started immediately. On February 19 Senator Eugene McCarthy demanded to know "under what authority . . . [are] American pilots bombing the Plain of Jars which is hundreds of miles from the Ho Chi Minh Trail and has nothing to do with the war in Vietnam?"

For years the joint chiefs wanted to send troops into Cambodia to eliminate the sanctuaries; Lyndon Johnson and Richard Nixon refused, hoping to avoid escalating the war. But the idea of widening the war into Laos and Cambodia to compensate for the troop withdrawal gained momentum. Nixon paved the way for invading Laos and Cambodia in 1969 by approving the expanded air strikes. At the time he viewed bombing as a compromise, something short of an invasion. The administration reacted quickly to persistent questions, denying the Cambodian raids outright and claiming that the air raids over Laos had been only at the request of the Laotian government to stop North Vietnamese aggression. At a March 6, 1970, press conference, Nixon assured reporters that there "are no American ground combat troops in Laos. . . . We have no plans for introducing ground combat forces into Laos." But two days later Captain John Bush of the United States Army was killed by North Vietnamese sappers who attacked his compound ten miles inside the Laotian border. J. William Fulbright, warning of another credibility crisis, charged that Nixon "does not have the authority, nor has Congress given him authority, to engage in combat operations in Laos, whether on the land, in the air or from the sea."

Critics also began asking questions about Cambodia. Since early in 1969 rumors had persisted that the United States was regularly bombing Vietcong and North Vietnamese units in Cambodia, but the administration denied the allegations. When confirmation of the Laotian involvement appeared in March 1970, questions naturally arose about Cambodia. On April 2, William P. Rogers told the Senate Foreign Relations Committee, "Our best policy is . . . to avoid any act which appears to violate the neutrality of Cambodia. . . . We have cautioned the South Vietnamese. . . . We think it is inadvisable to have cross-border operations." Three weeks later Rogers reassured the House Appropriations Committee, "We recognize that if we escalate and we get involved in Cambodia with our ground troops that our whole program is defeated."

Rogers had no idea what was going on. On March 27 and 28, American helicopters accompanied battalion-size ARVN forces on an invasion of Cambodia. Communist forces escaped to the west and began dumping their weapons on the Khmer Rouge, Cambodia's communist insurgents. Serious consideration of a joint U.S.-ARVN invasion had been under way for months, but Prince Norodom Sihanouk's neutrality was the problem. Sihanouk acquiesced in Operation Menu as well as Vietcong and North Vietnamese troops in Cambodian territory, but he wanted to maintain a formal neutrality. Actually, Sihanouk was trying desperately to save his country. If he did not allow North Vietnam use of the sanctuaries, they would provide assistance to the Khmer Rouge, who were trying to overthrow Sihanouk. When Sihanouk cooperated with Hanoi, the North Vietnamese limited their support of the Khmer Rouge. But by tacitly cooperating with Hanoi, Sihanouk risked the ire of the

United States. He wavered back and forth, walking a deadly political tightrope. MACV intelligence reports enticed Nixon, Kissinger, and Abrams with the prospects of capturing the elusive Central Office for South Vietnam. But Nixon could not invade Cambodia as long as Sihanouk was in power. It would be a violation of Cambodian sovereignty. What Nixon and Kissinger needed was a pro-American government in Phnom Penh.

Lon Nol was their man. Born in 1913 in French Cambodia, Lon Nol was educated in French colonial schools. Between 1935 and 1954 he held a number of important posts in the French colonial administration and became close to Sihanouk. After independence in 1954, Lon Nol became minister of national defense. A devout Buddhist and anticommunist, Nol urged Sihanouk throughout the early 1960s to side with the United States against the Vietcong, but the prince maintained Cambodian neutrality. Lon Nol started scheming. Sihanouk was a short, round man who loved Parisian suits but hated the fact that he wore a size 48 short. Each year he took off for the Côte d'Azur in France, where he spent a couple of months in a high-class fat farm. Lon Nol knew that no matter how desperate the political situation, the prince would never forgo the trips. Late in 1969 Sihanouk had already purchased fifty new suits, all of them 44 or 42 short. He left for France in January 1970, and Lon Nol immediately started maneuvering. In March, with Sihanouk in Paris, Lon Nol deposed the prince.

Lon Nol fanned political support by moving against the more than 400,000 Vietnamese living in Cambodia where ethnic hatreds were intense. Within days of assuming power, he launched murderous attacks on the Vietnamese community, slaughtering thousands of civilians and raising ethnic rivalries to a fever pitch. He also expressed to Richard Nixon his fears about the spread of the Vietnam War westward and the inability of Cambodian forces to handle the situation. Lon Nol doubled the size of the Cambodian army in a month and appealed to Nixon for arms. Nixon agreed.

On April 19 the president flew out to Hawaii to visit the crew of Apollo 13, who had just returned from a harrowing voyage to the moon. In Honolulu, Admiral John McCain, Jr., commander in chief of the United States Forces in the Pacific (CINCPAC), briefed him. An Annapolis graduate and a submariner during World War II, McCain replaced Ulysses S. Grant Sharp as CINCPAC in July 1968. Known as the "Red Arrow Man," McCain was a hard-boiled anticommunist given to placing red arrows on open world maps to show communist expansion around the globe. For reporters in Hawaii and Saigon, his briefings were laughably infamous, full of gloom-and-doom descriptions of "Reds," "Commies," and "Chicoms." McCain's son was a prisoner of war in North Vietnam, which only intensified his passion. McCain unfurled a map before Nixon, and, sure enough, there were the big red arrows,

"McCain's Claws" according to the reporters. Half the country was painted red, and the claws were reaching out for Malaysia and west to Thailand. "The Cambodians need more than a few thousand rifles," McCain told the president. "If you are going to withdraw another 150,000 troops from South Vietnam this year, you must protect Saigon's western flank by an invasion of the Cambodian sanctuaries."

Developments back home upset Nixon. In April the Senate rejected both of his nominations to fill the vacancy left on the Supreme Court by Abe Fortas's resignation. The Senate refused to confirm Clement Haynsworth because of his mediocre credentials and G. Harrold Carswell because of his racism. Nixon was so angry that he publicly called the sixty-one senators who voted against his appointments "vicious hypocrites." That month he watched private screenings of the film *Patton*. Nixon loved George C. Scott's portrayal of the lonely, misunderstood but tough general who defeated the Germans at the Battle of the Bulge. Cambodia became a way for Nixon to express his toughness, to seize the political initiative back from the Senate. "Those Senators think they can push me around," Nixon told Kissinger. "But I'll show them who's tough."

On April 30, 1970, President Nixon went on television with an important national security announcement. It was vintage Richard Nixon. He wanted to sound like George C. Scott being Patton. Sweat forming on his upper lip from the camera lights, Nixon stridently warned: "We live in an age of anarchy. We see mindless attacks on all the great institutions which have been created by free civilization in the last five hundred years. . . . Small nations all over the world find themselves under attack from within and without." He asserted that "only the power of the United States deters aggression." To protect American lives and guarantee Vietnamization, he had authorized an invasion of Cambodia. "We take this action not for the purpose of expanding the war . . . but for the purpose of ending the war in Vietnam, and winning the just peace." Searching for military victory, the killing machine moved into Cambodia.

It was a joint "incursion," as Nixon defined it. The United States First Cavalry Division (Airmobile) and the Eleventh Armored Cavalry Regiment, along with the First ARVN Armored Cavalry Regiment and the Third ARVN Airborne Brigade, invaded the Fishhook, a region of Cambodia about fifty miles northwest of Saigon. It was the ultimate search-and-destroy mission, the hunt for COSVN. If the troops could locate and annihilate the enemy's command headquarters, they could deal a death-blow to their effort. Melvin Laird remembered begging Nixon not to include in his speech any reference to COSVN: "Right up to the time he gave that speech I was pleading to have that out because COSVN was never a single headquarters. . . . So again the American people were misled by not having a real understanding of what it was about. But the speech . . . was made . . . COSVN was listed as a major military target."

Although COSVN had been nominally located in Tay Ninh Province of South Vietnam during much of the war, it was hardly what most American officers thought of as a command headquarters. It was not a fixed installation like MACV but a small number of senior officers and staff assistants.

The reports Nixon received on the first day of the invasion were so optimistic that he ordered the Pentagon "to take out all the sanctuaries. Make whatever plans are necessary and then just do it. Knock them all out so that they can't be used against us. Ever." Two weeks later the Twenty-fifth and Ninth Infantry Divisions attacked the Dog's Head, a region about twenty-five miles southwest of the Fishhook, and the Fourth Infantry Division invaded Cambodia west of Pleiku. Nixon renewed the bombing of North Vietnam, although he confined the strikes to areas just north of the Demilitarized Zone.

But the troops never found COSVN. Nearly 80,000 American and ARVN soldiers spent a couple of months slogging through eastern Cambodia, unloading tens of thousands of tons of explosives, but making little contact with the enemy. Communist troops were there, but the invasion actually drove them deeper—further west—into Cambodia. The destruction associated with the invasion sent a flood of refugees pouring into Phnom Penh. Creighton Abrams claimed that the invasion resulted in more than 11,000 enemy deaths, but the CIA disputed the claim, arguing that the bombardment had been so intense that "civilians and non-combatants [were] being included in the loss figure."

Although they never found COSVN, the troops captured a wealth of enemy supplies: 15 million rounds of ammunition, 143,000 rockets, 14 million pounds of rice, 23,000 firearms, 200,000 antiaircraft rounds, 5,487 mines, and 62,000 hand grenades. They destroyed 11,700 North Vietnamese bunker complexes. Nixon announced that the captured supplies and weapons were "enough to keep the North Vietnamese going for a year. They will be crippled now." Westmoreland defended the Cambodian invasion as the event that had finally pushed North Vietnam past the elusive crossover point. But there was so little contact with the enemy that Abrams could not afford to have the United States troops on a walking tour of Cambodia. All U.S.-ARVN ground operations in Cambodia were over by the end of June. No sooner had they left than new battalions of North Vietnamese troops moved down the Ho Chi Minh Trail and back into the Fishhook, Parrot's Beak, and Dog's Head, as did the enemy soldiers driven west into Cambodia by the initial invasion. The "incursion" was over, but like so many times in the past, the enemy was back.

In other ways the invasion was a disaster. Once in Cambodia, ARVN troops behaved badly, stealing everything in sight. North Vietnam gave strict orders to its troops to avoid the civilian population, and political cadres then went in behind the ARVN troops and appealed to the Khmer peasants, telling them that communism, not South Vietnam and the

United States, offered the best hope for freedom. When it was over, the invasion had given the Khmer Rouge new weapons as well as a civilian population ripe for recruitment.

The administration also paid a heavy political price at home. Nixon completely miscalculated the public reaction. On April 19, 1970, the Vietnam Moratorium Committee, sponsors of the huge, nationwide antiwar rallies in October and November 1969, announced that it would close its Washington office. The troop reductions convinced most Americans that Nixon was scaling down the war. That changed on April 30, 1970, when Nixon announced the Cambodia invasion. The invasion breathed new life into the antiwar movement. The president found himself facing one of the worst eruptions of civil disobedience in modern American history. On college campuses mass demonstrations disrupted classes. At Kent State University, National Guard troops called out by Ohio Governor James Rhodes to keep order fired into a crowd of students, killing four and creating martyrs for the antiwar movement. Similar violence occurred at Jackson State University in Mississippi. On May 8, some 100,000 people marched into Washington.

The extent of the protests cut deep into Nixon's paranoia. What had started out to be a military victory was turning into political disaster. In the White House, Nixon had an anxiety attack and could not sleep. After 10:30 P.M., he made nearly fifty phone calls to friends and political associates, seeking reassurance and vindication. Suddenly, in the middle of the night, he ordered the limousine to drive him over to the Lincoln Memorial to visit the camped protesters. But he was not at his best. Sleepless and tired, he talked with the students but not about the war. To a group of Ohio State students, Nixon rambled on and on about Woody Hayes and glory days. One student from California remembered the evening as a surrealistic experience: "Here we are protesting an immoral war and the president of the United States shows up in the middle of the night to tell us about baseball and how great the surfing is in California. It was unbelievable."

It was just as bad in Congress. Senators Mark Hatfield and George McGovern sponsored an amendment requiring total American withdrawal from South Vietnam by the end of 1971. Although the Hatfield-McGovern Amendment failed to pass in the Senate, it indicated the frustration many Americans felt about the war. Senators John Sherman Cooper and Frank Church were somewhat more successful. Cooper, a Republican from Kentucky, and Church, a Democrat from Idaho, sponsored an amendment prohibiting the United States without congressional approval from sending advisers into Cambodia, providing combat air support for Cambodian troops, or financing the sending of troops into Cambodia by other nations. On June 30, 1970, the amendment passed the Senate over bitter administration opposition, fifty-eight to thirty-seven.

Although the invasion resulted in the capture of valuable supplies and postponed North Vietnamese plans for offensive operations in South Vietnam, it was a strategic disaster for the United States. The administration did not locate COSVN, and the public reaction forced Nixon to accelerate the troop withdrawals even while Henry Kissinger was arguing that those reductions weakened his hand diplomatically. The historian William Turley argues that because of geostrategic realities that forced North Vietnam to exploit mountain regions and supply routes in Laos and Cambodia, they "for decades had considered Indochina a strategic unity, a single battlefield." The Cambodian invasion showed that the United States viewed Indochina in the same way. And, in the words of Senator Lee Metcalf of Montana, "With the Cambodian invasion, Nixon has made it his war."

10

The Fall of South Vietnam, 1970–1975

The real problem is that the enemy is willing to sacrifice in order to win, while the South Vietnamese simply aren't willing to pay that much of a price in order to avoid losing.
—Richard Nixon, 1972

They were probably the most influential antiwar group of all—the Vietnam Veterans against the War. Organized by six veterans in 1967, the VVAW had thousands of members by 1970. John Kerry, the VVAW spokesman, staged the Winter Soldier Investigation, and for three days between January 31 and February 2, 1971, 116 veterans testified of atrocities. Kerry argued that "the My Lai massacre was not an aberration, the isolated act of a ne'er-do-well second lieutenant gone berserk. . . . It was symbolic of a war gone berserk." With the world press focused on them, John Kerry's men testified that "at times they had personally raped, cut off ears, cut off heads, taped wires from portable telephones to human genitals and turned up the power, cut off limbs, blown up bodies, randomly shot at civilians, razed villages in fashion reminiscent of Genghis Khan, shot cattle and dogs for fun, poisoned food stocks." Their testimony was riveting, and the Nixon administration knew it. Time was running out on "peace with honor."

Nixon had to accelerate the troop withdrawals. The Third Brigade of the Ninth Infantry Division went home in October, and in December, Abrams lost the Fourth and the Twenty-fifth Infantry Divisions. At the end of 1970 he had 335,000 troops at his disposal, and the III Marine Amphibious Force, the First Marine Division, and the Eleventh Armored Cavalry were scheduled to leave in a few months. Already North Vietnam was increasing the infiltration of troops and supplies.

The Ho Chi Minh Trail had become a work of art maintained by 100,000 Vietnamese and Laotian workers. It included 12,000 miles of well-maintained trails, paved two-lane roads stretching from North Vietnam to Tchepone, just across the South Vietnamese border in Laos, and a four-inch fuel pipeline that reached all the way into the A Shau Valley. The CIA estimated that between 1966 and 1971 North Vietnam shipped 630,000 soldiers, 100,000 tons of food, 400,000 weapons, and 50,000 tons of ammunition into South Vietnam along the Ho Chi Minh Trail. Abrams wanted to invade Laos, cut the Ho Chi Minh Trail, and starve the North Vietnamese troops waiting in South Vietnam. But because the Cooper-Church Amendment prohibited the use of American troops outside South Vietnam, Abrams would have to rely on ARVN soldiers. During Nixon's first two years in office, nearly 15,000 American troops were killed in action.

The Nixon administration debated an invasion of Cambodia or an invasion of North Vietnam, but Abrams argued forcefully for severing the enemy supply lines in Laos. Nixon, Kissinger, and Westmoreland ultimately agreed with him. While the Winter Soldier Investigation was going on in Detroit, planning for the invasion of Laos was under way. Late in 1970 the United States 101st Airborne Division and the First Brigade of the Fifth Infantry Division reoccupied the former marine base at Khe Sanh as a staging area for the invasion. To divert enemy attention, a United States Navy task force with the Thirty-first Marine Amphibious Unit aboard hovered off the North Vietnamese city of Vinh, threatening an invasion. The ARVN objective was to drive west from Khe Sanh up Route 9 to Tchepone, about twenty-five miles away, cutting across the Ho Chi Minh Trail.

South Vietnam committed 21,000 troops to the invasion. Supported by B-52s and fighter-bombers from the United States Air Force and Navy, they invaded Laos on February 8, 1971. The attack was code-named Lam Son 719 after a small village in Thanh Hoa Province, the birthplace of Le Loi, the Vietnamese hero who defeated an invading Chinese army in 1428. But Laos was not Cambodia. North Vietnam was protecting its lifeline there, not isolated sanctuaries. The region surrounding Tchepone contained 36,000 NVA troops—nineteen antiaircraft battalions, twelve infantry regiments, one tank regiment, one artillery regiment, and elements of the NVA Second, 304th, 308th, 320th, and 324th Divisions.

For the first twelve miles, ARVN encountered only token resistance. The terrain was rugged, and the weather took a turn for the worse. Unexpected rains turned Route 9 into a muddy quagmire. ARVN stalled, and the North Vietnamese opened fire. The South Vietnamese troops fought well, but they were in an impossible position. ARVN air cavalry troops took Tchepone on March 6, but on March 9, 1971, Nguyen Van Thieu ordered a general withdrawal. It took two weeks of bitter fighting along Route 9 for the South Vietnamese to get back out of Laos, and without American air power they would not have made it at all. By the time they reached Khe Sanh, the South Vietnamese admitted to 1,200 men dead and 4,200 wounded, although MACV estimated the dead and wounded at 9,000 men.

General Creighton Abrams claimed publicly that Lam Son 719 had inflicted 14,000 casualties on the North Vietnamese. Back in Washington, President Nixon was even more effulgent, telling the White House press corps that "18 of 22 battalions conducted themselves with high morale, with greater confidence, and they are able to defend themselves man for man against the North Vietnamese." In a televised speech on April 7, the president proclaimed, "Tonight I can report that Vietnamization has succeeded." At the Pentagon, however, the private assessments were more grim. Most of the ARVN troops fought well, but North Vietnam inflicted a major military defeat on them and they had failed to sever the Ho Chi Minh Trail. The attack, as well as Vietnamization, was a failure.

Lam Son 719 had important strategic implications for both sides. For South Vietnam and the United States, it widened the field of battle, even though they would have fewer resources to fight. For the North Vietnamese, the victory proved that they could prevail over ARVN, even the new 1-million-man ARVN backed by American technology. It was clear to both sides that Vietnamization had not yet prepared ARVN to go it alone.

Not unexpectedly, Lam Son 719 inspired another series of antiwar protests. On April 20, 1971, more than 200,000 demonstrators gathered in Washington to protest the invasion. John Kerry had 1,000 Vietnam Veterans against the War, many of them paraplegics and amputees, as well as mothers of men killed in action, hold a memorial service at the Tomb of the Unknown Soldier. Nixon secured a court order prohibiting them from camping out on the Mall and laying wreaths on graves of fallen comrades at Arlington Cemetery. The press had a field day. The veterans and the mothers defied the order, and the administration declined to arrest them. On April 23 nearly 2,000 veterans threw medals they had won in Vietnam over police barricades on the Capitol steps. John Kerry said that they wanted to help the nation realize "the moral agony of America's Vietnam war generation—whether to kill on military orders and be a criminal, or to refuse to kill and be a criminal."

The Winter Soldier Investigation and the Laotian invasion devastated Daniel Ellsberg. Born in Chicago in 1931, Ellsberg grew up in a unique home. His parents were Jews who had converted to Christian Science, and Ellsberg was blessed, or perhaps cursed, with a moral passion and a sense of personal responsibility. He graduated *summa cum laude* from Harvard in 1952, spent a year at Cambridge University in England doing graduate work, and then joined the Marine Corps. He wanted to serve his country. When his marine tour ended in 1957, Ellsberg returned to Harvard for doctoral work. He left Harvard in 1959 for a job with the Rand Corporation, a civilian think tank. Ellsberg received the highest security clearances. When John Kennedy won the White House in 1960, Ellsberg got a leave of absence from Rand to serve on McGeorge Bundy's staff, and in 1964 he became special assistant to John McNaughton, deputy for foreign affairs at the Pentagon.

Of all the antiwar protesters, the most effective were the Vietnam Veterans Against the War—men who had served their country, experienced the war firsthand, and believed it was a futile effort.

DENNIS BRACK/BLACK STAR

Despondent about the breakup of his marriage in 1965, Ellsberg volunteered for the Marine Corps again. When the marines turned him down, Ellsberg secured a spot on Edward Lansdale's pacification team. He came back to the Defense Department convinced that success in Vietnam would require massive social and political changes, not just military victories. When Robert McNamara commissioned a study in 1967 of the history of American policy in Vietnam, Ellsberg was one of the senior researchers. A few months of research convinced Ellsberg that American policy in Vietnam was a disaster born of the political fact that "no American President, Republican or Democrat, wanted to be the President who lost the war. . . . That fear was sustained by years of duplicity, lies, exaggerations, and cover-ups."

By 1968 Ellsberg suffered from a profound guilt about his own role in formulating Vietnam policy. Throughout 1968 he called for a bombing halt and wrote policy papers for Senator Robert Kennedy and then Senator George McGovern. When Richard Nixon was elected in November, Ellsberg sank into a deep depression, and early in 1969 he began photocopying the secret Pentagon study and carrying it page by page to his Washington apartment. Ellsberg began secretly delivering the documents to Senator J. William Fulbright so "that the truths that changed me could help Americans free themselves and other victims from our longest war."

The Winter Soldier Investigation in February 1971 profoundly affected Ellsberg, deepening his sense of personal responsibility for the war. When he learned of the invasion of Laos later that month, he decided to hand over the secret documents to the *New York Times*. On June 13, 1971, the *Times* began publishing the documents, now dubbed the Pentagon Papers. Nixon was incensed. He ordered the wiretapping of dozens of administration officials to make sure no similar leaks of classified information occurred. The Justice Department secured a court order stopping the *New York Times* from publishing the documents, but the *Boston Globe* and the *Washington Post* continued to make the documents public. On June 29, 1971, Ellsberg was indicted for converting government property to his personal use, conspiracy, theft, and violation of the Espionage Act. The next day the Supreme Court, by a six to three vote, overturned the injunction against publishing the Pentagon Papers, citing the First Amendment freedoms of speech and the press. The Pentagon Papers proved conclusively the reality of the so-called credibility gap—government officials telling the public one thing and actively pursuing different military and political policies.

South Vietnamese politics only deepened public skepticism. President Nguyen Van Thieu was still embarrassed about the election of 1967, when he won office with only 35 percent of the total vote. The debacle in Laos in February and March exaggerated his need for an overwhelming political victory in the October elections. In March 1971 he exempted all civil servants and ARVN from paying income taxes, and the CIA provided Thieu with funds to bribe members of the National Assembly. He secured a bill requiring presidential candidates to receive nominations from forty legislators or 100 of the country's 554 city and provincial counselors. Thieu than eliminated all of Nguyen Cao Ky's supporters from the cabinet. When Ky submitted the nominations in July, the Supreme Court of South Vietnam disallowed them. In August several American newspapers revealed that Thieu already had elaborate plans for stuffing ballot boxes and jailing opposition leaders. On election day, 6.3 million people voted and gave Nguyen Van Thieu, the only candidate, a 94.3 percent plurality. Thieu finally had his "mandate from heaven."

While the antiwar protests, the controversy over the Pentagon Papers, and the South Vietnamese election were going on, American troops were leaving South Vietnam. In April 1971 the First Cavalry Division (Airmobile), the First Marine Division, and the Eleventh Armored Cavalry Regiment left South Vietnam, reducing the American troop levels to 240,000 men. Three months later the First Brigade of the Fifth Infantry Division and the 173d Airborne Brigade departed. The Americal Division left in November, just as President Nixon announced that all remaining American combat operations would be exclusively defensive in nature. On New Year's Day 1972, Creighton Abrams had only 157,000 troops left. If the United States was going to win the war, it would not happen on the battlefield. Richard Nixon and Henry Kissinger had to find another way.

"They're just a bunch of shits. Tawdry, filthy shits," exploded Henry Kissinger in frustration to Richard Nixon. Le Duc Tho was impossible, at least in Kissinger's mind. Tho was rigid and doctrinaire, his hatred of Western imperialism embedded in his psyche by years in French colonial prisons. He was also antiforeign to the point of xenophobia and fiercely patriotic, a "Vietnamese chauvinist" in the words of William Turley. Back in February 1971, at a small house on the Rue Darthe in the Paris suburb of Choisy-le-Roi, Kissinger held the first of many secret meetings with Le Duc Tho. But over the last year the house on Rue Darthe yielded nothing more than the formal talks at the Hotel Majestic. The United States was still approaching the negotiations on exclusively military terms, proposing a ceasefire, mutual withdrawal of American and North Vietnamese troops from South Vietnam, and an exchange of prisoners of war. Le Duc Tho insisted on a comprehensive political settlement: total withdrawal of all American troops, removal of Nguyen Van Thieu from office, immediate participation of the Provisional Revolutionary Government in the government of South Vietnam, exchanges of prisoners of war, and a cessation of hostilities—in that order. Four years of talking and fighting had not yielded a thing.

Well, they had achieved one thing. By early 1972 the negotiators in Paris had agreed on the shape of the table. What they had decided on was a circular table twenty-six feet in diameter, without name plates, place settings, flags, or identifying markings of any kind, where the chief negotiators would sit, and two rectangular tables, three by four and one-half feet each, placed eighteen inches from the circular table and at opposite sides. Nguyen Cao Ky remembered the table debate: "Oh! that table . . . it was of fundamental importance to us. There was no way we were prepared to negotiate with the NLF, who in our view were traitors, and therefore we insisted that the agreement not to distinguish the NLF as a separate party to the talks must be carried out to the letter—and this meant not sitting down 'officially' with them at the same table." After nearly one hundred sessions at the hotel, the diplomats had produced only an endless amount of copy for the press.

Le Duc Tho had a long memory. In 1954 the Vietminh accepted a military settlement at Geneva and agreed to postpone the political issues—the nebulous promise of free elections two years down the road.

The elections never took place. On his deathbed in 1969, Ho Chi Minh had warned Pham Van Dong and Le Duc Tho not to make the same mistake. It had cost them all fifteen years and more than a million deaths. The superpowers, all of them—the Soviet Union, France, the United States, and the People's Republic of China—were not to be trusted. "Don't sign the next agreement," Ho Chi Minh insisted, "until we're certain of the political outcome."

North Vietnamese stubbornness was compromising Kissinger's grand design for a new relationship among the superpowers. By 1971 the Chinese were more afraid of the Soviets than of the Americans, and Kissinger thought the time was ripe for the United States to seek a rapprochement. With increasingly powerful Vietnamese forces spread along China's southern border in Indochina, and huge Soviet forces arrayed along its northern frontier, Chinese leaders might be ready to talk. They were. Kissinger met secretly with Chinese representatives several times in 1971, and the talks were productive.

Kissinger further realized that improving American-Chinese relations would alarm the Soviets, increasing their willingness to negotiate in good faith, particularly on such critical issues as the Strategic Arms Limitation Talks then going on at Geneva. A unique opportunity to play the Soviets off against the Chinese and improve the United States' diplomatic position vis-à-vis both was at hand. Kissinger dubbed the new diplomatic initiative "détente," a mutual, morality-free process of cooperation and accommodation among the superpowers. Throughout 1971 and early 1972 Kissinger planned summit meetings in Moscow and Beijing so that Richard Nixon, the old "Red-Baiter," could reshape modern international politics. Nixon began that process in February 1972 with a triumphant visit to Beijing. The summit with the Soviet Union was scheduled for May.

One overwhelming problem stood between Kissinger and destiny— the Vietnam War. If the United States lost the war, the political repercussions back home would be severe. The right wing might rise up in self-righteous indignation and set off another McCarthy era, torpedoing any hopes Kissinger had of implementing a new relationship with the Soviets and the Chinese. If the United States withdrew without achieving "peace with honor," its reduced credibility would abort détente because neither the Soviets nor the Chinese would take the United States seriously. Kissinger needed an acceptable settlement of the war in Vietnam for détente to have any long-term hopes.

But the Soviets, Chinese, North Vietnamese, and Republican right wing were not Kissinger's only problems. Nixon worried constantly that the public would interpret endless negotiations as a sign of weakness. He was in his "tough" mood, as if George C. Scott's version of George S. Patton had become his alter ego. He was up for reelection and needed to do something to prove himself, to show the public that his "secret plan" of 1968 to end the war was more than campaign rhetoric. But at the end of 1971, Vietnamization was playing into Le Duc Tho's hands. If North Vietnam just waited a little while more, there would not be any United States troops left. As far as Nixon was concerned, Kissinger had a weak hand to play in Paris. The only military option left to the president was bombing, and he was ready to use it. He told Kissinger in the spring, "I'm going to show the bastards. Unless they deal with us I'm going to bomb the hell out of them." Nixon was in an anxious mood; the madman strategy was beginning to ring true.

In the spring of 1972 the North Vietnamese tested the "madman." With most of the American troops gone, they were certain the time was ripe for an all-out offensive in South Vietnam. The improving relations between the United States and China made some North Vietnamese feel a sense of urgency about winning the war as soon as possible. That fear was confirmed in late 1971 when the Chinese intimated that Vietnamese reunification might be a matter of years, not months. ARVN's dismal performance during the Lam Son invasion convinced the North Vietnamese that they could militarily win the war. A major figure behind that decision was Vo Nguyen Giap, who guaranteed "a great victory over the Americans and their Saigon puppets." The Politburo in 1971 decided on "a decisive victory" to force "the United States to end the war by negotiating from a position of defeat."

General Creighton Abrams had been expecting an attack. Since 1968 the North Vietnamese had used the Tet holidays for new offensives, and as early as October 1971 MACV had been warning ARVN to get ready. But February 1, 1972, came and went, with no attack. ARVN maintained an alert status throughout most of February, but the American warnings had a "cry wolf" refrain. ARVN commanders relaxed, and Giap traded the Vietnamese New Year holiday for the American Easter celebrations. The North Vietnamese offensive began on Good Friday, March 30, 1972. By that time there were 95,000 American troops still in South Vietnam, but only 6,000 of them were combat troops.

Under a heavy, advanced artillery barrage, more than 30,000 North Vietnamese troops, accompanied by 200 Soviet tanks, crossed the Demilitarized Zone and attacked Quang Tri Province in I Corps. Giap had moved long-range 130-mm artillery just north of the Hieu Giang River, bringing Quang Tri City and an area five miles south of the city under bombardment. Heavy cloud cover limited the effectiveness of American tactical air strikes. The NVA troops kept up the artillery bombardment of ARVN posts, and on April 27 they attacked Quang Tri City. Thousands of South Vietnamese refugees fled the city for the protection of Hue, but the North Vietnamese targeted the 130-mm artillery on Highway 1, exacting a heavy toll on the refugees. The ARVN Third Division was caught off guard and began falling back along Highway 1. On May 1, the 304th North Vietnamese Division took control of Quang Tri City.

Giap hoped to inspire a deployment of American and ARVN troops north into I Corps while he prepared for three other attacks. Another 35,000-man contingent of North Vietnamese troops, the now-reinforced remnants of those attacked in Cambodia in 1970 and Laos in 1971, assembled in Cambodia for an assault on Saigon, while 35,000 more soldiers prepared for an attack on Dak To in the Central Highlands. Giap hoped the battle in the north would distract ARVN forces, allowing the scheduled attacks in the Central Highlands and on Saigon to succeed. North Vietnamese troops moved out of Cambodia on April 2, attacking with tanks and armored personnel carriers. They moved down Highway 13, seized Loc Ninh, surrounded An Loc, and severed the route to Saigon. One week later North Vietnam attacked Dak To with the objective of taking Kontum. If Kontum fell, they planned on a drive for the South China Sea, where they could cut South Vietnam in half. To prepare for that possibility, two North Vietnamese divisions invaded Binh Dinh Province and took control of several districts along the South China Sea, cutting Highway 1 and the link between Hue and Saigon. The combined total of Vietcong and North Vietnamese troops committed to the offensive was 200,000 people.

The Eastertide offensive could not have come at a worse time for the Nixon administration. On April 2, Ambassador Ellsworth Bunker cabled Kissinger and Nixon that "ARVN forces are on the verge of collapse in I Corps." Back in his more naive days of 1969, Kissinger told several of his aides, "I can't believe that a fourth-rate power like North Vietnam doesn't have a breaking point." Now a military offensive led by North Vietnam threatened to derail everything. If the Eastertide offensive succeeded, even partially, Kissinger would lose bargaining power with Le Duc Tho. With so few troops left in South Vietnam, the United States had only one option: massive bombardment of North Vietnam and North Vietnamese forces to stop the invasion.

But Kissinger had scheduled a summit meeting for President Nixon with the Soviets in May. If the United States launched an all-out bombing campaign over North Vietnam, the Soviet Union might cancel the summit and destroy Kissinger's hopes for détente and the signing of a treaty limiting nuclear arms. Yet without the initiation of a heavy bombing campaign, the Eastertide offensive would overrun South Vietnam, inflict a military defeat on ARVN, and compromise the strategic position of the United States throughout the world. Kissinger was walking a tightrope.

The only advantage Nixon and Kissinger held was the intense Soviet desire to improve relations with the United States to offset the Chinese overtures to Washington. Nixon and Kissinger decided to unleash the B-52s. On April 6, 1972, they met in the White House with General John W. Vogt, new commander of the Seventh Air Force. Without American ground troops, Nixon's only option was air power, and he told Vogt "to get down there and use whatever air you need to turn this thing around. . . . Stop this offensive." Code-named Operation Linebacker, the bombing began later that day, the first sustained raids over North Vietnam since 1969. The president confined the attacks to targets within sixty miles of the Demilitarized Zone, but on April 10 Nixon extended the radius and by mid-month B-52s were attacking targets within a few miles of Hanoi and Haiphong. The raids elated the joint chiefs. Admiral Thomas Moorer, who replaced Earle Wheeler as chairman of the joint chiefs in 1970, remarked, "Finally we will be able to win the war."

On May 2 Kissinger met once again at the house on the Rue Darthe in Paris with Le Duc Tho, but the meeting was a complete failure. Kissinger tried to achieve some movement in the negotiations. But Le Duc Tho would not budge. Quang Tri City had fallen to NVA troops, Hue was threatened, Loc Ninh was taken, An Loc was under siege, and Saigon was bracing for an attack; and in the Central Highlands the NVA troops were preparing for a breakthrough that would carry them to the South China Sea. Le Duc Tho had one message for Kissinger on May 2, 1970: "What difference is all this talk going to make? The end is in sight." Kissinger was upset. Le Duc Tho was arrogant, even insulting. That night, when he got back to Washington, Kissinger met with Nixon. His restraint was gone. "Its time," he told Nixon, "to send them an undeniable message, to deliver a shock, to let them know that things might get out of hand if the offensive doesn't stop." Nixon was ready, too. "The bastards have never been bombed like they're going to be bombed this time." Two days later, on May 4, Nixon suspended the Paris peace talks after their 149th session.

On May 8 Nixon announced that Operation Linebacker would continue indefinitely and the United States Navy would mine the North Vietnamese ports of Haiphong, Cam Pha, Hon Gai, and Thanh Hoa and impose a naval blockade of the entire coast—all to cut the flow of supplies to North Vietnamese troops fighting in the South and to protect the lives of American forces still in Vietnam. Nixon hoped the raids would pressure North Vietnam into taking the Paris negotiations seriously. Privately, he hoped the B-52s would do what ARVN could not: stop the Eastertide offensive. Kissinger hoped the raids would not derail the upcoming Moscow summit.

Both Nixon and Kissinger received their wishes. Nixon shifted more than 100 B-52s from the Strategic Air Command and assigned them to tactical strikes over South Vietnam and strategic air raids over North Vietnam. The size of the Seventh Fleet nearly doubled, including the addition of four aircraft carriers and hundreds of fighter-bombers. By the end of May the United States was flying more than 2,200 sorties a month, up from only 700 in March, and most of the raids were concentrated on Quang Tri, Kontum, Dak To, An Loc, and Loc Ninh, and over selected strategic targets in North Vietnam. At An Loc and Quang Tri the B-52s struck every forty-five minutes, twenty-four hours a day, for weeks on end, pounding the North Vietnamese. They took a fearsome toll. On June 18 the NVA troops began pulling out of An Loc; the fighting petered out near Kontum, ending North Vietnam's hopes of driving to the South China Sea; and up north, the ARVN Airborne Division, First Division, and marines began a counterattack that lasted throughout the summer and eventually recaptured Quang Tri City. Eastertide was over.

The Soviets acted with restraint. They offered only the most tepid protest of the bombing and mining campaigns, decided not to challenge the naval blockade, and did not withdraw their invitation for Nixon to come to Moscow. The Chinese were equally circumspect, issuing a mild protest but also calling for a negotiated settlement. Pham Van Dong felt betrayed, condemning the Soviets and the Chinese for abandoning the "world revolutionary movement and acquiescing in the brutal violence of the American imperialists." Later in the month Nixon went to Moscow, drank champagne with a smiling Leonid Brezhnev, and signed the coveted Strategic Arms Limitation Treaty.

In Hanoi the Eastertide fiasco was a humiliating defeat for Vo Nguyen Giap. He had also fallen victim to Hodgkin's disease, a cancer of the lymphatic system, which prevented him from taking an active role in the government. Pham Van Dong began looking to General Van Tien Dung as his military chief. Born in Tonkin in 1917 to a peasant family, Dung joined the revolutionary movement in 1936 and fought against the French and then the Japanese during World War II. Shrewd and fearless, he exuded confidence, but his perpetually smiling countenance hid an all-consuming passion for Vietnamese independence. In the early 1950s Dung performed brilliantly as a Vietminh battalion commander, and Giap trained him in logistics and maneuvers. In 1953 Giap named Dung chief of staff, gave him command of the 320th Division, and charged him with logistical planning at Dienbienphu. For the next eighteen years Dung was Giap's closest associate.

When Dung assumed control of the North Vietnamese Army, he faced a complicated political and military situation. On August 23, 1972, the last American combat battalion—Third Battalion of the Twenty-first Infantry—left South Vietnam. ARVN troop strength had reached nearly 1.1 million troops, the highest since the beginning of the war, and with military equipment transfers from the United States, South Vietnam had a state-of-the-art fighting force. It was the fourth largest army in the world. With nearly 1,500 ships, the South Vietnamese Navy was the fifth largest in the world, and the South Vietnamese Air Force, with more than 2,000 aircraft, was the fourth largest in the world. Dung thought he faced a formidable enemy. Because Giap persisted in making repeated frontal assaults into fortified ARVN bunkers protected by massive American air support during Eastertide, fully half of the NVA combat divisions had been nearly bled to death. More than 100,000 of North Vietnam's best troops were dead, and Dung estimated it could take three years to restore the army to fighting strength. It was obvious to Dung that North Vietnam would not be able to contemplate a major offensive against South Vietnam anytime soon.

The political situation in the United States did not bode well either. Pham Van Dong and Le Duc Tho had been hoping ever since the Cambodian invasion in 1970 that the antiwar movement would sweep Richard Nixon from office and bring a Democrat to power who would be anxious to complete the American disengagement. They took heart when the Democrats nominated Senator George McGovern of South Dakota as their presidential candidate. A leading political figure in the antiwar movement since 1965, McGovern campaigned for an immediate, unilateral American withdrawal. For their purposes the North Vietnamese could not imagine a better American president.

But the McGovern campaign self-destructed. When the press found out that Senator Thomas Eagleton of Missouri, McGovern's vice-presidential running mate, had once been hospitalized for mental illness, the Democrats found themselves in a political mess. McGovern dumped Eagleton from the ticket and replaced him with Sargent Shriver, but the damage was done. Pham Van Dong and Le Duc Tho both knew that Richard Nixon would be reelected in November.

The military situation in South Vietnam and the political climate in the United States left North Vietnam with only one option: Negotiate a settlement to the war. Van Tien Dung played a central role in convincing the Politburo to return to the talks. Pham Van Dong and Le Duc Tho were more stubborn. Operation Linebacker, like the earlier Rolling Thunder bombing campaigns, made them more resentful of the United States and more intransigent. They did not want to give in to what they considered technological terrorism. But Dung saw no point in digging in. He could not launch an invasion of South Vietnam anyway, and no dramatic change appeared on the American political horizon. Why not reopen the talks, secure an end to the Linebacker attacks, rebuild the logistical network, and prepare for the final assault on South Vietnam?

Dung's logic was compelling, and in August, Kissinger resumed private talks with Le Duc Tho. Both sides wanted an accommodation. North Vietnam wanted an end to the Linebacker raids, and Nixon was looking ahead to the election, hoping to sign a peace treaty before November. In Paris at the end of September, Kissinger agreed to a complete withdrawal of American troops while allowing North Vietnamese soldiers to remain in place in South Vietnam, a major concession to Le Duc Tho. Kissinger felt he had little choice. Ten years of war and the greatest expenditure of firepower in history had not dislodged them. "We could not make it [NVA troop withdrawal] a condition for a final settlement. We had long since passed that threshold." Le Duc Tho dropped the long-standing North Vietnamese demand that Nguyen Van Thieu resign and a coalition government be created. At the end of September the outlines of a peace treaty had emerged: a mutual cease-fire and an end to American bombing; complete withdrawal of American troops; exchanges of prisoners of war; agreement to allow Vietcong, North Vietnamese, and South Vietnamese troops to remain in place; recognition of the Provisional Revolutionary Government of South Vietnam and the government of Nguyen Van Thieu as legitimate political entities in South Vietnam; and creation of a "council of national reconciliation" to work out the remaining problems.

In some ways the settlement was the easy part. Kissinger encountered opposition from the State Department, typical bureaucratic intransigence that, in his opinion, so often foiled modern diplomacy. When several State Department and National Security Council staff officials argued that the United States had caved in to the North Vietnamese position, Kissinger reacted violently, shouting at them in a White House briefing session: "I want to meet their terms. I want to reach an agreement. I want to end this war before the election. It can be done and it will be done. What do you want us to do? Stay there forever?"

In Saigon, President Nguyen Van Thieu believed a sellout was under way. He was apoplectic in his opposition to the treaty. Leaving fourteen divisions of North Vietnamese troops in South Vietnam and extending political recognition to the Provisional Revolutionary Government were unthinkable. When Kissinger met with Thieu in Saigon in mid-October, the South Vietnamese rejected the proposals out of hand, insisting on withdrawal of all North Vietnamese soldiers, recognition of the Demilitarized Zone as a sovereign international boundary, and a public American repudiation of the Provisional Revolutionary Government's legitimacy. When Kissinger termed the demands "insane and absurd," Thieu went mute with rage.

When Kissinger returned to Washington with the news that Thieu was going to sabotage the deal, Nixon flew into one of his own rages, ordering Kissinger to fly to Saigon and "tell that little son of a bitch to sign or else." Kissinger demurred and Nixon reconsidered, hoping that there was some way of finessing Thieu into agreement. On October 22, 1972, the administration scaled back the Linebacker raids to targets south of the twentieth parallel. The United States had staged more than 41,000 bombing sorties over North Vietnam since April 1, 1972. Thieu denounced the bombing halt and the draft treaty in a press conference on October 24, calling on South Vietnam to "wipe out the Vietcong and North Vietnamese invaders quickly and mercilessly." But Nixon was also getting cold feet. With the election just two weeks away, he did not want the settlement to appear politically contrived, and he thought that Thieu's demands might give the United States more bargaining power. Kissinger began another round of talks, which made Hanoi very suspicious. In a political dance inspired by the presidential elections and fear of losing the settlement outright, Kissinger held a press conference in which he promised that "peace is at hand. We believe that an agreement is within sight."

It was not, not quite yet at least. Nixon won a landslide victory in the election on November 7. When Kissinger renewed negotiations with Le Duc Tho after the elections, he presented to the North Vietnamese sixty-nine proposed changes in the treaty, all of them demanded by Nguyen Van Thieu. The North Vietnamese found the proposals unacceptable, and later in the month they began introducing new proposed changes of their own. The agreement, which had seemed so close back in October, was disintegrating.

Nixon then decided to use the carrot instead of the stick with South Vietnam, promising Thieu that if "North Vietnam violates the agreement and stages offensive operations against you, the United States will take swift and severe retaliatory action." Thieu knew better than anyone that South Vietnamese survival depended on that retaliation. Only massive American bombing had stopped the Eastertide offensive. Without American air support and military assistance, South Vietnam would not survive another attack. Thieu still would not budge. Pham Van Dong, however, saw the feud between the United States and South Vietnam as an opportunity. If he could stall the talks, raise more procedural issues, and delay a final settlement, North Vietnam might be able to strengthen the air defenses around Hanoi and Haiphong, repair the rail lines to China, and adjust its supply routing to compensate for the American blockade. The changing diplomatic wind was unsettling. On December 13 Le Duc Tho suspended the negotiations and returned to Hanoi "for consultations."

The next day Nixon gave Pham Van Dong an ultimatum: "Resume serious negotiations within seventy-two hours or suffer the consequences." Nixon was reaching the end of his emotional rope. He wanted a signed peace treaty before the inauguration on January 20, 1973. He was even more blunt to Admiral Thomas Moorer, instructing him to develop immediate plans for massive bombing of North Vietnam: "I don't want any more of this crap about the fact that we couldn't hit this target or that one. This is your chance to use military power to win this war, and if you don't, I'll hold you responsible." On December 18, 1972, Moorer followed orders and launched Operation Linebacker II, a final eleven-day bombing campaign that evolved into one of the heaviest aerial assaults of the war. B-52s, F-105s, F-4s, and F-111s flew nearly 2,000 sorties over North Vietnam, employing highly accurate laser-guided, television-targeted bombs—"Christmas bombs"—to strike rail yards, power plants, communication facilities, air defense radar sites, bridges, highways, docks and shipping facilities, petroleum stores, ammunition supply depots, air bases, military installations, and transportation facilities.

Early in January 1973 Le Duc Tho indicated a willingness to resume the negotiations. Van Tien Dung had been right all along. It was best to wait for a better opportunity, sometime in the future, to plan the final offensive. The only roadblock to a settlement was Nguyen Van Thieu, but Richard Nixon was not about to let a peace treaty slip through his hands again. On January 5, 1973, he secretly communicated with Thieu, sending him a threat and a promise:

> Gravest consequences would then ensue if [you] . . . reject the agreement. . . . It is imperative for our common objectives that your government take no further actions . . . that make more difficult the acceptance of the settlement by all parties. . . . Should you decide . . . to go with us, you have my assurance of continued assistance in the post-settlement period and that we will respond with full force should the settlement be violated by North Vietnam.

Thieu got the message. With or without him, Nixon was going to sign a treaty. Refusal to cooperate would mean an end to United States military assistance and certain defeat. Stone-faced, his teeth tightly clenched, Thieu told Ambassador Ellsworth Bunker that he would sign. Kissinger met with Le Duc Tho in Paris on January 8; Nixon halted all military operations against North Vietnam on January 15; and all four parties— the United States, North Vietnam, South Vietnam, and the Provisional Revolutionary Government of South Vietnam—signed the treaty in Paris on January 27, 1973. The treaty provided for release of all American prisoners of war and withdrawal of all United States military personnel within sixty days; a cease-fire to be monitored by a four-nation International Commission of Control and Supervision; cessation of all foreign military activity in Laos and Cambodia; United States provision of replacement military aid and unlimited economic assistance to South Vietnam; and formation of a Council of National Reconciliation and Concord, composed of representatives from the Saigon regime, the Provisional Revolutionary Government of South Vietnam, and a neutral body, to resolve outstanding political questions and organize elections in South Vietnam.

The settlement came none too soon. When Congress convened in January, the Democratic caucuses of both houses voted overwhelmingly to eliminate all funds for military operations in Indochina, and polls of the new Congress indicated huge majorities for the end of American involvement in the region. There were only 24,000 American troops still in South Vietnam. Political support for the war in the United States had completely evaporated. Nixon had no choice but to get the treaty signed and sealed.

In a national television address, he announced that within sixty days all American troops would be out of South Vietnam and the prisoners of war would be home. "South Vietnam," he said, "has gained the right to determine its own future. . . . Let us be proud that America did not settle for a peace that would have betrayed our ally." Nguyen Cao Ky watched the speech, noting, "I could not stomach [it], so nauseating was its hypocrisy and self-delusion. . . . This is an enormous step toward the total domination of Vietnam and there is no reason why they [the Communists] should stop now. . . . I give them a couple of years before they invade the South."

There were a few good months before it all started to unravel. On February 12, 1973, the first of 591 American prisoners of war returned home, and the rest were in the United States by the end of March. Nixon and Kissinger hosted them at the White House, and the soldiers paid homage to the president who had ended the war. On February 21 the Royal Laotian government signed a cease-fire with the communist Pathet Lao guerrillas. The International Commission of Control and Supervision, composed of Canada, Indonesia, Hungary, and Poland, went into operation in March. A relieved Henry Kissinger remarked to the press, "It should be clear by now that no one in the war has had a monopoly of anguish and that no one has a monopoly of insight. Together with healing the wounds in Indochina, we can begin to heal the wounds in America."

But those wounds continued to fester, and the Nixon administration was unable to deliver on its promise to rescue South Vietnam if Hanoi broke the agreement. Richard Nixon's insecurities and paranoia, his resentment of the press and the eastern establishment, were about to catch up with him. The Watergate scandal enveloped him, and when the final North Vietnamese offensive came in 1975, Richard Nixon would be living in exile in San Clemente, California.

During the election campaign of 1972, the Nixon administration orchestrated a series of illegal and unethical campaign programs, all directed at undermining the political efforts of liberal Democrats. On June 22, 1972, police caught several men attempting to wiretap Democratic Party National Headquarters in the Watergate Building in Washington. A few days later, when it was clear that a number of top administration officials were involved in planning and financing the break-in, Nixon ordered a cover-up of the entire affair. Two enterprising reporters from the *Washington Post*—Robert Woodward and Carl Bernstein—eventually exposed the whole story.

Two of the president's closest advisers, John Ehrlichman and H. R. Haldeman, resigned on April 30, 1973, when they were implicated in the cover-up, and on May 11 a federal judge dismissed charges against Daniel Ellsberg when he learned that the Justice Department had illegally wiretapped his phone and administration officials, with CIA assistance, had burglarized the files of Ellsberg's psychiatrist to "find some dirt" about him. Senator Sam Ervin of North Carolina headed up the Select Committee on Presidential Campaign Activities, and the televised hearings dominated the news for the next six months. The testimony indicated that Nixon had been personally involved in the cover-up, despite

President Richard Nixon's popularity would never be higher than it was early in 1973 when the American POWs returned home from captivity in North Vietnam.
UPI/BETTMANN NEWSPHOTOS

his self-righteous denials, from the very beginning, and that he had tape-recorded most of his White House conversations. Throughout 1973 and much of 1974 Congress, the press, and the special Justice Department prosecutor wanted copies of those tapes, which the administration refused to provide. The House Judiciary Committee began impeachment proceedings against the president late in 1973, and when the Supreme Court forced Nixon to hand over the tapes, and the tapes clearly implicated him in the cover-up, Nixon resigned from office. Gerald Ford became the thirty-eighth president of the United States on August 9, 1974.

During the Watergate controversy, Nixon's presidential authority steadily eroded, and he was unable to keep control over Southeast Asia policy. Late in June 1973 Congress attached a rider to a supplemental appropriations bill cutting off funds for American bombing in Cambodia. Nixon vetoed the bill on June 27, but when it became clear that an override was a distinct possibility, he compromised, guaranteeing to

Congress that all American military activity in Cambodia would be over by August 15, 1973. Congress passed legislation ending all American combat activities in Indochina by August 15. Nixon signed the bill on July 1.

By that time there were already signs that the peace agreement was not working. With no more American bombing of Cambodia and Laos, North Vietnam initiated massive increases in the infiltration of troops and supplies, and provided matériel to the Khmer Rouge guerrillas in Cambodia and the Pathet Lao in Laos. The Soviet Union increased shipments of weapons and financial assistance to North Vietnam by 400 percent. To counter that assistance, the United States funneled $3.2 billion in military assistance to South Vietnam. When it became clear in August 1973 that North Vietnam had no intention of abiding by the Treaty of Paris, Canada withdrew from the International Commission of Control and Supervision. Iran became the fourth member nation. The Council of National Reconciliation and Concord remained stillborn.

In Laos and Cambodia the prospects were equally dismal. The Khmer Rouge gained ground in Cambodia, and the Lon Nol government seemed impotent. The situation in Laos was just as precarious. The Pathet Lao controlled most of northern Laos by 1974. Prince Souvanna Phouma hoped to maintain a neutralist government, but the North Vietnamese were making that difficult. Although Souvanna Phouma had signed the cease-fire on February 21, in which the North Vietnamese agreed to withdraw their troops from Laos, he was skeptical. In a plea to Henry Kissinger, Phouma said: "If pressure is kept on the North Vietnamese to understand the risk they run from violating the Agreement, then perhaps they will respect the Agreement. . . . Therefore we must count on our great friends the Americans to help us survive. We hope, we dream, that this wish will be granted." It was a futile plea. Kissinger met with Le Duc Tho in Hanoi on February 10 and learned that North Vietnam would withdraw *after* a political settlement in Laos between the government and the Pathet Lao, not before. There was nothing Kissinger could do about it.

The continuing fighting in Indochina triggered a movement in Congress to restrict the authority of the president. In July, Congress began debating a joint resolution requiring the president to report to Congress within forty-eight hours if he committed American forces to a foreign conflict or he "substantially" increased the number of combat troops in a foreign country. Unless Congress approved the president's actions within sixty days, the president would have to end the commitment. At the insistence of the Senate, a loophole was inserted allowing the deadline to be extended another thirty days if the president certified that more time was necessary to complete the evacuation of American forces. Congress could also order an immediate withdrawal within the sixty- or ninety-day period by passing a concurrent resolution, which could not be vetoed.

Congress passed the War Powers Resolution at the end of October. Nixon vetoed it, but on November 7, 1973, Congress overrode the veto and the measure became law.

The North Vietnamese were watching Washington politics very closely. The Canadians were right. North Vietnam had no intention of abandoning the dream of unification and independence. It was only a question of time. Pham Van Dong and Le Duc Tho were cautious about the next offensive. They knew that the Nixon administration was weakening under the pressures of Watergate, but they did not underestimate the president. Le Duc Tho in particular was certain that if Nixon had a chance, he would unleash the B-52s again. Van Tien Dung was cautious for another reason. The last thing he wanted was another Eastertide offensive. He could not afford the casualties. They all watched with interest the political debates in Congress. In mid-1974 Congress limited aid to Vietnam to $1.1 billion, down from $3.2 billion the year before, and the funding for fiscal 1975 was cut to only $700 million, which included shipping costs to South Vietnam. A major American intervention seemed unlikely.

South Vietnam was also facing severe economic problems. Ever since the early 1960s the economy had been driven by massive American aid and the spending power of hundreds of thousands of United States soldiers. Army construction projects alone employed 100,000 South Vietnamese workers. With the troops gone and American aid declining, the economy fluttered out of control. Inflation hit 65 percent, and urban unemployment reached 40 percent. The fact that the government supported an army of 1.1 million people only worsened the economic situation. President Nguyen Van Thieu's support among the general population, never really very high, plummeted even more.

The war had forever transformed Saigon. In less than a decade its population had swelled from 1 million to nearly 4 million people, without any real improvements in housing or city services. People came to the city for homes or jobs, for access to the sea of American money, for the security that was absent in the countryside. It had become a city of prostitutes, pimps, black marketeers, petty thieves, drug dealers, assassins, orphans, refugees, deserters, Vietcong, terrorists, and opportunists. The GIs said they could get anything in Saigon—"laid and waylaid, diarrhea and gonorrhea, drugs and slugs." For more traditional Vietnamese, especially Buddhists, the material worldliness of Saigon was an abomination.

In Saigon the regime of Nguyen Van Thieu became even more authoritarian. In 1971 Thieu abolished village elections and raised Buddhist ire. Thieu established the Dan Chu (Democracy) party in March 1973 and then promptly did the most undemocratic things—forcing all civil servants to join, manipulating the National Assembly elections, abolishing rival political parties, closing down newspapers, and maintaining a martial law state. A variety of protest movements developed in 1973 and 1974, the most influential of which was led by Father Tran Huu Thanh, a Roman Catholic priest who accused Thieu of subverting anticommunism in order to line his own pockets. Late in 1974 Thieu tried to deal with Thanh's increasing power by firing several hundred patently corrupt military officers and civilian officials, but it was only a token attempt at reform. The regime remained an authoritarian, single-party state.

Le Duan decided the time was ripe for the final offensive. The United States was out of Vietnam for good. The Arab oil embargo of 1973 had triggered higher unemployment and inflation in the United States, and the Watergate scandal, the corruption in Saigon, the increasing power of the Pathet Lao in Laos and the Khmer Rouge in Cambodia, and the intense congressional opposition to continuing involvement in Indochina guaranteed, as far as Le Duan was concerned, that the United States would not be able to save South Vietnam. Planning for the offensive accelerated.

General Van Tien Dung decided to begin the offensive cautiously, and he predicted it could take years to succeed, particularly if the United States intervened with air power. By the end of 1974 Dung had twenty-two fully equipped infantry divisions, complete with hundreds of tanks and thousands of artillery pieces, already in place in South Vietnam. Improvements in the Ho Chi Minh Trail gave the North Vietnamese Army more mobility than ever before.

But rather than an all-out offensive, Dung decided to attack Phuoc Long, a sparsely populated province that bordered Cambodia on the west and whose southern tip was only forty miles from Saigon. Such an offensive would yield two important pieces of information: Was ARVN prepared for serious resistance, and would the United States intervene? If ARVN collapsed, the United States did not intervene, and Phuoc Long fell, North Vietnam would gain a critically important psychological and logistical victory. North Vietnamese troop movements would be unimpeded all the way from Hanoi to within forty miles of Saigon.

Nguyen Van Thieu felt that North Vietnam was still too weak in 1975 to launch an all-out offensive. But Van Tien Dung had already moved the NVA Third and Seventh Divisions into position. The NVA artillery bombardment began on December 26, 1974. On January 5, 1975, the North Vietnamese attacked with two full divisions, T-54 tanks, and 130-mm field-gun batteries. Thieu sent in only one ARVN battalion to defend Phuoc Long, but it was woefully inadequate. Most important, the dreaded B-52s did not appear over Phuoc Long. Le Duan summed it up best in a speech to the Politburo in Hanoi: "Never have we had military and political conditions so perfect or a strategic advantage so great as we have now."

Van Tien Dung, Le Duc Tho, and Pham Van Dong decided their next step would be to cut South Vietnam in half, driving from the Central Highlands to the South China Sea. From Phuoc Long they decided to attack Ban Me Thuot. Dung spent the next two months moving his troops, tanks, artillery, and supplies into place, and on March 9, 1975, the NVA 316th, Tenth, and 320th Divisions attacked. Assuming North Vietnam would not attack unless it was a diversion, ARVN defenders at Ban Me Thuot were not prepared, and the NVA took the city on March 12. Once again, there had been no B-52s overhead or American fighter-bombers from the South China Sea.

The fall of Ban Me Thuot had immediate consequences. In Saigon on March 14, over the opposition of all of his senior military advisers, President Nguyen Van Thieu made the fateful decision to abandon the Central Highlands and redeploy ARVN forces to the major cities—an enclave strategy designed to protect the major population centers. On the same day, General Van Tien Dung decided to attack up Route 14 and seize Pleiku and Kontum. In the process he encountered hundreds of thousands of South Vietnamese refugees fleeing the Central Highlands and tens of thousands of ARVN troops withdrawing. He cut them to pieces with heavy artillery. More than 100,000 civilians and 15,000 ARVN troops died in the wholesale flight out of the highlands.

In Cambodia the Khmer Rouge pushed toward victory. By the end of 1974, the Lon Nol government was dying. The Khmer Rouge guerrillas sealed off the Mekong River as a source of commerce for Phnom Penh, and they surrounded the capital, tightening the noose day by day. They controlled 80 percent of the country. In fact, there were no ground transportation routes open into the capital. More than 2.7 million Cambodians crowded into Phnom Penh, and there was no way of supplying them. American ambassador John Gunther Dean reported that Cambodia was doomed.

Events in Laos were just as bad. On March 27, the Pathet Lao launched an offensive against the Souvanna Phouma government, attacking Vang Pao and Sala Phou Khoun and then driving south along Route 13 toward the capital city of Vientiane. Antigovernment demonstrations and riots erupted in Vientiane during the offensive, and Souvanna Phouma was unable to suppress them. Similar antigovernment insurgency developed in other towns and cities throughout the country. The Pathet Lao also infiltrated guerrilla soldiers into Vientiane and such cities as Pakse, Savannakhet, and Thakhek along the border with Thailand. Like the Khmer Rouge and the North Vietnamese, the Pathet Lao could smell victory.

A week after the ARVN debacle in the Central Highlands, Van Tien Dung surprised South Vietnam again with a major offensive in I Corps. The NVA 341st Division attacked out of Quang Tri Province and headed South along Route 1 toward Hue, while the NVA 324B and 325C Divisions came east out of the mountains of Quang Nam Province and drove to the South China Sea, cutting off Route 1 and isolating Hue. On March 20, 1975, Nguyen Van Thieu abandoned Hue, hoping to hold the line at Danang. North Vietnam took Hue on March 24. But no sooner had Hue been abandoned than the NVA Second Division seized Tam Ky on Route 1, cutting off Danang. The NVA 711th and 304th Divisions then moved on Danang. The South Vietnamese Air Force and Navy evacuated 50,000 refugees and 16,000 ARVN troops before Danang fell on March 29. Left behind were more than 2 million civilians and 25,000 ARVN soldiers, who surrendered to the North Vietnamese. To make sure that the few Americans still in the city got away, North Vietnamese troops did not reach the docks at Danang until March 30. Van Tien Dung was taking no chances on angering the United States and inspiring intervention.

The collapse of South Vietnamese forces in the Central Highlands and in I Corps caught everyone off guard. The fall of Indochina to communism seemed imminent. In Washington, President Gerald Ford and Henry Kissinger, who had replaced William P. Rogers as secretary of state in 1973, went to Congress for emergency assistance. In January they had unsuccessfully lobbied Congress for $300 million for South Vietnam and $222 million for Cambodia, but early in February Ford returned with a request for $1.3 billion for South Vietnam and $497 million for Cambodia. Senate Majority Leader Mike Mansfield reacted angrily to the request, saying that he was "sick and tired of pictures of Indochinese men, women, and children being slaughtered by American guns with American ammunition in countries in which we have no vital interests." Ford failed. He tried again in April with a new request for $722 million, but he received only $300 million, and it was confined to humanitarian assistance and funds to help evacuate Americans if necessary. South Vietnam, Cambodia, and Laos were on their own.

South Vietnam was imploding. For years the United States had trained ARVN to fight a conventional war with the support of enormous firepower, a strategy that, although incapable of achieving military victory, had at least staved off defeat. But Vietnamization had taken American troops out of the strategic picture, and opposition to the war in the United States gradually eliminated the firepower. Only the B-52s had stopped the Eastertide offensive in 1972. The South Vietnamese did not have that support in 1975. They did not even have much American money anymore. But between 1970 and 1975, when ARVN lost its American support, the war expanded all across Indochina, increasing the field of battle and stretching ARVN's resources to the breaking point. Those strategic factors, combined with a crumbling economy and an isolated political regime, guaranteed defeat.

On March 31, 1975, Le Duan cabled Van Tien Dung with orders to take Saigon. He called it a "once in a thousand years opportunity to liberate Saigon before the rainy season." The offensives in I Corps and the Central Highlands had decimated ARVN forces. South Vietnam had lost 150,000 troops to death, capture, or desertion, along with more than $1 billion in military equipment. President Nguyen Van Thieu had isolated himself in the presidential palace, and the Joint General Staff was doing nothing to get ready for the North Vietnamese attack. Le Duan was right. Van Tien Dung had a "once in a thousand years opportunity."

On April 3, 1975, Ambassador John Gunther Dean asked President Gerald Ford for permission to evacuate all Americans from Phnom Penh. The 1.7 million people in the city were starving. The Khmer Rouge had cut off all routes into Phnom Penh, including the Mekong River, and the airlift of supplies was becoming precarious because the guerrillas were closing in on Pochentong Airport. The communists were pouring 107-mm rockets into the city constantly. Lon Nol had abdicated two days before to a military coalition and left the city for Indonesia, on his way to Hawaii. Hoping to work out a last-minute arrangement for the return of Prince Norodom Sihanouk to power, Kissinger delayed the American evacuation. The Khmer Rouge were on the outskirts of Phnom Penh on April 11. President Ford then implemented Operation Eagle Pull. Naval helicopters from the Seventh Fleet landed on the embassy grounds and evacuated 276 Cambodian and American embassy personnel and their families, with Ambassador John Gunther Dean the last to leave, carrying the United States embassy flag, neatly folded in a plastic bag, at his side. The Khmer Rouge swept through the streets of Phnom Penh six days later.

By that time the North Vietnamese were ready for a final assault of their own. Le Duc Tho was so excited that he came down the Ho Chi Minh Trail to stay in Loc Ninh at Dung's headquarters. During late March and early April, Dung moved eighteen NVA divisions into place within a forty-mile radius of Saigon. Poised due east of the city were the Third, 304th, 325th, and 342B Divisions, charged with taking out the ARVN First Airborne Brigade at Ba Ria and the 951st ARVN Ranger Group and Fourth Airborne Brigade near Long Thanh. Northeast of Saigon, Dung placed the Sixth, Seventh, and 314th Divisions and assigned them to hit Bien Hoa. To the north, the 320B, 312th, and 338th Divisions were assigned the conquest of the ARVN Fifth Division at Ben Cat and the ARVN Ninth Ranger Brigade at Lai Thieu. Northwest of Saigon, Dung had the Seventh, 316th, 320th, and 968th Divisions ready to pounce on the ARVN Twenty-fifth Division at Trang Bang and Cu Chi. In the west, the Third, Fifth, Ninth, and Sixteenth divisions were poised to attack the ARVN Twenty-second Division at Tan An and Ben Luc and the Seventh and Eighth Ranger Brigades just outside of Saigon. To the southwest, the NVA Eighth Division prepared to attack the ARVN Seventh Division at My Tho.

The end was near. President Nguyen Van Thieu resigned on April 21, 1975. Duong Van ("Big") Minh, Thieu's longtime rival, assumed the presidency. Graham Martin, the United States ambassador to South

During the final evacuations in 1975, panic-stricken South Vietnamese who had worked for the Americans tried desperately to get out of the country. At Nha Trang on April 1, 1975, an American punches a Vietnamese man trying to get on the overloaded helicopter.

UPI/BETTMANN NEWSPHOTOS

Vietnam who had replaced Ellsworth Bunker in 1973, cabled Henry Kissinger two days later telling him that Operation Frequent Wind, the American evacuation of Saigon, was only a few days away. Worried about his career, Martin complained to Kissinger that "the only person whose ass isn't covered is me." Kissinger cabled back: "My ass isn't covered. I can assure you it will be hanging several yards higher than you when this is all over."

The end came eleven days later. Van Tien Dung launched the "Ho Chi Minh Campaign" on April 26, 1975, and ARVN immediately collapsed in toward Saigon. With television cameras broadcasting the entire series of events throughout the world, the North Vietnamese moved in on the city. President Gerald Ford implemented Operation Frequent Wind on April 29, and in the next several days American helicopters airlifted 7,100 American and South Vietnamese military and civilian personnel out of Saigon, many of them from the roof of the United States embassy, while naval ships ferried more than 70,000

South Vietnamese to American vessels in the South China Sea. Duong Van Minh surrendered unconditionally on April 29. Graham Martin left the embassy on April 30. The NVA 325th, 471st, and 968th Divisions then headed for Laos, setting the stage for the Pathet Lao victory several months later. Twenty-one years after the Geneva Convention of 1954, Indochina had fallen to the communists.

On the afternoon of April 30, 1975, after Graham Martin and the last Americans were out of Saigon, a column of North Vietnamese tanks appeared on Thong Nhut Avenue and rumbled across Cong Ly Boulevard toward Independence Palace. The tank column crashed through the gates of the palace and lined up on the lawn. A soldier, bearing the blue-and-red flag with the yellow star of the Provisional Revolutionary Government, emerged from the belly of the lead tank and triumphantly waved the flag from the palace steps. Neil Davis, a war correspondent from Reuters, went up to the young man and asked his name. "Nguyen Van Thieu," the soldier replied. The Vietnam War was over.

Although the design of the Vietnam Veterans Memorial triggered a storm of protest in the United States, the "wall" eventually became a sacred shrine to millions of people who visited it.

PAUL HOSEFROS/NYT PICTURES

11

Distorted Images, Missed Opportunities, 1975–1995

No more Vietnams.

—Richard Nixon, 1985

It was not at all like the Iwo Jima monument. On that point nearly everyone agreed. Probably the most famous American war monument, the Iwo Jima statue stands proud in Arlington, Virginia, an eloquent reminder of a simpler, more straightforward war. Frozen in bronze are the five marines thrusting the American flag into the soil on top of Mount Surabachi. Its style is heroic realism, a faithful attempt to reproduce the award-winning photograph. It traffics in uncomplex emotions that border on clichés: the "good war," John Wayne in the Pacific, go get 'em boys, "I shall return." Not far from the Iwo Jima monument, across the Potomac River, broods the Vietnam War Memorial. Between the Washington Monument and the Lincoln Memorial, the Vietnam Memorial rises out of a depression in the ground, shifts direction a bit, and then descends back into the ground. Its surface is polished black granite, an inscrutable veneer that reflects the image of the viewer and the landscape that faces it. Cut into the granite are the names of the more than 58,000 men and women who died in the war. What did they die for? What caused the war? What was the nature of the conflict? If you look for the answers in the silent black stone, all you will see is yourself.

From its inception the memorial generated controversy. It was too vague, some said, too abstract, not heroic enough. Others complained loudly and bitterly about the architect, Yale student Maya Ying Lin. The war had been against Asians. Students had been the most outspoken opponent of the war. Should an Asian-American student memorialize the war? Many veterans answered no. Emotion ran high. The memorial, meant to commemorate sacrifice, opened old wounds. The questions about the meaning of the war returned with fresh force. To satisfy veterans' protests, another sculpture was commissioned. This one, the work of Frederick Hart, is a realistic rendition of soldiers. Both memorials were dedicated on November 13, 1982.

The controversy died quickly. Good for a few stories on nightly news shows and a handful of editorials, by 1983 it had become old news. The polished black stone took its place near the other stones—some polished, some not—which memorialize other events and other wars and other men. Tourists dutifully visited it along with the others. Most were pleased by what they saw, agreeing that it was "a pretty nice" memorial after all. They came, they saw, they passed judgment, and they left. Their reflections lasted only a moment. In some very special way, the memorial was like the war itself—so misunderstood and complex and even abstract. Americans went to a land few understood. They fought a war full of sound and fury. And then they returned home. And within a short time Vietnam left the news shows and the news magazines, replaced by other stories.

Within months of the dedication of the Vietnam War Memorial, women veterans began to campaign for recognition of their role in Indochina. Former army nurse Diane Carlson Evans served in Vietnam in 1968 and 1969, and the idea of a memorial to women germinated in her mind in 1983. For years she struggled to secure the necessary congressional approval and to raise $2.5 million. By 1991 she had the money and the authorization, and Glenna Goodacre received the commission to design the memorial. Goodacre produced a larger-than-life bronze sculpture of three women cradling a wounded GI. The more than 11,000 women nurses who served during the Vietnam conflict treated 153,000 wounded soldiers. The memorial was unveiled and dedicated on Veterans Day in 1993.

The struggle of Americans to come to terms with the Vietnam War was contested largely outside the corridors of power. Politicians, diplomats, and military leaders lost their chance to influence popular opinion. Many Americans no longer trusted their answers to fundamental questions. With the war lost and the peace concluded, politicians gave way to intellectuals and artists and media executives, a diverse collection of historians, writers, and film and television producers. It was now their turn to explain the war and its impact on American society. The time to ask, "What should we do?" had passed. Now the questions "What did we do?" and "Why did we do it?" occupied center stage.

Americans struggled with three central issues. First, the veterans of the war. How did Vietnam change them? Could they peacefully return to American society? How did their experiences scar them? Second, the war itself. What did it accomplish? What did it mean? How did it change America? Third, the loss of the war. Why did the United States lose? Who or what was to blame? How did that experience change America?

At first the Vietnam veteran had loomed large in American popular culture. He came to symbolize the war that the nation wished to forget, and far from being portrayed as a hero, he was transformed into a

The Vietnam Women's Memorial, dedicated in 1993, commemorated the service and sacrifice of tens of thousands of American women who spent part of their lives in Vietnam.
MARKEL/LIAISON

villain. Somehow his participation in the "immoral" war, even if it had not been voluntary, set him apart from the civilians at home and made him a misfit. Often he was seen as a person not to pity or hate or love but to fear, for he was a ticking time bomb waiting to explode, waiting to carry the war home.

The psychotic or maladjusted Vietnam War veteran was portrayed as a product of the war. In most cases, he is a man without a background, a man without a home or parents or life before his service in Vietnam. It is almost as if he were bred in the country's steamy jungles and fertile rice fields. All he knows is war, and when he returns to the United States he continues to ply his trade. Sometimes he joins an outlaw motorcycle gang in which violence is a way of life and a reason for being. Such B-movies as *Angels from Hell* (1968), *Satan's Sadists* (1969), *Chrome and Hot Leather* (1971), and *The Losers* (1971) transport the veteran from a helicopter to a Harley. Other times the veteran remains a loner. But once again the potential for violence seethes beneath the surface. In *Taxi Driver* (1976) Travis Bickle (Robert De Niro) ticks quietly in New York City. He has no past and no future; he seems to invent both out of thin air. Although he writes his parents, he fills his letters with lies, and one suspects that his parents are part of his fantasy life. The only reality in his life is the war that he cannot articulate but that drives him toward violence as surely as he drives his taxi. As Seth Cagin and Philip Dray observe: "Travis Bickle is the prototypical movie vet: In ways we can only imagine, the horror of the war unhinged him. He's lost contact with other human beings, he doesn't hear them quite properly, and his speaking rhythms are off. He's edgy; he can't sleep at night, not even with the help of pills, so he takes a job as a taxi driver on the night shift." And he waits to explode. That in the end he kills a pimp is irrelevant. He might just as easily have killed a politician or anyone else, including himself. His violence knows no reason. It is not directed toward society or politicians or any particular person. It just is.

Violence is given greater direction and logic in *Tracks* (1976), a low-budget film directed by Henry Jaglom. In the film an army sergeant, played by Dennis Hopper, escorts the body of a friend killed in Vietnam back to the soldier's home for burial. On the cross-country train trip he tries to tell his fellow passengers about the dead soldier, a black hero who saved his life. He asks the civilians about the war and wonders why the United States was in Vietnam. Most of the other passengers are not interested in the sergeant, his dead comrade, or his questions; some are hostile, a few embarrassed. His war is not their war; his sufferings are not their sufferings. The film ends with the burial. Alone, the sergeant watches the coffin being lowered into the ground. Then he jumps in after it. When he emerges from the hole, he is dressed for battle and fully armed. "You want to go to Nam?" he cries out. "I'll take you there." A sympathetic character has once again been transformed into violence incarnate. Avenging angel or not, violence is implicit in his being, the answer to an uncaring nation.

Even when the veteran wishes to avoid violence it follows him like an albatross. In Karel Reisz's *Who'll Stop the Rain* (1978), based on Robert Stone's novel *Dog Soldiers* (1974), the action centers on a veteran who is involved in smuggling a shipment of heroin into the United States. Not only does he bring the corruption of Saigon back home with him—for the heroin will ruin civilians just as it did soldiers—but violence and death follow in his wake. As in the other films, the ultimate threat of the veterans is the Vietnamization of the United States. The image of the troubled Vietnam veteran would be an enduring one. As late as 1994, two films played on that theme. Tommy Lee Jones's character in *Between Heaven and Earth* and Kevin Costner's in *The War* both revolved around men who returned from Vietnam carrying debilitating psychological baggage.

But for the most part, starting in the late 1970s the image of the Vietnam veteran began to change. Hollywood signaled the shift with two successful movies—*Coming Home* (1978) and *The Deer Hunter* (1978). In *Coming Home,* director Hal Ashby continued his interest in

Vietnam. Three years earlier he had directed *Shampoo,* a film about wealthy southern Californians set during the 1968 presidential election. As the characters in *Shampoo* get ready for a Nixon victory party, news of the horrors of Vietnam assaults them from radios and televisions. But they pay no mind; it is not their war, not their concern. *Coming Home* brings the war to southern California. Its central characters are Luke Martin (Jon Voight), a bitter paraplegic, and Sally Hyde (Jane Fonda), the wife of a marine captain (Bruce Dern) serving a tour in Vietnam. Viewed from the perspective of the 1990s, *Coming Home* is sentimental stuff. It is too pat. During the course of the film the conservative, sexually repressed Sally flowers into a liberal, liberated woman. She puts on Levis, allows her hair to follow its natural frizzy disposition, and experiences an orgasm—with Luke—for the first time in her life. Luke also is transformed. Bitter and angry at the start of the film, he becomes introspective and gentle. *Coming Home* suggests that love can cure the trauma of Vietnam, that understanding can erase the pain of bad memories.

In 1978, however, *Coming Home* was an original film. Frank Rich of *Time* magazine called it "one long, low howl of pain," and other reviewers agreed that it was an important statement. It also showed Hollywood that a film about the Vietnam War could be political and profitable. At the same time it contributed to the rehabilitation of the popular image of the Vietnam veteran. Influenced by paraplegic Ron Kovic's book *Born on the Fourth of July* (1976), *Coming Home* portrays the veteran as not only someone who needs to be healed but also as a healer. Luke is not a loner; he is not a ticking bomb; he is not a threat to society. His anger flows from the unwillingness of America to recognize his plight. "When people look they don't see me," Luke tells Sally. He wants America to take notice and to remember, for his crippled body is an important legacy of Vietnam. Toward the end of the film he tells a group of high school students, "There was a lot of shit over there I find fucking hard to live with. But I don't feel sorry for myself. I'm just saying that there's a choice to be made." And that choice is as present in the United States as it was in Vietnam. Luke has to decide whether he will live consumed by bitterness or use his pain to help others. He chooses the latter course and is reintegrated into society.

The Deer Hunter contains the same message. Directed by Michael Cimino, the film shows how the war changed the lives of three men from a western Pennsylvania steel town. Of the three, the most important is Michael (Robert De Niro). He begins the film as a loner, and violence seems an integral part of his character. He kills a deer with one shot and is intolerant of his friends' shortcomings. In Vietnam, it seems, surrounded by death and terror, he finds compassion. He saves the lives of his two friends, and when one becomes addicted to heroin and Russian roulette, Michael even risks his own life in an attempt to reach him. "I love you," he says just before Nicky's (Christopher Walken) luck runs out and he loses his final game of Russian roulette.

Vietnam changes Michael for the better. It purges him of his aggression and anger. He no longer wants to kill deer or any other living animals. He is at peace with himself and his surroundings. He can even love and now is able to relate to women. The film ends on a note of affirmation. After Nicky's funeral, Michael joins his other friends—women as well as men—in singing "God Bless America." He is finally a whole person, reconciled with himself, his community, and his country. That same message comes through in Oliver Stone's 1990 film *Born on the Fourth of July,* in which Tom Cruise portrays Ron Kovic, a paraplegic Vietnam veteran who finally comes to terms with the war.

After 1980 the popular image of the Vietnam veteran began to change on television. Like Michael in *The Deer Hunter* and Luke in *Coming Home,* the veteran was transformed into a figure of compassion and imbued with a sense of justice. Rather than threaten society, the new television veteran defends society, upholds justice, and restores order. In Vietnam he learned how to fight, use sophisticated weapons, and function in a tight-knit group, but the experience did not rob him of his compassion. Indeed, it is suggested that the very traits that led him to Vietnam now compel him to battle evil and injustice in the United States. Television showcased this new veteran in such shows as *Magnum, P.I., The A-Team, Riptide,* and *Air Wolf.* Most of the heroes of these shows are unmarried, but their bachelorhood is not viewed as negative. The group functions as their family, and they display a healthy attraction to women that is amply reciprocated. Furthermore, they are not scarred emotionally or physically by their service in Vietnam. No guilt troubles their thoughts, no injuries plague their days.

Although these heroes were once in the military, they no longer act on behalf of the government. Crippled by red tape and bureaucratic lethargy, the modern state seems unable to act with speed and justice. The veteran heroes are part of the private sector—the United States of Ronald Reagan—and they function outside official channels. But they always get the job done; they ensure justice. As the viewer is told each week at the beginning of *The A-Team,* "If you have a problem, if no one else can help, and if you can find them . . . you can hire the A-Team." But if the veteran heroes work outside of the government, they are still willing to fight for their country. Often they combat external threats—drug smuggling, terrorism, and spying. Occasionally they travel outside the United States to solve problems. This they willingly do, for their cause is always just and on television ends justify means. Perhaps, as Lisa M. Heilbronn writes, they "represent a desire on the part of the public to see our control secured beyond the boundaries of the United States."

The transformation of the Vietnam veteran on television since 1980 is part of the more general rehabilitation of the popular image of the United States military. During the 1970s films and television portrayed the military as a corrupt, bloodthirsty institution. Although enlisted men were occasionally presented as decent people, officers were invariably pictured as incompetent, self-serving, and destructive. "The bullshit piled up so fast in Vietnam you needed wings to stay above it," Captain Willard remarks in *Apocalypse Now* (1979). And in the same movie, Lieutenant Colonel Kilgore orders his men into battle to secure a strip of beach that has "good surf." In such films as *An Officer and a Gentleman* (1982), *Taps* (1981), *Lords of Discipline* (1983), *Private Benjamin* (1980), and *Stripes* (1981), Hollywood revitalized the military. Instead of being an institution that kills boys, it is viewed as a place where boys become men, or in the case of *Private Benjamin,* spoiled girls become independent women.

In part, the promilitary films reflect the economy of the late 1970s and early 1980s. High-paying jobs in heavy industry were becoming scarce, and there was little glamour or money in flipping hamburgers at McDonald's. For many young Americans the military became "a great place to start." Enlistments in the armed forces jumped in the 1980s, and enrollment in ROTC programs doubled. The mood of Reagan's era—with its overt patriotism and promise of restored greatness—contributed to the popularity of the films. It contrasted especially with the malaise and perceived impotency of the Carter years. Americans yearned for a return to greatness. They wanted a military with teeth, equipped to act and fortified by a commitment to a higher code.

As Americans reappraised the Vietnam veteran and the military, they also attempted to understand the war itself. Historians sifted through the "facts" of the war. Aided by the illegally released Pentagon Papers, they searched for its causes. During the 1960s and most of the 1970s two schools of thought emerged. The first believed that the war, in Arthur Schlesinger, Jr.'s words, was a "tragedy without villains." It resulted from unfortunate decisions made by well-meaning officials. The second school rejected this benign view and asserted that the war was the result of an imperialistic American foreign policy. Such historians as William Appleman Williams, Walter LaFeber, and Gabriel Kolko claimed that the United States had a history of expansion and domination and that at least since the turn of the century it had been establishing its hegemony over the Pacific. The Vietnam War marked a setback in this policy of expansion, but the decision to fight in Vietnam was very much a part of the policy.

During the 1980s a third school of historical thought gained ascendancy. It maintained that the war was a "noble crusade" against communism, a shining expression of American commitment to democracy and liberty. Not only did these historians believe that the United States should have fought in Vietnam, but they also argued that the military could have won the war. These historians absolve the military of all guilt. As Guenter Lewy writes in *America in Vietnam* (1978), "The sense of guilt created by the Vietnam War in the minds of many Americans is not warranted and the charges of officially condoned illegal and grossly immoral conduct are without substance." Instead of being the villains, the soldiers who fought the war were the heroes; they did their duty under taxing circumstances. That the war was ultimately lost was not their fault. Rather, civilians back home—both inside and outside the government—failed to understand what the war was about and refused to live up to their country's honorable commitment to South Vietnam. Of course, this perception reflected the changing political face of the United States. By 1980 politicians were once again talking about falling dominoes and the obligations the United States had to countries struggling to stay free. In 1980 Ronald Reagan said that the United States had "an inescapable duty to act as the tutor and protector of the free world."

This academic search for an understanding of the Vietnam War was expressed in popular culture. Many of the novelists who wrote about the war had served in Vietnam, and for them the war was a morass. Raised on World War II films that ooze moral certainty and enshrine a sporting ethos and the notion of fair play, these writers confront in Vietnam a world of shadows and moral ambiguities. Their schoolboy rules belonged to a distant continent. "It was the dawn of creation in the Indochina bush," writes Philip Caputo in *A Rumor of War* (1977), "an ethical as well as a geographical wilderness. Out there, lacking restraints, sanctioned to kill, confronted by a hostile country and a relentless enemy, we sank into a brutish state." The same sense of uncertainty is expressed in Tim O'Brien's *Going after Cacciato* (1978). His protagonist

> didn't know who was right, or what was right; he didn't know if it was a war of self-determination or self-destruction, outright aggression or national liberation; he didn't know which speeches to believe, which books, which politicians; he didn't know if nations would topple like dominoes or stand separate like trees; he didn't know who started the war, or why, or when, or with what motives; he didn't know if it mattered.

This profound sense of confusion about the meaning of and the reasons for the war also found its way into the films about the war. Francis Ford Coppola's *Apocalypse Now* attempted to translate that confusion into a narrative film. "The most important thing I wanted to do in the making of *Apocalypse Now*," Coppola wrote in the program notes for the film, "was to create a film experience that would give the audience a sense of the horror, the madness, the sensuousness, and the moral dilemma of the Vietnam War." Captain Willard's voyage up the river into the "heart of darkness" is as much a quest for answers as it is a mission of death. In trying to understand the sanity behind Colonel Kurtz's insanity, Willard is attempting to fathom the logic of the illogical conflict. Everywhere there is madness. The coldly unemotional military and civilian officials who tell Willard that Kurtz's command must be "terminated with extreme prejudice" are mad. They speak the language of madness; the meanings of their words cannot be found in a dictionary. Kilgore is mad. He attacks the enemy not to win the war but to secure a good surfing beach. Even Willard remarks, "After seeing the way Kilgore fought the war, I began to wonder what they had against Kurtz." And Kurtz, well, he is quite mad. He is like a computer thrown into an Alice-in-Wonderland world and fed bits of illogical data. His response to his environment is to become insane, for as the film demonstrates, only the insane survive.

Apocalypse Now may be the best film about the war, and its theme of madness may be accurate on a psychological level, but it does not help the viewer understand how or why the United States became involved in the war. It does not deal with what the war accomplished or how it changed the country. Its major political criticism is aimed not at the war itself but at the management of the war. Willard describes his superior officers as "a bunch of four star clowns who are giving the whole circus away." He openly sympathizes with the outlaw Kurtz: "Charging someone with murder in a place like this is like handing out speeding tickets at the Indianapolis 500."

Platoon (1986) similarly does not address questions of causation or results. Instead, it revolves around a conflict of good and evil. The war becomes a stage, and although there is an attempt to relate something of the combat experience, the meaning of the war is irrelevant. In one voice-over, Chris Taylor (Charlie Sheen), the leading character in the film, remarks, "I think now, we did not fight the enemy, we fought ourselves. And the enemy was in us." This is the soul of the film—the enemy within. It happens to be set in Vietnam. It just as easily could have been set in World War II or peacetime. Like *Apocalypse Now, Coming Home,* and *The Deer Hunter, Platoon* is about self-discovery, not war.

Films that have taken a political stand have not been particularly successful at the box office. *Go Tell the Spartans* (1978) deals with the early years of the American combat presence in Vietnam. In theory these were years of youthful innocence, a time when the struggle for "hearts and minds" was taken seriously by Americans in Vietnam and in the United States. But as the film illustrates, the war was already over. The United States had lost but had not yet realized the fact. The film's final scene—a long shot of a cemetery of war dead—suggests that the only act remaining in the war was death; futile, meaningless death.

If filmmakers dealt poorly with the origins and meaning of the war, they were even worse at coming to terms with defeat. To be sure, most of the films depict a thoroughly corrupt or stupid officer corps. But beyond this limited explanation of failure few producers were willing to go. Part of the reason was financial; industry leaders maintained that Americans would not pay to watch a film about their country's losing a war. During the 1970s when there was a mood of self-criticism in the country, few films about the war were made. And when producers turned to the subject of the war, the age of self-criticism had passed. The Reagan years affirmed patriotic values. Heroes dominated popular culture. Rock star Bruce Springsteen, at his 1986 concert in Dallas, expressed frustration that his anti-Vietnam megahit "Born in the U.S.A." had actually become, in the popular mind, a patriotic anthem.

The best expression of this new mood was Sylvester Stallone's films *First Blood* (1982) and *Rambo: First Blood II* (1985). In the first film John Rambo is an ex-Green Beret who is mistaken for a hippie. By nature a loner and even a peaceful man, he is forced by a series of inept government officials to defend his freedom in the wilds of the Pacific Northwest. The movie suggests that men like John Rambo did not lose the war; politicians back home did. In the climactic scene Rambo tells his former Special Forces commanding officer: "Nothing is over, nothing! You just don't turn it off. It wasn't my war—you asked me, I didn't ask you . . . and I did what I had to do to win—but somebody wouldn't let us win." Yet there is no examination of just what "winning" in the context of the war in Vietnam means. It is enough for Rambo and his audience that the war *could* have been won.

In the second film Rambo returns to Vietnam to find and rescue Americans missing in action (MIAs) from Vietnam—a popular scenario in the mid-1980s that was central to such films as *Uncommon Valor* (1983), *Missing in Action* (1984), *Missing in Action II* (1985), *P.O.W.: The Escape* (1986), and *The Hanoi Hilton* (1987). But Rambo was really returning to Vietnam to win the war. When Colonel Trautman (Richard Crenna), his former commander, tells him, "The old war's dead, John," Rambo replies, "I'm alive. It's still alive." And later Rambo asks, "Do we get to win this time?" Trautman answers, "This time it's up to you." And since winning is again never defined, Rambo rewrites history. He "wins."

Complete redemption of the American military did not really occur until the outbreak of the Gulf War. On August 2, 1990, Saddam Hussein sent Iraqi troops into the tiny, oil-rich nation of Kuwait. The invasion threatened Saudi Arabia and the vital sea lanes of the Persian Gulf, through which most of Japan's and the Western world's oil flowed. President George Bush carefully constructed a United Nations–backed coalition and ordered Iraqi forces out of Kuwait. When Saddam Hussein refused to withdraw, the president ordered a massive military buildup. On January 17, 1991, after giving the Iraqis another chance to retreat, Bush unleashed Operation Desert Storm. Allied bombers pounded Iraq, and Iraqi forces in Kuwait, for more than five weeks, and on February

24 the ground offensive began. The war was over four days later—a stunning victory for the American military.

During the war, General Norman Schwarzkopf, the field commander of Allied forces, conducted a brilliant military campaign, crushing Iraqi forces and achieving a public relations tour de force. Americans watched navy and air force pilots carrying out pin-point bombing campaigns using laser-guided "smart bombs," marines storming Persian Gulf beaches, and armored divisions sweeping across the deserts of the Middle East. When the war was over, the GIs returned triumphant to a grateful nation. Whatever images of an incompetent military still lingered in American popular culture were rapidly put to rest. And in the victory parades that took place across the country in 1991 and 1992, thousands of Vietnam veterans spontaneously joined the marchers down Main Street, getting the attention they deserved, but never received, during the Vietnam War era.

While American filmmakers "Ramboized" the conflict, Vietnam labored to construct a viable nation out of the rubble of war. As the last American helicoptered from the roof of the United States embassy in Saigon in 1975, North Vietnamese troops crashed through the gates. Saigon, whose very name was associated with American domination, was renamed Ho Chi Minh City, a salute to the dead Vietnamese hero. North Vietnamese and Vietcong celebrated the creation of a new country, the fulfillment of the centuries-old dream.

The war of liberation had ended, but the struggle continued. The Socialist Republic of Vietnam (SRV), as the united nation was named, faced pressing problems. At the core of the new struggle was a nation battered by three decades of fighting. American bombing had destroyed the infrastructure of Vietnam. Roads and bridges, power plants and factories lay in ruins. Ports suffered from damage and neglect. For a generation the resources of Vietnam had been used to fuel the war machines, and with the war over, conversion to a peacetime economy presented difficult, at times almost insurmountable, problems. Raw materials were in short supply, and investment capital had left with the Americans. Machines that had been imported from the United States broke down, and spare parts were impossible to obtain. If peace brought hope, it also brought the specter of economic ruin.

Vietnamese communism smothered the country with a stifling bureaucracy. The communists tried to implement Ho Chi Minh's dream— political reunification of the two Vietnams and imposition of a socialist economic order. North Vietnamese cadres and Vietcong took control of South Vietnam, seized private property, collectivized plantations and farms, squeezed out small businesses, and hunted down South Vietnamese political and military officials. The government forcibly moved nearly

1 million civilians from Ho Chi Minh City, Hue, Danang, and Nha Trang to "New Economic Zones" in abandoned sections of South Vietnam. The SRV—blessed with a strategic location, a huge capacity for producing rice, and an enterprising people—declined into Third World poverty complete with high unemployment, crippling food shortages, and starvation. Along with the direct results of the war—hundreds of thousands of orphans, paraplegics, and amputees, and the physical destruction wrought by the American military—the ideology of communism transformed Vietnam into one of the poorest countries in the world. The average worker made the equivalent of 300 dong a month in 1980. That same year a pair of cotton trousers cost 400 dong and a new bicycle 20,000 dong. Malnutrition became a normal condition. As one Soviet professor in Vietnam privately confided, "How much poverty in Vietnam? We have nothing like this in Moscow. Their party has made so many mistakes."

The SRV also failed in its attempt to de-Westernize the country. Western ideas and aspirations lingered in the south. Reeducation along socialist lines failed to alter old habits. A number of critics even contended that southerners "Westernized" northerners. The official party newspaper *Nhan Dan* warned that the "new-colonial culture" of the south was "expanding to the north" and threatened to "spoil our younger generation and wreck our revolution." French food, American beer, and Western ideas became black-market commodities. Governmental corruption, always a staple in the south, wound its way north. As one loyal northerner admitted, "I've been a Communist all my life. But now, for the first time, I have seen the realities of Communism. It is a failure—mismanagement, corruption, privilege, repression. My ideals are gone."

As conditions in Vietnam worsened, hundreds of thousands of Vietnamese fled the food and electricity rationing, de-Westernization, grinding poverty, and countless other daily hardships. Ethnic Chinese, the business leaders and merchants in Ho Chi Minh City, left the country in droves. The "boat people"—desperate Vietnamese willing to flee the SRV at all costs—risked the dangers of the South China Sea to find a new home. Tens of thousands drowned at sea when their rickety ships sank, and thousands more were killed by pirates. Tens of thousands were caught by Vietnamese authorities before they had gone very far. Indonesia and Malaysia frequently rejected them when they did make landfall. Although exact statistics are difficult to obtain, as many as 250,000 Vietnamese boat people died during their escape attempt.

Diplomatic woes compounded domestic unrest. In 1977 President Jimmy Carter cautiously extended the olive branch to the SRV. Determined to improve the image of the United States among Third World countries, soon after his election Carter announced that he "would be perfectly glad to support the admission of Vietnam to the United Nations and to normalize relations with Vietnam." That autumn he made good on his promise, and the two countries allowed academic and other cultural exchanges. At that moment what the SRV most needed was the investment capital and technological expertise of the United States. But in 1978 the SRV committed several critical mistakes, the most important of which was to demand reparations as a precondition for normalization. This demand prompted a quick reaction in Congress, opening still fresh psychological wounds. Carter's decision to pardon all Americans who had fled to Canada during the war to avoid the draft and to all those who had deserted from the armed forces had a similar effect. Carter's initiatives—Vietnam's best hope of recovery and economic stability—died on the floor of Congress.

In 1978 the SRV made a second disastrous mistake. It invaded the newly named Kampuchea (formerly Cambodia). In comparison with Kampuchea, Vietnam's problems seemed insignificant. Recalling the mid-1970s, the *New York Times* correspondent Sydney H. Schanberg remarked: "Everybody, Cambodians and foreigners alike, looked with hopeful relief to the collapse of the city, for they felt that when the Communists came and the war finally ended, at least the suffering would be over. All of us were wrong." When Pol Pot and the Khmer Rouge roared into downtown Phnom Penh in armored personnel carriers and trucks in April 1975, they brought a demanding, ruthless ideology with them. They began emptying the cities of Cambodia, forcing people into the countryside for reeducation. For Pol Pot it was the beginning of a new age—"Year Zero" for the new country of Kampuchea. Dreaming of a preindustrial, agricultural utopia, he launched an assault on cities, teachers, intellectuals, professionals, and the middle class. He completely evacuated Phnom Penh, turning the city of 3 million people into a ghost town. He ordered the destruction of libraries, temples, schools, colleges, businesses, and whole cities. He transformed Kampuchea into a concentration camp, a huge "killing field" where 2 million Kampucheans lost their lives.

The Vietnamese watched the horrors with growing anxiety. A revolt in eastern Kampuchea in 1977 sent hundreds of thousands of frightened Kampucheans fleeing across the border into Vietnam. By 1978 the SRV had had enough of Pol Pot's megalomania. Vietnamese troops invaded Kampuchea, drove Pol Pot and the Khmer Rouge into the jungles, and established the People's Republic of Kampuchea. But the invasion did not end the suffering. Coming as it did during the planting season, peasant farmers lost their rice crop, and widespread starvation resulted. Pol Pot regrouped his forces and, with 35,000 troops, began a guerrilla action against the invasion. The Khmer People's National Liberation Front, supplied by the United States, fielded 15,000 of its own guerrillas, and there was another 9,000-person guerrilla army loyal to Prince Norodom Sihanouk. The three groups fought guerrilla wars against one another and the Vietnamese. With the Vietnamese in Kampuchea, the premeditated killing of civilians stopped, but once again the flames of war swept across Indochina.

The centuries-old animosities between Vietnamese and Kampucheans stirred other ancient hatreds and fears. China did not want to see the SRV extend its influence. On February 17, 1979, Deng Xiaoping sent the People's Liberation Army across the border into Tonkin. The bloody war lasted less than one month, but 35,000 people died before it was over. On their way out of Tonkin, the Chinese destroyed several towns, blew up vital railway links, and obliterated important power plants and a phosphate mine responsible for most of Vietnam's fertilizer.

The border war against China and the guerrilla war against Kampuchea further strained the Vietnamese economy. Before the two wars the SRV had been attempting to secure desperately needed loans from China, Japan, and several Western countries. As the fighting became hotter, the international financial community became colder. To make matters worse, the SRV had the added cost of maintaining a standing army of more than 1 million men and stationing 140,000 troops in Kampuchea. By the mid-1980s the SRV had become one of the poorest nations in the world, but its army was the fourth largest in the world. In 1989 Vietnam withdrew its troops from Kampuchea, raising the specter of the return of Pol Pot and the Khmer Rouge to power. Visions of genocide, of the holocaust portrayed in David Putnam's 1984 film *The Killing Fields,* once again plagued the people of Indochina. The American war in Vietnam was over. The older war, with origins in the ancient past, continued. Then after nineteen years as Kampuchea, it readopted Cambodia as its official name.

For the money needed to keep its country solvent, Vietnam turned to the Soviet Union. The loans the Soviet Union provided—$1.5 billion annually—carried strings that stretched back to Moscow. To many people inside and outside of Vietnam, it soon appeared that Soviet domination had simply replaced American domination. Just as American advisers and experts flocked to Vietnam twenty years earlier, so now the Soviets came. "Americans without dollars," the Vietnamese called them. One Vietnamese joke reflected the new relationship with the Soviet Union. After appealing to the Soviets for loans, Vietnam receives the cable: "Tighten your belts." Vietnam replies: "Send belts."

By the mid-1980s the SRV had sunk to its lowest point. Economic reorganization had failed. Emigrants—often valuable professionals whom the country needed—continued to leave. The guerrilla war in Kampuchea dragged on. And Soviet advisers worked to turn the SRV into Cuba East. Finally, in 1986 the SRV committed itself to a radical change. At the Sixth Communist Party Congress, party leaders admitted that their experiment in communism had failed. The old guard retired and a new set of leaders, led by Nguyen Van Linh, took office. Linh, who had been born in Hanoi but had lived the majority of his life in the south, symbolized the desire for true national unification. He realized that the economic and foreign policies of Pham Van Dong were bankrupt. Boldly, and with a firm sense of resolve, he once again looked West.

Undoubtedly influenced by the ideas and actions of Mikhail Gorbachev, Linh opened Vietnam to increasing amounts of democracy and capitalism. He permitted politicians to openly contest for assembly seats, and he released political prisoners. He sanctioned limited free enterprise and trimmed the glutted governmental bureaucracy. He even opened up Vietnam to Western goods. As the historian Terry H. Anderson notes, "Western T-shirts and tapes of Madonna" were sold on the streets of Hanoi. Where a few years earlier the SRV had frightened away Western investment capital, it now courted Western bankers and industrialists by enacting a liberal foreign investment code. An "underdeveloped nation such as Vietnam," Linh emphasized, "needs even more to look to the capitalist world for lessons."

Vietnam had little choice but to turn to the West. Throughout the 1980s, in spite of Mikhail Gorbachev's *glasnost* and *perestroika* reforms, the economy of the Soviet Union continued its downward spiral. Ever since the early 1960s, infusions of financial aid from the Soviet Union had kept the North Vietnamese economy afloat, and after 1975, the process of rebuilding Vietnam required even more money. For a decade, the influx of Russian rubles at least partially masked the economic disaster Vietnamese communists brought to their country. But in the late 1980s, the Soviet Union had to cut back on the assistance. It could no longer prop up the economies of its satellites because its own economy was imploding. The Soviet Union could no longer even control its former satellites. With stunning rapidity beginning in 1989, the Soviet bloc in Eastern Europe disintegrated. Poland, East Germany, Czechoslovakia, and Hungary went their separate ways. A rebellion succeeded in overthrowing the communist government of Romania. Yugoslavia broke up into petty warring states. And in 1991 the Soviet Union itself collapsed and ceased to exist. The river of rubles dried up. Vietnam's choice was simple: turn to the West and liberalize its economy or face economic collapse and political ruin.

The emergence of new forms in popular culture reflected Vietnam's political and economic changes. Such American films as *Platoon* played to crowded houses in Ho Chi Minh City and Hanoi. And the Vietnamese film industry started to make films that showed the emotional complexity of the war. In *Ahn va em* (Brothers and Relations, 1986) a veteran returns from war to find a changed Vietnamese society. Hanoi is wallowing in consumerism, his family has betrayed the ideas of socialism, and government corruption hampers efforts to reconstruct Vietnam. The veteran questions why he fought. In the end of the film, he turns away from the modern Vietnam and withdraws to the traditional, "unprogressive" life of the rural village.

The image of Americans is also revamped in the recent Vietnamese films. American soldiers are portrayed as victims of a senseless and unjust war—confused, frustrated, and angry but not evil. Films such as Hong Sen's *The Abandoned Field—Free Fire Zone* (1979) endow the machines of war, not the soldiers, with evil intentions. The filmmaker anthropomorphizes helicopters, giving them malevolent qualities. They drop from the sky like prehistoric birds of prey. They, not their pilots, are blamed for the destruction. In the last scene of the film the Vietnamese shoot down a helicopter. In the wreckage they discover a dead pilot. "It is a sad moment," notes film critic Karen Jaehne, made "all the sadder for a photo of the pilot's family carried away from the carnage on the wind."

Altogether the films signal a shift in Vietnam's attitude toward the United States. Since 1986 the SRV has promoted cultural exchanges with the United States by liberalizing its visa policy and allowing American writers and journalists greater access to Vietnam. American tourists can now visit Hue, Dienbienphu, and the Cu Chi tunnels. The government has allowed Vietnamese Amerasian children to emigrate to the United States to reunite with their parents. Through actions and words, the SRV has conveyed the simple message that the war is over and the time to forgive is at hand.

The message, however, was at odds with American foreign policy in the 1980s. During his two terms as president, Ronald Reagan consistently ignored Vietnamese efforts to normalize relations between the two countries. Rather than emphasize areas of agreement, he stressed fields of discord. Reagan focused on two issues: Vietnam's continued occupation of Kampuchea and the POW-MIA controversy. The first was a concrete problem. The SRV expressed a willingness to withdraw from Kampuchea— and in fact began to withdraw in 1988—but the prospect of the return of Pol Pot to power complicated matters. Given the centuries of hostilities between the Vietnamese and the Khmer, the SRV was not anxious to see the Khmer Rouge extend its power. In addition, other world powers feared the return of Pol Pot would initiate a new phase in his genocidal war against all Western influences within Kampuchea. Nevertheless, the Vietnamese completed their withdrawal from Kampuchea in 1989.

The POW-MIA issue was largely imaginary. Fueled by a series of POW-MIA movies and the incendiary rhetoric of the Reagan administration, a large portion of the American public became convinced that there were thousands of prisoners of war and other American soldiers listed as missing in action still alive in Vietnam. This emotionally charged issue blocked talks between the United States and the Socialist Republic of Vietnam for almost a decade. It also defied logic and impartial investigation. Although several government investigations of the issue reached the conclusion that there are no live POWs or MIAs in Vietnam, still the suspicion lingers. Criticizing the Reagan administration for its intractable stand, Terry H. Anderson observes:

Technically, it is impossible for *any* Vietnamese government to find "all recoverable remains" under fifteen years of jungle growth. . . . Also MIAs are not just an American problem. The French still have 20,000 MIAs from their war in Indochina, and the Vietnamese list over 200,000. Furthermore, the United States still has 80,000 MIAs from World War II and 8,000 from the Korean War, figures that represent 20 and 15 percent, respectively, of the confirmed dead in those conflicts; the percentage is 4 percent for the Vietnam War. . . . The real "noble cause" for [the Reagan] administration is not the former war but its emotional and impossible crusade to retrieve "all recoverable remains."

Beginning in 1988, Vietnam started working diligently at improving its foreign relations. It completed the withdrawal from Kampuchea and tried to address the POW-MIA charges. High-level contacts between United States and Vietnamese diplomats increased in number and significance late in the Reagan administration. In September 1988, the two countries agreed to joint field investigations in Vietnam to identify the remains of American MIAs. In April 1992 President George Bush eased the U.S. trade embargo in Vietnam by allowing the sales of products for humanitarian needs, primarily grain and medicines. At the end of 1992, Bush agreed to permit U.S. companies to open offices in Vietnam, sign business contracts, and begin feasibility studies.

During the first year of the Clinton administration, efforts to improve economic relations between the two countries began to bear fruit, and the president dropped American opposition to settlement of Vietnam's debts with the International Monetary Fund. The move toward normalization of relations, however, ran into a roadblock late in 1993 when circumstantial evidence from former Soviet archives and Vietnamese defectors indicated that several hundred American prisoners-of-war remained in Indochina after the return of the 591 POWs in 1973. Pentagon officials immediately went to work trying to confirm the stories, but they were unable to find any evidence corroborating the charges. Few politicians, however, were willing to risk promoting normalization until Vietnam became more cooperative. Bob Smith, a New Hampshire Republican who visited Vietnam frequently to investigate the issue, remarked late in 1993: "I don't know if anyone is alive today, but I do know that we don't have all the facts."

Anxious to get on the good side of administration officials in Washington, D.C., Vietnamese leaders early in 1994 began releasing more and more information about American soldiers missing-in-action and worked more diligently at returning the remains of MIAs. To acknowledge the Vietnamese effort and to encourage them to be even more forthcoming, in February 1994 President Clinton lifted the trade embargo, opening up Vietnam and most of Indochina to American business. Only one step remained in the normalization process: U.S. diplomatic recognition of the Socialist Republic of Vietnam.

Early in 1995, the Clinton administration began testing the political waters, leaking stories to the press about possible diplomatic recognition. Many Vietnamese-Americans opposed the move, insisting that the United States should withhold recognition until the communist regime had collapsed. Republican presidential hopefuls Robert Dole of Kansas and Phil Gramm of Texas voiced opposition as well. So did POW-MIA advocacy groups, such as the National League of Families of Vietnam POWs and MIAs. Clinton lined up some heavy hitters of his own. Senator John McCain, an Arizona Republican and former POW, backed the idea, as did Senator John Kerry, a Massachusetts Democrat and Vietnam veteran, and Senator Bob Kerrey, a Nebraska Democrat who had lost a leg in Vietnam.

While the Clinton administration was moving toward recognition, the Vietnamese were preparing for the twentieth anniversary of the fall of Saigon, planning parades, parties, and solemn observances throughout the country. They wanted to make the most of history, to remember better days when a Third World nation had humbled the greatest superpower. At the end of April 1995, a score of years had passed since the ignominious collapse of South Vietnam. Images of the North Vietnamese Army's triumphant march toward the U.S. Embassy in Saigon still stirred the hearts of tens of thousands of Vietnamese; Vo Nguyen Giap was a military genius and living icon; and Ho Chi Minh had become a demigod to his country.

But Vietnamese leaders also found themselves in a quandary. After twenty years of communist rule, and a generation of property seizures and reeducation camps, the economy was in shambles. Disillusionment ran deep, especially in southern Vietnam, where millions could still remember capitalism's virtues. The Communist party still ruled Vietnam, not because the Vietnamese believed in its bankrupt ideology but because the party could legitimately take credit for Vietnamese independence and unification. People tend to have short memories, however, especially the young, and in 1995 Vietnam was a very young country. More than half of all Vietnamese were under the age of twenty-five, with few or no memories of the war. They yearned for a better life, and ironically, for tens of millions of them, the beacon of freedom and opportunity was the United States. To appease the young and to attract investment capital, Vietnamese leaders needed the United States, and they were not about to let any raucous, self-righteous twentieth-anniversary celebrations anger influential Americans. Vietnam moved forward with the anniversary preparations, but the Politburo made sure to keep them subdued.

What stoked the still burning embers of the Vietnam War in the spring of 1995 and postponed normalization efforts, however, was not anything perpetrated by the Vietnamese. To coincide with the twentieth anniversary of the fall of South Vietnam, Random House published *In Retrospect,* the memoirs of former Secretary of Defense Robert McNamara. For twenty-eight years after leaving the Johnson administration, McNamara had kept his peace, refusing to answer any questions about the Vietnam War. To most antiwar activists, he was a *persona non grata,* the arrogant, "whiz-kid" architect of an unnecessary war that killed 3 million Vietnamese and nearly 60,000 Americans, a war that polarized the country and created a nation of cynics.

Random House hyped the book as McNamara's *mea culpa,* the confessions of a troubled man who wanted to come clean. They booked him on every talk show in every major media market, and he responded to questions directly, his voice sometimes cracking and his eyes welling up in tears. In conducting the Vietnam War, he admitted, the Kennedy and Johnson administrations mistakenly saw a communist Vietnam as a grave threat to national security, underestimated the power of Vietnamese nationalism, overestimated the influence of communism, and tried to find a military solution to what was essentially a political problem. In short, he acceded to every major criticism the antiwar movement had offered in the 1960s. "It seems beyond understanding, incredible," he wrote, "that we did not force ourselves to confront such issues head-on. But then, it is very hard, today, to recapture the innocence and confidence with which we approached Vietnam in the early days. . . . We were wrong, terribly wrong."

The book rocketed to the top of the bestseller lists, not because Americans accepted McNamara's confession or endorsed his ideas, but because he managed to enrage liberals as well as conservatives and antiwar protesters as well as veterans, unleashing an avalanche of hostility. Skeptics charged that the man who had sent millions of boys to Vietnam and brought hundreds of thousands home in body bags or on hospital gurneys was just as arrogant as ever, and greedy as well, poised to make millions off the book, rendering his confession tawdry and self-serving. Former critics of the war wondered why he had remained so silent for so long, if indeed he had realized his mistakes ever since 1966. McNamara's disclaimer about not speaking up earlier—"I didn't know any way to do it. At that point my voice wouldn't have made any difference"—fell on deaf ears. "It's the same McNamara as ever," one former antiwar activist claimed. "He still thinks he's one of the best and the brightest. Those are crocodile tears he sheds."

Veterans organizations were even more critical. Such groups as the American Legion and Veterans of Foreign Wars reacted angrily to McNamara's belated confession. The Gulf War had resurrected the reputation of America's soldiers, and the luster of Vietnam veterans was brighter than ever. Just when the country was finally taking note of their sacrifice, the architect of the war cast aspersions on the American effort there and, as far as many veterans were concerned, tarnished the men who had fought there. "That no good son-of-a-bitch," remarked

Wendell Johnson, a purple-hearted marine who lost part of his foot near Chu Lai. "He's making a couple of million now, going to the bank with his blood money. You would think he'd at least have the good sense to donate the profits to some handicapped veterans he sent off to war. Hell, I'd be satisfied if he gave the money to wounded Vietnamese. Anything but keep it himself. Has he no sense of decency?"

The Clinton administration was forced to postpone temporarily its plans for diplomatic recognition. McNamara's book had stirred up a political hornet's nest of controversy, and even though the Vietnamese victory celebrations were low key, the president decided to hold off until media attention had died down. Early in July 1995, two months after the end of the anniversary celebrations, and with Robert McNamara off the television screens, Bill Clinton moved forward with his plans. Public opinion polls indicated that most Americans supported normalization. On July 11, 1995, at a brief White House ceremony, the president extended diplomatic recognition to Vietnam. "This moment," Clinton said in a prepared statement, "offers us the opportunity to bind up our own wounds. They have resisted time for so long. We can now move on to common ground."

12

The Vietnam War:
The American Heritage

*I don't think the whole of Southeast Asia, as related to the
present and future safety and freedom of the people of this
country, is worth the life or limb of a single American.*
— General David Shoup, 1966

For the generation after the fall of Saigon in 1975, the American people
wondered how it had happened, how the Vietnam War had gone out of
control, how the richest country in the world could sacrifice hundreds of
billions of dollars and tens of thousands of young men and women in a
military effort that seemed, in the end, to have so little significance.
Vietnam, Laos, and Cambodia fell to communism, but the rest of Asia
survived. Only three dominoes went down. During the 1970s and 1980s
the victorious Socialist Republic of Vietnam slipped into stupefying poverty, while the United States recovered from its malaise and enjoyed a
period of unprecedented growth and prosperity. Around the world there
were nearly 60,000 graves covering the bodies of Americans who lost
their lives, but few people in the United States knew whether their
sacrifice meant anything at all. Communism had taken over Indochina
in the end, and the United States was just fine anyway.

Back in the late 1940s, when the American crusade began, it had all
seemed so simple, so clear, the threat so real and the sacrifice so necessary. Communism was on the march—in Europe and in Asia—and it
appeared to be enjoying great success. Much of Eastern Europe was
under Soviet domination, and in 1949 China fell to Mao Zedong's cadres.
Ho Chi Minh threatened to do the same to Vietnam, Laos, and Cambodia. In the United States, the fear of communist expansion became a
paranoia, and American leaders vowed to hold the line, to fight the
Marxist menace at home and abroad. The policy became known as containment, and the United States looked to apply it all around the world.
Because Southeast Asia seemed crucial to the economic recovery of Japan and Western Europe, United States policymakers committed themselves to the survival of the French empire, even though it left a bad
taste in the mouths of many. Given a choice between European colonial-

ism and communism, they chose the former. Nationalism and democracy took a backseat to anticommunism.

For most American policymakers in the Truman and Eisenhower administrations, Vietnam was like Eastern Europe and Korea—just a blatant case of communist military aggression that had to be stopped. The memories of Munich were still clear. European leaders had given Adolf Hitler an inch in Czechoslovakia, and he had taken hundreds of thousands of square miles of territory across the continent. Ho Chi Minh was just another dictator who needed his bluff called. The United States assumed it would be a relatively simple task. Surely no poor Southeast Asian guerrilla could stand up to the American killing machine. American leaders did not see Ho Chi Minh for what he was—a communist who also happened to be a Vietnamese hero.

In order to stand up to Ho Chi Minh, however, the United States committed itself to upholding a tiny elite in South Vietnam—an urban, Roman Catholic minority that had nothing in common with the masses of rural Buddhist and Confucian peasants. The government of South Vietnam—with its arrogance and corruption—was never able to win the loyalties of its own people, and large numbers of them gravitated instead to the Vietcong. When the United States tried to win the war militarily by bludgeoning the Vietcong and North Vietnamese with massive firepower, there were inordinately large numbers of civilian casualties, which only made the problem of winning political loyalty more acutely difficult.

Throughout most of the war, however, the United States did not worry much about peasant loyalties. The Kennedy and Johnson administrations decided to fight a war of attrition, to kill so many enemy troops and inflict so much damage on North Vietnam that continuation of the war would be impossible. Long before there was any hope of finally converting the peasants, Kennedy and Johnson expected the war to be over, with the communists licking their wounds and retreating back across the seventeenth parallel. What the Americans did not know was the extent of the communists' commitment to reunification and independence. They were fighting a war to the death, an open-ended commitment to risk everything, including annihilation, for victory. The United States commitment fell far short of that, and the Vietcong and North Vietnamese were willing to wait until the American public reached its political and economic limit.

Slowly but surely the United States found itself getting deeper and deeper into the war, not out of any forthright commitment to military victory but out of compromise and moderation, taking the middle road between those Neanderthals who wanted to bomb the enemy back into the stone age and the weak-kneed pacifists who wanted out at any cost. Each escalation of the conflict was undertaken as a compromise, and each step was taken with the conviction that just a little more firepower

While much healing and reconciliation has occurred in the twenty years since the end of the war, the experience of the Vietnam War remains indelible and the pain and loss, for many, is irreparable.
WENDY WATRISS/WOODFIN CAMP

would win the day. None of the presidents who increased the volume of American assets in Indochina viewed himself as an extremist. On the contrary, each was acting prudently, carefully, and moderately. But the sum total of dozens of small escalations was the dreaded land war in Asia.

Even when American policymakers began to see Vietnam for the quagmire it was, disengagement was excruciatingly difficult. Presidents Eisenhower, Kennedy, Johnson, and Nixon all expressed the fear of becoming the first American president to lose a war. Each of them remembered the political abuse Harry Truman had taken from the Republican right wing over the "loss" of China to the Reds, and none of them wanted to be the target of similar abuse for "losing" Vietnam. Domestic politics, as much as the perceived need to stop communism in Vietnam, kept the United States in the war against the better judgment of a number of prominent leaders. Even in the early 1970s, when the war had become an albatross to the Nixon administration, blanket withdrawal was not an option because of the need to maintain "American credibility" around the world. What started out as a righteous crusade in the late 1940s to save Southeast Asia and ultimately the rest of the world from global communism ended up in the 1970s as a face-saving game to get out of an impossible mess without looking too bad. The war was a colossal blunder born of an odd mixture of paranoia and arrogance. Blind to history, the United States saw only communism, not nationalism, in Vietnam, and, naively confident about its role as the premier power on earth, the United States applied military solutions to a problem that was essentially political and cultural. Vietnam was the wrong war in the wrong place at the wrong time for the wrong reason.

> And the end of the fight is a tombstone white with
>   the name of the late deceased,
> In the epitaph drear: "A fool lies here who tried
>   to hustle the East."

And the end of the Vietnam War is a black wall in Washington with 58,175 names, an epitaph to a loss that is every American's.

Bibliography

Long before Americans ever heard of Vietnam—indeed long before the United States even existed—the people of Indochina had been struggling to secure their place in the world. Keith Weller Taylor's *The Birth of Vietnam* (1983) surveys the ancient period. For general surveys, see Joseph Buttinger, *The Smaller Dragon: A Political History of Vietnam* (1958) and Georges Coedes, *The Making of Southeast Asia* (1964). The nineteenth-century presence of China in Vietnam is the subject of Henry McAleavy's *Black Flags in Vietnam: The Story of the Chinese Intervention* (1968), while Edgar Wickberg's *Historical Interaction of China and Vietnam* (1969) takes a longer view. Van-Kiem Thai's *Viet Nam Past and Present* (1956) provides a Vietnamese perspective. There are several useful reference works dealing with more recent wars. An excellent bibliography is Richard Dean Burns and Milton Leitenberg, *The Wars in Vietnam, Cambodia, and Laos, 1945–1982* (1983). Two useful encyclopedias are James S. Olson, ed., *Dictionary of the Vietnam War* (1988) and Harry G. Summers, Jr., *Vietnam War Almanac* (1985). Shelby L. Stanton's *Vietnam Order of Battle* (1981) provides excellent coverage of individual military units.

There are a number of important works on Vietnamese culture. A good survey is F. Raymond Iredell, *Vietnam: The Country and the People* (1966). Ann Crawford's *Customs and Culture of Vietnam* (1966) provides a brief survey of Vietnamese culture. Danny J. Whitfield's *Historical and Cultural Dictionary of Vietnam* (1976) is an encyclopedia of Vietnamese historical figures, geography, and customs. For a discussion of religion in Vietnam, see Gustave Dumoutier, *Annamese Religions* (1955) and Pierro Gheddo, *The Cross and the Bo-Tree: Catholics and Buddhists in Vietnam* (1970). Bernard Philippe Groslier, *The Art of Indochina* (1962) is a useful survey. Also see Nguyen Dinh Hoa's *The Vietnamese Language* (1961). The best work on the Montagnard people is Gerald C. Hickey's *Free in the Forest: An Ethnohistory of the Vietnamese Central Highlands, 1954–1976* (1982) and his *Sons of the Mountains: Ethnohistory of the Vietnamese Central Highlands to 1954* (1982).

The seminal event in the nineteenth century is the arrival of the French. John Cady's *The Roots of French Imperialism in Asia* (1954) looks at the early penetration of Indochina by French missionaries and entrepreneurs. Milton E. Osborne, *The French Presence in Cochinchina and*

Cambodia: Rule and Response 1859–1905 (1969) looks at the nineteenth century. Raymond F. Betts's *Assimilation and Association in French Colonial Theory* (1961) analyzes the policy implications of French racial attitudes. For an indigenous look at French imperialism, see Ngo Vinh Long, *Before the Revolution: The Vietnamese Peasants under the French* (1973). Nguyen Khac Vien's *Tradition and Revolution in Vietnam* (1974) shows that Vietnamese nationalism long predated the arrival of the French, although French rule sharpened it. Joseph Buttinger's *Vietnam: A Dragon Embattled,* volume 1, *From Colonialism to Vietminh* (1967) is a masterful survey of French colonialism and the Vietnamese reaction to it. Ellen J. Hammer's *The Struggle for Indochina* (1954) is a good supplement. David G. Marr's *Vietnamese Anticolonialism 1885–1925* (1971) and *Vietnamese Tradition on Trial 1920–1945* (1981) describe the political resistance to the French among the Vietnamese. Also see William Duiker, *The Rise of Nationalism in Vietnam, 1900–1941* (1976). For a Marxist perspective on Vietnamese nationalism, see Thomas Hodgkin, *Vietnam: The Revolutionary Path* (1981).

The leading Vietnamese nationalist was, of course, Ho Chi Minh. Charles Fenn's *Ho Chi Minh: A Biographical Introduction* (1973) is the memoirs of an OSS officer who knew Ho Chi Minh during World War II. For two highly readable biographies, see Jean Lacouture, *Ho Chi Minh: A Political Biography* (1968) and David Halberstam, *Ho* (1971). For Lacouture's recollections, see *Ho Chi Minh and His Followers: A Personal Memoir* (1968). Also see William Warbey, *Ho Chi Minh and the Struggle for an Independent Vietnam* (1972). Some of Ho Chi Minh's own writings are also illuminating, especially *Selected Works* (1960–1962) and *Prison Diary* (1966). For descriptions of other Vietnamese leaders, see Bernard B. Fall, *The Viet-Minh Regime* (1956) and Huynh Kim Khanh, *Vietnamese Communism 1925–1945* (1982). Joseph Buttinger's portraits can be found in *Vietnam: A Dragon Embattled,* volume 2, *Vietnam at War* (1967). Two good but not very accessible reference works are the CIA's *Who's Who in Vietnam* (1969) and the U.S. State Department's *Who's Who in North Vietnam* (1972). Also see Robert J. O'Neill, *General Giap: Politician and Strategist* (1969). Truong Chinh's *Primer for Revolt: The Communist Takeover in Vietnam* (1963) is an excellent first-hand account. A good deal can also be learned from Tran Van Dinh, *This Nation and Socialism Are One: Selected Writings of Le Duan* (1977).

Anti-French nationalism culminated in the first Indochina War. For the history of French politics, see Alexander Werth, *France 1940–1954* (1956). Ellen Hammer's *The Struggle for Indochina* (1954) and Donald Lancaster's *The Emancipation of French Indochina* (1961) are both useful surveys. So is Robert F. Turner's *Vietnamese Communism: Its Origins and Developments* (1975). Bernard Fall, a leading journalist who observed the first Indochina War and died in the second, describes Vietnamese insurgency in *Street Without Joy: Insurgency in Vietnam, 1946–*

1963 (1963). David G. Marr's *Vietnamese Tradition on Trial* explains how the Vietminh displaced the other Vietnamese nationalist groups. Vo Nguyen Giap's *People's War, People's Army* (1962) is an anthology of his writings about the French war. Lucien Bodard's *The Quicksand War* (1967) provides a good description of the war from 1946 to 1950. The best account of the war is Giap's *Unforgettable Days* (1978). On the battle at Dienbienphu, see Jules Roy, *The Battle of Dien Bien Phu* (1965) and Bernard Fall, *Hell in a Very Small Place: The Siege of Dien Bien Phu* (1966). For the Geneva Conference, see Robert F. Randle, *Geneva 1954* (1969) and Philippe Devillers and Jean Lacouture, *End of a War: Indochina 1954* (1969).

The best writing on Vietnam remains the property of journalists, not historians. Stanley Karnow, who spent years in Vietnam as a reporter, wrote *Vietnam: A History* in 1983. It is full of anecdotal material about the leading figures in the war. David Halberstam, who won a Pulitzer Prize for his early reporting of the war, subsequently wrote *The Making of a Quagmire* (1964), a book that proved prophetic in its prediction of the outcome of the war. Halberstam's *The Best and the Brightest* (1972) is outstanding in its description of leading American policymakers. The best book of all is Neil Sheehan's *The Bright and Shining Lie: John Paul Vann and America in Vietnam* (1988), a devastating critique of United States policy. Peter Arnett, a former AP reporter in Vietnam, and Michael Maclear wrote *The Ten Thousand Day War* (1981).

There are also a number of general works by historians. One of the most recent is George Donelson Moss, *Vietnam: An American Ordeal* (1989). Also see Philip Davidson, *Vietnam at War: The History, 1945–1975* (1988). An early history which romanticizes the communists is Frances FitzGerald's *Fire in the Lake* (1972). Chester Cooper's *The Last Crusade: America in Vietnam* (1970) is well-informed by its author's policy-making role in the war, as is Paul Kattenburg's *The Vietnam Trauma in American Foreign Policy, 1945–1975* (1980). Guenter Lewy's *America in Vietnam* (1978) is a revisionary work which seeks to justify the United States involvement. Norman Podhoretz's *Why We Were in Vietnam* (1982) follows a similar vein. Two of the best surveys are George C. Herring's *America's Longest War: The United States and Vietnam, 1950–1975* (1986) and William S. Turley's *The Second Indochina War: A Short Political and Military History, 1954–1975* (1986). Turley is especially good in his discussion of Vietcong and North Vietnamese politics. Also see William J. Duiker's *Sacred War* (1995).

The reasons behind the American commitment to Southeast Asia have been the focus of intense debate. President Franklin D. Roosevelt flirted with the idea of trusteeship for Indochina, but he was merely expressing a concern rather than developing a policy; see Christopher Thorne, *Allies of a Kind: The United States, Britain, and the War Against Japan, 1941–1945* (1978) and William Roger Louis, *Imperial-*

ism at Bay: The United States and the Decolonization of the British Empire (1978). One school argues that the United States became involved because of its fear of Soviet expansionism in Europe. For that point of view, see George C. Herring, "The Truman Administration and the Restoration of French Sovereignty in Indochina," *Diplomatic History* 1 (1977), 97–117. Richard J. Barnet's *Roots of War* (1972) argues that the United States simply defined its national interests too broadly. Leslie H. Gelb and Richard K. Betts, in *The Irony of Vietnam: The System Worked* (1978), claim that American politicians were unable, because of the realities of domestic politics, to withdraw without committing political suicide. A more recent argument attempts to integrate complex economic and political factors in Europe, Japan, and Southeast Asia. See Robert M. Blum, *Drawing the Line: The Origin of the American Containment Policy in East Asia* (1982); Andrew J. Rotter, *The Path to Vietnam: Origins of the American Commitment to Southeast Asia* (1987); and Gabriel Kolko, *Anatomy of a War* (1985).

For information on the growing commitment in the 1950s, see Stephen E. Ambrose, *Eisenhower,* volume 2, *President and Elder Statesman, 1952–1969* (1984) and Townsend Hoopes, *The Devil and John Foster Dulles* (1973). Also see Stephen Jurika, Jr., ed., *From Pearl Harbor to Vietnam: The Memoirs of Admiral Arthur W. Radford* (1980). The decision whether or not to intervene at Dienbienphu in 1954 is the subject of John Prados's *The Sky Would Fall: Operation Vulture: The U.S. Bombing Mission in Indochina, 1954* (1983) and Matthew B. Ridgway, *Soldier: The Memoirs of Matthew B. Ridgway* (1956). Robert Shaplen's *The Lost Revolution* (1966) is an especially good survey of the period.

For discussions of events inside South Vietnam during the 1950s, see Edward G. Lansdale, *In the Midst of Wars* (1972) and J. Lawton Collins, *Lightning Joe: An Autobiography* (1979). The early role played by the United States military is described in J. Lawton Collins, *The Development and Training of the South Vietnamese Army, 1950–1972* (1975); Robert H. Whitlow, *U.S. Marines in Vietnam: The Advisory and Combat Assistance Era, 1954–1964* (1976); Ronald H. Spector, *United States Army in Vietnam: Advice and Support: The Early Years* (1985); and Edwin Hooper et al., *The United States Navy and the Vietnam Conflict: The Setting of the Stage to 1959* (1976). Denis Warner's *The Last Confucian* (1963) and Anthony Bouscaren's *The Last of the Mandarins: Diem of Vietnam* (1965) describe the Diem regime.

Good general surveys on communist insurgency can be found in Frances FitzGerald's *Fire in the Lake* and in the second volume of Joseph Buttinger's *Vietnam.* For the connection between North Vietnam and the southern communists, see P. J. Honey, *Communism in North Vietnam* (1963). Also see King C. Chen's "Hanoi's Three Decisions and the Escalation of the Vietnam War," *Political Science Quarterly* 90 (1975). One of the earliest scholarly works on the insurgency was Douglas

Pike's *Viet Cong* (1966). Also see Pike's *The Viet Cong Strategy of Terror* (1970). William Henderson's *Why the Vietcong Fought: A Study of Motivation and Control in a Modern Army* (1979) is a psychological portrait of the guerrillas. William Duiker's *The Communist Road to Power* is first-rate. A number of books look at insurgency on the local level. See William R. Andrews, *The Village War: Vietnamese Communist Revolutionary Activities in Dinh Tuong Province, 1960–1964* (1973); Stuart Herrington, *Silence Was a Weapon* (1982); and Jeffrey Race, *War Comes to Long An: Revolutionary Conflict in a Vietnamese Village* (1972). For Vietcong memoirs, see Nguyen Thi Dinh, *No Other Road to Take* (1976) and Truong Nhu Tang, *A Vietcong Memoir* (1985). An outstanding oral history is David Chanoff and Doan Van Toai, *Portrait of the Enemy* (1986). Also see Kate Webb, *On the Other Side: 23 Days with the Viet Cong* (1972).

For an even-handed history of the Kennedy years, see Herbert Parmet's *JFK: The Presidency of John F. Kennedy* (1983). Bruce Miroff's *Pragmatic Illusions: The Presidential Politics of John F. Kennedy* (1976) is a New Left critique. Two works that specialize on Kennedy and Vietnam are R. B. Smith, *An International History of the Vietnam War,* volume 2, *The Kennedy Strategy* (1985) and William J. Rust, *Kennedy in Vietnam* (1985). Among the books by administration officials, see George T. Ball, *The Past Has Another Pattern* (1982) and Roger Hilsman, *To Move a Nation: The Politics of Foreign Policy in the Administration of John F. Kennedy* (1967). Also see Walt W. Rostow, *The Diffusion of Power, 1957–1972* (1972); Henry Cabot Lodge, Jr., *The Storm Has Many Eyes: A Personal Narrative* (1973); and Maxwell D. Taylor, *Swords and Ploughshares* (1972). Warren Cohen's *Dean Rusk* (1980) looks at the secretary of state. For the events in South Vietnam during the Kennedy years, see Mieczyslaw Maneli, *War of the Vanquished* (1971) and John Mecklin, *Mission in Torment: An Intimate Account of the U.S. Role in Vietnam* (1974). Joseph Buttinger's second *Vietnam* volume is also good, as is David Halberstam's *The Making of a Quagmire*. Frederick Nolting, the United States ambassador to South Vietnam in the early 1960s, wrote *From Triumph to Tragedy: The Political Memoirs of Frederick Nolting* (1988). For the events leading up to Diem's assassination, see Ellen J. Hammer, *A Death in November: America in Vietnam, 1963* (1987). Also see John Newman, *John F. Kennedy and Vietnam* (1992).

A number of books look at counterinsurgency. The best survey is Larry E. Cable, *Conflict of Myths: The Development of American Counterinsurgency Doctrine and the Vietnam War* (1986). Douglas S. Blauburg's *The Counterinsurgency Era: U.S. Doctrine and Performance 1950 to the Present* (1977) is also excellent. Robert W. Komer discusses how badly the United States underestimated the insurgency in *Bureaucracy Does Its Thing* (1972). Milton E. Osborne's *Strategic Hamlets in South Vietnam* (1965) is an early study of that disaster. Sir Robert

Thompson discusses his role in *Defeating Communist Insurgency* (1966) and *Peace Is Not at Hand* (1974). For a look at the Marine Corps pacification programs, see Michael E. Petersen's *The Combined Action Platoons: The U.S. Marines' Other War in Vietnam* (1989). Shelby L. Stanton's *Green Berets at War* (1985) and Charles M. Simpson III's *Inside the Green Berets: The First Thirty Years* (1983) provide descriptions of Special Forces pacification efforts. Andrew F. Krepinevich's *The Army and Vietnam* (1986) has an excellent chapter on army counterinsurgency.

Lyndon B. Johnson's decision to escalate the war, of course, enjoys a voluminous literature. Although flawed by a self-serving defensiveness, Johnson's *The Vantage Point: Perspectives of the Presidency, 1963–1969* (1971) is a necessary starting point. Vaughn Robert's *The Presidency of Lyndon B. Johnson* (1983) is the best history of the administration. For a revealing portrait of Johnson, see Doris Kearns, *Lyndon Johnson and the American Dream* (1976). Robert Caro's *The Years of Lyndon Johnson: The Path to Power* (1982) and *The Years of Lyndon Johnson: Means of Ascent* (1990) are a savage critique. For the events surrounding the Gulf of Tonkin incident, see John Galloway, *The Gulf of Tonkin Resolution* (1970) and Eugene C. Windchy, *Tonkin Gulf* (1971). There are several excellent books that describe the decision-making process in Washington. Especially good are Henry Graff's interviews with administration officials, published as *The Tuesday Cabinet: Deliberation and Decision on Peace and War under Lyndon B. Johnson* (1970). Equally good are two books by Larry Berman—*Planning a Tragedy: The Americanization of the War in Vietnam* (1982) and *Lyndon Johnson's War: The Road to Stalemate in Vietnam* (1989). Also see Henry Brandon, *Anatomy of Error: The Inside Story of the Asian War on the Potomac, 1954–1969* (1969). There is no really good biography on McNamara, but see Henry L. Trewhitt, *McNamara: His Ordeal in the Pentagon* (1971). Alain Enthoven and K. Wayne Smith provide an inside look at McNamara in *How Much Is Enough? Shaping the Defense Program, 1961–1969* (1971). Gregory Palmer's *The McNamara Strategy and the Vietnam War: Program Budgeting in the Pentagon, 1960–1968* (1978) is highly critical of the secretary of defense. For the role played by such elder statesmen as Dean Acheson and W. Averell Harriman, see Walter Isaacson and Evan Thomas, *The Wise Men: Six Friends and the World They Made* (1986). David Di Leo's *George Ball, Vietnam, and the Rethinking of Containment* (1991) is excellent. Also see Robert McNamara, *In Retrospect: The Tragedy and Lessons of Vietnam* (1995).

The question of strategy remains highly controversial. David Richard Palmer's *Summons for a Trumpet* (1978) argues that the attrition strategy was hopelessly inadequate, while Guenter Lewy's *America in Vietnam* claims that the United States should have focused on pacification.

Andrew F. Krepinevich argues in *The Army and Vietnam* that United States military policy should have focused on light infantry formations, firepower restraint, and solving political and social problems, not conventional warfare. The best survey of the army effort is Shelby L. Stanton, *The Rise and Fall of an American Army: U.S. Ground Forces in Vietnam, 1965–1973* (1985). For arguments that the American command and control function during the war was badly designed, see Robert L. Gallucci, *Neither Peace Nor Honor: The Politics of American Military Policy in Vietnam* (1975) and George S. Eckhart, *Command and Control, 1950–1969* (1974). Another school of thought argues that the United States should have isolated North Vietnam from South Vietnam. See Harry G. Summers, Jr., *On Strategy: The Vietnam War in Context* (1981) and Bruce Palmer, Jr., *The 25-Year War: America's Military Role in Vietnam* (1984). Finally, some argue that the United States did not apply enough firepower. This point of view is clearly expressed in two memoirs: William Westmoreland, *A Soldier Reports* (1976) and Ulysses S. Grant Sharp, *Strategy for Defeat: Vietnam in Retrospect* (1978). Also see William Colby and Alexander Burnham, *Lost Victory* (1990). Wilbur Morrison summarizes this argument in *Vietnam: The Winnable War* (1990). Also see H. G. Moore and Joseph Galloway, *We Were Soldiers Once and Young* (1992); Christian Appy, *Working-Class War* (1993); and Eric Bergerud, *Red Thunder, Tropic Lightning: The World of a Combat Division in Vietnam* (1993).

The literature on American women in Vietnam is just beginning to grow. For a look at the role played by nurses in the war, see Dan Freedman and Jacqueline Rhoads, *Nurses in Vietnam: The Forgotten Veterans* (1987) and Elizabeth Norman, *Women at War* (1990). Also see Lynda Van Devanter, *Home before Morning: The Story of an Army Nurse in Vietnam* (1983). The best oral history is Kathryn Marshall's *In the Combat Zone: An Oral History of American Women in Vietnam, 1965–1975* (1987). Also see Shelley Saywell, *Women in War* (1985); Keith Walker, *A Piece of My Heart: The Stories of 26 American Women Who Served in Vietnam* (1985); and Patricia Walsh, *Forever Sad the Hearts* (1982). For a more recent description of American women in Vietnam, see Winnie Smith, *American Daughters Gone to War* (1992).

The effectiveness of the air war over Vietnam is quite controversial. For general surveys see Raphael Littauer and Norman Uphoff, eds., *The Air War in Indochina* (1972) and Bernard C. Nalty et al., *The Air War over Vietnam* (1971). William Momyer's *Air Power in Three Wars* praises the air force from an insider's perspective. In a similar vein is John B. Nichols and Barrett Tillman, *On Yankee Station: The Naval Air War over Vietnam* (1987). William A. Buckingham, Jr.'s *Operation Ranch Hand: The United States Air Force and Herbicides in Southeast Asia, 1961–1971* (1982) is important reading. Criticisms of the air war can be found in James Clay Thompson, *Rolling Thunder: Undertaking Policy and Program Failure* (1980) and Mark Clodfelter, *The Limits of Air Power: The American Bombing of North Vietnam* (1989).

For the Vietnamese perspective on the American military effort, there are a number of valuable works. Jon M. Van Dyke's *North Vietnam's Strategy for Survival* (1972) describes how North Vietnam adjusted to the strategy of attrition. Also see Patrick J. McGarvey, ed., *Visions of Victory: Selected Vietnamese Communist Military Writings, 1964–1968* (1969), which describes North Vietnamese debates over military strategy. William Duiker's *The Communist Road to Power in Vietnam* is excellent. North Vietnam's official history of the conflict is entitled *The Anti-U.S. Resistance for National Salvation 1954–1975* (1980). For discussions of communist strategy, see Vo Nguyen Giap's *Big Victory, Big Task* and *Banner of People's War: The Party's Military Line* (1970). Tran Van Tra's *Ending the Thirty Years War* (1982) is also revealing. Douglas Pike's *PAVN: People's Army of Vietnam* (1986) is an outstanding portrait of the North Vietnamese army. An excellent survey of the war from the communist perspective is Nguyen Khac Vien, *The Long Resistance 1958–1974* (1975). Nguyen Thi Dinh's *No Other Road to Take* (1976) describes the efforts of the People's Liberation Army of Vietnam. For descriptions of South Vietnamese politics, see Charles A. Joiner, *The Politics of Massacre* (1974) and Allen E. Goodman, *Politics in War* (1973). The best survey of South Vietnam is the book by Anthony James Joes, *The War for South Viet Nam, 1954–1975* (1989). The best series of oral histories collected from ordinary people in South Vietnam is Don Luce and John Sommer, *Vietnam: The Unheard Voices* (1969). For Vietnamese recollections, see Cao Van Vien and Dong Van Khuyen, *Reflections on the Vietnam War* (1980); Hoang Ngoc Lung, *The General Offensives of 1968–69* (1981); Tran Van Don, *Our Endless War* (1978); and Nguyen Cao Ky, *Twenty Years and Twenty Days* (1976).

The watershed event in the war was the Tet offensive of 1968. Don Oberdorfer's *Tet!* (1971) is a highly readable account by a journalist who was there. Also see his *Tet: The Turning Point of the War* (1983). Walter Isaacson and Evan Thomas in *The Wise Men* provide excellent descriptions of the frustration in Washington. For the political implications of Tet, see Herbert Y. Schandler, *The Unmaking of a President: Lyndon Johnson and Vietnam* (1977). Peter Baestrup's *Big Story* (1977) criticizes the press for its reporting of Tet. For histories of two key battles, see Keith W. Nolan, *Battle for Hue: Tet, 1968* (1983) and Robert Pisor, *The End of the Line: The Siege of Khe Sanh* (1982). In *The Viet Cong Tet Offensive* (1969), Pham Von Son and Le Van Duong provide a local perspective. Ronald H. Spector's *After Tet* (1993) is especially illuminating.

For a survey of the antiwar movement, see Nancy Zaroulis and Gerald Sullivan, *Who Spoke Up? American Protest Against the War in Vietnam, 1963–1975* (1984). Also see Thomas Powers's two books, *The War at*

Home: Vietnam and the American People (1973) and *Vietnam, the War at Home: The Antiwar Movement, 1964–1968* (1984). On the issue of draft resistance, see Lawrence M. Baskir and William A. Strauss, *Chance and Circumstance: The Draft, the War, and the Vietnam Generation* (1978) and David S. Surrey, *Choice of Conscience: Vietnam Era Military and Draft Resisters in Canada* (1982). For two recent books on the antiwar movement, see Kenneth Heineman, *Campus Wars* (1993) and Tom Wells, *The War Within: America's Battle over Vietnam* (1994).

The available sources on the Nixon administration are more limited than for Eisenhower, Kennedy, and Johnson. For Richard Nixon's perspective, see his memoirs, *RN: The Memoirs of Richard Nixon* (1978) and *In the Arena* (1990). Also see his *No More Vietnams* (1985). Kissinger's point of view is expressed in his memoirs, *White House Years* (1979) and *Years of Upheaval* (1983). Also see William Safire, *Before the Fall* (1975); U. Alexis Johnson, *The Right Hand of Power* (1984); John Ehrlichman, *Witness to Power* (1982); and H. R. Haldeman, *The Ends of Power* (1978). For an evenhanded version of Nixon's early years, see Stephen E. Ambrose, *Nixon: The Education of a Politician, 1913–1962* (1987). Nixon's approach to foreign policy is explained in C. L. Sulzberger, *The World and Richard Nixon* (1987) and Robert S. Litwack, *Detente and the Nixon Doctrine: American Foreign Policy and the Pursuit of Stability, 1969–1976* (1984). For a highly sympathetic view of Henry Kissinger, see Marvin Kalb and Bernard Kalb, *Kissinger* (1974). Contrast it with Seymour M. Hersh, *The Price of Power: Kissinger in the Nixon White House* (1983). Also see Robert D. Schulzinger, *Henry Kissinger: Doctor of Diplomacy* (1989); Roger Morris, *An Uncertain Greatness: Henry Kissinger and American Foreign Policy* (1977); and John Stoessinger, *Kissinger: The Anguish of Power* (1976).

Vietnam as an international issue is surveyed in R. B. Smith, *An International History of the Vietnam War*, volume 1, *Revolution versus Containment, 1955–61* (1983) and volume 2, *The Kennedy Strategy* (1985). Also see Paul M. Kattenburg's *The Vietnam Trauma in American Foreign Policy*. Douglas Pike's *Vietnam and the Soviet Union: Anatomy of an Alliance* (1987) analyzes Soviet foreign policy, as does Leif Rosenberger's *The Soviet Union and Vietnam* (1986). For the impact of the Vietnam War on China, see Robert G. Sutter, *Chinese Foreign Policy after the Cultural Revolution: 1966–1977* (1978) and Ray Hemen, *China's Vietnam War* (1983). Also see Daniel S. Papp, *Vietnam: The View from Moscow, Peking, and Washington* (1981). Two books deal with Canada: Douglas A. Ross, *In the Interests of Peace: Canada and Vietnam, 1954–1973* (1984) and Charles Taylor, *Snow Job: Canada, the United States and Vietnam, 1954–1973* (1984). For the Japanese perspective, see Thomas R. H. Havens, *Fire across the Sea: The Vietnam War and Japan 1965–1975* (1987). On the British, see George Rosie, *The British in Vietnam* (1970). For the Australians, see Peter King, *Australia's Vietnam* (1983). Also see

Robert Larsen and James Lawton Collins, Jr., *Allied Participation in Vietnam* (1975).

A number of books deal with the end of the war. For negotiations leading to the Paris agreements of 1974, see the memoirs of Nixon and Kissinger as well as Gareth Porter's *A Peace Denied: The United States, Vietnam, and the Paris Agreement* (1975). Allan Goodman's *The Lost Peace* (1978) is critical of the treaty. On the Christmas bombing of 1972, see Mark Clodfelter, *The Limits of Air Power*, as well as Martin F. Herz, *The Prestige Press and the Christmas Bombing* (1980). For the offensive that inspired the bombing campaign, see G. H. Turley, *The Easter Offensive: Vietnam, 1972* (1985). Ngo Quang Truong, *The Easter Offensive of 1972* (1980) provides a Vietnamese perspective. Also see A.J.C. Lavelle, ed., *Airpower and the 1972 Spring Invasion* (1976).

P. Edward Haley's *Congress and the Fall of South Vietnam and Cambodia* argues that Congress severely limited the effectiveness of Presidents Nixon and Ford. Two works highly critical of the settlement are William F. LaGro, *Vietnam from Cease-Fire to Capitulation* (1981) and Stuart A. Herrington, *Peace with Honor?* (1983). A.J.C. Lavelle's *Last Flight from Saigon* (1978) describes the hectic final hours at the end of April 1975. John Pilzer's *The Last Day* (1976) is highly readable. For a scathing attack on Ambassador Graham Martin's failure to anticipate the communists' final offensive, see Frank Snepp, *Decent Interval: An Insider's Account of Saigon's Indecent End* (1977). Three books deal with the spring 1975 offensive: Alan Dawson, *55 Days: The Fall of South Vietnam* (1977); Tiziano Terzani, *Giai Phong! The Fall and Liberation of South Vietnam* (1977); and David Butler, *The Fall of Saigon* (1985). Stephen T. Hosmer's *The Fall of South Vietnam* (1980) consists of interviews with former South Vietnamese officials. See Cao Van Vien's *The Final Collapse* (1982) for another South Vietnamese account. Tran Van Tra's *Ending the Thirty Years War* and Van Tien Dung's *Our Great Spring Victory* (1977) give the communist view.

Laos and Cambodia have also received considerable attention. Charles Stevenson offers a highly critical account in *The End of Nowhere: American Policy Toward Laos Since 1954* (1973). For histories of the 1971 invasion of Laos, see Nguyen Duy Hinh, *Lam Son 719* (1981) and Keith William Nolan, *Into Laos: The Story of Dewey Canyon/Lam Son 719* (1986). An outstanding look at communist insurgency in Laos is MacAlister Brown and Joseph J. Zasloff, *Apprentice Revolutionaries: The Communist Movement in Laos, 1930–1985* (1986). Perala Ratnam's *Laos and the Super Powers* (1980) summarizes the diplomatic issues. The catastrophe in Cambodia is the subject of David P. Chandler's *A History of Cambodia* (1983). For the background to the struggle, see Wilfred Burchet, *The China-Cambodia-Vietnam Triangle* (1982) and Michael Leifer, *Cambodia: The Search for Security* (1967). The 1970 invasion is covered in Shelby L. Stanton's *The Rise and Fall of an American Army* and Tran

Dinh Tho, *The Cambodian Incursion* (1979). Arnold Isaacs deals with the fall of Cambodia to the Khmer Rouge in *Without Honor,* as does Craig Etcheson in *The Rise and Demise of Democratic Kampuchea* (1984). Also see Michael Vickery, *Cambodia, 1975–1982* (1984). For a critique of American policy, see William Shawcross, *Sideshow: Kissinger, Nixon, and the Destruction of Cambodia* (1979). Several books deal with the Khmer Rouge's genocidal assault on Cambodia in the late 1970s. See William Shawcross, *The Quality of Mercy: Cambodia, Holocaust, and the Modern Conscience* (1984); George Hildebrand and Gareth Porter, *Cambodia: Starvation and Revolution* (1976); and Francois Ponchaud, *Cambodia: Year Zero* (1978). For the most recent books on the holocaust in Cambodia, see Usha Welarafua, *Beyond the Killing Fields* (1993) and David A. Chandler, *Brother Number One: A Biography of Pol Pot* (1992).

The steady decline of Vietnam after the final victory is the subject of Nguyen Van Canh's *Vietnam under Communism, 1975–1982* (1983) and Nguyen Long's *After Saigon Fell* (1981). William Duiker describes the state of Vietnam in the late 1970s in *Since the Fall of Saigon* (1980). For post–1975 conflict in Indochina, see Ray Hemen, *China's Vietnam War.* Also see David P. Elliott, ed., *The Third Indochina Conflict* (1981). The best general survey is Nayan Chanda, *Brother Enemy: The War after the War* (1986).

The legacy of the Vietnam War for Americans continues to generate interest and debate. One survey of the topic is James F. Veninga and Harry A. Wilmer, eds., *Vietnam in Remission* (1985). Several books deal with the impact of the war on American culture. See Philip D. Beidler, *American Literature and the Experience of Vietnam* (1982) and John Hellman, *American Myth and the Legacy of Vietnam* (1986) for the part played by Vietnam in recent literature. Also see W. D. Ehrhart, ed., *Carrying the Darkness: American Poetry of the Vietnam War* (1985) and Timothy J. Lomperis, *Reading the Wind: The Literature of the Vietnam War* (1986). James C. Wilson's *Vietnam in Prose and Film* (1982) surveys the films of the 1970s. Also see Andrew V. Martin, "Critical Approaches to American Cultural Studies: The Vietnam War in History, Literature, and Film," Ph.D. dissertation, University of Iowa, 1987. For the war's impact on foreign policy, see Anthony Lake, ed., *The Legacy of Vietnam: The War, American Society and the Future of American Foreign Policy* (1976). Also see Earl C. Ravenal, *Never Again: Learning from America's Foreign Policy Failures* (1978) and Ole R. Holsti and James N. Rosenau, *American Leadership in World Affairs: Vietnam and the Breakdown of Consensus* (1984). Several books deal with the question of American identity. See Walter H. Capps, *The Unfinished War: Vietnam and the American Conscience* (1982) and Myra MacPherson, *Long Time Passing* (1984).

Finally, there is an increasing volume of documentary source material becoming available to scholars. The starting place, of course, is the Pentagon Papers. Neil Sheehan and several other scholars and journalists wrote an early introduction to the papers which is still useful; see *The Pentagon Papers as Published by the New York Times* (1971). The best edition of the papers is U.S. Congress, Senate, Subcommittee on Public Buildings and Grounds, *The Pentagon Papers,* The Senator Gravel Edition, 4 vols. (1971). Also see George H. Herring, ed., *The Secret Diplomacy of the Vietnam War: The Negotiating Volumes of the Pentagon Papers* (1983). Gareth Porter's two-volume documents collection—*Vietnam: The Definitive Documentation of Human Decisions* (1979)—is very useful. Less useful, because of how it is organized, is the 12-volume *Department of Defense, U.S.–Vietnam Relations, 1945–1967* (1971). During the last several years the State Department, National Security Council, and CIA have released a series of research reports and classified reports through the "Indochinese Research Collections" of University Publications of America. For the U.S. military side of the conflict, scholars should consult Records Group 338 (Vietnam War: MACV/USARV Records) at the Washington National Records Center in Suitland, Maryland. There is also a valuable oral history collection called the Senior Officer Oral History Program, at the U.S. Army Military History Institute, Carlisle Barracks, Pennsylvania, which contains the reminiscences of major American army officers.

For those individuals interested in the policy debates taking place in the Kennedy and Johnson administrations, there are invaluable resources at the John F. Kennedy Presidential Library in Boston, Massachusetts and the Lyndon B. Johnson Presidential Library in Austin, Texas. At the JFK Library, scholars should look at the Presidential Office Files, particularly the sections on Counterinsurgency, on Vietnam, and on Vietnam Security. They should also see the National Security Files, especially the Vietnam section. At the LBJ Library, the most revealing materials on the policy debates can be found in the National Security File and the White House Central Files. There are also oral histories at the LBJ Library by William Bundy, George Christian, Clark Clifford, Chester Cooper, Alain Enthoven, W. Averell Harriman, Lyndon B. Johnson, Cyrus Vance, Paul Warnke, and William Westmoreland.

Documentary sources for the communists are far more limited. Cornell University maintains a microfilmed *Catalog of Viet Cong Documents,* while the Library of Congress has on microfilm a series of *Communist Vietnamese Publications.* At the Center for Research Libraries in Chicago, there is a very useful *Documents of the National Liberation Front of South Vietnam* on microfilm. Finally, there is the State Department's *Working Paper of North Viet-Nam's Role in the War in South Viet-Nam* (1968).

A Vietnam War Chronology

1945

Sept. 2 Ho Chi Minh proclaims the Democratic Republic of Vietnam.
26 A. Peter Dewey, head of the OSS mission in Saigon, is shot by Vietminh troops, becoming the first American to die in the Vietnam War.

1946

Mar. 6 Franco-Vietnamese Accords signed.
June 1 The Fontainebleau Conference convenes.
Dec. 19 The Vietminh attack French forces in Tonkin, formally beginning the first Indochina War.

1948

June 5 The French name Bao Dai head of state of Vietnam.

1949

Mar. 8 Elysée Agreement signed.
Oct. 1 Mao Zedong proclaims the People's Republic of China.

1950

Jan. 14 Ho Chi Minh again proclaims establishment of the Democratic Republic of Vietnam.
June 27 President Harry S. Truman announces increased U.S. military assistance to Vietnam.
Aug. 3 United States Military Assistance and Advisory Group arrives in Saigon.
Dec. 30 United States signs a Mutual Defense Assistance Agreement with France, Vietnam, Cambodia, and Laos.

1952

Nov. 4 Dwight D. Eisenhower is elected president.

1953

July 27 Korean War armistice is signed.

1954

Mar. 13 Vietminh attack the French fortress at Dienbienphu.
20 Admiral Arthur Radford proposes Operation Vulture to assist the French in defending Dienbienphu.

Apr. 7 President Dwight D. Eisenhower uses the domino analogy to explain the political significance of Indochina.

25 Winston Churchill and the British refuse to participate in Operation Vulture.

29 President Eisenhower announces that the United States will not provide air support to the French garrison at Dienbienphu.

May 7 The Vietminh conquer Dienbienphu.

8 The Geneva Conference opens.

July 20 France signs a cease-fire ending hostilities in Indochina.

Aug. 1 The first of nearly 1 million refugees from North Vietnam cross into South Vietnam.

Sept. 8 United States signs the Manila Treaty forming the Southeast Asia Treaty Organization.

1955

Mar. 28 Ngo Dinh Diem attacks the Binh Xuyen.

June 5 Ngo Dinh Diem attacks the Hoa Hao.

July 6 Ngo Dinh Diem repudiates the Geneva Agreements and refuses to plan for open elections throughout the country.

Oct. 26 Ngo Dinh Diem proclaims the Republic of Vietnam with himself as president.

1957

May 5–19 Ngo Dinh Diem visits the United States.

1959

Apr. 4 President Eisenhower makes his first commitment to maintain South Vietnam as a separate nation.

22 Christian A. Herter replaces John Foster Dulles as secretary of state.

July 1 General Lyman Lemnitzer replaces General Maxwell Taylor as chief of staff, U.S. Army.

8 First American servicemen (Major Dale Bius and Master Sergeant Chester Ovnard) killed by Vietcong attack at Bien Hoa.

Dec. 1 Thomas S. Gates, Jr., replaces Neil H. McElroy as secretary of defense.

31 Approximately 760 U.S. military personnel in Vietnam.

1960

Oct. 1 General George Decker replaces General Lyman Lemnitzer as chief of staff, U.S. Army.

Dec. 20 National Liberation Front established.

31 Approximately 900 U.S. military personnel in Vietnam.

1961

Jan. 21 John F. Kennedy succeeds Dwight D. Eisenhower as president. Dean Rusk succeeds Christian A. Herter as secretary of state. Robert S. McNamara succeeds Thomas S. Gates, Jr., as secretary of defense. McGeorge Bundy succeeds Gordon Gray as national security adviser.

28 Kennedy approves a Vietnam counterinsurgency plan.

Mar. 23 Kennedy insists that a Laotian ceasefire must precede negotiations to establish a neutral Laos.

May 9–15 Vice President Lyndon Johnson visits South Vietnam and recommends a strong American commitment there. Geneva Conference on Laos opens.

June 9 President Ngo Dinh Diem asks for U.S. military advisers to train the South Vietnamese Army.

July 1 General Maxwell Taylor is appointed military adviser to President John F. Kennedy.

Nov. 3 General Maxwell Taylor concludes that U.S. military, financial, and political aid will bring victory without a U.S. takeover of the war. He advises Kennedy to send 8,000 U.S. combat troops to Vietnam.

Dec. 15 Kennedy restates U.S. commitment to an independent South Vietnam.

31 U.S. military personnel in Vietnam now number 3,205.

1962

Feb. 6 MACV (U.S. Military Assistance Command, Vietnam) established in Saigon under the command of General Paul Harkins. The major buildup of American forces begins.

14 Kennedy authorizes U.S. military advisers in Vietnam to return fire if fired upon.

Mar. 22 United States launches the Strategic Hamlet (rural pacification) Program.

July 23 Geneva Accords on Laos signed.

Oct. 1 General Earle Wheeler replaces General George Decker as chief of staff, U.S. Army. General Maxwell Taylor replaces General Lyman Lemnitzer as chairman, Joint Chiefs of Staff.

Dec. 31 U.S. military personnel in Vietnam now number 11,300.

1963

Aug. 21 South Vietnamese troops attack Buddhist pagodas.

22 Henry Cabot Lodge replaces Frederick Nolting as U.S. ambassador to Vietnam.

Nov. 1 Military coup overthrows the government of President Ngo Dinh Diem.

2 Diem and his brother Ngo Dinh Nhu assassinated.

22 President John F. Kennedy assassinated.

Dec. 31 U.S. military personnel in Vietnam now number 16,300.

1964

Feb. 7 Johnson removes American dependents from South Vietnam.

June 20 General William Westmoreland replaces General Paul Harkins as head of MACV.

23 General Maxwell Taylor replaces Henry Cabot Lodge as U.S. ambassador to South Vietnam.

30 Admiral Ulysses S. Grant Sharp replaces Admiral Harry D. Felt as CINCPAC.

July 3 General Harold Johnson replaces General Earle Wheeler as chief of staff, U.S. Army.

Aug. 2 U.S. destroyer *Maddox* allegedly attacked by North Vietnamese patrol boats in the Gulf of Tonkin.

4 U.S. destroyer *Turner Joy* claims attack by North Vietnamese patrol boats.

7 U.S. Congress passes Gulf of Tonkin Resolution.

Oct. 1 U.S. Army Fifth Special Forces Group arrives in Vietnam.

Nov. 1 Vietcong attack Bien Hoa Air Base. Six U.S. B-57 bombers destroyed; five American service personnel killed.

2 Johnson defeats Senator Barry Goldwater in presidential election.

Dec. 24 Vietcong kill two U.S. soldiers in an attack on the Brinks Hotel in Saigon.

31 U.S. military personnel in Vietnam now number 23,300.

1965

Feb. 7 Vietcong launch a widespread attack on American military installations in South Vietnam.

Mar. 2 Operation Rolling Thunder begins.

8 First American combat troops (U.S. Third Marine regiment) arrive in Vietnam to defend Danang.

24 First teach-in held at the University of Michigan.

Apr. 6 Johnson permits U.S. ground combat troops to conduct offensive operations in South Vietnam.

17 Students for a Democratic Society hold antiwar rally in Washington, D.C.

May 15 National Teach-In held throughout the country.

June 8 State Department reports that Johnson has authorized the use of U.S. troops in direct combat if the South Vietnamese Army requests assistance.

July 8 Henry Cabot Lodge succeeds Maxwell Taylor as U.S. ambassador to South Vietnam.

Oct. 15–16 Antiwar protests in forty American cities.

Nov. 14–16 Battle of the Ia Drang Valley.

Dec. 25 Johnson suspends bombing of North Vietnam (Operation Rolling Thunder) and invites North Vietnam to negotiate.

31 U.S. military personnel in Vietnam now number 184,300; 636 U.S. military personnel killed in action to date; 22,420 Allied troops in Vietnam.

1966

Jan. 31 Bombing of North Vietnam (Operation Rolling Thunder) resumes.

Feb. 4 Senate Foreign Relations Committee opens televised hearings on the Vietnam War.

6 President Lyndon Johnson convenes the Honolulu Conference.

Mar. 1 Senate refuses to repeal the Gulf of Tonkin Resolution.

20 President Lyndon Johnson convenes the Guam Conference.

Apr. 1 Walt Rostow replaces McGeorge Bundy as national security adviser.

7 President Lyndon Johnson offers the Johns Hopkins Speech.

May 1 U.S. forces bombard Vietcong targets in Cambodia.

June 29 United States bombs oil facilities in Haiphong and Hanoi.

Oct. 26 Johnson visits U.S. troops in Vietnam.

Dec. 31 U.S. military personnel in Vietnam now number 385,300; 6,644 U.S. military personnel killed in action to date; 52,500 Allied military personnel in Vietnam.

1967

Jan. 8 Operation Cedar Falls begins.

26 Operation Cedar Falls ends.

Feb. 22 Operation Junction City begins.

Apr. 15 One hundred thousand antiwar protesters rally in New York.

May 1 Ellsworth Bunker replaces Henry Cabot Lodge as U.S. ambassador to South Vietnam.

9 Robert Komer appointed deputy to the MACV commander.

14 Operation Junction City ends.

19 U.S. planes bomb a power plant in Hanoi.

July 7 Congressional Joint Economic committee estimates the war will cost $4 billion to $6 billion more in 1967 than the $20.3 billion requested by Johnson.

Sept. 3 Nguyen Van Thieu elected president of South Vietnam.

29 Johnson offers to stop bombing of North Vietnam if they will immediately come to the negotiating table (San Antonio Formula).

Oct. 21 Fifty thousand antiwar activists protest at the Pentagon.

Dec. 31 U.S. military personnel in Vietnam now number 485,600; 16,021 U.S. military personnel killed in action to date.

1968

Jan. 3 Senator Eugene McCarthy announces his decision to seek the Democratic presidential nomination.

21 NVA siege of Khe Sanh begins.

30 Tet offensive begins.

31 Vietcong and NVA capture Hue.
General Leonard F. Chapman replaces General Wallace M. Greene as Marine Corps commandant.

Feb. 1 Richard M. Nixon announces his candidacy for the presidency.

25 ARVN and U.S. troops reconquer Hue.

27 Westmoreland requests 206,000 more troops.

	CBS anchorman Walter Cronkite predicts over the evening news that the war cannot be won.
Mar. 12	Eugene McCarthy almost defeats Lyndon Johnson in the New Hampshire Democratic presidential primary.
16	Senator Robert Kennedy announces his decision to seek the Democratic presidential nomination.
	My Lai massacre takes place.
25–26	Senior Advisory Group on Vietnam recommends deescalation of the American commitment in Vietnam.
31	Lyndon Johnson announces his decision not to run for reelection.
Apr. 23	Columbia University demonstrations begin.
26	Two hundred thousand people in New York City demonstrate against the war.
27	Vice President Hubert Humphrey announces his decision to seek the Democratic presidential nomination.
May 3	Johnson announces that formal peace talks will take place in Paris.
12	Vietnam peace talks open in Paris.
June 6	Robert Kennedy is assassinated.
July 1	General Creighton Abrams replaces General William Westmoreland as head of MACV.
3	General William Westmoreland replaces General Harold Johnson as chief of staff, U.S. Army.
31	Admiral John McCain replaces Admiral U.S. Grant Sharp as CINCPAC.
Aug. 28	Antiwar protests and riots in Chicago during the Democratic National Convention.
Oct. 31	Johnson announces end of bombing of North Vietnam.
	Operation Rolling Thunder ends.
Nov. 5	Richard Nixon defeats Hubert Humphrey in the 1968 presidential election.
Dec. 31	U.S. military personnel in Vietnam now number 536,000; 30,610 U.S. military personnel killed in action to date; 65,600 Allied troops in Vietnam.

1969

Jan. 22	Operation Dewey Canyon begins.
	Richard Nixon inaugurated as president.
	William Rogers becomes secretary of state.
	Melvin Laird becomes secretary of defense.
	Henry Kissinger becomes national security adviser.
Mar. 18	Operation Dewey Canyon ends.
	Operation Menu begins.
26	Women Strike for Peace demonstration in Washington, D.C.
Apr. 30	The number of U.S. military personnel in Vietnam reaches 543,300.
May 10	Operation Apache Snow begins.

14 Nixon proposes peace plan for Vietnam involving mutual troop withdrawal.

June 7 Operation Apache Snow ends.

8 Nixon announces the removal of 25,000 troops from Vietnam.

July 25 Richard Nixon proclaims the Nixon Doctrine.

Aug. 27 U.S. Ninth Infantry Division withdraws from Vietnam.

Sept. 3 Ho Chi Minh dies.

Oct. 15 National Moratorium antiwar demonstrations staged throughout the United States.

Nov. 15 The New Mobilization Committee to End the War in Vietnam sponsors a demonstration of 250,000 in Washington, D.C.

16 My Lai massacre described in the press.

30 U.S. Third Division withdraws from Vietnam.

Dec. 11 U.S. Third Brigade, Eighty-second Airborne Division, withdraws from Vietnam.

31 U.S. military personnel strength in Vietnam declines to 475,200; 40,024 U.S. military personnel killed in action to date. Allied military personnel in Vietnam totals 70,300.

1970

Feb. 20 Henry Kissinger opens secret peace negotiations in Paris.

Mar. 18 Prince Norodom Sihanouk of Cambodia deposed by General Lon Nol.

Apr. 15 U.S. First Infantry Division withdraws from Vietnam.

29 Operations in Cambodia begin.

30 United States invades Cambodia.

May 4 National Guard troops kill four students at Kent State University during demonstrations against the Cambodian invasion.

June 30 Operations in Cambodia end.

Oct. 11 U.S. Third Brigade, Ninth Infantry Division, leaves Vietnam.

Nov. 21 Unsuccessful raid on the Son Tay Prison in North Vietnam.

Dec. 7 U.S. Fourth Infantry Division leaves Vietnam.

8 U.S. Twenty-fifth Infantry Division withdraws from Vietnam.

22 U.S. Congress prohibits U.S. combat forces or advisers in Cambodia and Laos.

31 U.S. military personnel strength in Vietnam declines to 334,600; 44,245 U.S. military personnel killed in action to date. Allied military personnel declines to 67,700.

1971

Jan. 30 Operation Lam Son 719 begins.

31 Winter Soldier Investigation begins in Detroit.

Mar. 3 U.S. Fifth Special Forces Group leaves Vietnam.

5	U.S. Eleventh Armored Cavalry Regiment withdraws from Vietnam.
29	Lieutenant William L. Calley, Jr., found guilty of murder.
Apr. 6	Operation Lam Son 719 ends.
14	U.S. III Marine Amphibious Force withdraws from Vietnam.
20	Demonstrators in Washington, D.C., and San Francisco call for an end to the war.
29	U.S. First Cavalry Division withdraws from Vietnam.
30	U.S. Second Brigade, Twenty-fifth Infantry Division, withdraws from Vietnam.
May 3–5	People's Coalition for Peace and Justice demonstrates against the war in Washington, D.C.
June 13	*New York Times* starts publishing the Pentagon Papers.
30	Supreme Court allows publication of the Pentagon Papers.
Aug. 25	U.S. 173d Airborne Brigade withdraws from Vietnam.
27	U.S. First Brigade, Fifth Infantry Division, withdraws from Vietnam.
31	Royal Thai Army withdraws from Vietnam.
Nov. 12	Nixon confines U.S. ground forces to a defensive role.
Dec. 26	Nixon orders resumption of bombing of North Vietnam.
31	U.S. military personnel strength declines to 156,800; 45,626 U.S. military personnel killed in action to date. Allied military personnel in Vietnam declines to 53,900.

1972

Feb. 21	Nixon seeks détente with the People's Republic of China by visiting Beijing.
Mar. 10	U.S. 101st Airborne Division leaves Vietnam.
23	United States suspends Paris peace talks until North Vietnam and the NLF enter into "serious discussions."
30	Eastertide Offensive begins.
Apr. 7	Battle of An Loc begins.
15	U.S. bombing of Hanoi begins again.
15–20	Widespread antiwar demonstrations across the United States.
27	Paris peace talks resume.
May 1	North Vietnamese conquer Quang Tri.
4	United States suspends the Paris peace talks.
8	U.S. Navy mines North Vietnamese ports.
June 18	NVA forces an end to the battle of An Loc.
22	Watergate break-in and arrests.
26	U.S. Third Brigade, 1st Cavalry Division, withdraws from Vietnam.
29	U.S. 196th Infantry Brigade withdraws from Vietnam.
July 1	General Bruce Palmer, Jr., becomes acting chief of staff, U.S. Army.
13	Paris peace talks resume after ten weeks.

Aug. 23	U.S. Third Battalion, Twenty-first Infantry, withdraws from Vietnam.
Sept. 15	ARVN forces recapture Quang Tri.
26–27	Henry Kissinger conducts secret talks with North Vietnamese diplomats in Paris.
Oct. 16	General Creighton Abrams becomes chief of staff, U.S. Army.
17	Peace talks begin in Laos.
19–20	Kissinger meets with President Nguyen Van Thieu in Saigon to secure South Vietnamese support for the pending Paris Peace Accords.
Nov. 7	Nixon is reelected president in a landslide over Senator George McGovern.
20–21	Kissinger and Le Duc Tho put finishing touches on the Paris Peace Accords.
Dec. 13	Paris peace talks stall.
18–29	Operation Linebacker II conducted.
31	U.S. military personnel strength declines to 24,000; 45,926 U.S. military personnel killed in action to date. Allied military personnel drops to 35,500. SVNAF personnel killed in action to date numbers 195,847.

1973

Jan. 8–12	Kissinger and Le Duc Tho convene more private negotiations.
15	Nixon halts all U.S. offensive action against North Vietnam.
27	Peace pact signed in Paris by the United States, South Vietnam, North Vietnam, and the National Liberation Front.
30	Elliot L. Richardson becomes secretary of defense.
Feb. 12	First of American POWs released by North Vietnam.
21	Peace agreement signed in Laos.
Mar. 16	ROK Capital Division and Ninth Infantry Division withdraw from Vietnam.
29	MACV headquarters removed. Last of American POWs released by North Vietnam.
June 13	Implementation accord signed in Paris by the United States, South Vietnam, North Vietnam, and the National Liberation Front.
24	Graham Martin becomes U.S. ambassador to South Vietnam. Congress prohibits all bombing in Cambodia after August 15.
July 2	James Schlesinger becomes secretary of defense.
Aug. 14	All direct American military operations end in all of Indochina.
Sept. 22	Henry Kissinger becomes secretary of state.
Nov. 7	War Powers Resolution becomes law despite a presidential veto.
Dec. 31	U.S. military personnel in South Vietnam drops to 50. To

date, 46,163 U.S. military personnel killed in action. No
Allied military personnel remain in Vietnam.

1974

Aug. 9	Nixon resigns the presidency.
	Gerald Ford is inaugurated as president of the United States.
20	Congress reduces aid to South Vietnam from $1 billion to $700 million.
Sept. 4	General Creighton Abrams dies.
16	Ford offers clemency to draft evaders and military deserters.
Oct. 3	General Frederick Weyand becomes chief of staff, U.S. Army.
Dec. 13	Combat between NVA and ARVN is conducted in Phuoc Long Province.
31	U.S. military personnel in Vietnam remains at 50.

1975

Jan. 6	NVA troops take control of Phuoc Long Province.
8	North Vietnam decides on a massive invasion of South Vietnam.
Mar. 10	NVA captures Ban Me Thuot.
14	President Nguyen Van Thieu withdraws ARVN forces from Central Highlands.
19	NVA captures Quang Tri Province.
26	Hue falls to the NVA.
30	Danang falls to the NVA.
Apr. 1	Cambodian President Lon Nol flees Cambodia in face of Khmer Rouge invasion. South Vietnam abandons the northern half of the country to North Vietnam.
8–20	Battle of Xuan Loc.
11–13	Operation Eagle Pull removes U.S. embassy personnel from Phnom Penh, Cambodia.
12	President Nguyen Van Thieu resigns.
17	Cambodia falls to Khmer Rouge troops.
29–30	Operation Frequent Wind evacuates all American personnel and some South Vietnamese from Vietnam.
	NVA captures Saigon.
30	Vietnam War ends.
May 12	*Mayaguez* seized in Kampuchean waters.

Glossary and Guide to Acronyms

AID: Agency for International Development.

Airborne: People or matériel delivered by helicopter.

Amtrack: An amphibious vehicle, equipped with armor, primarily used by the Marine Corps to transport troops and matériel.

ARVN: Army of the Republic of Vietnam.

Base Area: An area of installations, defensive fortifications, or other physical structures used by the enemy.

Base Camp: A semipermanent field headquarters and center for a given unit, usually within the unit's tactical area of responsibility.

Battalion Days in the Field: Days when battalions are patrolling in the field. It was a standard measure of battalion productivity.

Body Bags: Plastic bags used for retrieval of bodies in the field.

Charlie, Charles, Chuck: Nickname used by American troops for the Vietcong.

Chieu Hoi: An amnesty program offered to the Vietcong by the government of the Republic of Vietnam.

CIA: Central Intelligence Agency.

CIDG: Civilian Irregular Defense Group.

CINCPAC: Commander in Chief, Pacific (U.S. Navy).

Clear and Hold: An American military tactic in which U.S. troops tried to capture and permanently hold an area.

CORDS: Civil Operations and Revolutionary Development Support.

COSVN: Central Office of South Vietnam.

DeSoto: U.S. Navy destroyer patrols in the South China Sea.

DMZ: Demilitarized Zone.

DRV: Democratic Republic of Vietnam (North Vietnam).

Firebase: A temporary artillery firing position, often secured by infantry.

Firefight: An exchange of small-arms fire between opposing units.

I Corps: Northernmost military region in South Vietnam.

IV Corps: Southernmost military region in South Vietnam, located in the Mekong Delta.

Frag: To kill or attempt to kill one's own officers or sergeants.

Free Fire Zone: Any area in which permission was not required prior to firing on targets.

Gooks: Slang term, brought to Vietnam by Korean War veterans, for anyone of Asian descent.

Green Berets: U.S. Special Forces troops.

Guerrilla Warfare: Military operations conducted in hostile territory by irregular, primarily indigenous forces.

GVN: Government of Vietnam (South Vietnam).

Hedgehogs: Isolated outposts in which the French high command concentrated troops.

Hot Pursuit: Policy allowing American troops to chase Vietcong and NVA soldiers across the border into Cambodia.

JCS: Joint Chiefs of Staff.

Khmer Rouge: Cambodian communists.

Light at the End of the Tunnel: Term used to describe the imminent demise of the Vietcong and North Vietnamese.

MAAG: Military Assistance and Advisory Group.

MACV: Military Assistance Command, Vietnam (Mac-Vee).

Main Force: Vietcong and North Vietnamese military units.

M-16: The standard American rifle used in Vietnam after 1966.

Napalm: An incendiary used by French and Americans as a defoliant and as an antipersonnel weapon.

NLF: National Liberation Front (the political organization of the Vietcong until 1969).

NVA: North Vietnamese Army.

Pacification: Several programs of the South Vietnamese and the U.S. governments to destroy the Vietcong in the villages, gain civilian support for the Republic of South Vietnam, and stabilize the countryside.

Pathet Lao: Laotian communists.

PAVN: People's Army of Vietnam (North Vietnamese Army, NVA).

PLVN: People's Liberation Army of Vietnam (Vietcong troops).

PRGVN: Provisional Revolutionary Government of South Vietnam (the political organization of the Vietcong after 1969).

Punji Stake: A razor-sharp bamboo stake sometimes coated with poison or feces and usually hidden under water, along trails, at ambush sites, or in deep pits.

ROKs: Troops from the Republic of Korea.

Ruff-Puffs: South Vietnamese Regional Forces and Popular Forces; paramilitary forces usually of squad or platoon size recruited and utilized in a hamlet or village.

RVN: Republic of Vietnam (South Vietnam).

SAM: Soviet-made surface-to-air missiles.

Sappers: North Vietnamese or Vietcong demolition commandos.

Search and Destroy: Offensive operations designed to find and destroy enemy forces rather than establish permanent government control.

II Corps: Central Highlands military region in South Vietnam.

Seventeenth Parallel: Temporary division line between North and South Vietnam.

Sortie: One aircraft making one takeoff and landing to conduct a mission for which it was scheduled.

Special Forces: U.S. soldiers, popularly known as Green Berets, trained in techniques of guerrilla warfare.

SRV: Socialist Republic of Vietnam.

Tet: Vietnamese Lunar New Year holiday period.

III Corps: Military region between Saigon and the Central Highlands.

Vietcong: Communist forces fighting in South Vietnam.

Vietminh: Communist forces fighting the French before 1954.

Vietnamization: President Nixon's program to gradually turn the war over to the South Vietnamese while phasing out American troops.

Index